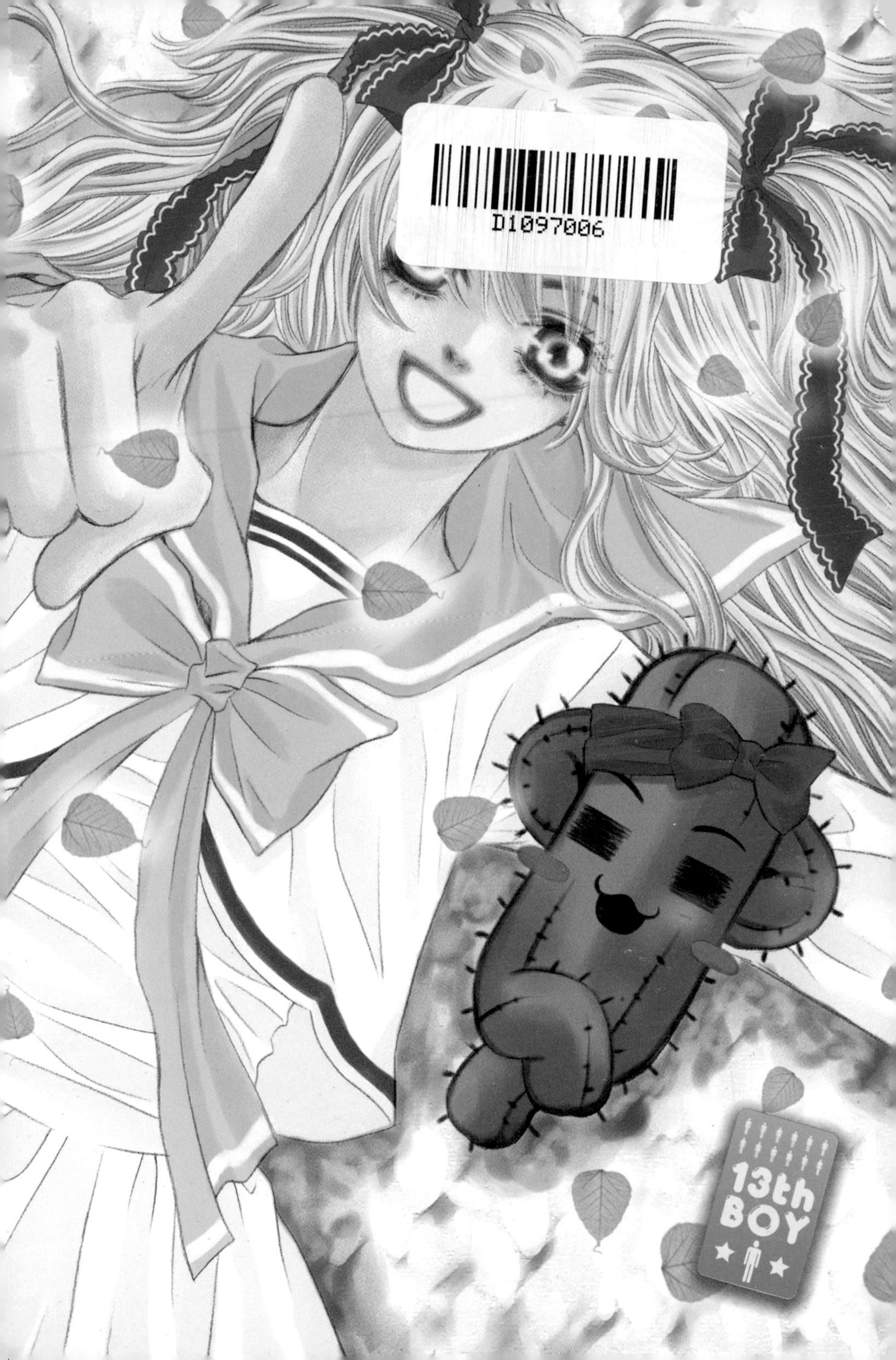
13th
BOY

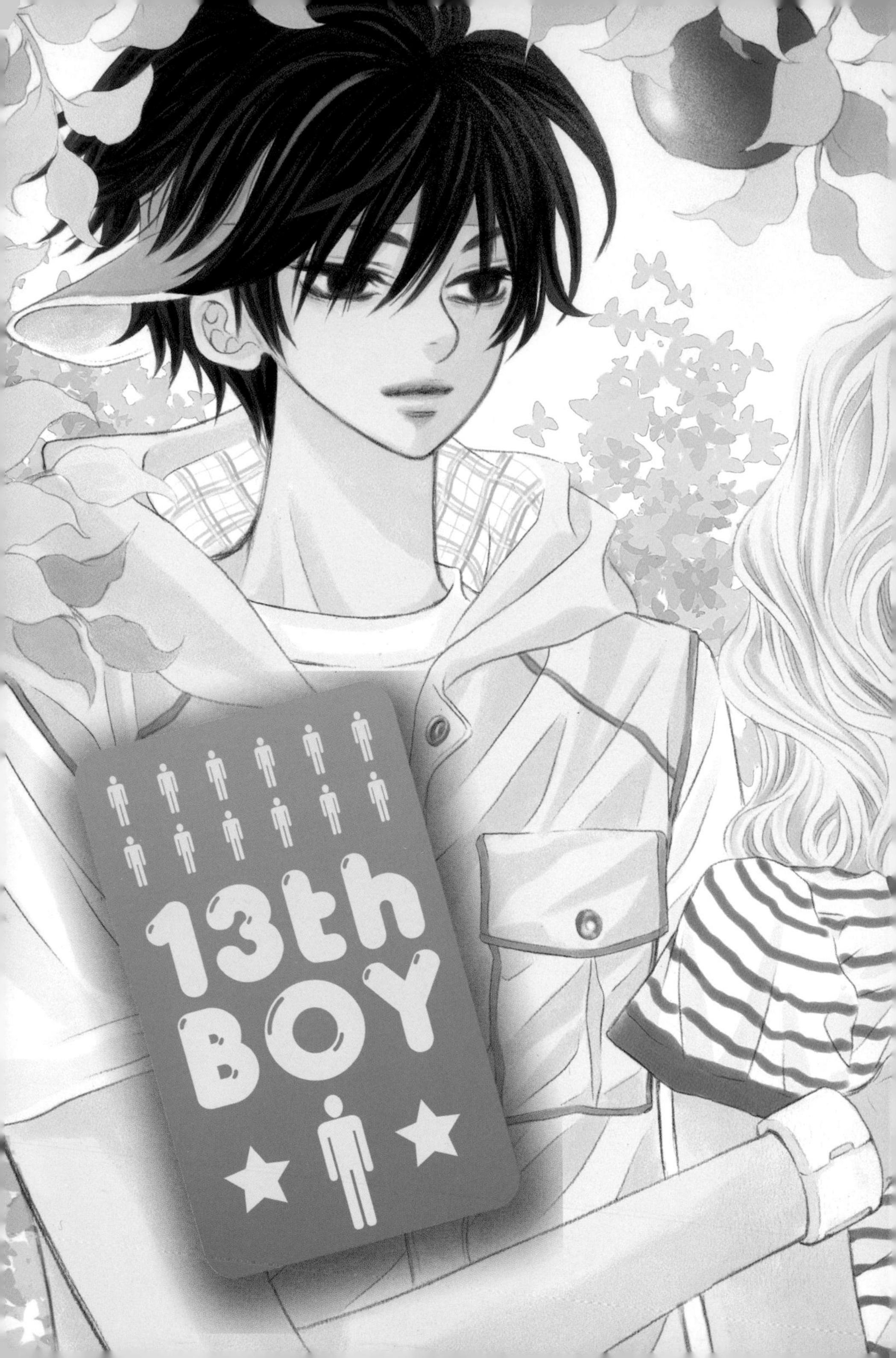
13th
BOY

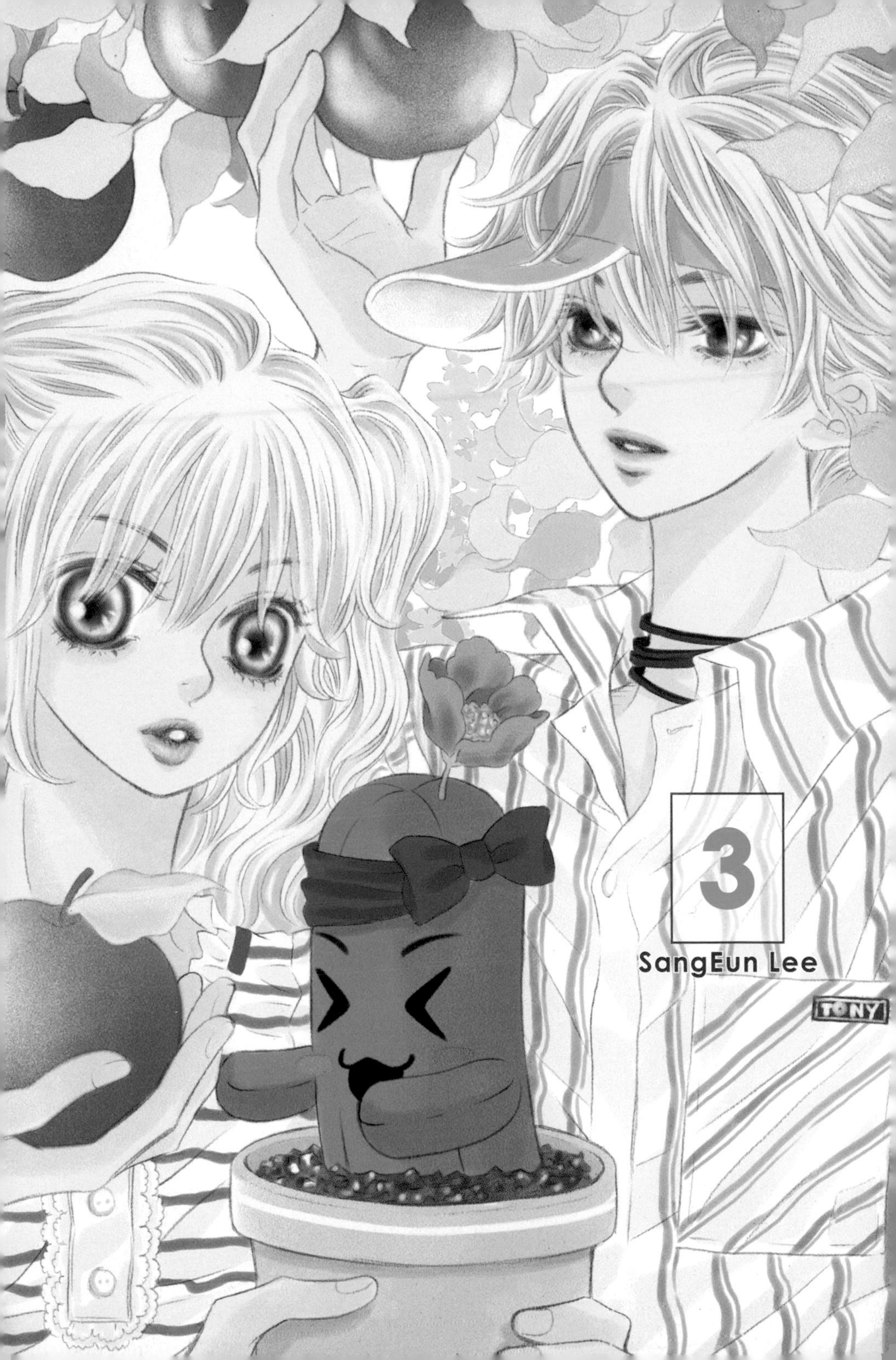
3
SangEun Lee
TONY

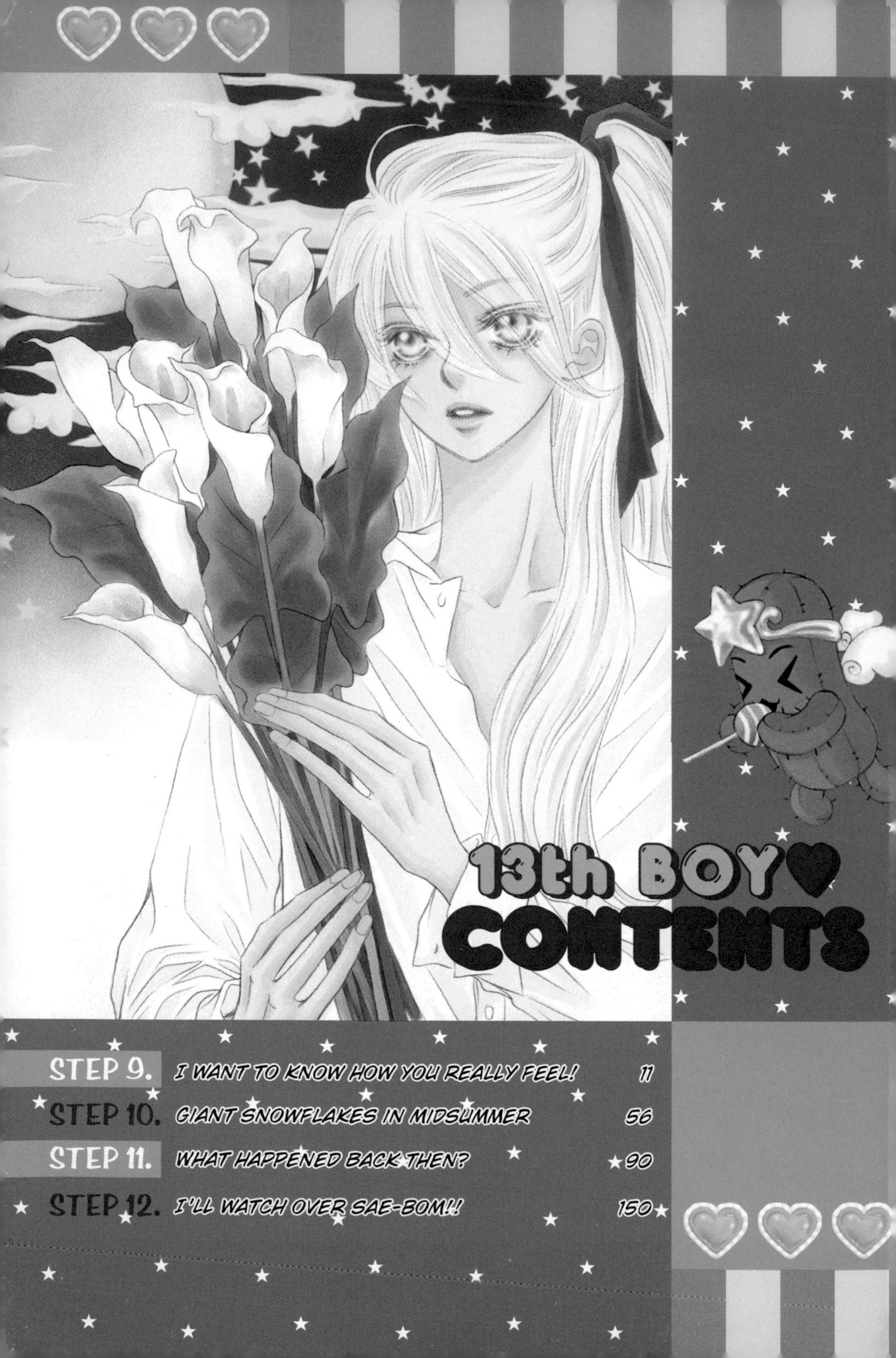

13th BOY♥ CONTENTS

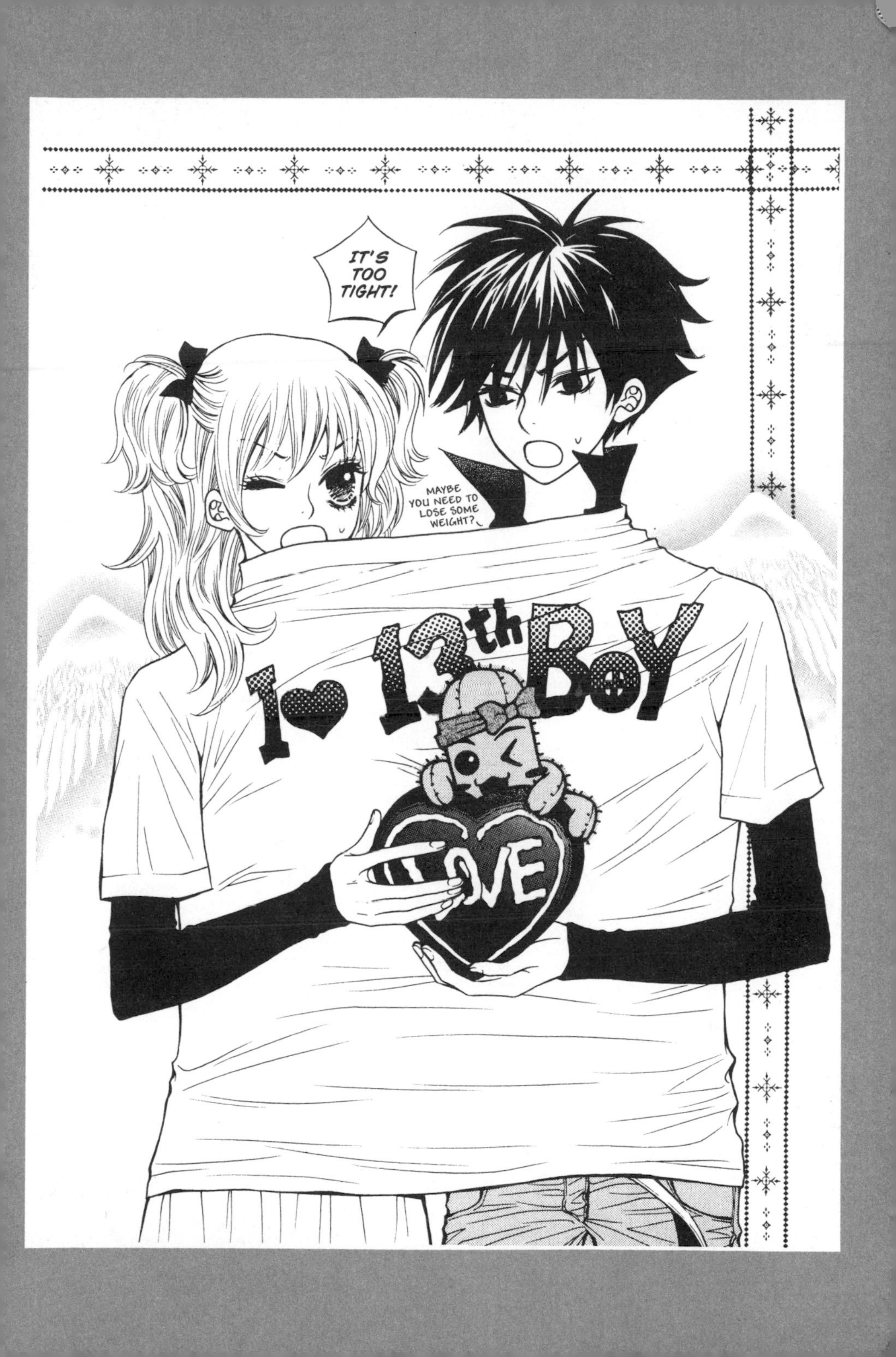
IT'S TOO TIGHT!
MAYBE YOU NEED TO LOSE SOME WEIGHT?
I ♥ 13th BOY
LOVE

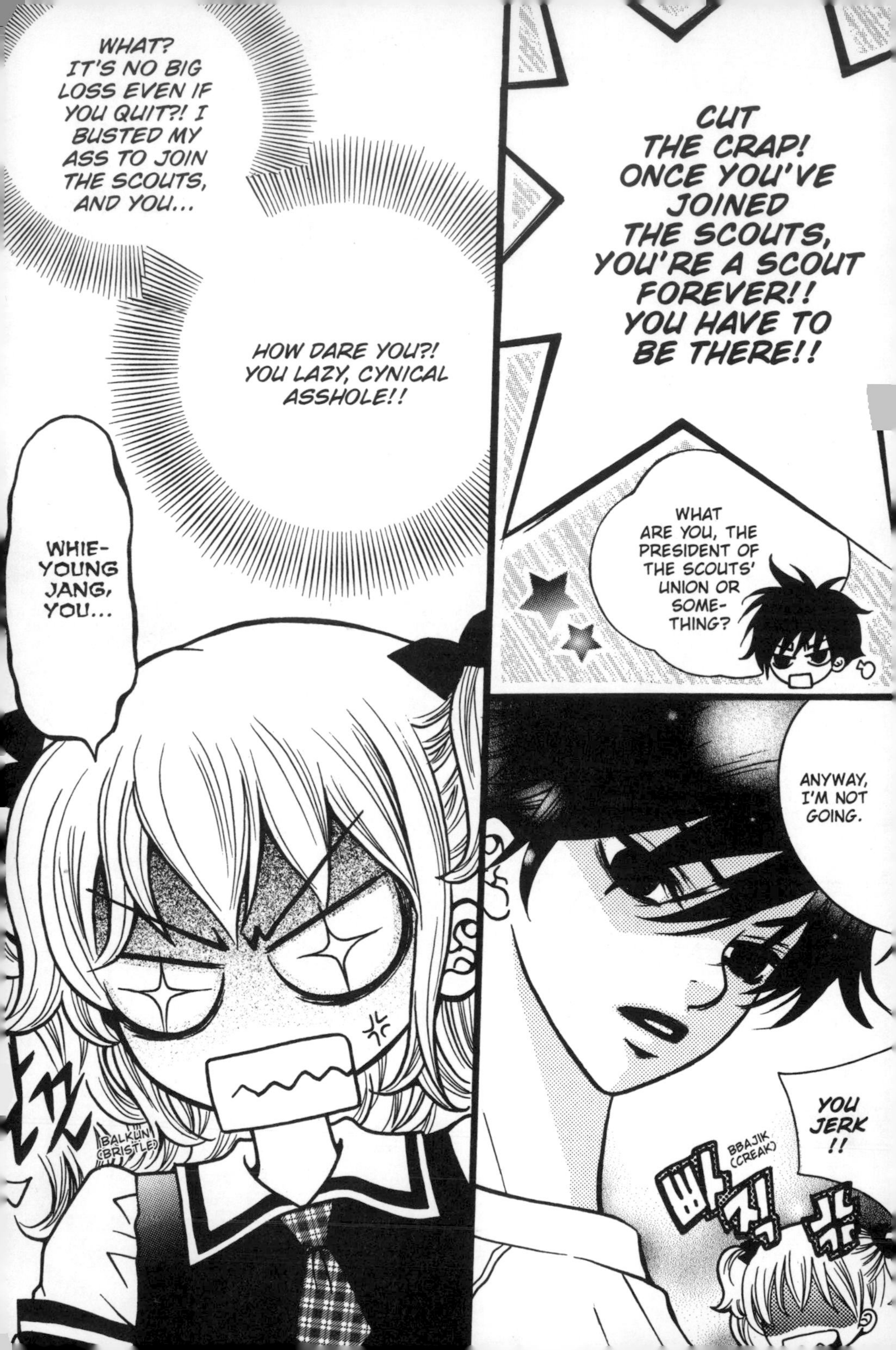
WHAT? IT'S NO BIG LOSS EVEN IF YOU QUIT?! I BUSTED MY ASS TO JOIN THE SCOUTS, AND YOU...
HOW DARE YOU?! YOU LAZY, CYNICAL ASSHOLE!!
WHIE-YOUNG JANG, YOU...
BALKUN (BRISTLE)
CUT THE CRAP! ONCE YOU'VE JOINED THE SCOUTS, YOU'RE A SCOUT FOREVER!! YOU HAVE TO BE THERE!!
WHAT ARE YOU, THE PRESIDENT OF THE SCOUTS' UNION OR SOME-THING?
ANYWAY, I'M NOT GOING.
YOU JERK!!
BBAJIK (CREAK)

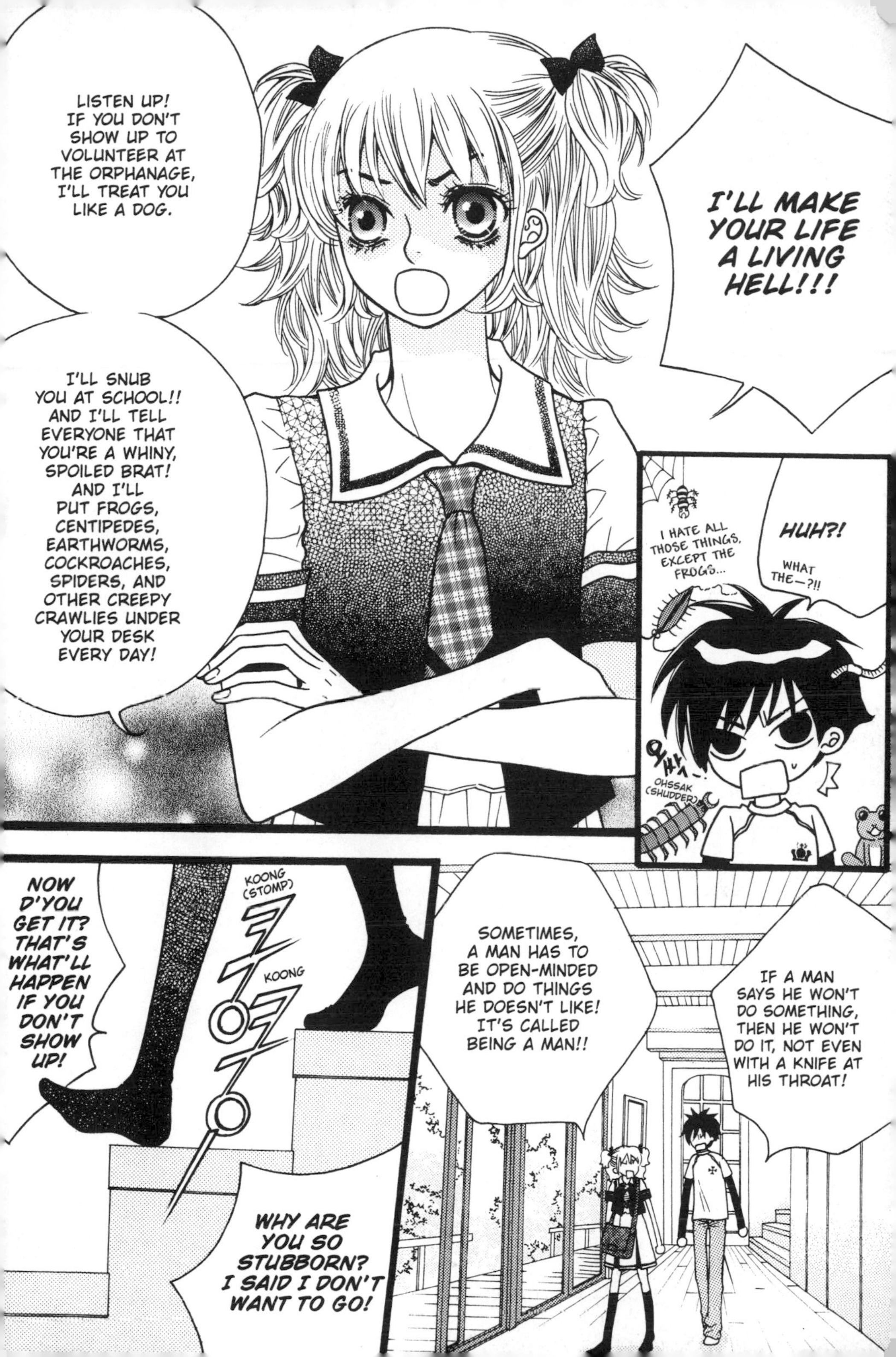
LISTEN UP! IF YOU DON'T SHOW UP TO VOLUNTEER AT THE ORPHANAGE, I'LL TREAT YOU LIKE A DOG.
I'LL MAKE YOUR LIFE A LIVING HELL!!!
I'LL SNUB YOU AT SCHOOL!! AND I'LL TELL EVERYONE THAT YOU'RE A WHINY, SPOILED BRAT! AND I'LL PUT FROGS, CENTIPEDES, EARTHWORMS, COCKROACHES, SPIDERS, AND OTHER CREEPY CRAWLIES UNDER YOUR DESK EVERY DAY!
I HATE ALL THOSE THINGS, EXCEPT THE FROGS...
HUH?!
WHAT THE—?!!
OHSSAK (SHUDDER)
NOW D'YOU GET IT? THAT'S WHAT'LL HAPPEN IF YOU DON'T SHOW UP!
KOONG (STOMP)
KOONG
WHY ARE YOU SO STUBBORN? I SAID I DON'T WANT TO GO!
SOMETIMES, A MAN HAS TO BE OPEN-MINDED AND DO THINGS HE DOESN'T LIKE! IT'S CALLED BEING A MAN!!
IF A MAN SAYS HE WON'T DO SOMETHING, THEN HE WON'T DO IT, NOT EVEN WITH A KNIFE AT HIS THROAT!

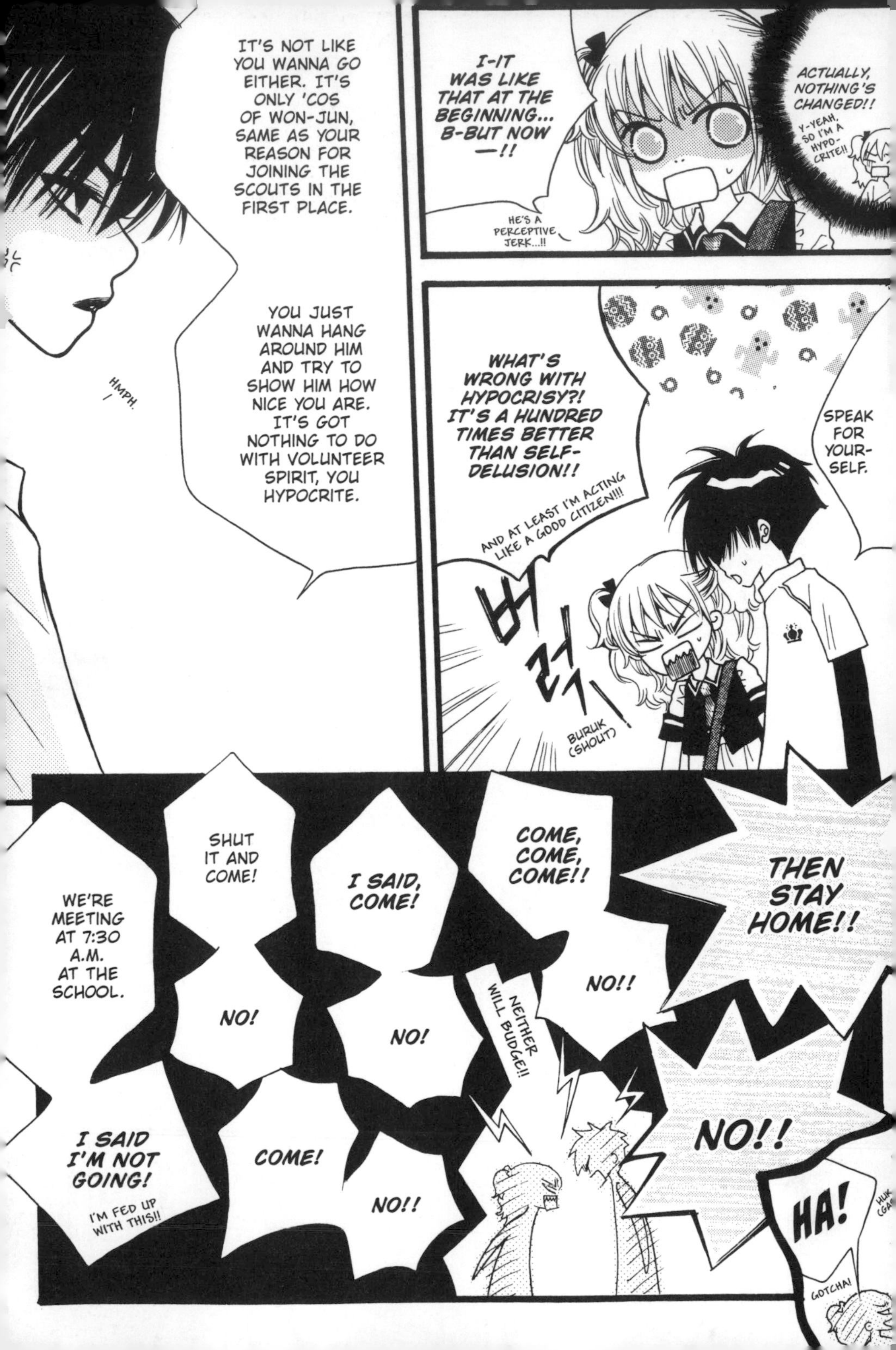

IT'S NOT LIKE YOU WANNA GO EITHER. IT'S ONLY 'COS OF WON-JUN, SAME AS YOUR REASON FOR JOINING THE SCOUTS IN THE FIRST PLACE.
HMPH.
YOU JUST WANNA HANG AROUND HIM AND TRY TO SHOW HIM HOW NICE YOU ARE. IT'S GOT NOTHING TO DO WITH VOLUNTEER SPIRIT, YOU HYPOCRITE.
I-IT WAS LIKE THAT AT THE BEGINNING... B-BUT NOW—!!
HE'S A PERCEPTIVE JERK...!!
ACTUALLY, NOTHING'S CHANGED!!
Y-YEAH, SO I'M A HYPOCRITE!!
WHAT'S WRONG WITH HYPOCRISY?! IT'S A HUNDRED TIMES BETTER THAN SELF-DELUSION!!
AND AT LEAST I'M ACTING LIKE A GOOD CITIZEN!!!
SPEAK FOR YOURSELF.
버럭
BURUK (SHOUT)
WE'RE MEETING AT 7:30 A.M. AT THE SCHOOL.
I SAID I'M NOT GOING!
I'M FED UP WITH THIS!!
SHUT IT AND COME!
NO!
COME!
I SAID, COME!
NO!
NO!!
COME, COME, COME!!
NO!!
NEITHER WILL BUDGE!!
THEN STAY HOME!!
NO!!
HA!
GOTCHA!

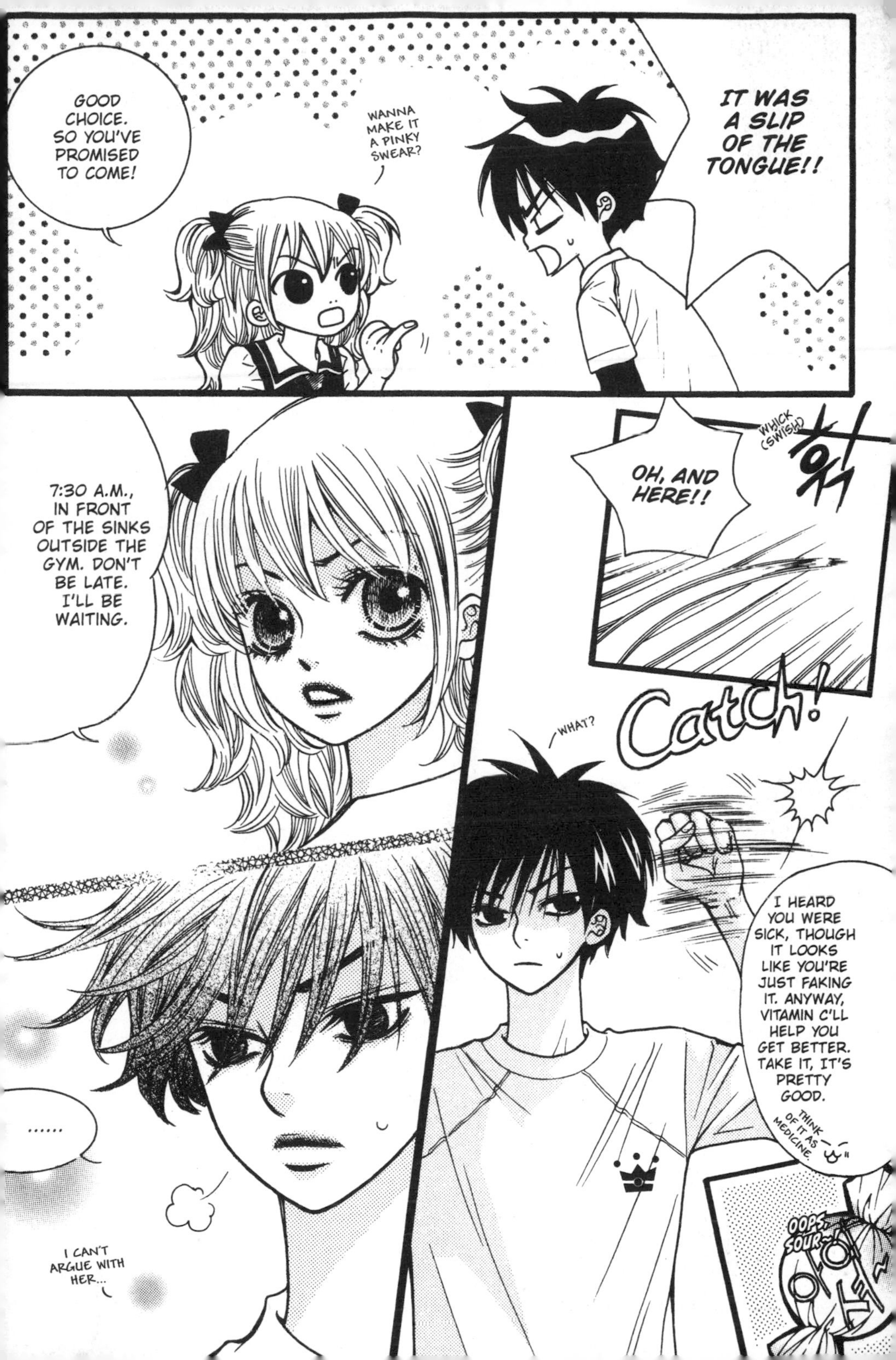
GOOD CHOICE. SO YOU'VE PROMISED TO COME!
WANNA MAKE IT A PINKY SWEAR?
IT WAS A SLIP OF THE TONGUE!!
7:30 A.M., IN FRONT OF THE SINKS OUTSIDE THE GYM. DON'T BE LATE. I'LL BE WAITING.
......
I CAN'T ARGUE WITH HER...
WHICK (SWISH)
OH, AND HERE!!
Catch!
WHAT?
I HEARD YOU WERE SICK, THOUGH IT LOOKS LIKE YOU'RE JUST FAKING IT. ANYWAY, VITAMIN C'LL HELP YOU GET BETTER. TAKE IT, IT'S PRETTY GOOD.
THINK OF IT AS MEDICINE.
OOPS, SOUR~!

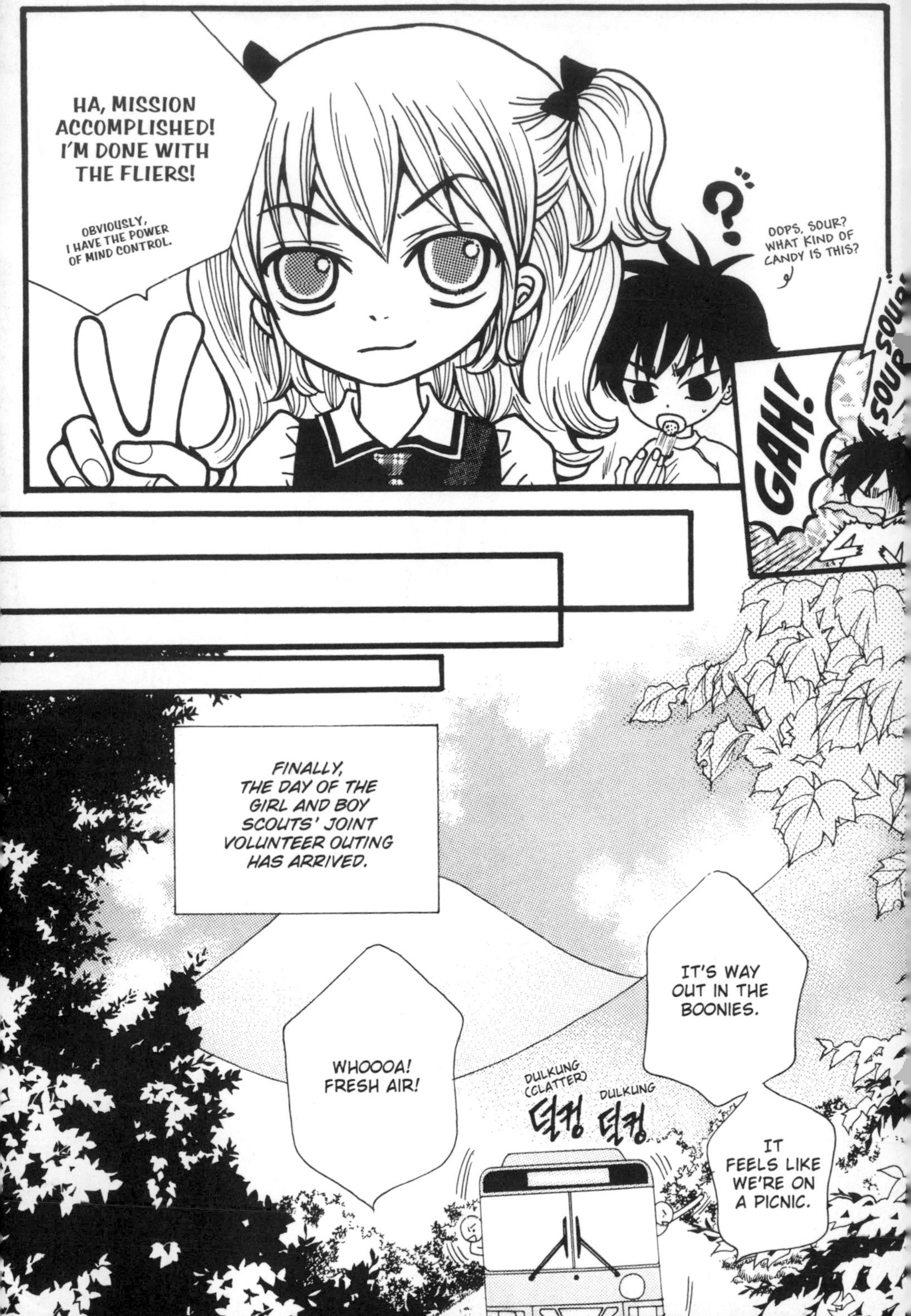
HA, MISSION ACCOMPLISHED! I'M DONE WITH THE FLIERS!
OBVIOUSLY, I HAVE THE POWER OF MIND CONTROL.
?
OOPS, SOUR? WHAT KIND OF CANDY IS THIS?
GAH!
SOUR SOUR
FINALLY, THE DAY OF THE GIRL AND BOY SCOUTS' JOINT VOLUNTEER OUTING HAS ARRIVED.
WHOOOA! FRESH AIR!
DULKUNG (CLATTER) DULKUNG
덜컹 덜컹
IT'S WAY OUT IN THE BOONIES.
IT FEELS LIKE WE'RE ON A PICNIC.

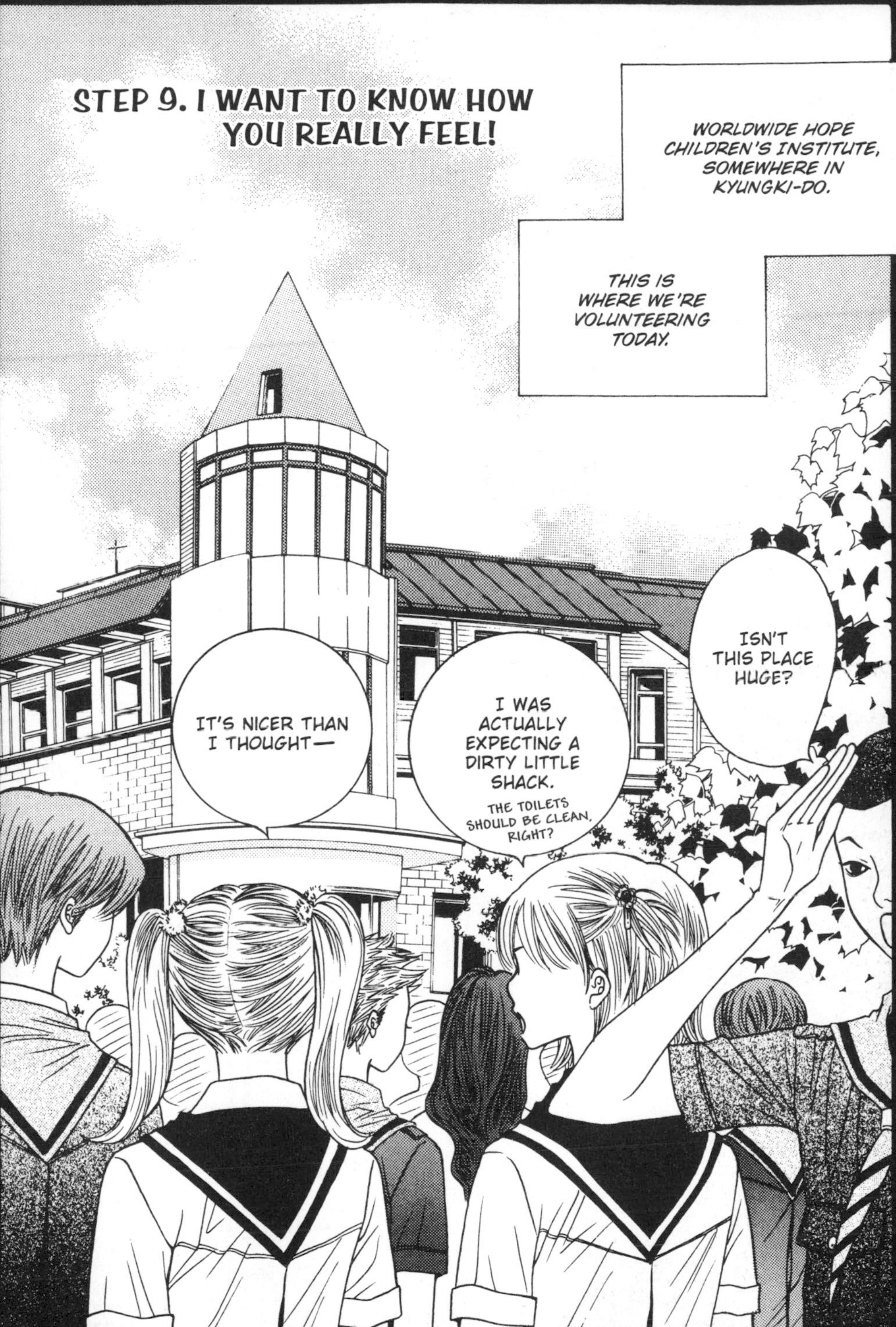
STEP 9. I WANT TO KNOW HOW YOU REALLY FEEL!
WORLDWIDE HOPE CHILDREN'S INSTITUTE, SOMEWHERE IN KYUNGKI-DO.
THIS IS WHERE WE'RE VOLUNTEERING TODAY.
ISN'T THIS PLACE HUGE?
I WAS ACTUALLY EXPECTING A DIRTY LITTLE SHACK.
THE TOILETS SHOULD BE CLEAN, RIGHT?
IT'S NICER THAN I THOUGHT—

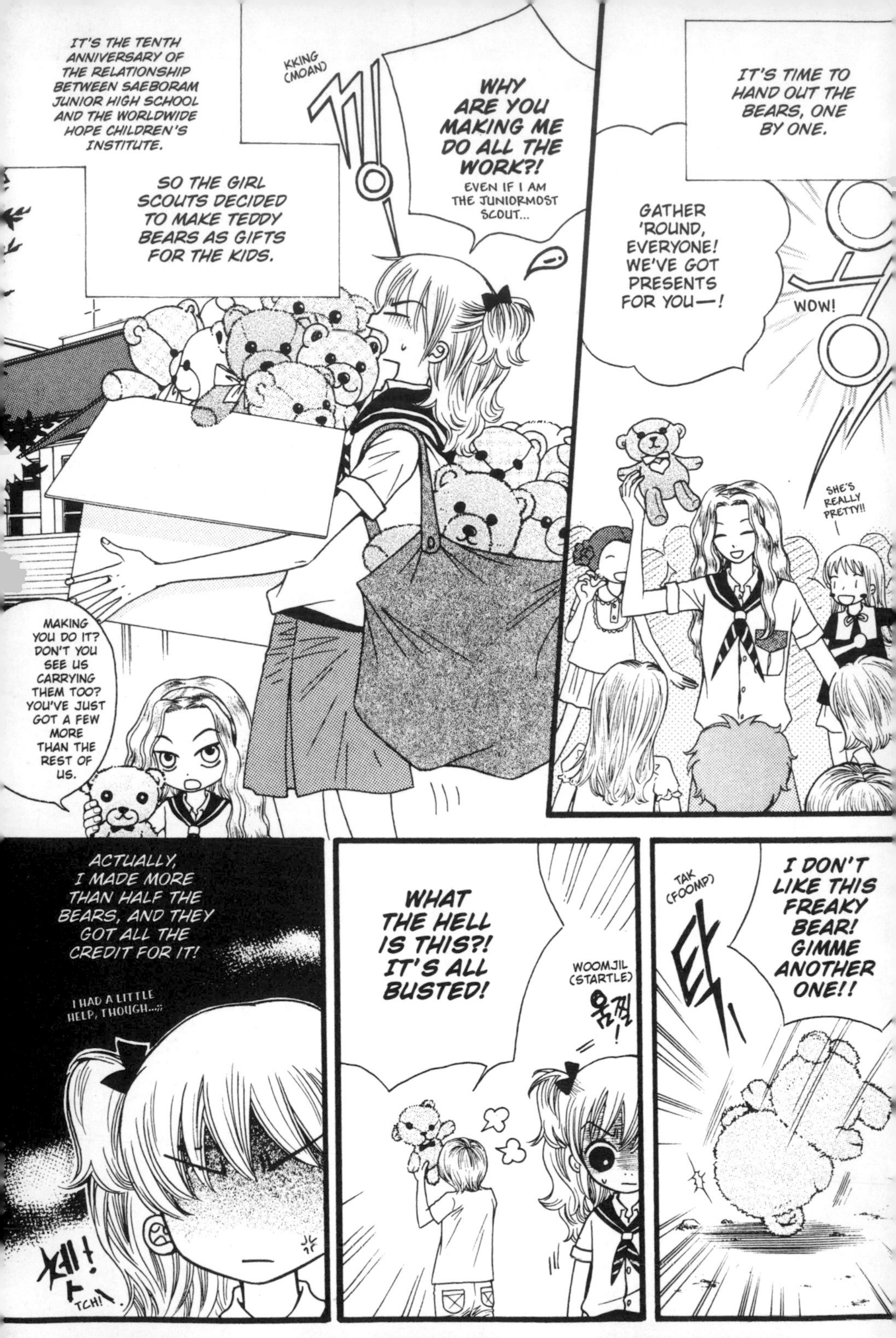
IT'S THE TENTH ANNIVERSARY OF THE RELATIONSHIP BETWEEN SAEBORAM JUNIOR HIGH SCHOOL AND THE WORLDWIDE HOPE CHILDREN'S INSTITUTE.
SO THE GIRL SCOUTS DECIDED TO MAKE TEDDY BEARS AS GIFTS FOR THE KIDS.
KKING (MOAN)
WHY ARE YOU MAKING ME DO ALL THE WORK?!
EVEN IF I AM THE JUNIORMOST SCOUT...
MAKING YOU DO IT? DON'T YOU SEE US CARRYING THEM TOO? YOU'VE JUST GOT A FEW MORE THAN THE REST OF US.
IT'S TIME TO HAND OUT THE BEARS, ONE BY ONE.
GATHER 'ROUND, EVERYONE! WE'VE GOT PRESENTS FOR YOU—!
WOW!
SHE'S REALLY PRETTY!!
ACTUALLY, I MADE MORE THAN HALF THE BEARS, AND THEY GOT ALL THE CREDIT FOR IT!
I HAD A LITTLE HELP, THOUGH...;;
TCH!
WHAT THE HELL IS THIS?! IT'S ALL BUSTED!
WOOMJIL (STARTLE)
TAK (FOOMP)
I DON'T LIKE THIS FREAKY BEAR! GIMME ANOTHER ONE!!

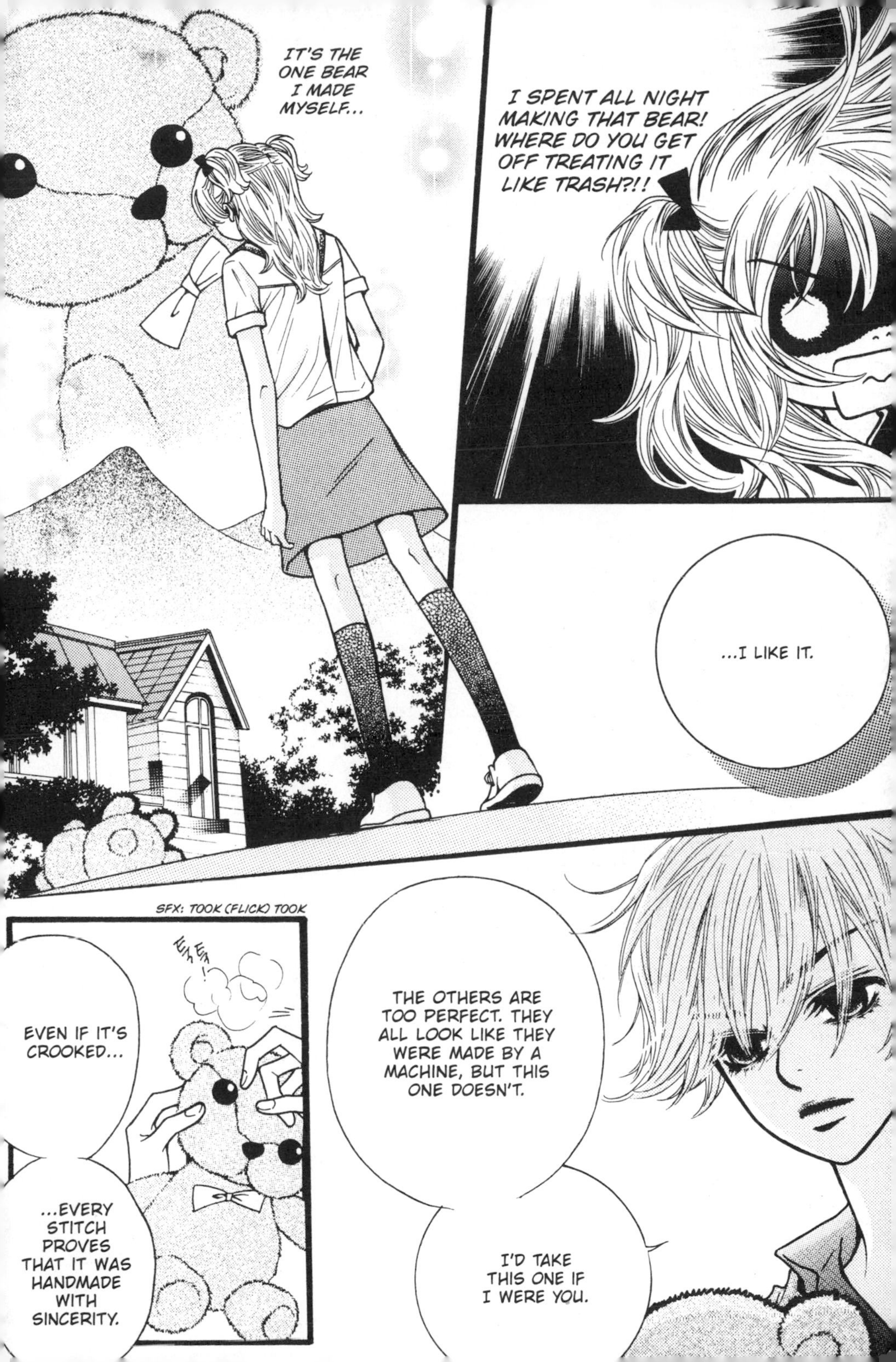
IT'S THE ONE BEAR I MADE MYSELF...
I SPENT ALL NIGHT MAKING THAT BEAR! WHERE DO YOU GET OFF TREATING IT LIKE TRASH?!!
...I LIKE IT.
SFX: TOOK (FLICK) TOOK
EVEN IF IT'S CROOKED...
...EVERY STITCH PROVES THAT IT WAS HANDMADE WITH SINCERITY.
THE OTHERS ARE TOO PERFECT. THEY ALL LOOK LIKE THEY WERE MADE BY A MACHINE, BUT THIS ONE DOESN'T.
I'D TAKE THIS ONE IF I WERE YOU.

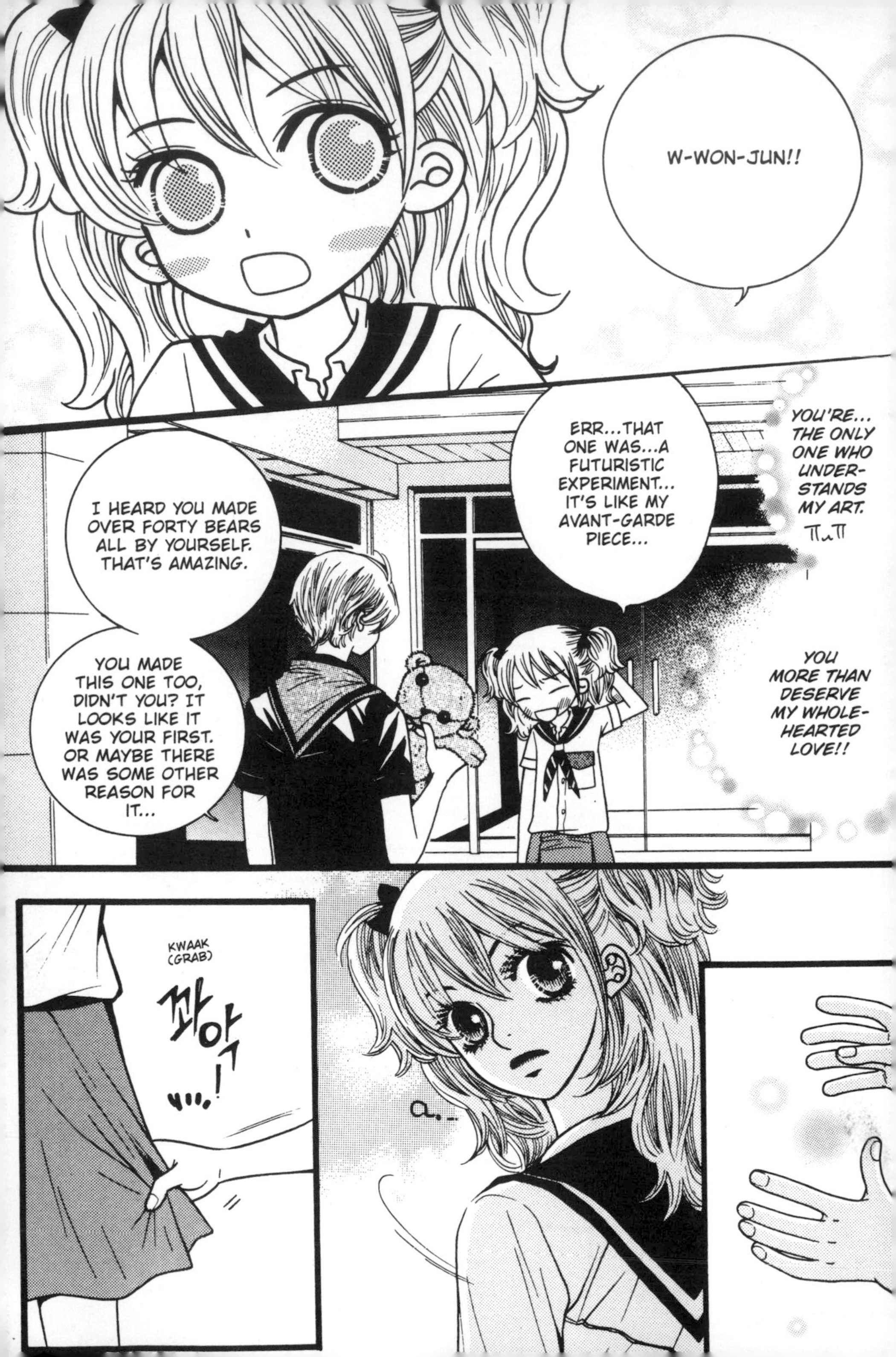
W-WON-JUN!!
I HEARD YOU MADE OVER FORTY BEARS ALL BY YOURSELF. THAT'S AMAZING.
YOU MADE THIS ONE TOO, DIDN'T YOU? IT LOOKS LIKE IT WAS YOUR FIRST. OR MAYBE THERE WAS SOME OTHER REASON FOR IT...
ERR...THAT ONE WAS...A FUTURISTIC EXPERIMENT... IT'S LIKE MY AVANT-GARDE PIECE...
YOU'RE... THE ONLY ONE WHO UNDER-STANDS MY ART.
YOU MORE THAN DESERVE MY WHOLE-HEARTED LOVE!!
KWAAK (GRAB)
꽈악

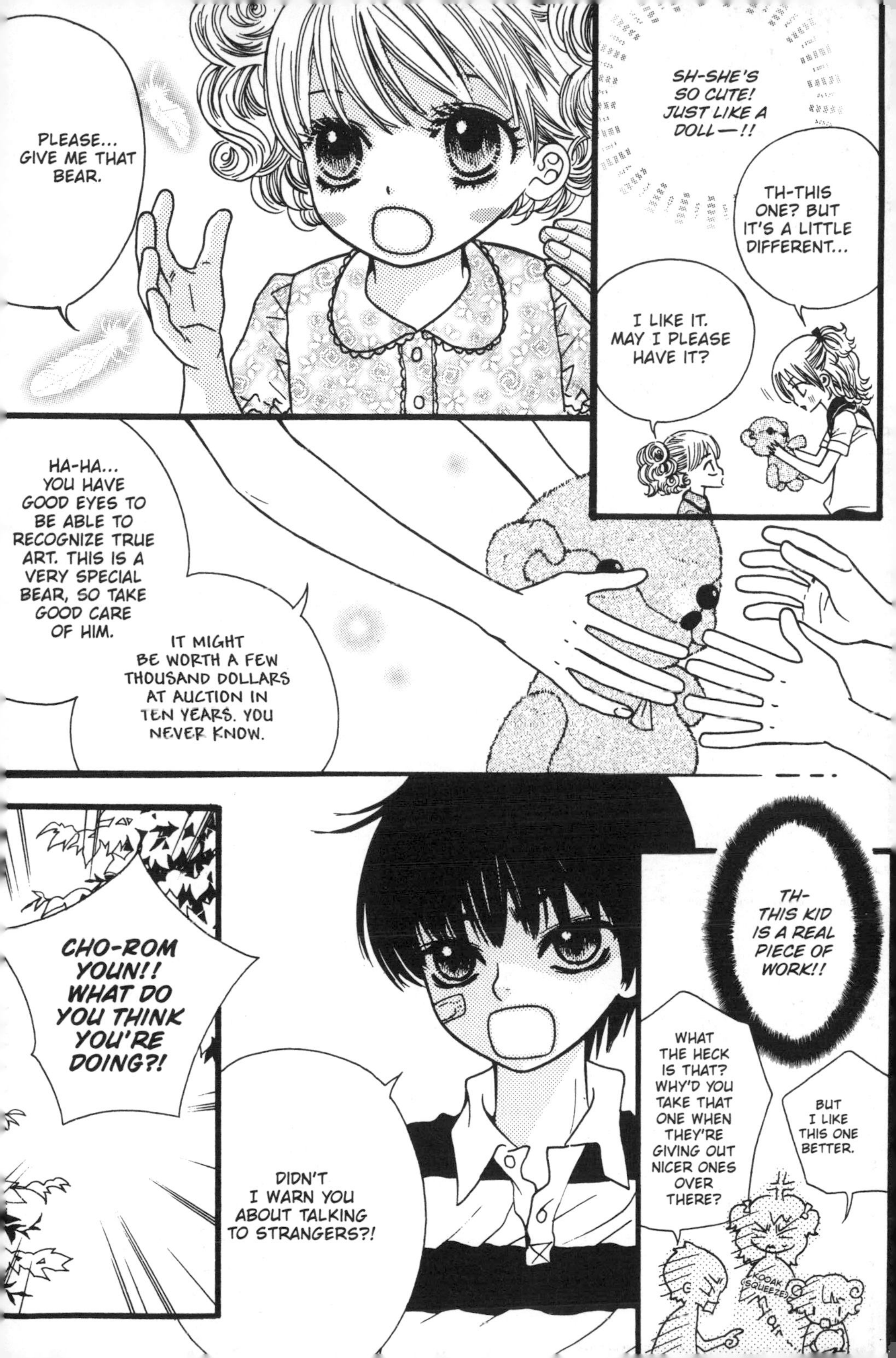
PLEASE... GIVE ME THAT BEAR.
SH-SHE'S SO CUTE! JUST LIKE A DOLL—!!
TH-THIS ONE? BUT IT'S A LITTLE DIFFERENT...
I LIKE IT. MAY I PLEASE HAVE IT?
HA-HA... YOU HAVE GOOD EYES TO BE ABLE TO RECOGNIZE TRUE ART. THIS IS A VERY SPECIAL BEAR, SO TAKE GOOD CARE OF HIM.
IT MIGHT BE WORTH A FEW THOUSAND DOLLARS AT AUCTION IN TEN YEARS. YOU NEVER KNOW.
CHO-ROM YOUN!! WHAT DO YOU THINK YOU'RE DOING?!
DIDN'T I WARN YOU ABOUT TALKING TO STRANGERS?!
TH-THIS KID IS A REAL PIECE OF WORK!!
WHAT THE HECK IS THAT? WHY'D YOU TAKE THAT ONE WHEN THEY'RE GIVING OUT NICER ONES OVER THERE?
BUT I LIKE THIS ONE BETTER.
KOOAK (SQUEEZE)

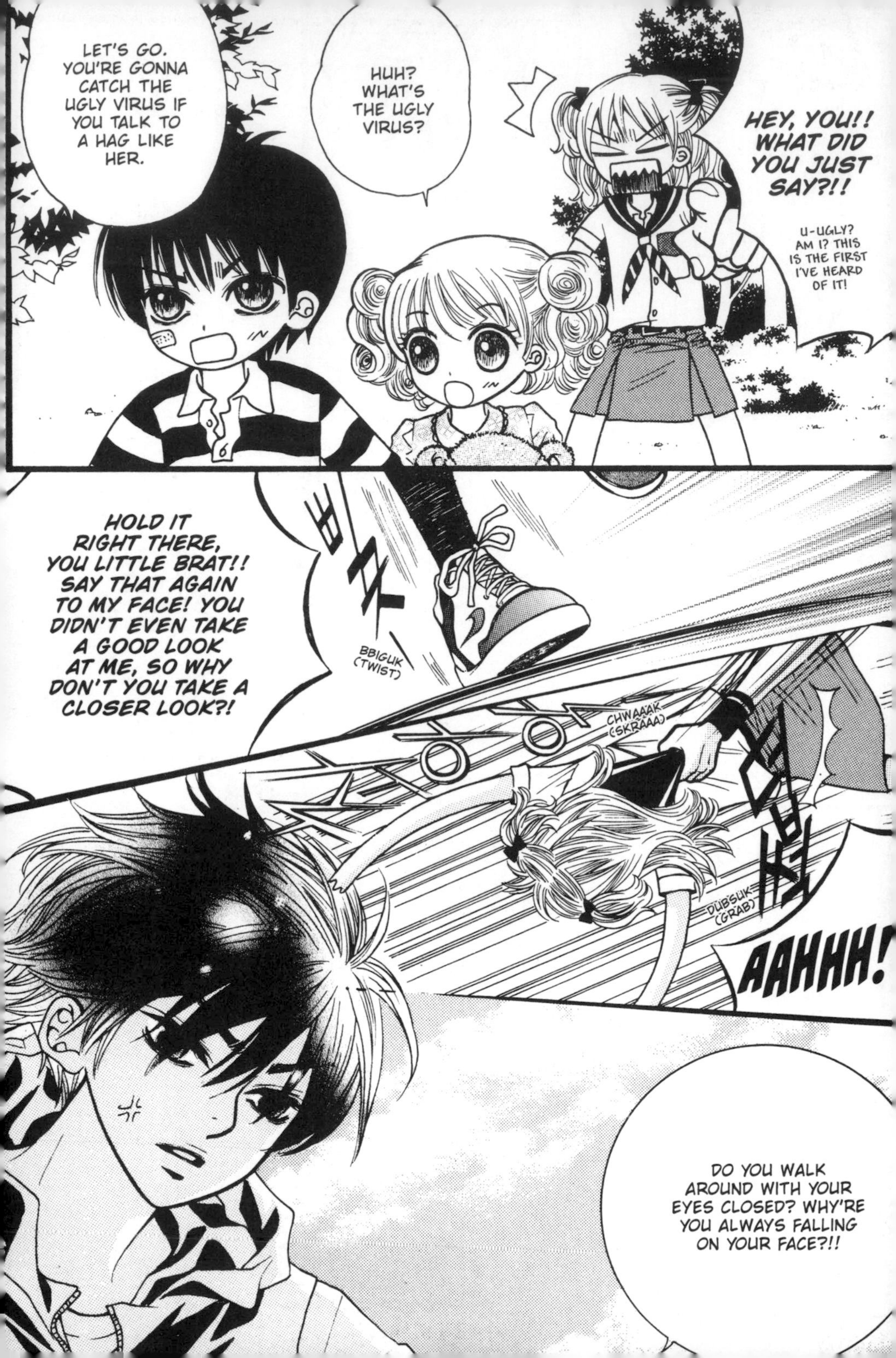
LET'S GO. YOU'RE GONNA CATCH THE UGLY VIRUS IF YOU TALK TO A HAG LIKE HER.
HUH? WHAT'S THE UGLY VIRUS?
HEY, YOU!! WHAT DID YOU JUST SAY?!!
U-UGLY? AM I? THIS IS THE FIRST I'VE HEARD OF IT!
HOLD IT RIGHT THERE, YOU LITTLE BRAT!! SAY THAT AGAIN TO MY FACE! YOU DIDN'T EVEN TAKE A GOOD LOOK AT ME, SO WHY DON'T YOU TAKE A CLOSER LOOK?!
BBIGUK (TWIST)
CHWAAAK (SKRAAA)
DUBSUK (GRAB)
AAHHH!
DO YOU WALK AROUND WITH YOUR EYES CLOSED? WHY'RE YOU ALWAYS FALLING ON YOUR FACE?!!

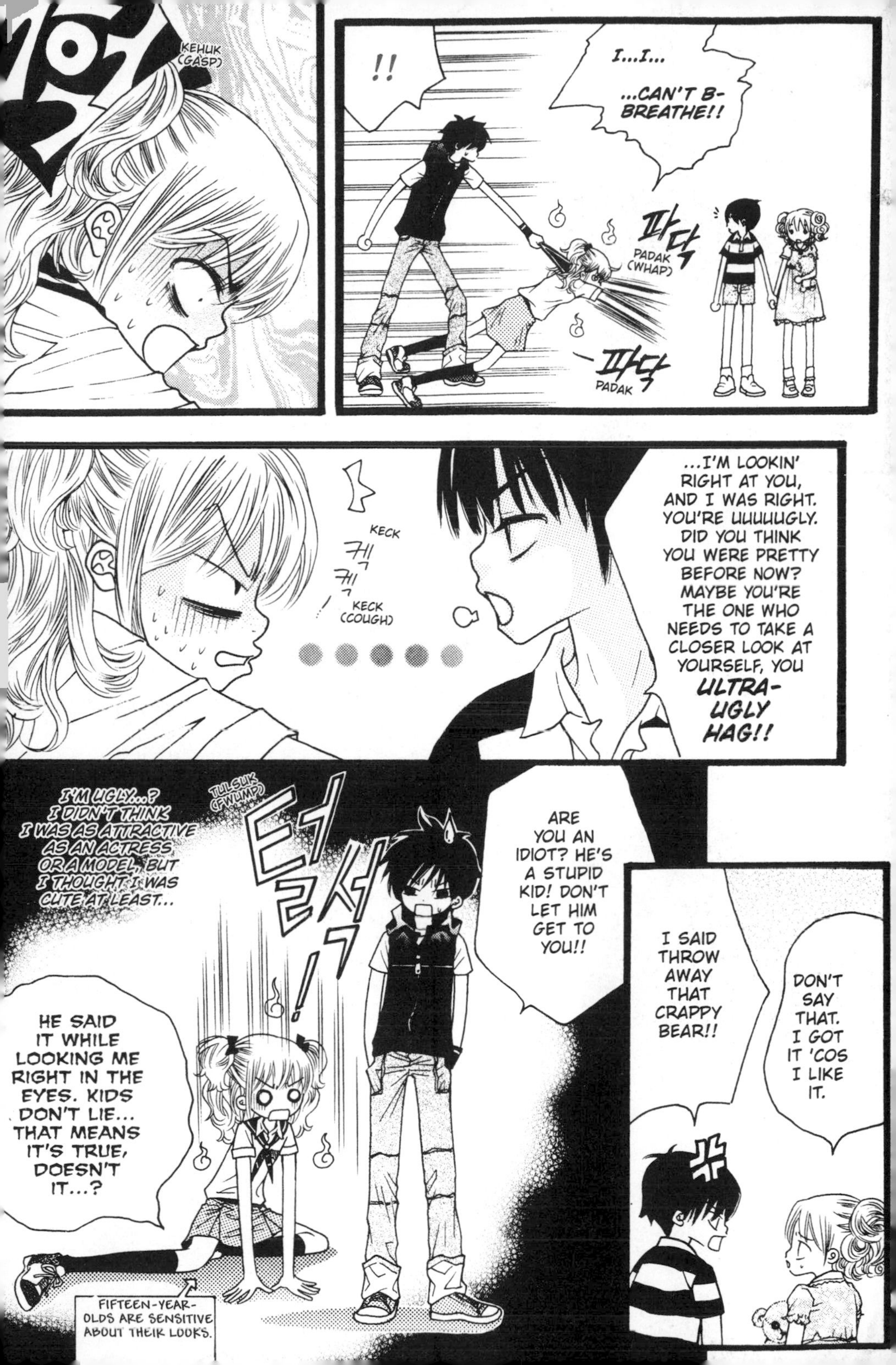

KEHUK (GASP)
!!
I...I...
...CAN'T B-BREATHE!!
파닥
PADAK (WHAP)
파닥
PADAK
켁
켁
KECK
KECK (COUGH)
...I'M LOOKIN' RIGHT AT YOU, AND I WAS RIGHT. YOU'RE UUUUUGLY. DID YOU THINK YOU WERE PRETTY BEFORE NOW? MAYBE YOU'RE THE ONE WHO NEEDS TO TAKE A CLOSER LOOK AT YOURSELF, YOU ULTRA-UGLY HAG!!
I'M UGLY...? I DIDN'T THINK I WAS AS ATTRACTIVE AS AN ACTRESS OR A MODEL, BUT I THOUGHT I WAS CUTE AT LEAST...
TULSUK (FWUMP)
털썩
ARE YOU AN IDIOT? HE'S A STUPID KID! DON'T LET HIM GET TO YOU!!
HE SAID IT WHILE LOOKING ME RIGHT IN THE EYES. KIDS DON'T LIE... THAT MEANS IT'S TRUE, DOESN'T IT...?
FIFTEEN-YEAR-OLDS ARE SENSITIVE ABOUT THEIR LOOKS.
I SAID THROW AWAY THAT CRAPPY BEAR!!
DON'T SAY THAT. I GOT IT 'COS I LIKE IT.

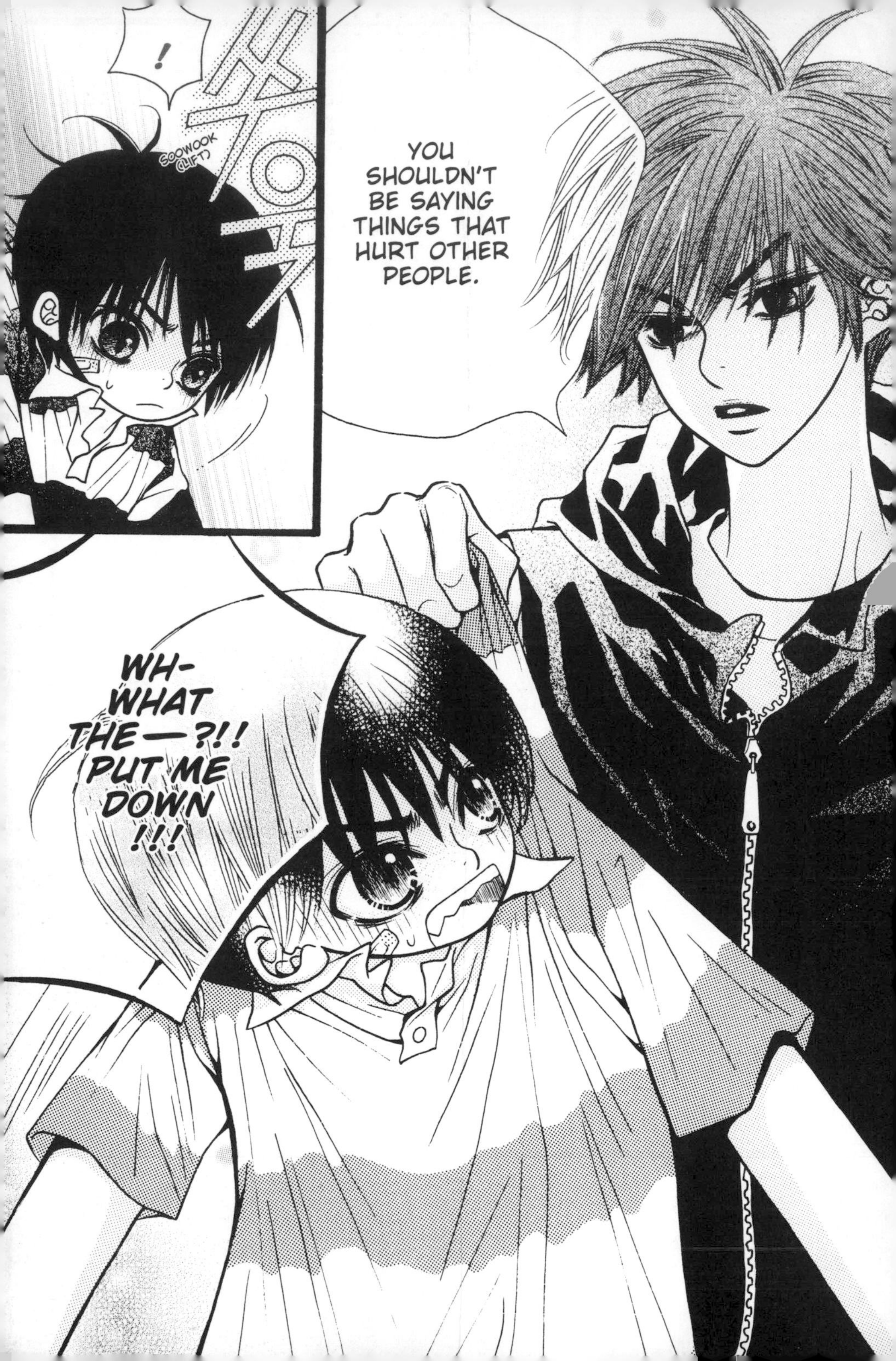
!
SOOWOOK (LIFT)
YOU SHOULDN'T BE SAYING THINGS THAT HURT OTHER PEOPLE.
WH- WHAT THE—?!! PUT ME DOWN!!!

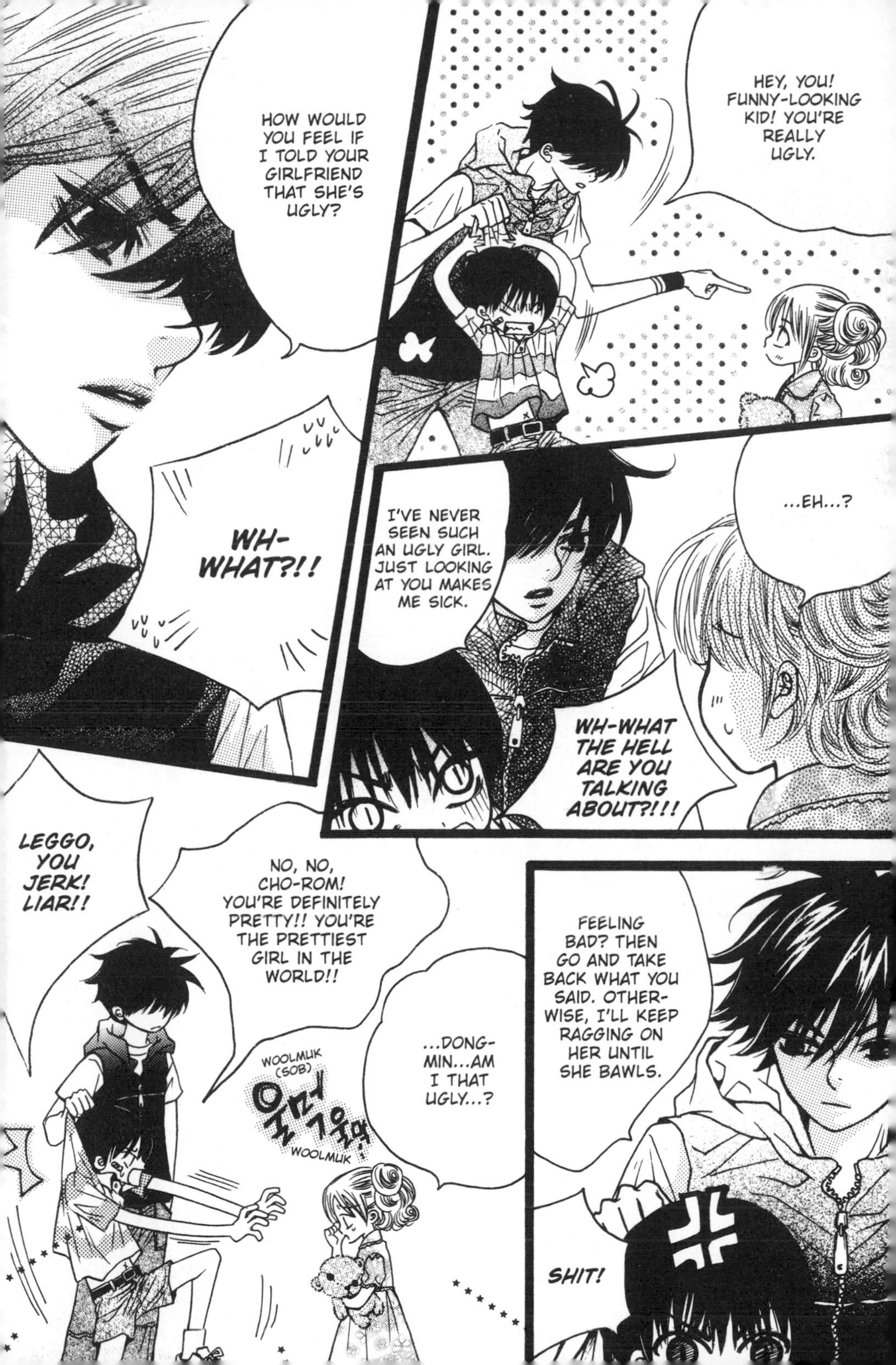
HOW WOULD YOU FEEL IF I TOLD YOUR GIRLFRIEND THAT SHE'S UGLY?
WH-WHAT?!!
HEY, YOU! FUNNY-LOOKING KID! YOU'RE REALLY UGLY.
I'VE NEVER SEEN SUCH AN UGLY GIRL. JUST LOOKING AT YOU MAKES ME SICK.
...EH...?
WH-WHAT THE HELL ARE YOU TALKING ABOUT?!!!
LEGGO, YOU JERK! LIAR!!
NO, NO, CHO-ROM! YOU'RE DEFINITELY PRETTY!! YOU'RE THE PRETTIEST GIRL IN THE WORLD!!
WOOLMUK (SOB)
WOOLMUK
...DONG-MIN...AM I THAT UGLY...?
FEELING BAD? THEN GO AND TAKE BACK WHAT YOU SAID. OTHERWISE, I'LL KEEP RAGGING ON HER UNTIL SHE BAWLS.
SHIT!

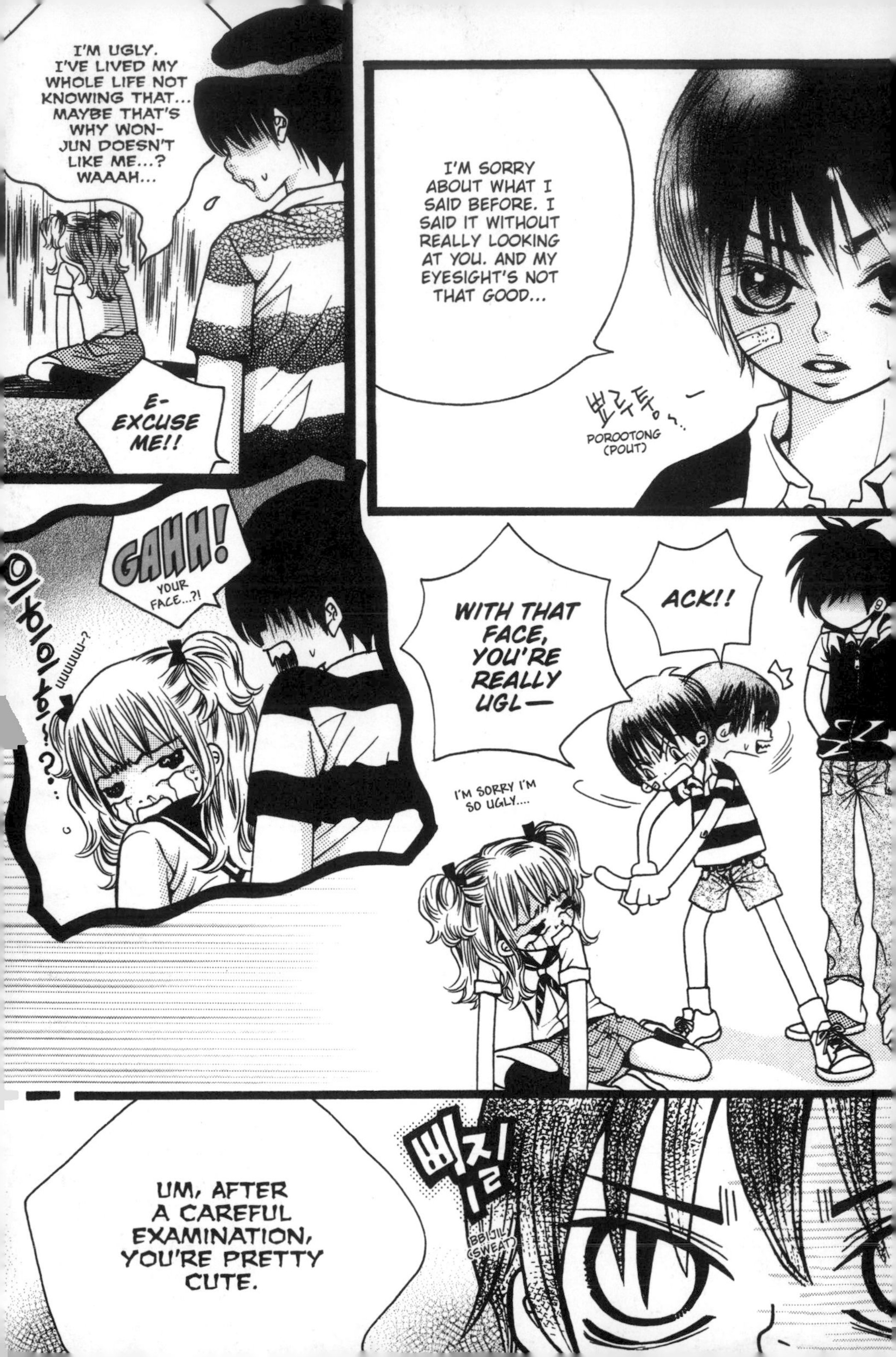
I'M UGLY. I'VE LIVED MY WHOLE LIFE NOT KNOWING THAT... MAYBE THAT'S WHY WON-JUN DOESN'T LIKE ME...? WAAAH...
E-EXCUSE ME!!
I'M SORRY ABOUT WHAT I SAID BEFORE. I SAID IT WITHOUT REALLY LOOKING AT YOU. AND MY EYESIGHT'S NOT THAT GOOD...
뾰루퉁
POROOTONG (POUT)
GAHH!
YOUR FACE...?!
WITH THAT FACE, YOU'RE REALLY UGL—
ACK!!
I'M SORRY I'M SO UGLY....
UM, AFTER A CAREFUL EXAMINATION, YOU'RE PRETTY CUTE.
삐질
BBIJIL (SWEAT)

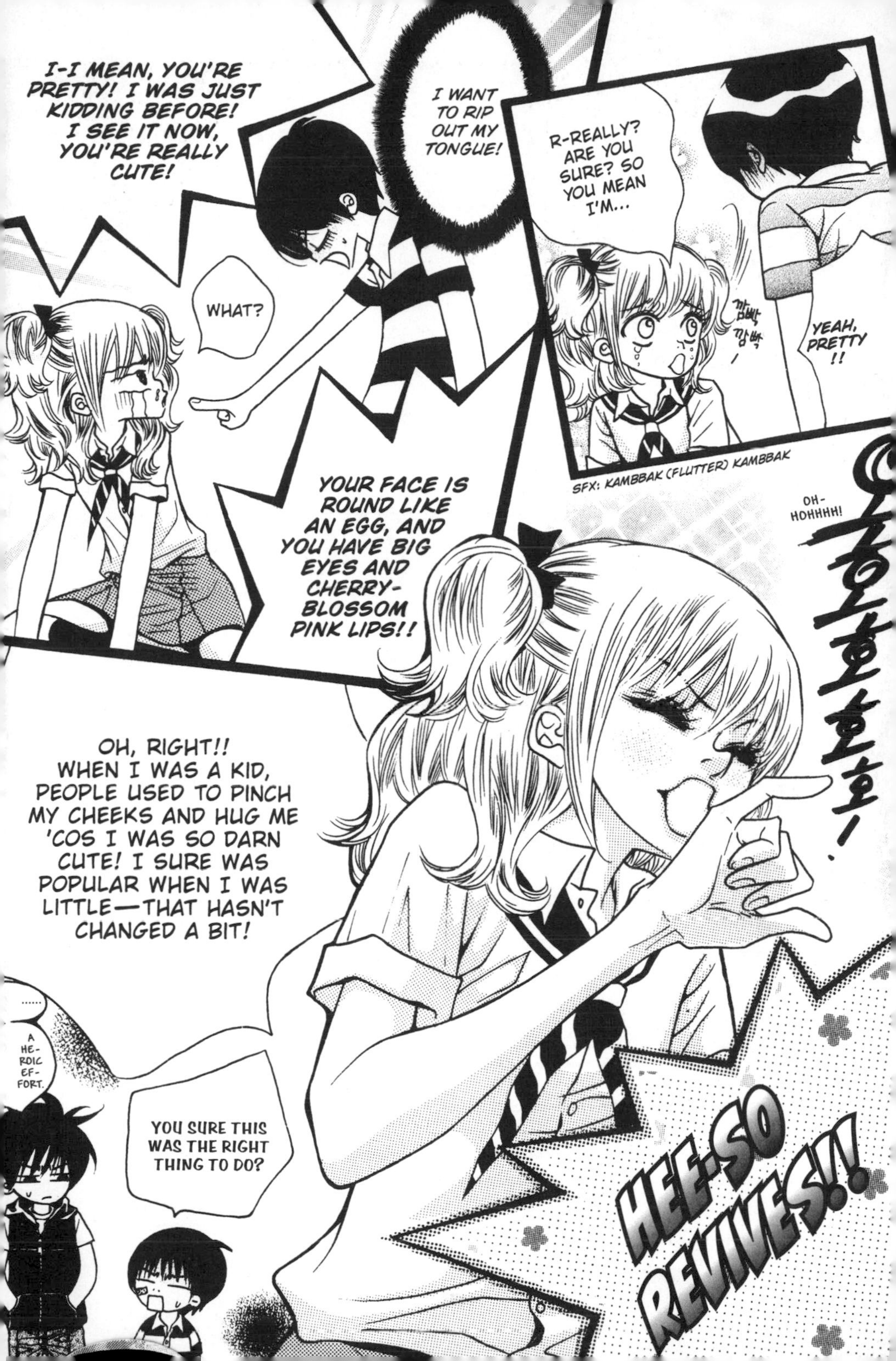
I-I MEAN, YOU'RE PRETTY! I WAS JUST KIDDING BEFORE! I SEE IT NOW, YOU'RE REALLY CUTE!
I WANT TO RIP OUT MY TONGUE!
WHAT?
YOUR FACE IS ROUND LIKE AN EGG, AND YOU HAVE BIG EYES AND CHERRY-BLOSSOM PINK LIPS!!
R-REALLY? ARE YOU SURE? SO YOU MEAN I'M...
깜빡 깜빡
YEAH, PRETTY!!
SFX: KAMBBAK (FLUTTER) KAMBBAK
OH-HOHHHH!
OH, RIGHT!! WHEN I WAS A KID, PEOPLE USED TO PINCH MY CHEEKS AND HUG ME 'COS I WAS SO DARN CUTE! I SURE WAS POPULAR WHEN I WAS LITTLE—THAT HASN'T CHANGED A BIT!
......
A HE-ROIC EF-FORT.
YOU SURE THIS WAS THE RIGHT THING TO DO?
HEE-SO REVIVES!!

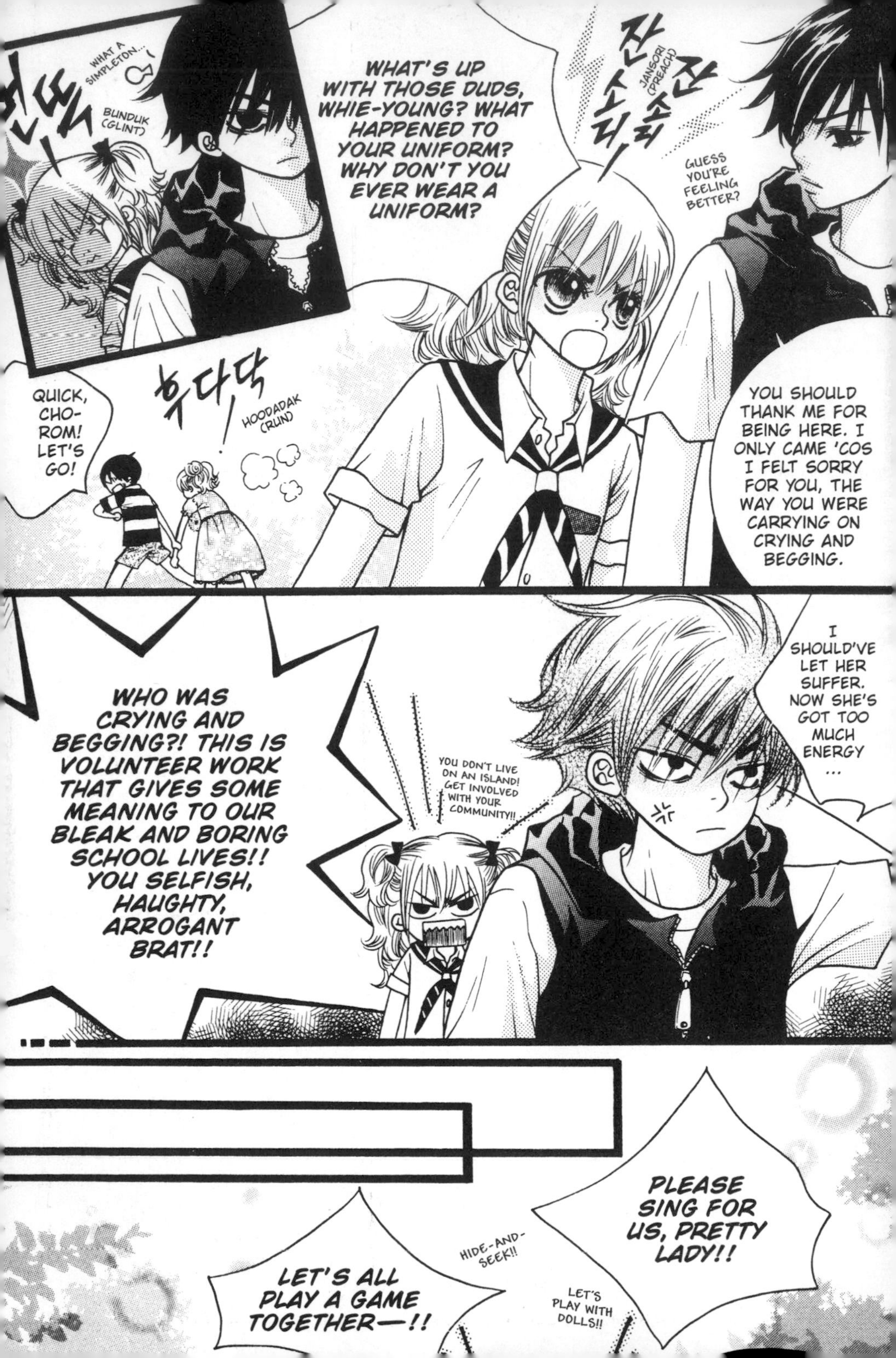

WHAT A SIMPLETON...
번뜩
BUNDUK (GLINT)
WHAT'S UP WITH THOSE DUDS, WHIE-YOUNG? WHAT HAPPENED TO YOUR UNIFORM? WHY DON'T YOU EVER WEAR A UNIFORM?
잔소리 잔소리
JANSORI (PREACH)
GUESS YOU'RE FEELING BETTER?
QUICK, CHO-ROM! LET'S GO!
후다닥
HOODADAK (RUN)
YOU SHOULD THANK ME FOR BEING HERE. I ONLY CAME 'COS I FELT SORRY FOR YOU, THE WAY YOU WERE CARRYING ON CRYING AND BEGGING.
WHO WAS CRYING AND BEGGING?! THIS IS VOLUNTEER WORK THAT GIVES SOME MEANING TO OUR BLEAK AND BORING SCHOOL LIVES!! YOU SELFISH, HAUGHTY, ARROGANT BRAT!!
YOU DON'T LIVE ON AN ISLAND! GET INVOLVED WITH YOUR COMMUNITY!!
I SHOULD'VE LET HER SUFFER. NOW SHE'S GOT TOO MUCH ENERGY ...
PLEASE SING FOR US, PRETTY LADY!!
HIDE-AND-SEEK!!
LET'S ALL PLAY A GAME TOGETHER—!!
LET'S PLAY WITH DOLLS!!

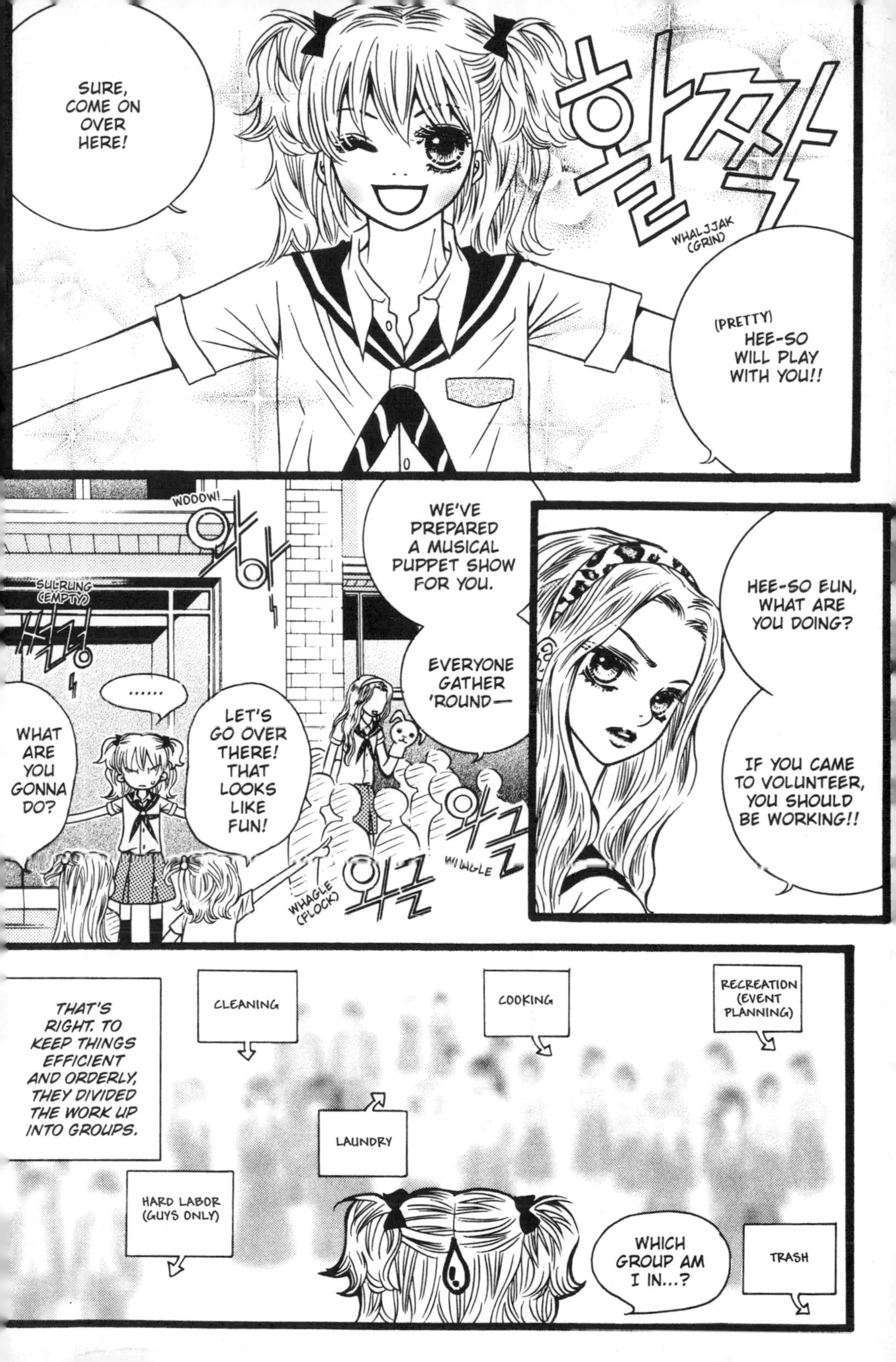
SURE, COME ON OVER HERE!
활짝
WHALJJAK (GRIN)
(PRETTY) HEE-SO WILL PLAY WITH YOU!!
WOOOW!
와아
SUL-RUNG (EMPTY)
썰렁
WHAT ARE YOU GONNA DO?
......
LET'S GO OVER THERE! THAT LOOKS LIKE FUN!
WE'VE PREPARED A MUSICAL PUPPET SHOW FOR YOU.
EVERYONE GATHER 'ROUND—
WHAGLE (FLOCK)
와글
WHAGLE
HEE-SO EUN, WHAT ARE YOU DOING?
IF YOU CAME TO VOLUNTEER, YOU SHOULD BE WORKING!!
THAT'S RIGHT. TO KEEP THINGS EFFICIENT AND ORDERLY, THEY DIVIDED THE WORK UP INTO GROUPS.
CLEANING
COOKING
RECREATION (EVENT PLANNING)
LAUNDRY
HARD LABOR (GUYS ONLY)
WHICH GROUP AM I IN...?
TRASH

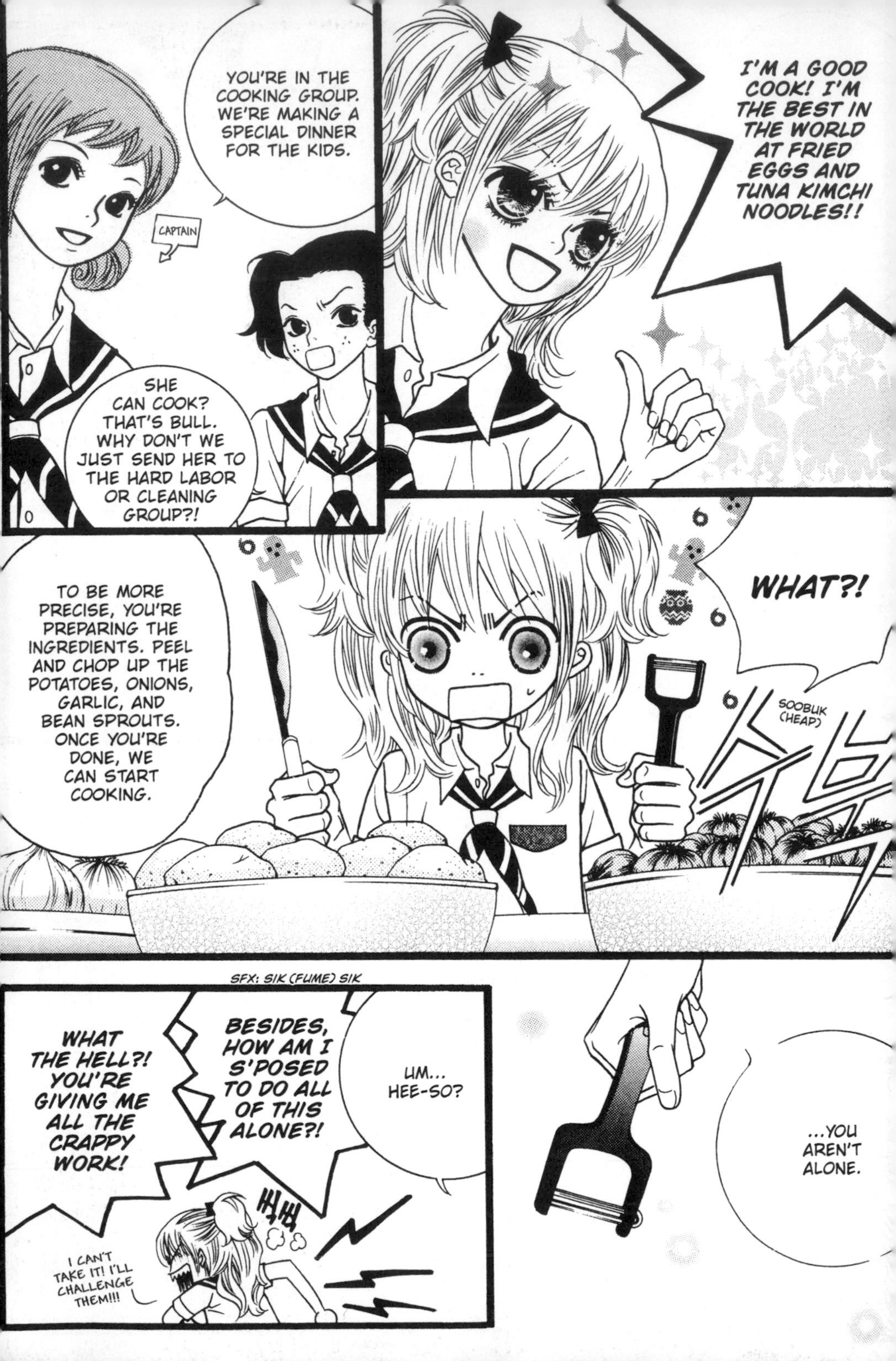
YOU'RE IN THE COOKING GROUP. WE'RE MAKING A SPECIAL DINNER FOR THE KIDS.
CAPTAIN
SHE CAN COOK? THAT'S BULL. WHY DON'T WE JUST SEND HER TO THE HARD LABOR OR CLEANING GROUP?!
I'M A GOOD COOK! I'M THE BEST IN THE WORLD AT FRIED EGGS AND TUNA KIMCHI NOODLES!!
TO BE MORE PRECISE, YOU'RE PREPARING THE INGREDIENTS. PEEL AND CHOP UP THE POTATOES, ONIONS, GARLIC, AND BEAN SPROUTS. ONCE YOU'RE DONE, WE CAN START COOKING.
WHAT?!
SOOBUK (HEAP)
SFX: SIK (FUME) SIK
WHAT THE HELL?! YOU'RE GIVING ME ALL THE CRAPPY WORK!
BESIDES, HOW AM I S'POSED TO DO ALL OF THIS ALONE?!
UM... HEE-SO?
I CAN'T TAKE IT! I'LL CHALLENGE THEM!!!
...YOU AREN'T ALONE.

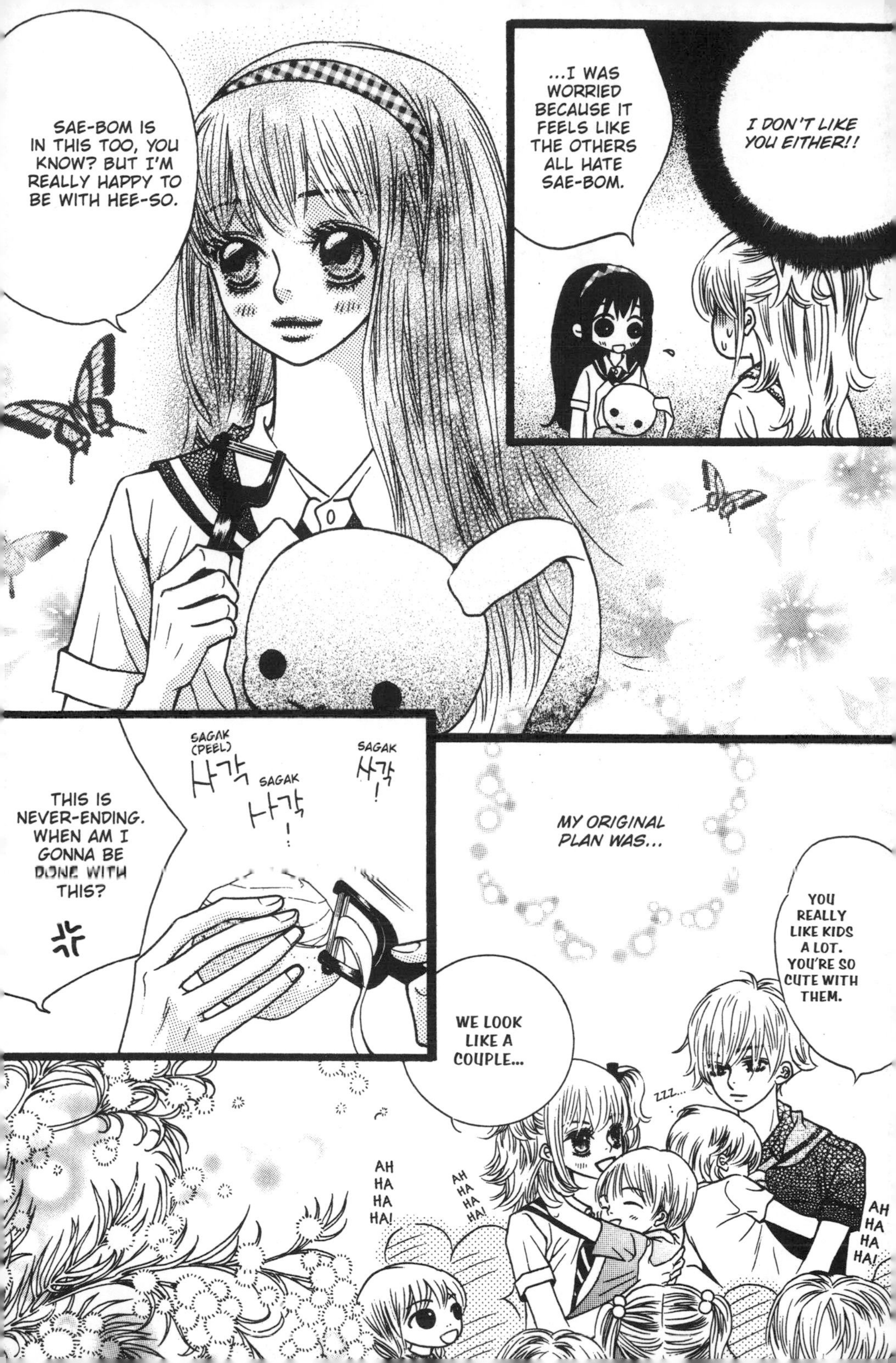
SAE-BOM IS IN THIS TOO, YOU KNOW? BUT I'M REALLY HAPPY TO BE WITH HEE-SO.
...I WAS WORRIED BECAUSE IT FEELS LIKE THE OTHERS ALL HATE SAE-BOM.
I DON'T LIKE YOU EITHER!!
SAGAK (PEEL) 사각
SAGAK 사각!
SAGAK 사각!
THIS IS NEVER-ENDING. WHEN AM I GONNA BE DONE WITH THIS?
MY ORIGINAL PLAN WAS...
YOU REALLY LIKE KIDS A LOT. YOU'RE SO CUTE WITH THEM.
WE LOOK LIKE A COUPLE...
ZZZ...
AH HA HA HA!
AH HA HA HA!
AH HA HA HA!

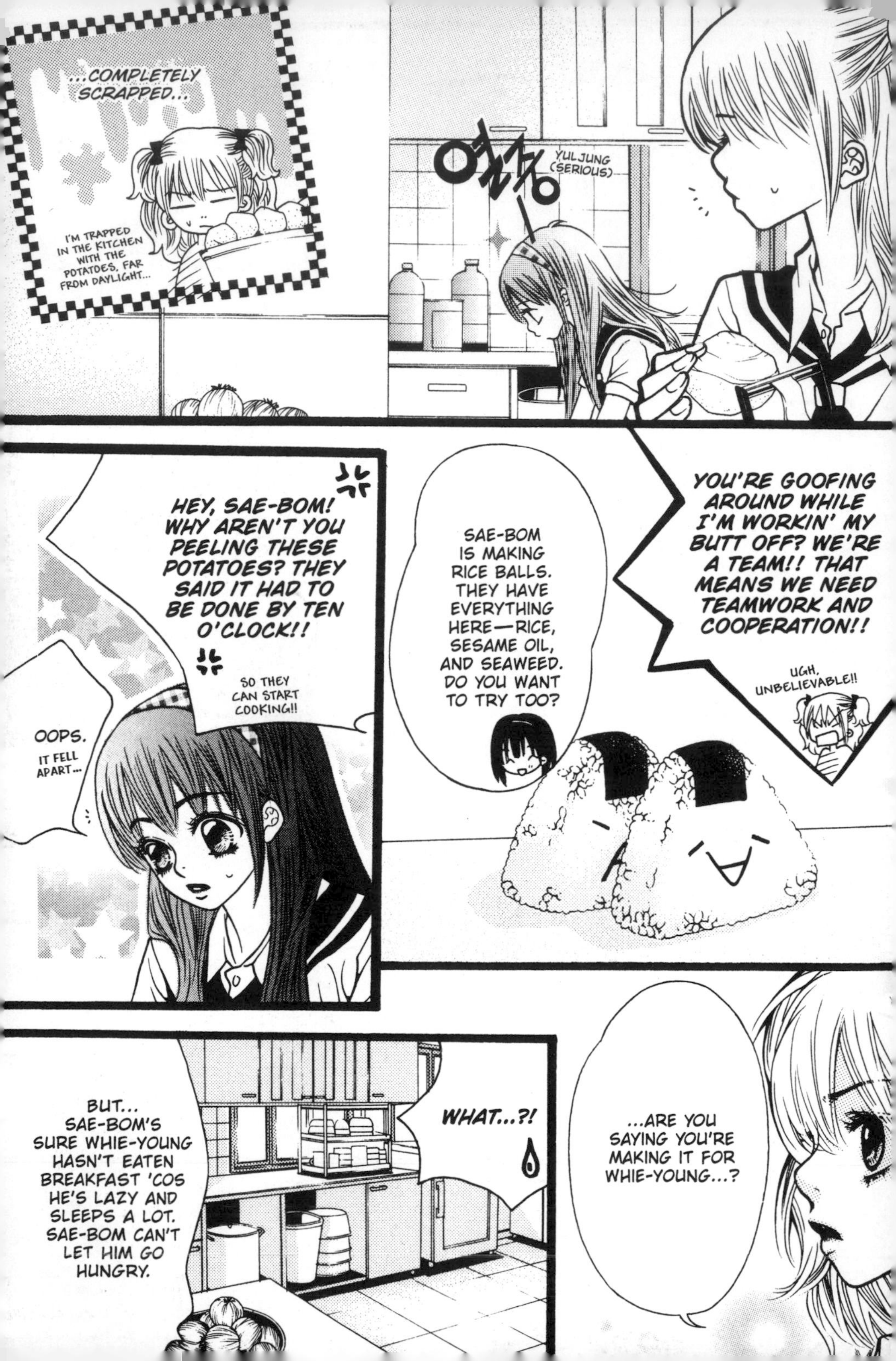
...COMPLETELY SCRAPPED...
I'M TRAPPED IN THE KITCHEN WITH THE POTATOES, FAR FROM DAYLIGHT...
YULJUNG (SERIOUS)
HEY, SAE-BOM! WHY AREN'T YOU PEELING THESE POTATOES? THEY SAID IT HAD TO BE DONE BY TEN O'CLOCK!!
SO THEY CAN START COOKING!!
OOPS.
IT FELL APART...
SAE-BOM IS MAKING RICE BALLS. THEY HAVE EVERYTHING HERE—RICE, SESAME OIL, AND SEAWEED. DO YOU WANT TO TRY TOO?
YOU'RE GOOFING AROUND WHILE I'M WORKIN' MY BUTT OFF? WE'RE A TEAM!! THAT MEANS WE NEED TEAMWORK AND COOPERATION!!
UGH, UNBELIEVABLE!!
BUT... SAE-BOM'S SURE WHIE-YOUNG HASN'T EATEN BREAKFAST 'COS HE'S LAZY AND SLEEPS A LOT. SAE-BOM CAN'T LET HIM GO HUNGRY.
WHAT...?!
...ARE YOU SAYING YOU'RE MAKING IT FOR WHIE-YOUNG...?

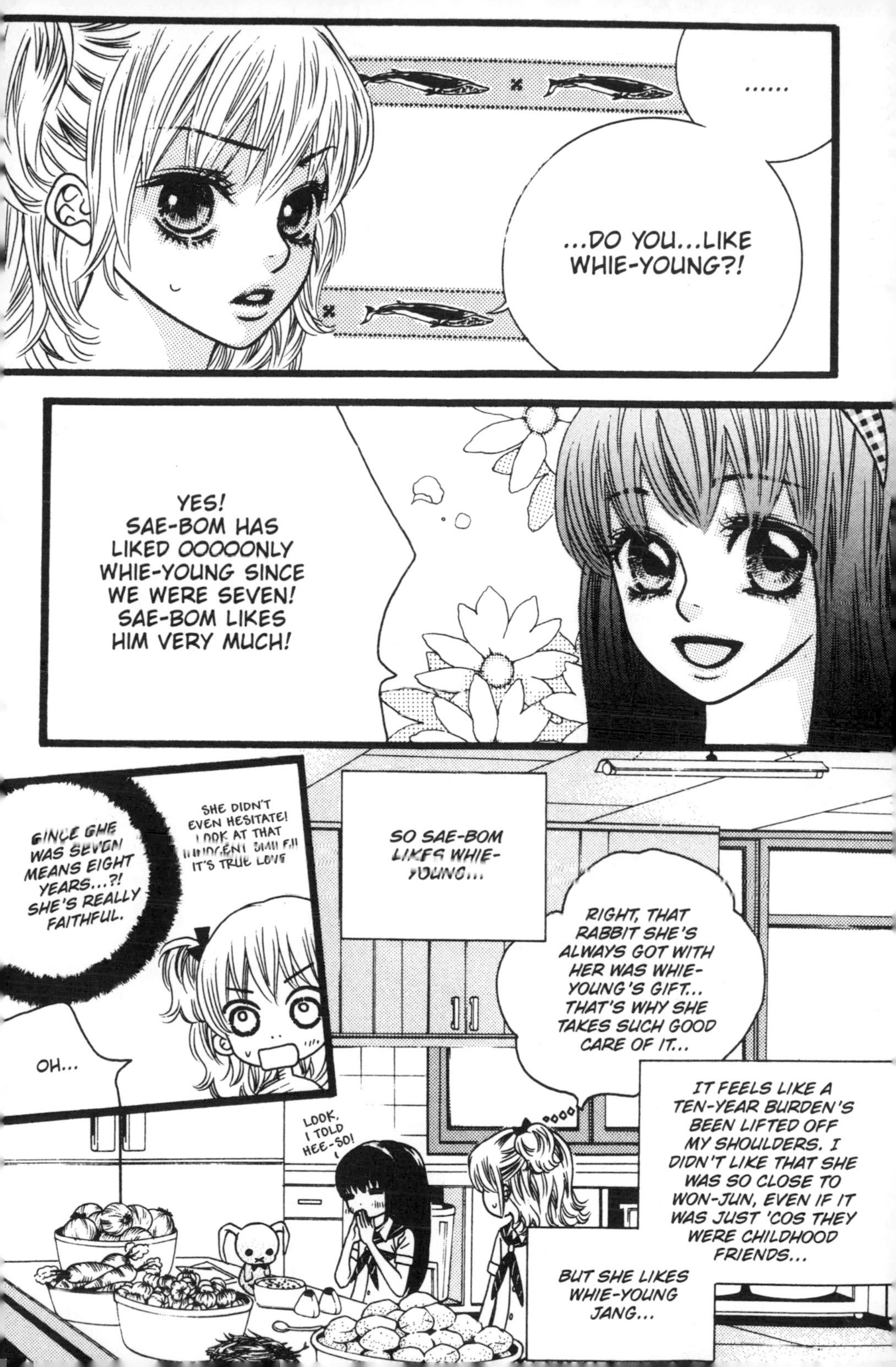

......
...DO YOU...LIKE WHIE-YOUNG?!
YES! SAE-BOM HAS LIKED OOOOONLY WHIE-YOUNG SINCE WE WERE SEVEN! SAE-BOM LIKES HIM VERY MUCH!
SINCE SHE WAS SEVEN MEANS EIGHT YEARS...?! SHE'S REALLY FAITHFUL.
SHE DIDN'T EVEN HESITATE! LOOK AT THAT INNOCENT SMILE!! IT'S TRUE LOVE
OH...
SO SAE-BOM LIKES WHIE-YOUNG...
RIGHT, THAT RABBIT SHE'S ALWAYS GOT WITH HER WAS WHIE-YOUNG'S GIFT... THAT'S WHY SHE TAKES SUCH GOOD CARE OF IT...
LOOK, I TOLD HEE-SO!
IT FEELS LIKE A TEN-YEAR BURDEN'S BEEN LIFTED OFF MY SHOULDERS. I DIDN'T LIKE THAT SHE WAS SO CLOSE TO WON-JUN, EVEN IF IT WAS JUST 'COS THEY WERE CHILDHOOD FRIENDS...
BUT SHE LIKES WHIE-YOUNG JANG...

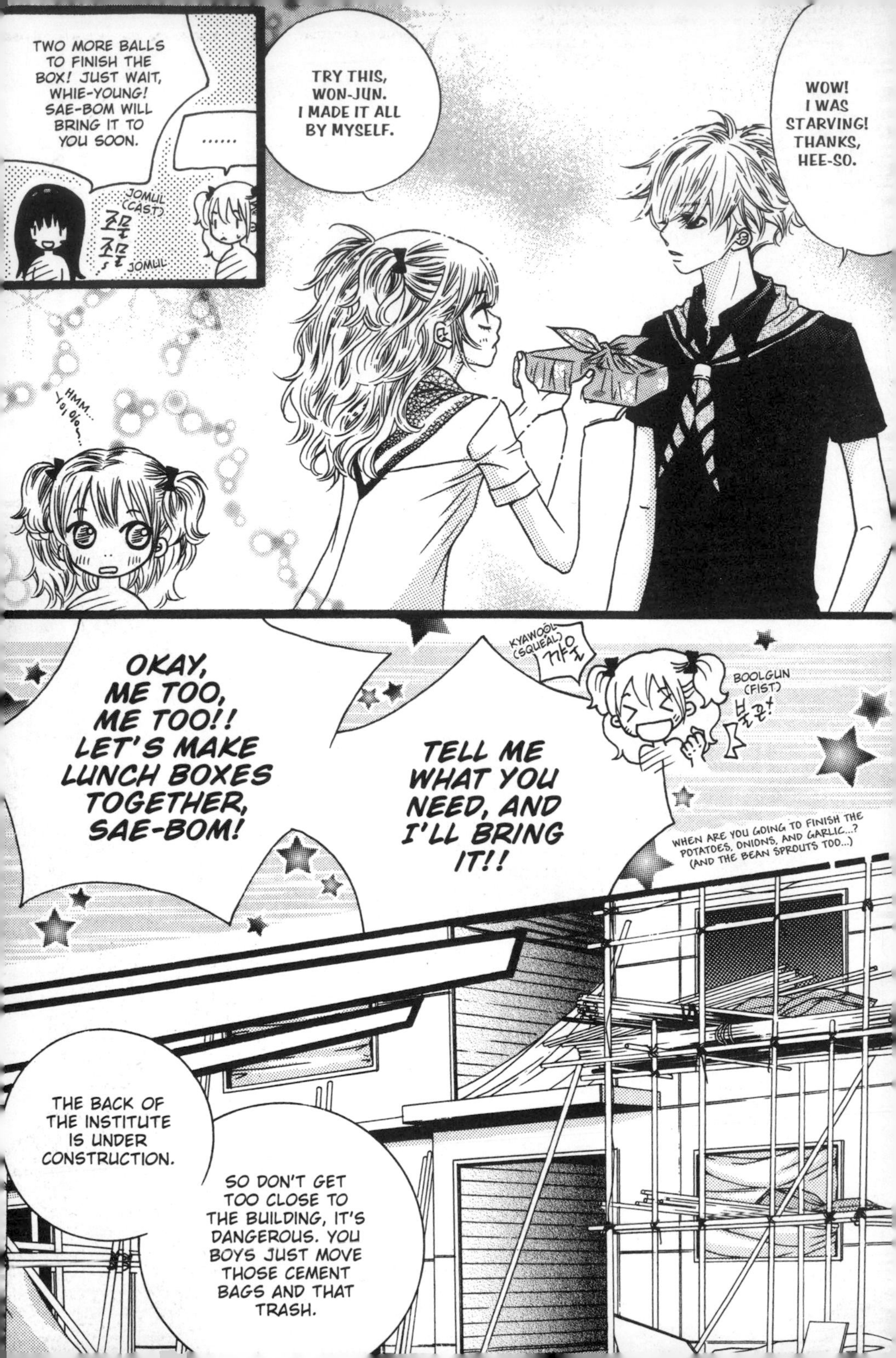
TWO MORE BALLS TO FINISH THE BOX! JUST WAIT, WHIE-YOUNG! SAE-BOM WILL BRING IT TO YOU SOON.
......
JOMUL (CAST)
조물조물
JOMUL
TRY THIS, WON-JUN. I MADE IT ALL BY MYSELF.
WOW! I WAS STARVING! THANKS, HEE-SO.
HMM...
OKAY, ME TOO, ME TOO!! LET'S MAKE LUNCH BOXES TOGETHER, SAE-BOM!
TELL ME WHAT YOU NEED, AND I'LL BRING IT!!
KYAWOOL (SQUEAL)
BOOLGUN (FIST)
불끈!
WHEN ARE YOU GOING TO FINISH THE POTATOES, ONIONS, AND GARLIC...? (AND THE BEAN SPROUTS TOO...)
THE BACK OF THE INSTITUTE IS UNDER CONSTRUCTION.
SO DON'T GET TOO CLOSE TO THE BUILDING, IT'S DANGEROUS. YOU BOYS JUST MOVE THOSE CEMENT BAGS AND THAT TRASH.

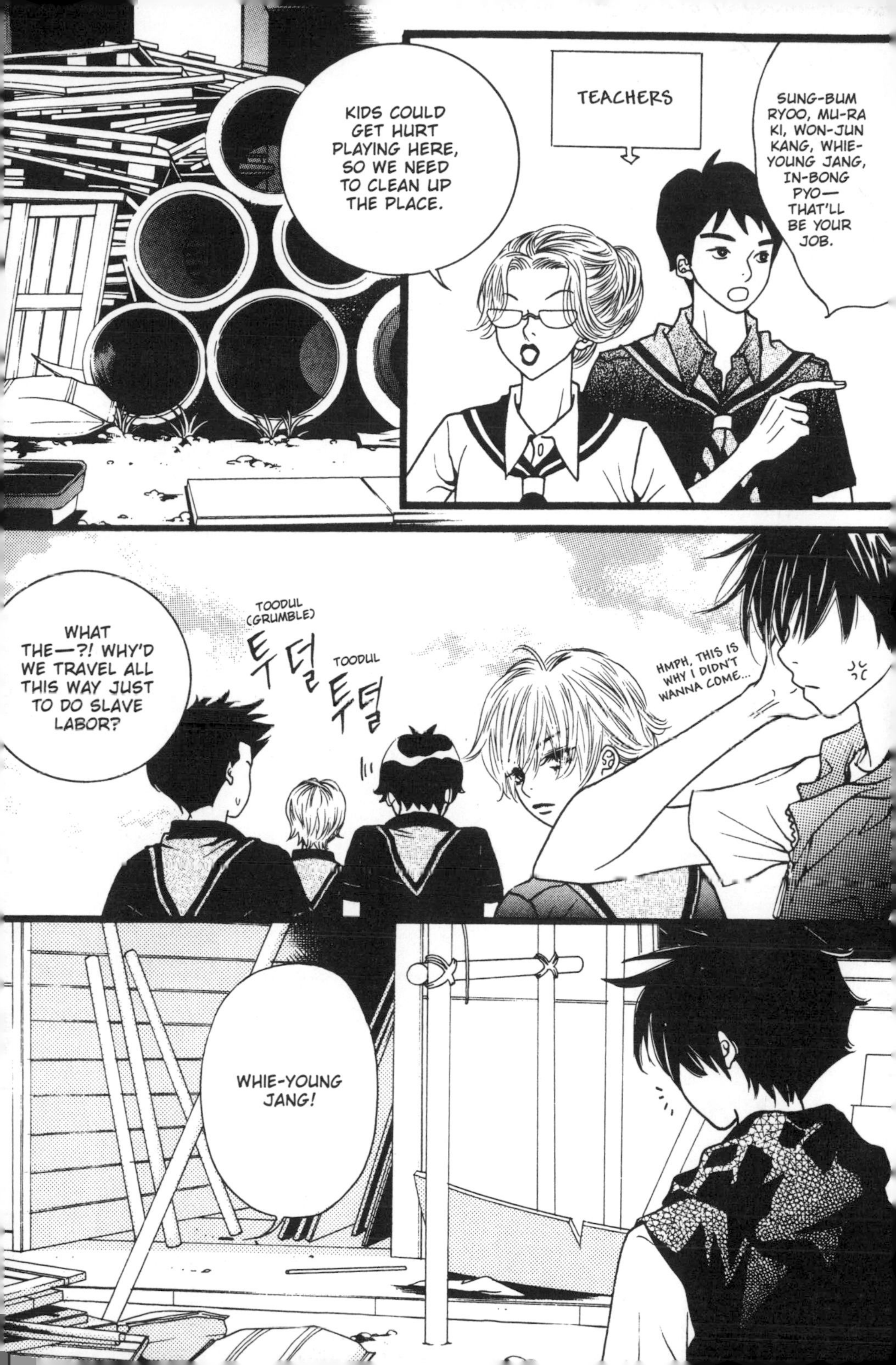
KIDS COULD GET HURT PLAYING HERE, SO WE NEED TO CLEAN UP THE PLACE.
TEACHERS
SUNG-BUM RYOO, MU-RA KI, WON-JUN KANG, WHIE-YOUNG JANG, IN-BONG PYO— THAT'LL BE YOUR JOB.
WHAT THE—?! WHY'D WE TRAVEL ALL THIS WAY JUST TO DO SLAVE LABOR?
TOODUL (GRUMBLE)
투덜
TOODUL
투덜
HMPH, THIS IS WHY I DIDN'T WANNA COME...
WHIE-YOUNG JANG!

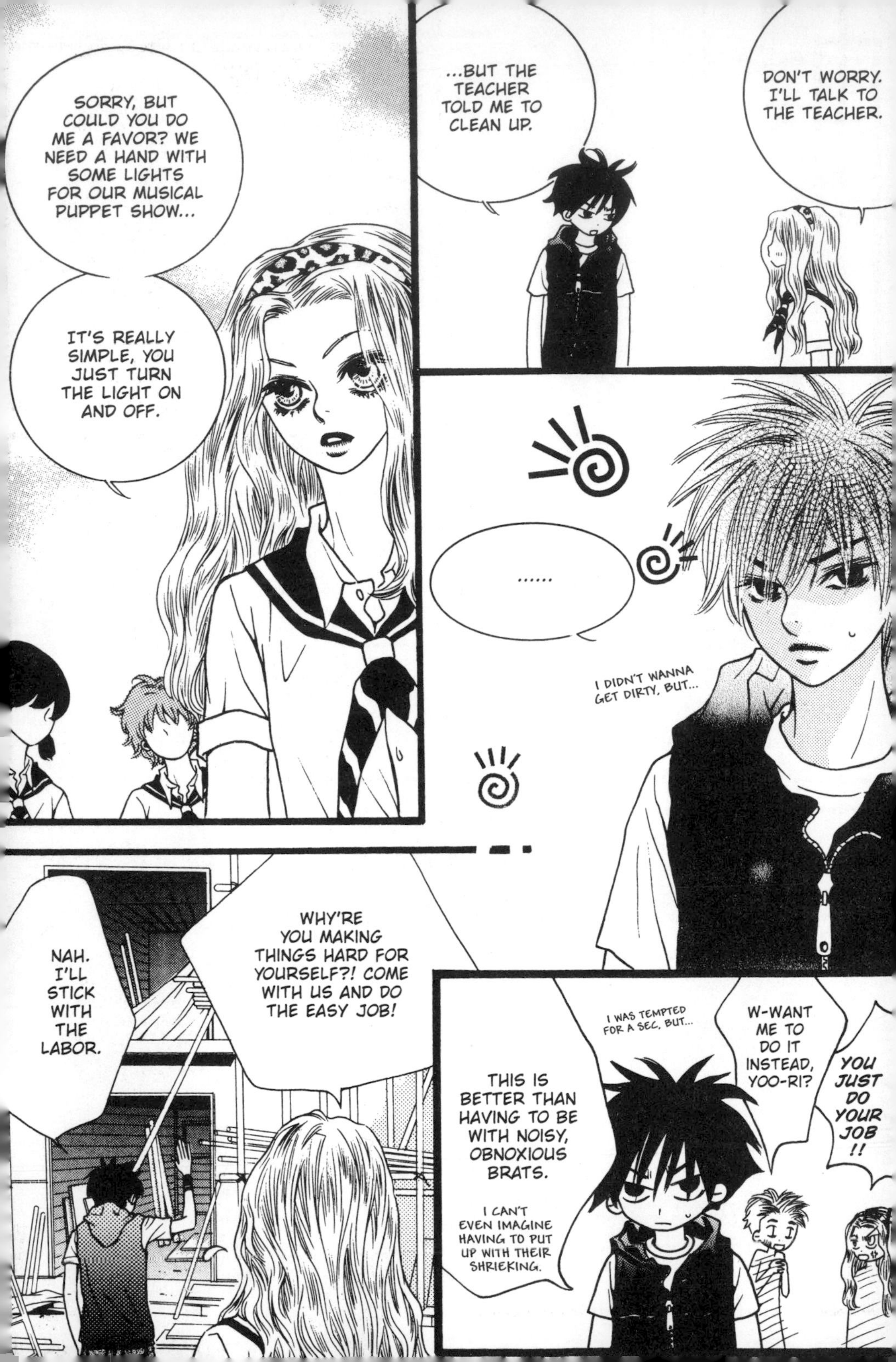
SORRY, BUT COULD YOU DO ME A FAVOR? WE NEED A HAND WITH SOME LIGHTS FOR OUR MUSICAL PUPPET SHOW...
IT'S REALLY SIMPLE, YOU JUST TURN THE LIGHT ON AND OFF.
...BUT THE TEACHER TOLD ME TO CLEAN UP.
DON'T WORRY. I'LL TALK TO THE TEACHER.
......
I DIDN'T WANNA GET DIRTY, BUT...
WHY'RE YOU MAKING THINGS HARD FOR YOURSELF?! COME WITH US AND DO THE EASY JOB!
NAH. I'LL STICK WITH THE LABOR.
I WAS TEMPTED FOR A SEC, BUT...
THIS IS BETTER THAN HAVING TO BE WITH NOISY, OBNOXIOUS BRATS.
I CAN'T EVEN IMAGINE HAVING TO PUT UP WITH THEIR SHRIEKING.
W-WANT ME TO DO IT INSTEAD, YOO-RI?
YOU JUST DO YOUR JOB!!

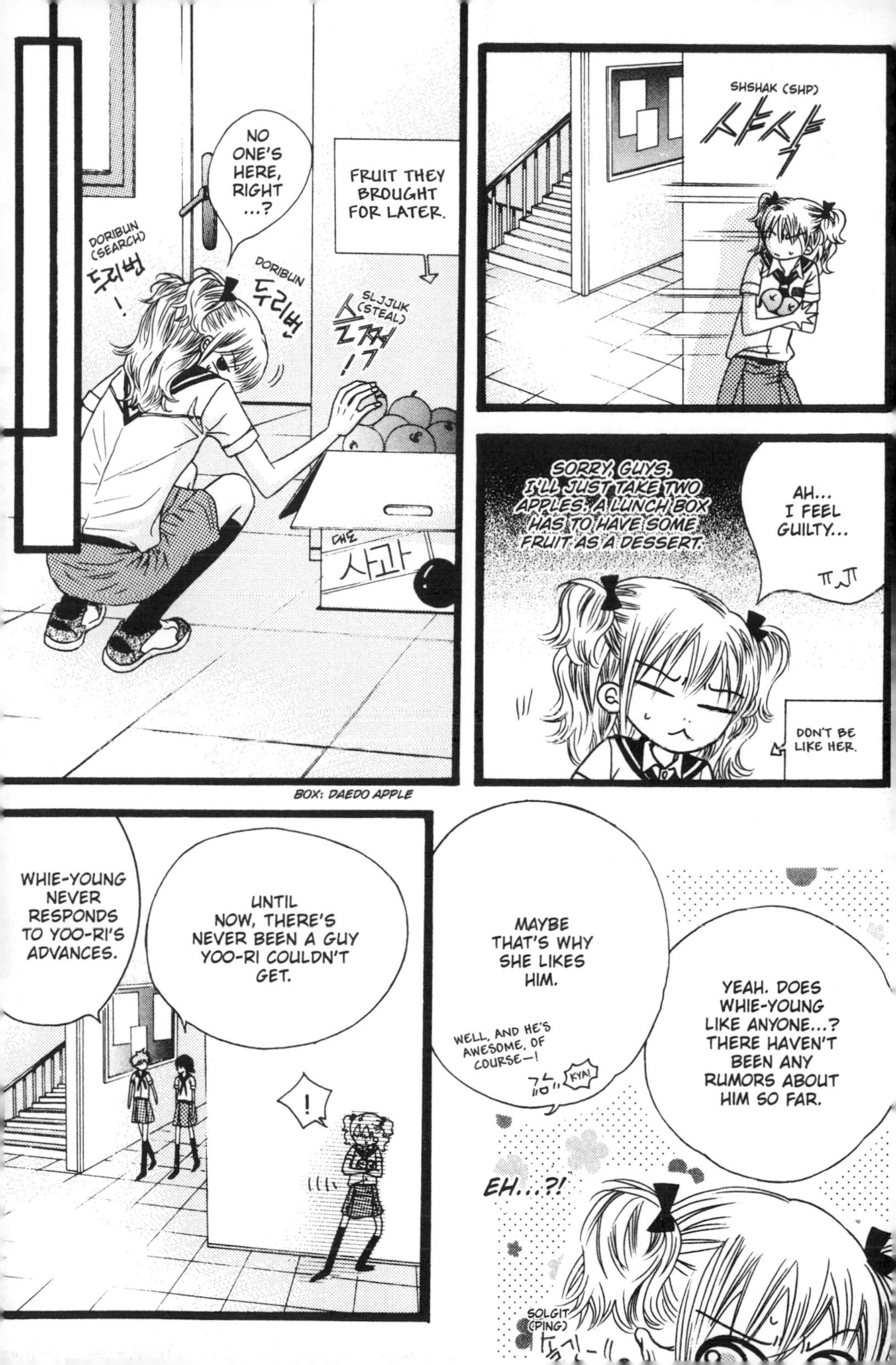
DORIBUN (SEARCH)
두리번
!
NO ONE'S HERE, RIGHT ...?
DORIBUN
두리번
FRUIT THEY BROUGHT FOR LATER.
SLJJUK (STEAL)
슬쩍
!?
대도
사과
SHSHAK (SHP)
샤샥
SORRY, GUYS. I'LL JUST TAKE TWO APPLES. A LUNCH BOX HAS TO HAVE SOME FRUIT AS A DESSERT.
AH... I FEEL GUILTY...
ㅠ_ㅠ
DON'T BE LIKE HER.
BOX: DAEDO APPLE
WHIE-YOUNG NEVER RESPONDS TO YOO-RI'S ADVANCES.
UNTIL NOW, THERE'S NEVER BEEN A GUY YOO-RI COULDN'T GET.
!
MAYBE THAT'S WHY SHE LIKES HIM.
WELL, AND HE'S AWESOME, OF COURSE—!
KYA!
YEAH. DOES WHIE-YOUNG LIKE ANYONE...? THERE HAVEN'T BEEN ANY RUMORS ABOUT HIM SO FAR.
EH...?!
SOLGIT (PING)

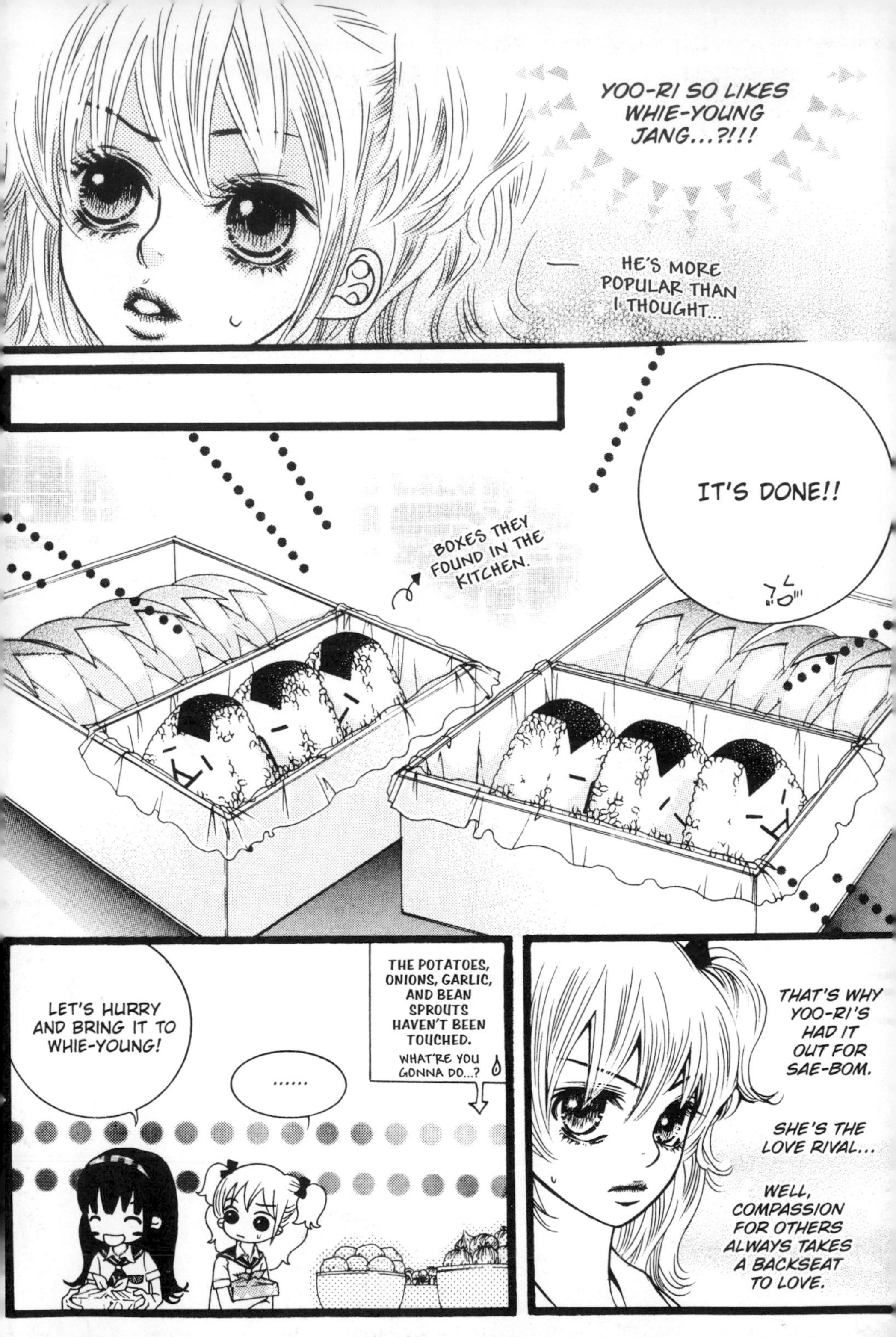
YOO-RI SO LIKES WHIE-YOUNG JANG...?!!!
HE'S MORE POPULAR THAN I THOUGHT...
IT'S DONE!!
BOXES THEY FOUND IN THE KITCHEN.
LET'S HURRY AND BRING IT TO WHIE-YOUNG!
......
THE POTATOES, ONIONS, GARLIC, AND BEAN SPROUTS HAVEN'T BEEN TOUCHED.
WHAT'RE YOU GONNA DO...?
THAT'S WHY YOO-RI'S HAD IT OUT FOR SAE-BOM.
SHE'S THE LOVE RIVAL...
WELL, COMPASSION FOR OTHERS ALWAYS TAKES A BACKSEAT TO LOVE.

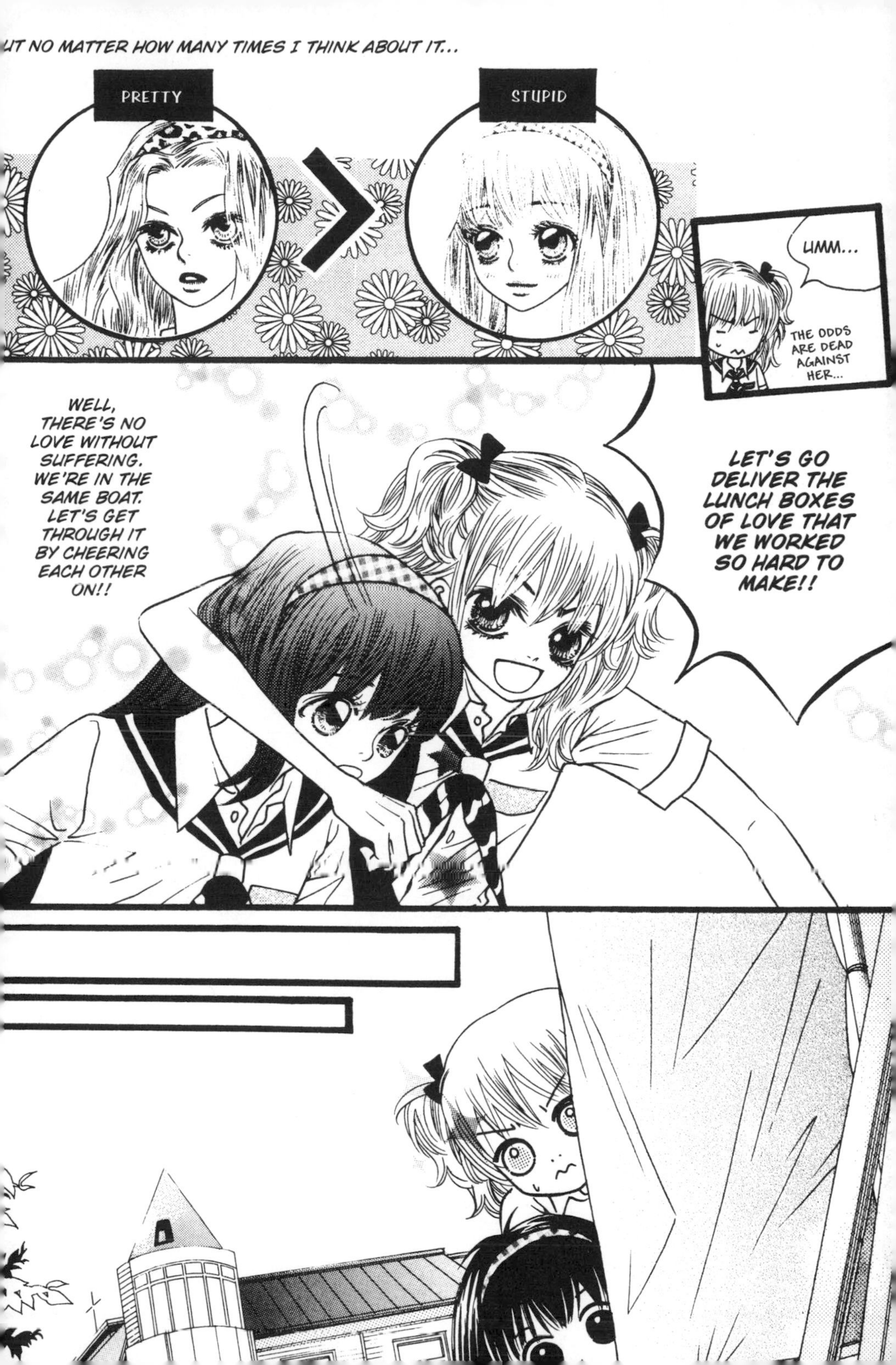
UT NO MATTER HOW MANY TIMES I THINK ABOUT IT...
PRETTY
STUPID
UMM...
THE ODDS ARE DEAD AGAINST HER...
WELL, THERE'S NO LOVE WITHOUT SUFFERING. WE'RE IN THE SAME BOAT. LET'S GET THROUGH IT BY CHEERING EACH OTHER ON!!
LET'S GO DELIVER THE LUNCH BOXES OF LOVE THAT WE WORKED SO HARD TO MAKE!!

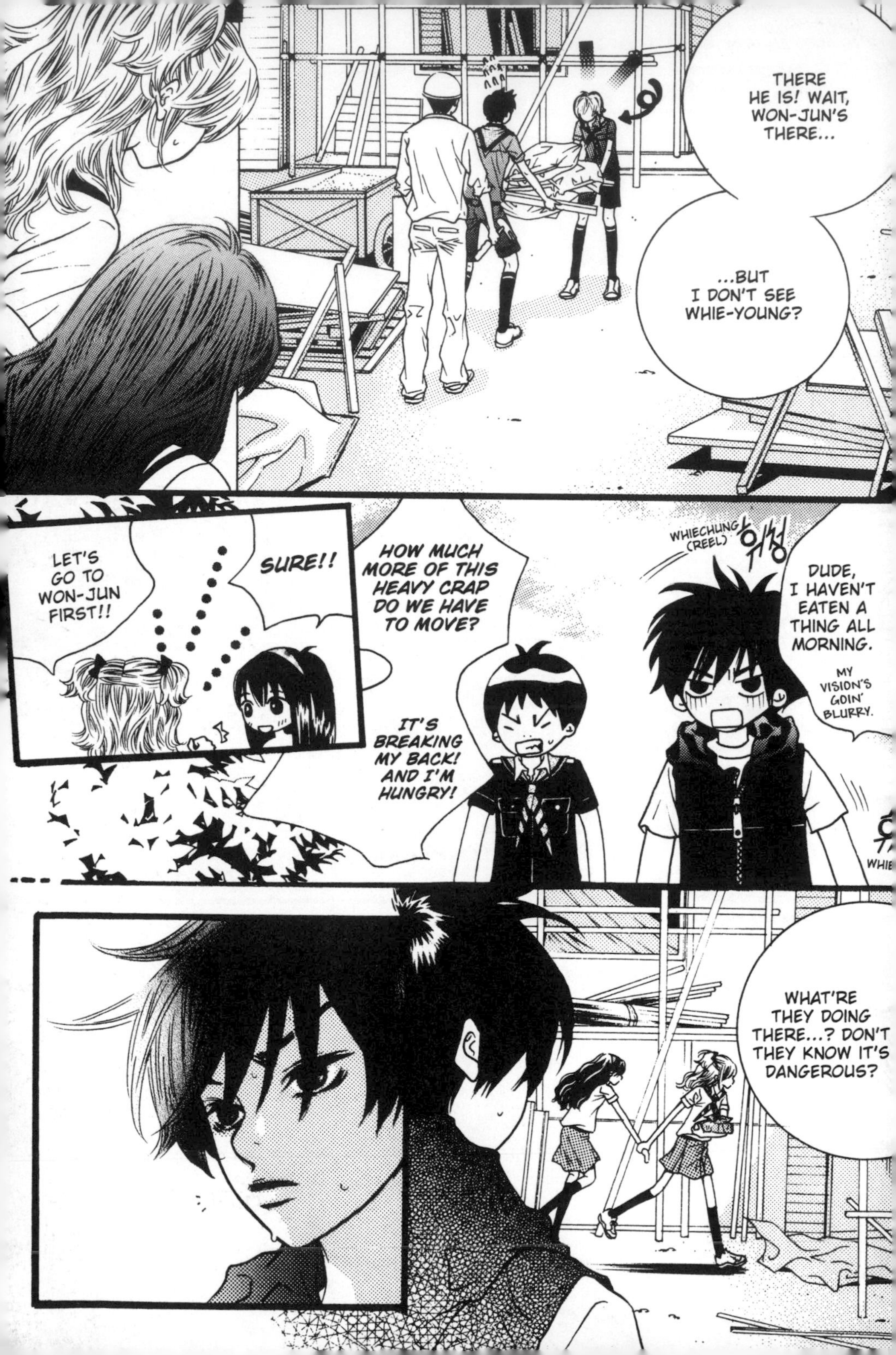

THERE HE IS! WAIT, WON-JUN'S THERE...
...BUT I DON'T SEE WHIE-YOUNG?
LET'S GO TO WON-JUN FIRST!!
SURE!!
HOW MUCH MORE OF THIS HEAVY CRAP DO WE HAVE TO MOVE?
IT'S BREAKING MY BACK! AND I'M HUNGRY!
WHIECHUNG (REEL)
DUDE, I HAVEN'T EATEN A THING ALL MORNING.
MY VISION'S GOIN' BLURRY.
WHAT'RE THEY DOING THERE...? DON'T THEY KNOW IT'S DANGEROUS?

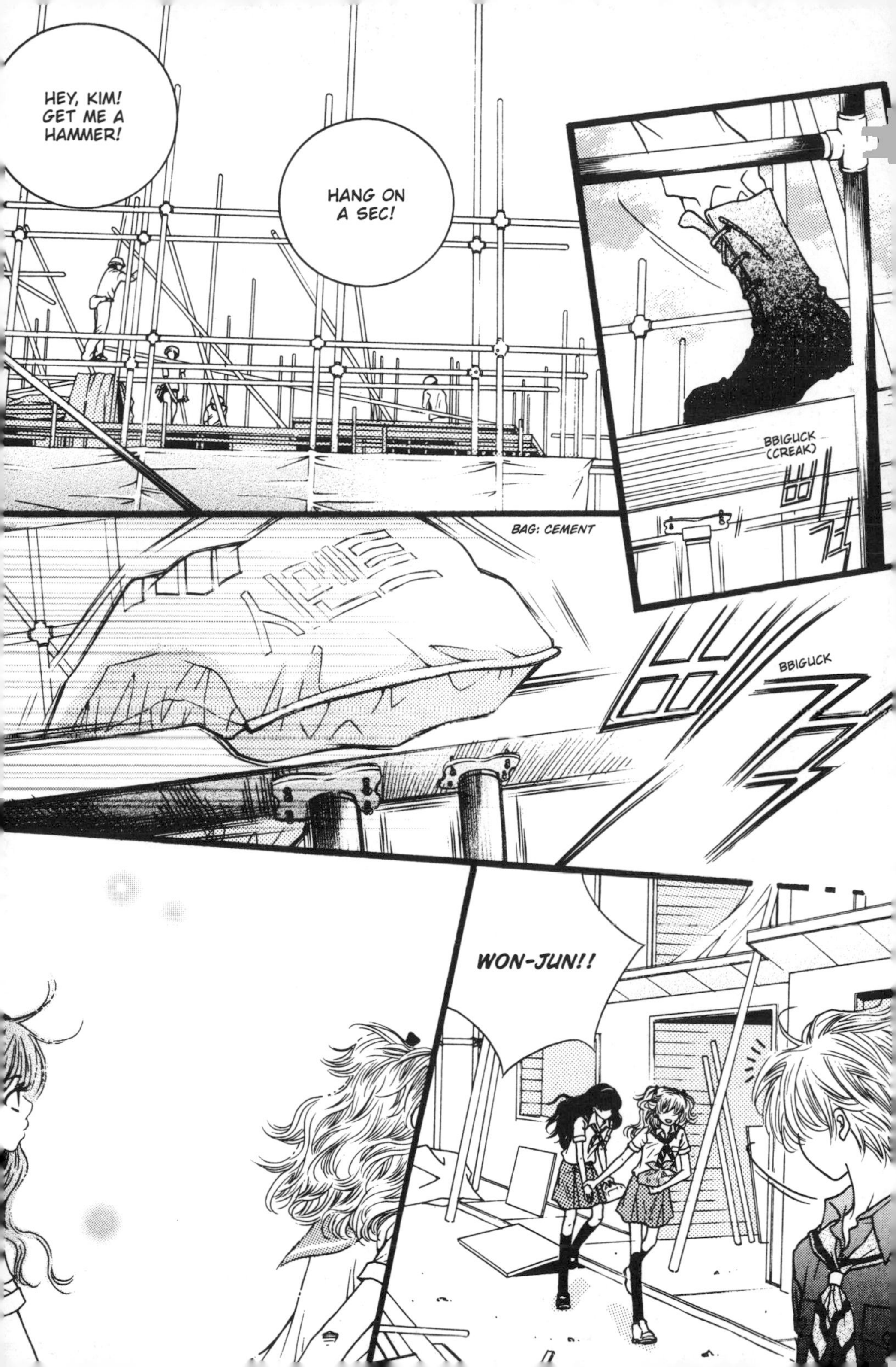
HEY, KIM! GET ME A HAMMER!
HANG ON A SEC!
BBIGUCK (CREAK)
BAG: CEMENT
BBIGUCK
WON-JUN!!

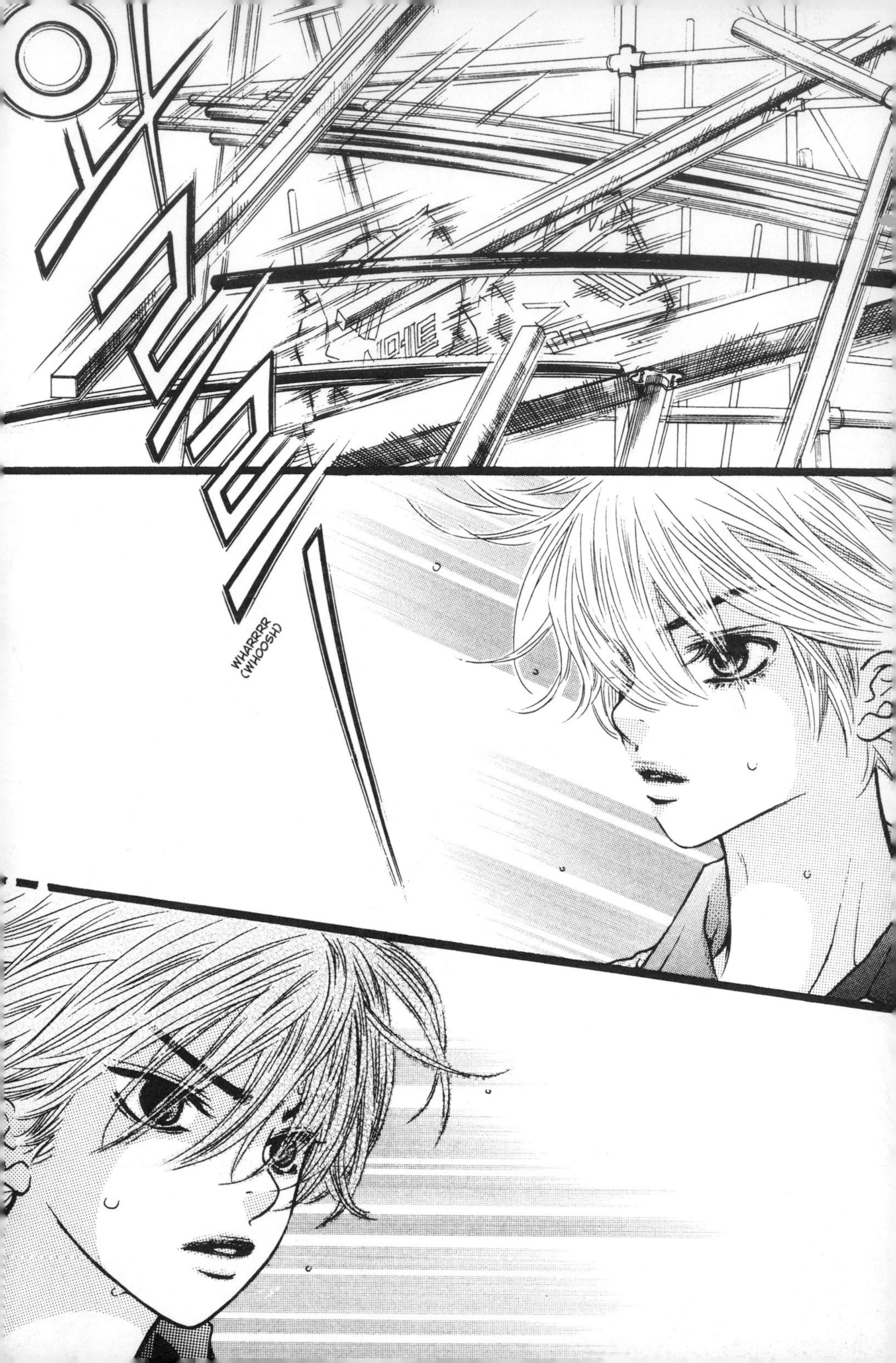
WHARRRR
(WHOOSH)

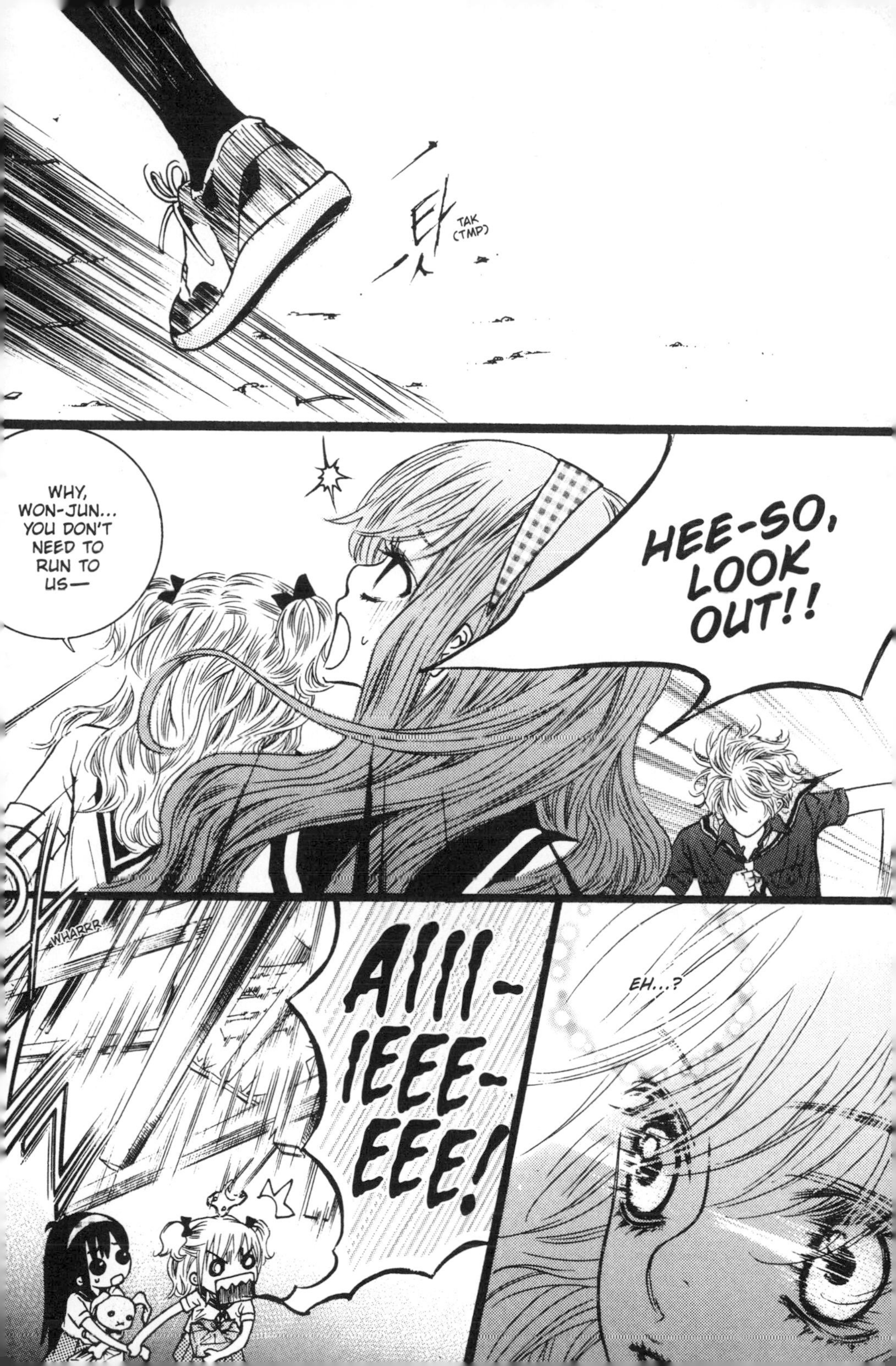
TAK (TMP)
WHY, WON-JUN... YOU DON'T NEED TO RUN TO US—
HEE-SO, LOOK OUT!!
WHARRR
AIII-IEEE-EEE!
EH...?

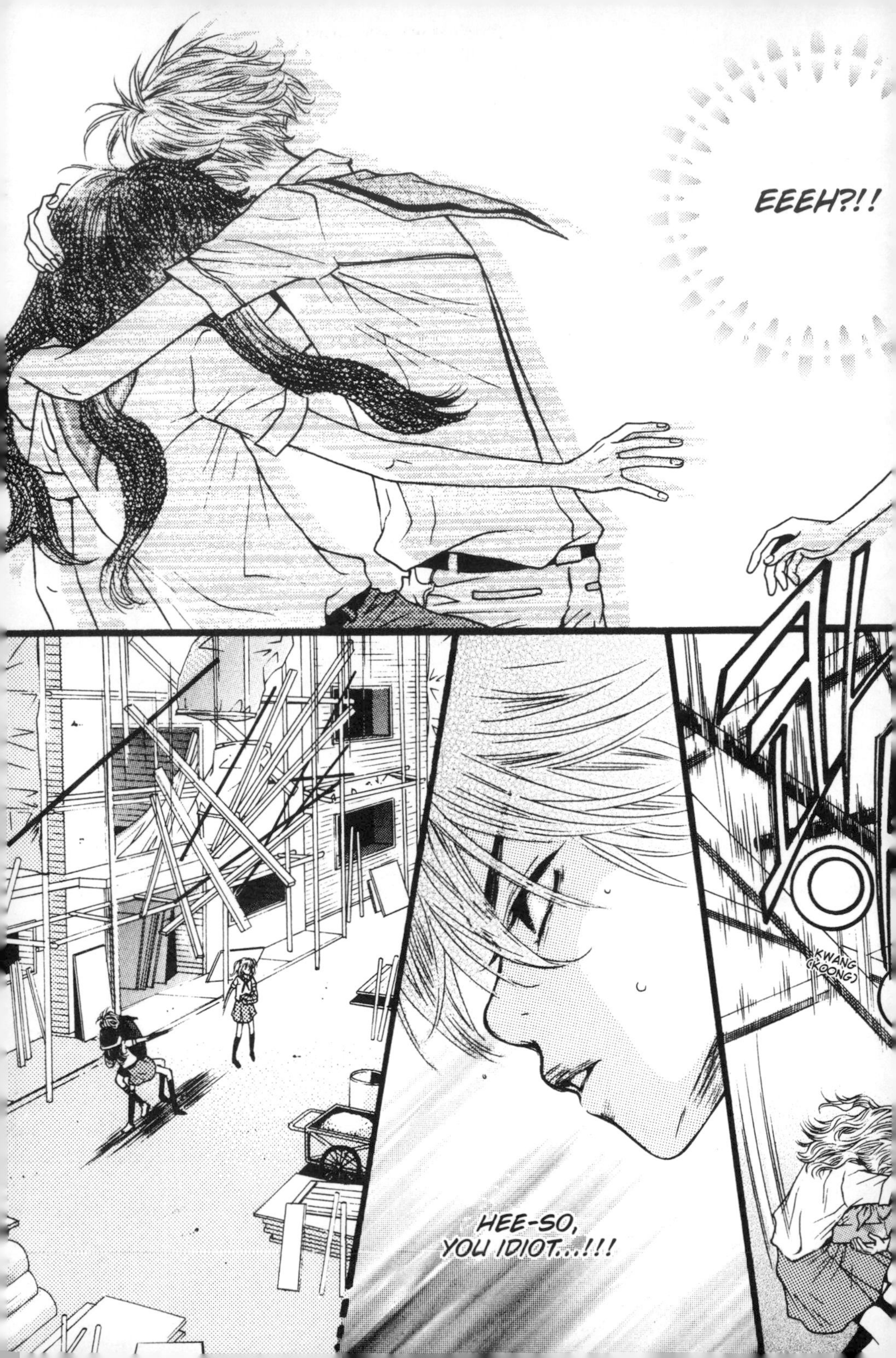
EEEH?!!
HEE-SO, YOU IDIOT...!!!
KWANG (KOONG)

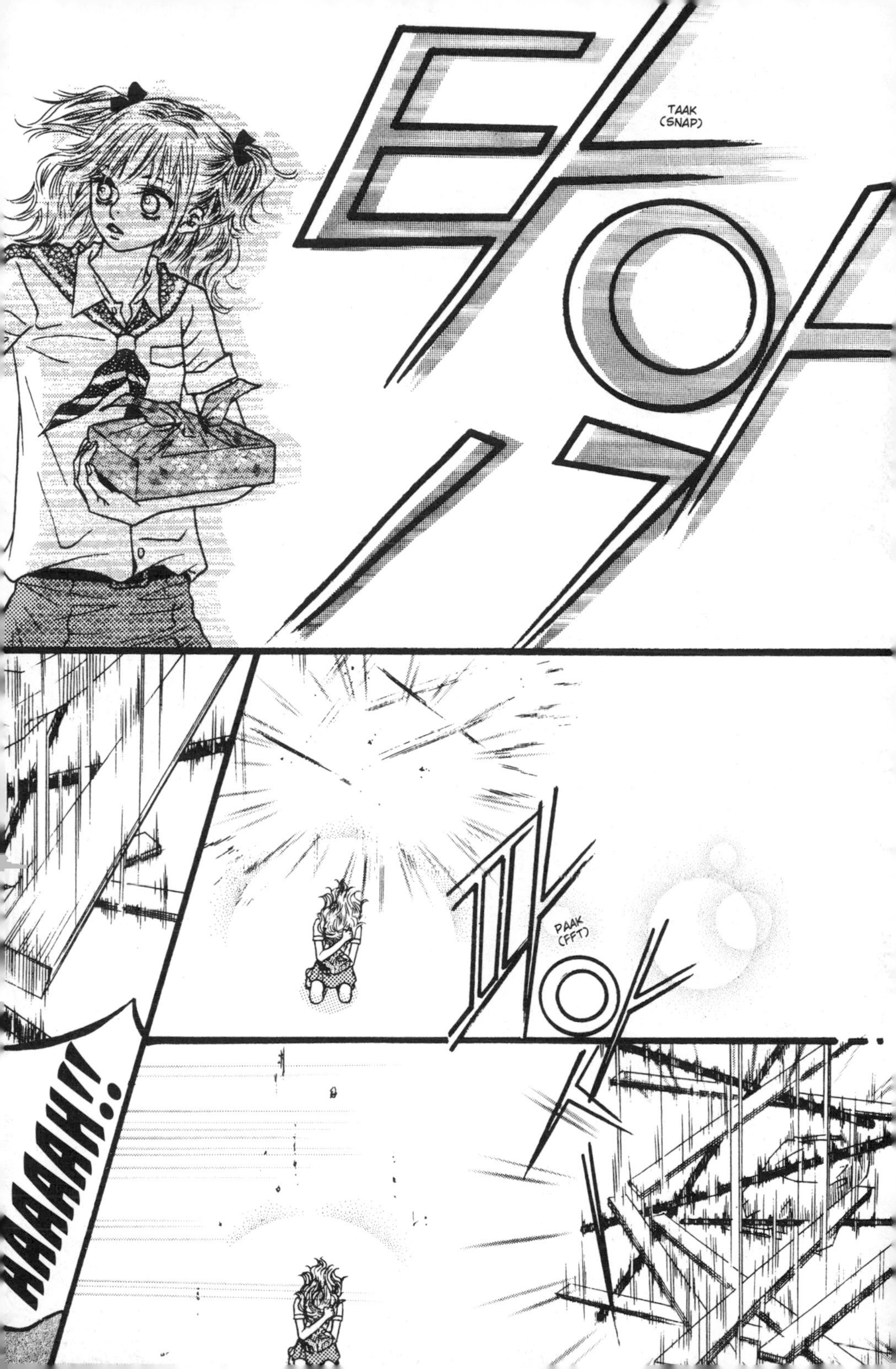
TAAK
(SNAP)
PAAK
(FFT)
HAAAAH!!

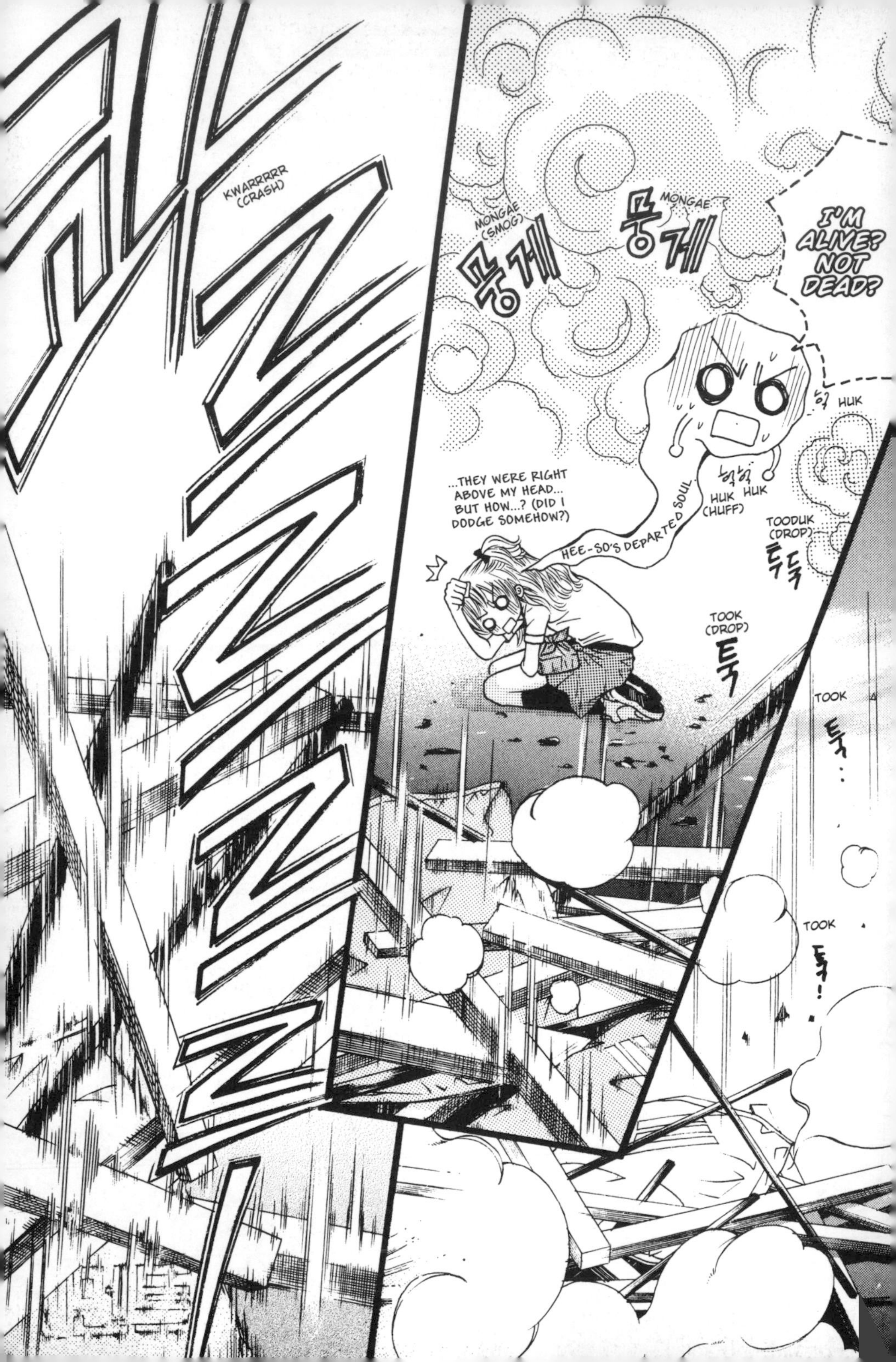
KWARRRR (CRASH)
MONGAE (SMOG)
뭉게
MONGAE
뭉게
I'M ALIVE? NOT DEAD?
헉 HUK
...THEY WERE RIGHT ABOVE MY HEAD... BUT HOW...? (DID I DODGE SOMEHOW?)
HEE-SO'S DEPARTED SOUL
헉헉 HUK HUK (HUFF)
TOODUK (DROP)
투둑
TOOK (DROP)
툭
TOOK
툭...
TOOK
툭!

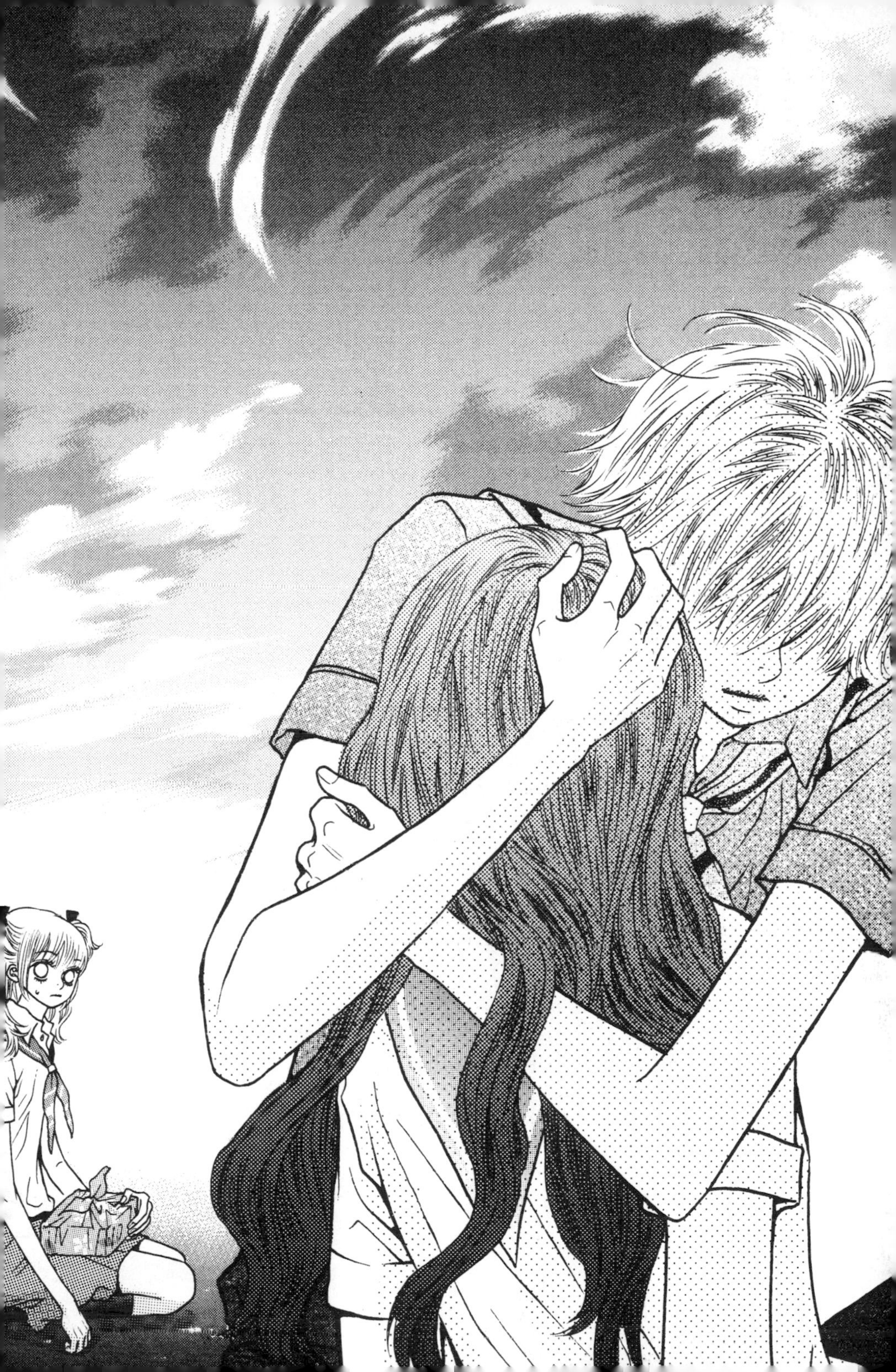

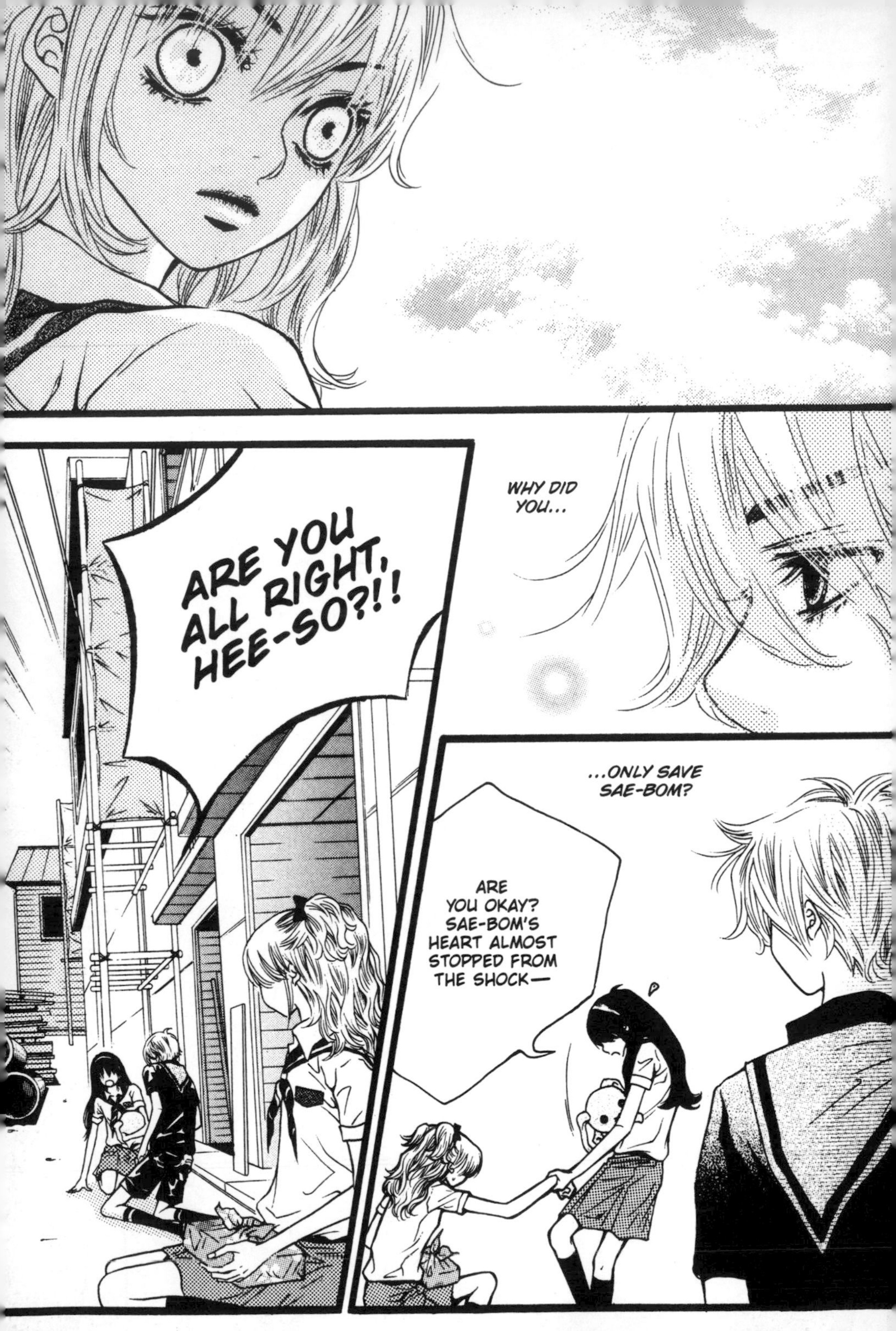

ARE YOU ALL RIGHT, HEE-SO?!!
WHY DID YOU...
...ONLY SAVE SAE-BOM?
ARE YOU OKAY? SAE-BOM'S HEART ALMOST STOPPED FROM THE SHOCK—

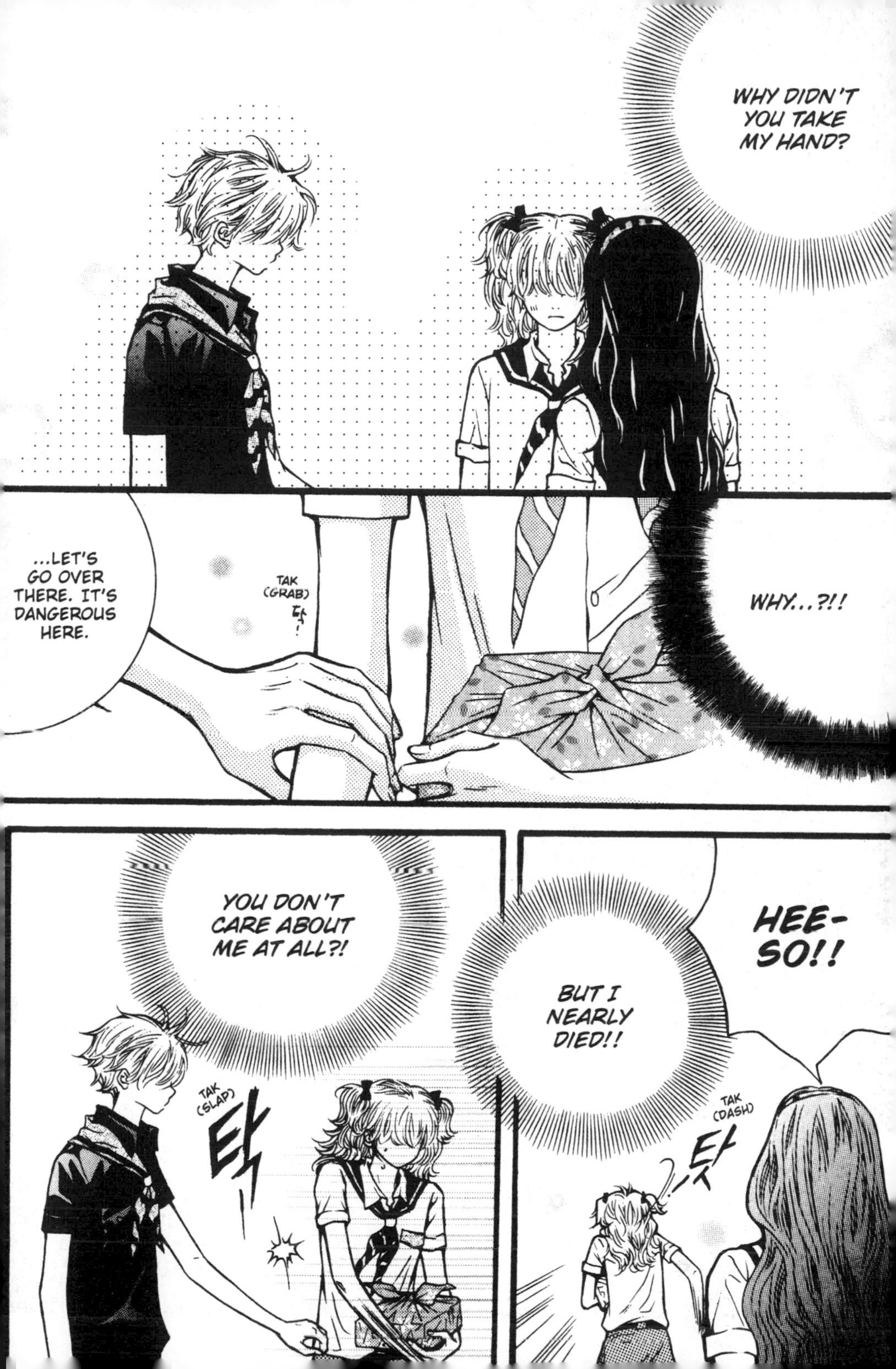
WHY DIDN'T YOU TAKE MY HAND?
...LET'S GO OVER THERE. IT'S DANGEROUS HERE.
TAK (GRAB)
탁
WHY...?!!
YOU DON'T CARE ABOUT ME AT ALL?!
TAK (SLAP)
탁
BUT I NEARLY DIED!!
HEE-SO!!
TAK (DASH)
탁

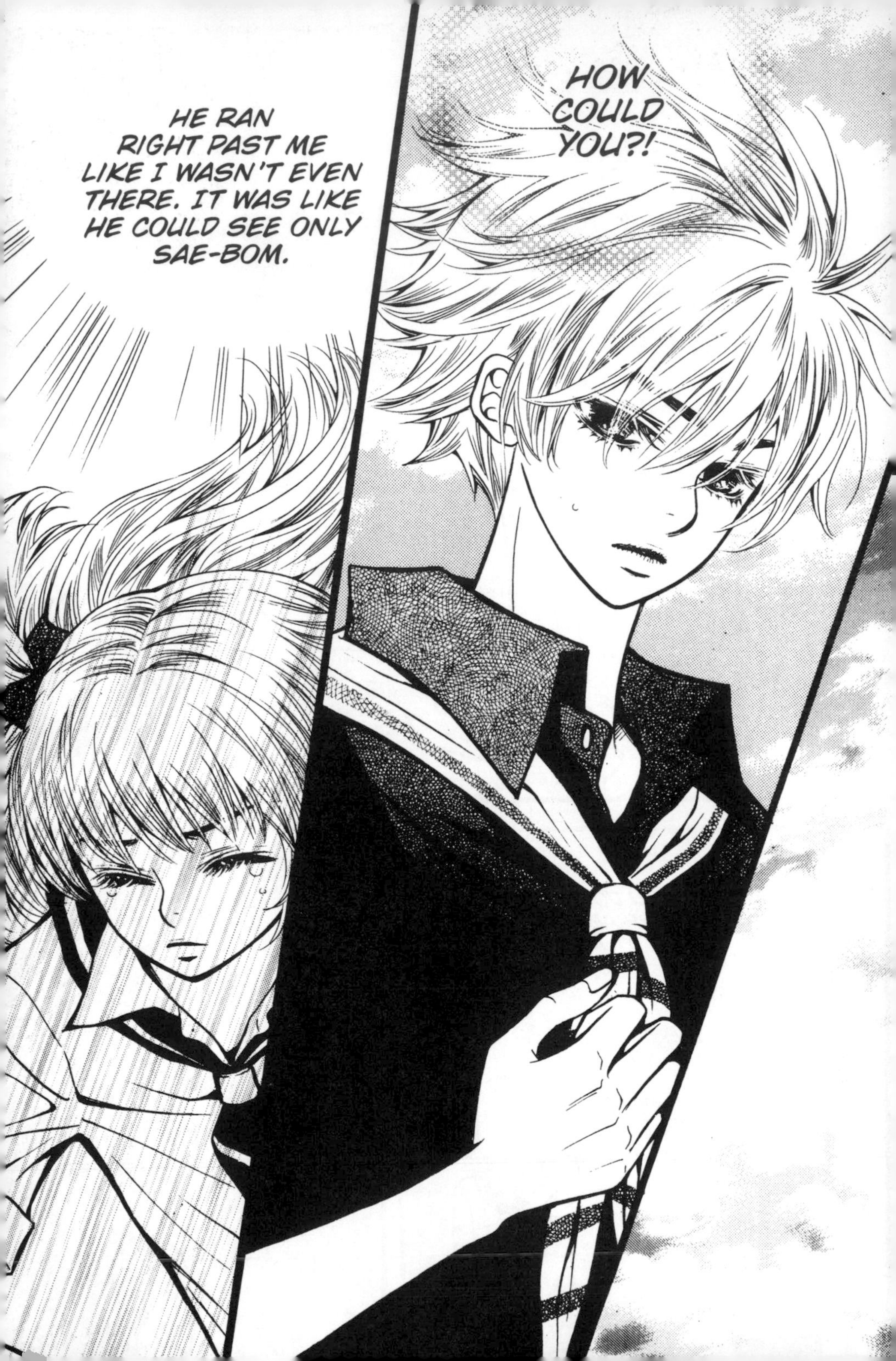
HE RAN RIGHT PAST ME LIKE I WASN'T EVEN THERE. IT WAS LIKE HE COULD SEE ONLY SAE-BOM.
HOW COULD YOU?!

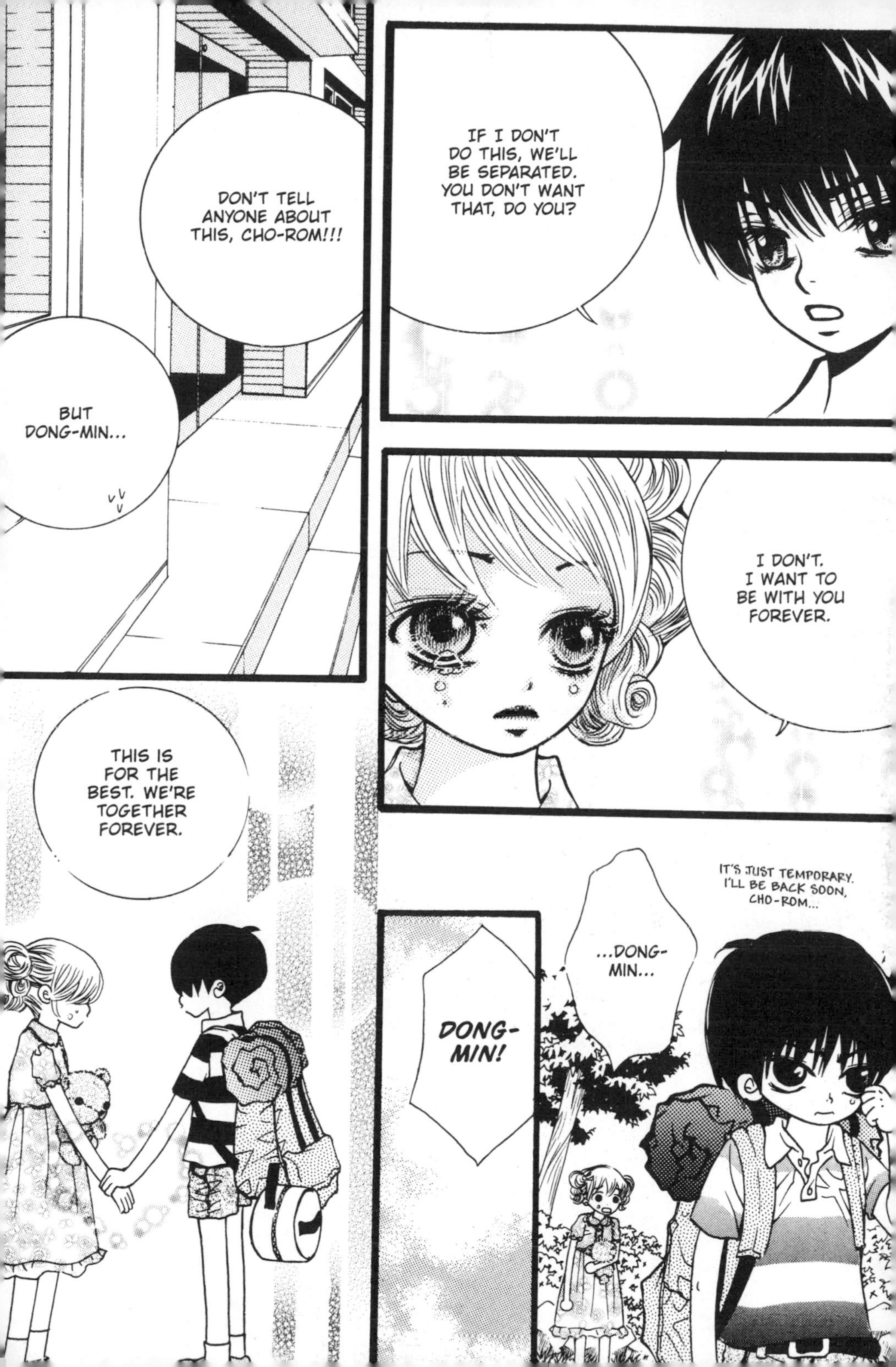

DON'T TELL ANYONE ABOUT THIS, CHO-ROM!!!
BUT DONG-MIN...
IF I DON'T DO THIS, WE'LL BE SEPARATED. YOU DON'T WANT THAT, DO YOU?
I DON'T. I WANT TO BE WITH YOU FOREVER.
THIS IS FOR THE BEST. WE'RE TOGETHER FOREVER.
...DONG-MIN...
IT'S JUST TEMPORARY. I'LL BE BACK SOON, CHO-ROM...
DONG-MIN!

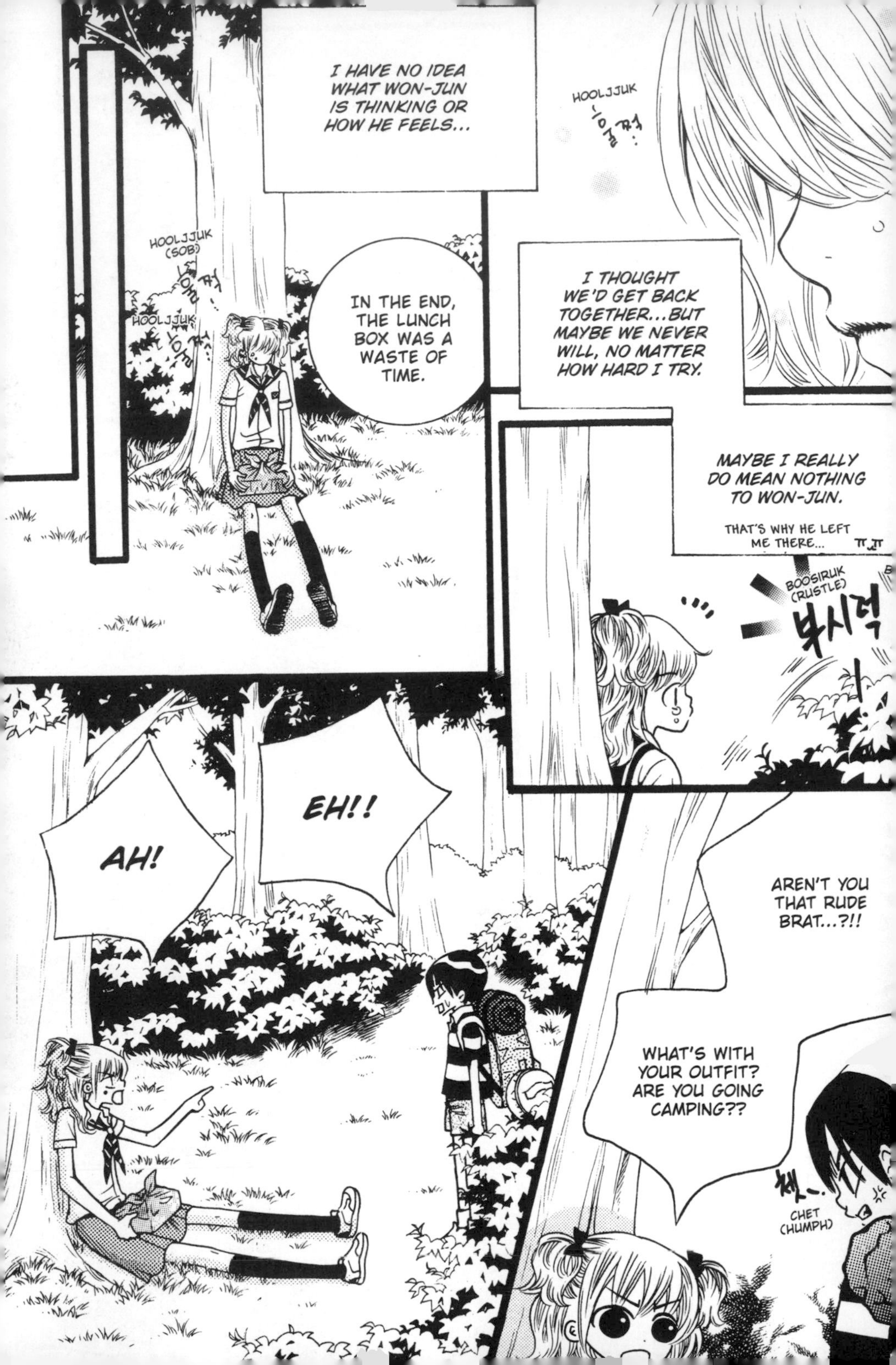
I HAVE NO IDEA WHAT WON-JUN IS THINKING OR HOW HE FEELS...
HOOLJJUK (SOB)
훌쩍
HOOLJJUK
훌쩍
IN THE END, THE LUNCH BOX WAS A WASTE OF TIME.
HOOLJJUK
훌쩍..
I THOUGHT WE'D GET BACK TOGETHER...BUT MAYBE WE NEVER WILL, NO MATTER HOW HARD I TRY.
MAYBE I REALLY DO MEAN NOTHING TO WON-JUN.
THAT'S WHY HE LEFT ME THERE... ㅠ.ㅠ
BOOSIRUK (RUSTLE)
부시럭
AH!
EH!!
AREN'T YOU THAT RUDE BRAT...?!!
WHAT'S WITH YOUR OUTFIT? ARE YOU GOING CAMPING??
쳇..
CHET (HUMPH)

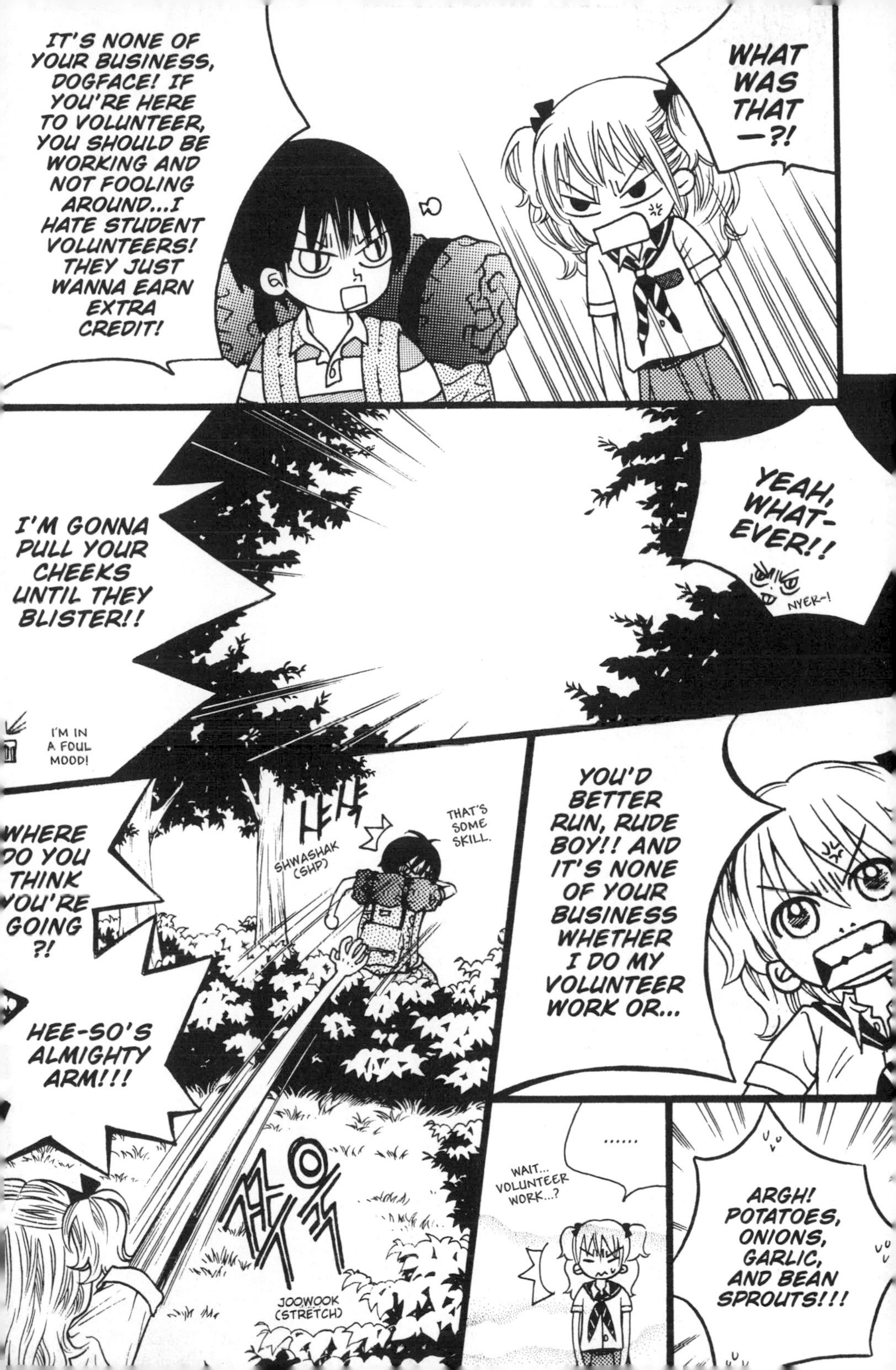
IT'S NONE OF YOUR BUSINESS, DOGFACE! IF YOU'RE HERE TO VOLUNTEER, YOU SHOULD BE WORKING AND NOT FOOLING AROUND...I HATE STUDENT VOLUNTEERS! THEY JUST WANNA EARN EXTRA CREDIT!
WHAT WAS THAT—?!
I'M GONNA PULL YOUR CHEEKS UNTIL THEY BLISTER!!
YEAH, WHATEVER!!
NYER-!
I'M IN A FOUL MOOD!
WHERE DO YOU THINK YOU'RE GOING?!
SHWASHAK (SHP)
THAT'S SOME SKILL.
HEE-SO'S ALMIGHTY ARM!!!
JOOWOOK (STRETCH)
YOU'D BETTER RUN, RUDE BOY!! AND IT'S NONE OF YOUR BUSINESS WHETHER I DO MY VOLUNTEER WORK OR...
......
WAIT... VOLUNTEER WORK...?
ARGH! POTATOES, ONIONS, GARLIC, AND BEAN SPROUTS!!!

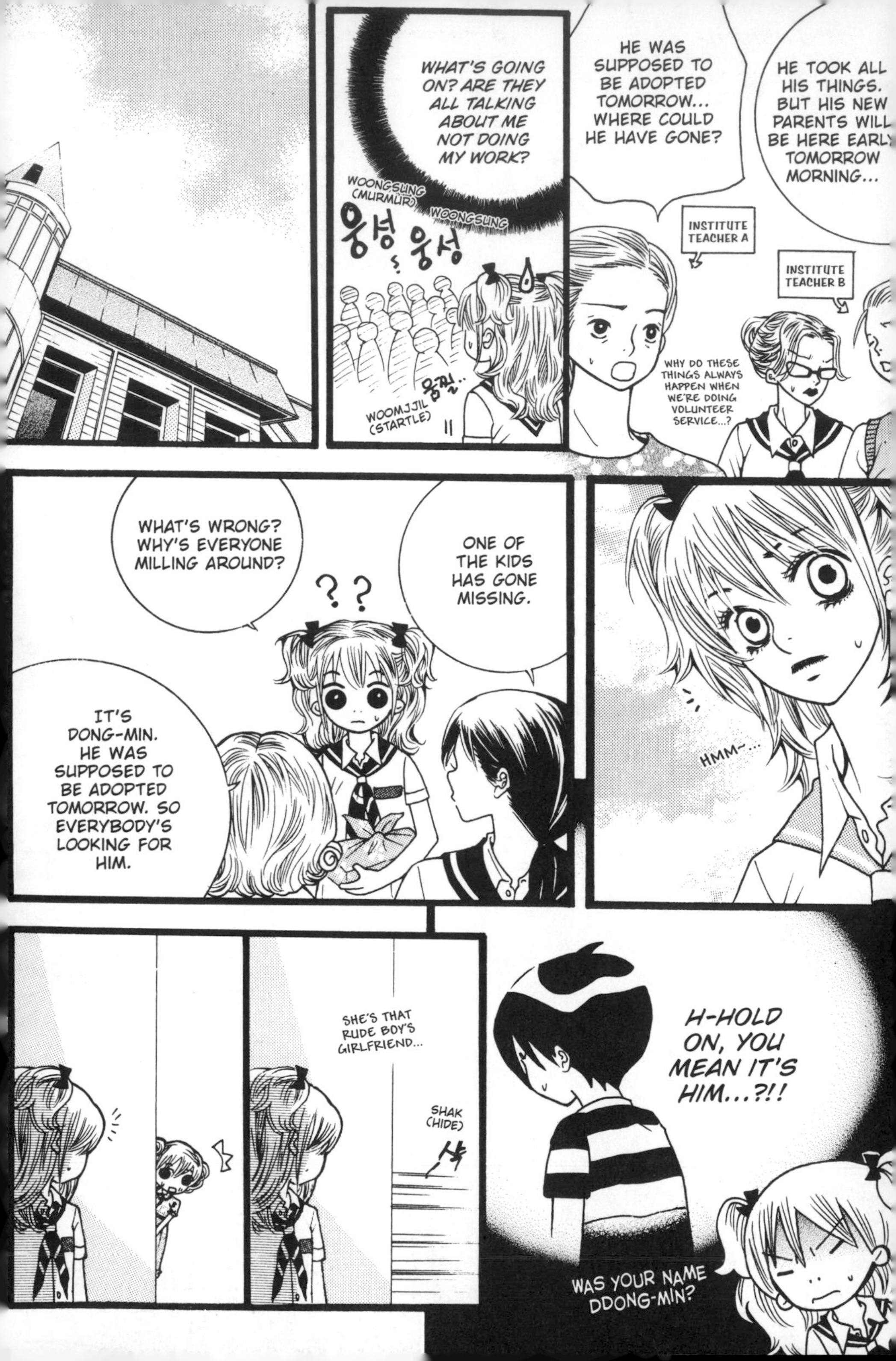
WHAT'S GOING ON? ARE THEY ALL TALKING ABOUT ME NOT DOING MY WORK?
WOONGSUNG (MURMUR) WOONGSUNG
웅성 웅성
움찔
WOOMJJIL (STARTLE)
HE WAS SUPPOSED TO BE ADOPTED TOMORROW... WHERE COULD HE HAVE GONE?
HE TOOK ALL HIS THINGS. BUT HIS NEW PARENTS WILL BE HERE EARLY TOMORROW MORNING...
INSTITUTE TEACHER A
INSTITUTE TEACHER B
WHY DO THESE THINGS ALWAYS HAPPEN WHEN WE'RE DOING VOLUNTEER SERVICE...?
WHAT'S WRONG? WHY'S EVERYONE MILLING AROUND?
??
ONE OF THE KIDS HAS GONE MISSING.
IT'S DONG-MIN. HE WAS SUPPOSED TO BE ADOPTED TOMORROW. SO EVERYBODY'S LOOKING FOR HIM.
HMM~...
SHE'S THAT RUDE BOY'S GIRLFRIEND...
SHAK (HIDE)
H-HOLD ON, YOU MEAN IT'S HIM...?!!
WAS YOUR NAME DDONG-MIN?

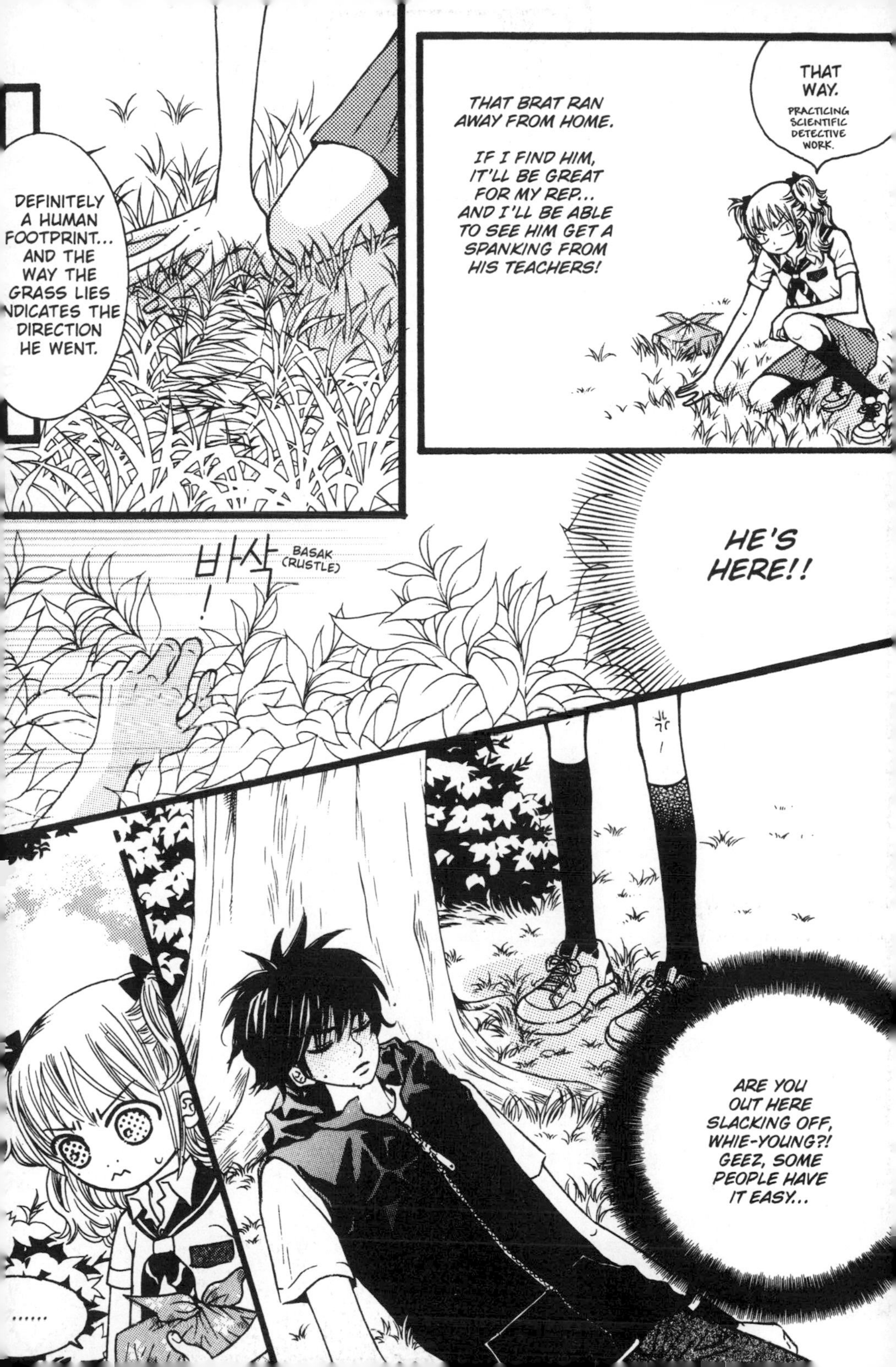
DEFINITELY A HUMAN FOOTPRINT... AND THE WAY THE GRASS LIES INDICATES THE DIRECTION HE WENT.
THAT BRAT RAN AWAY FROM HOME.
IF I FIND HIM, IT'LL BE GREAT FOR MY REP... AND I'LL BE ABLE TO SEE HIM GET A SPANKING FROM HIS TEACHERS!
THAT WAY.
PRACTICING SCIENTIFIC DETECTIVE WORK.
바삭
BASAK (RUSTLE)
HE'S HERE!!
......
ARE YOU OUT HERE SLACKING OFF, WHIE-YOUNG?! GEEZ, SOME PEOPLE HAVE IT EASY...

13th Boy

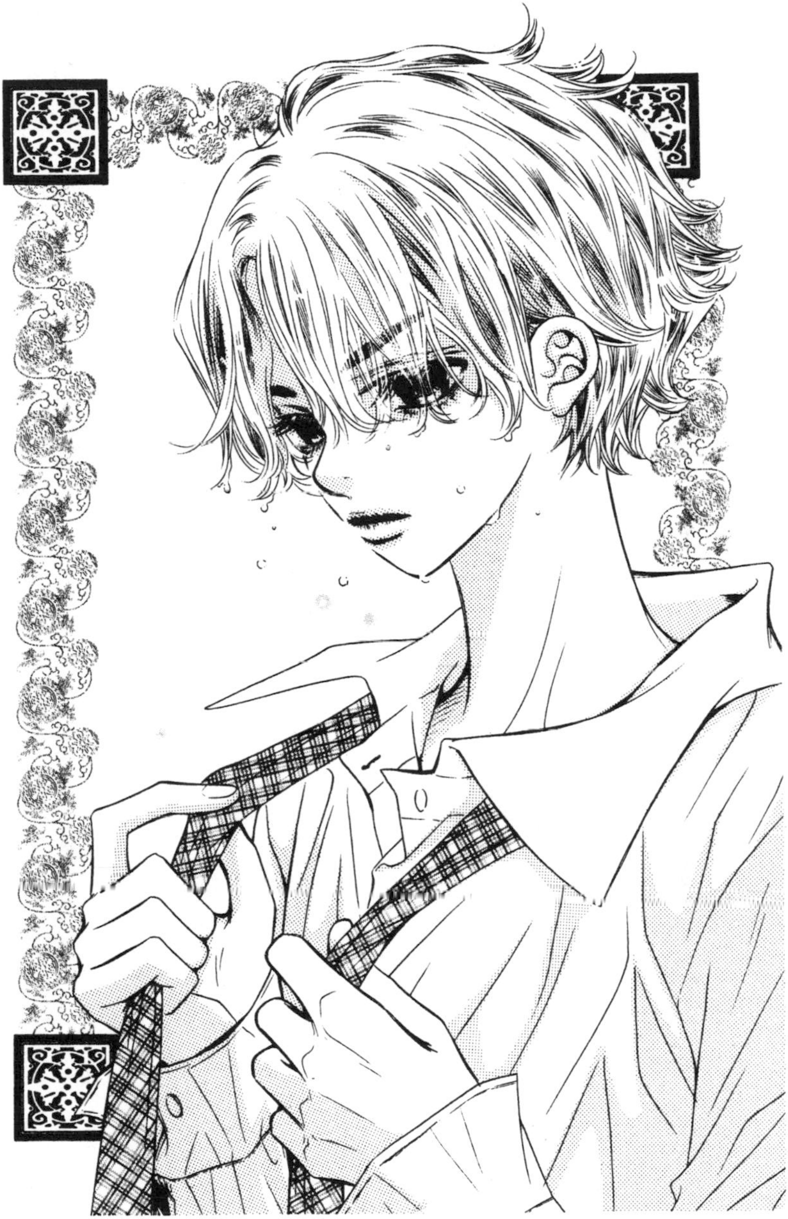

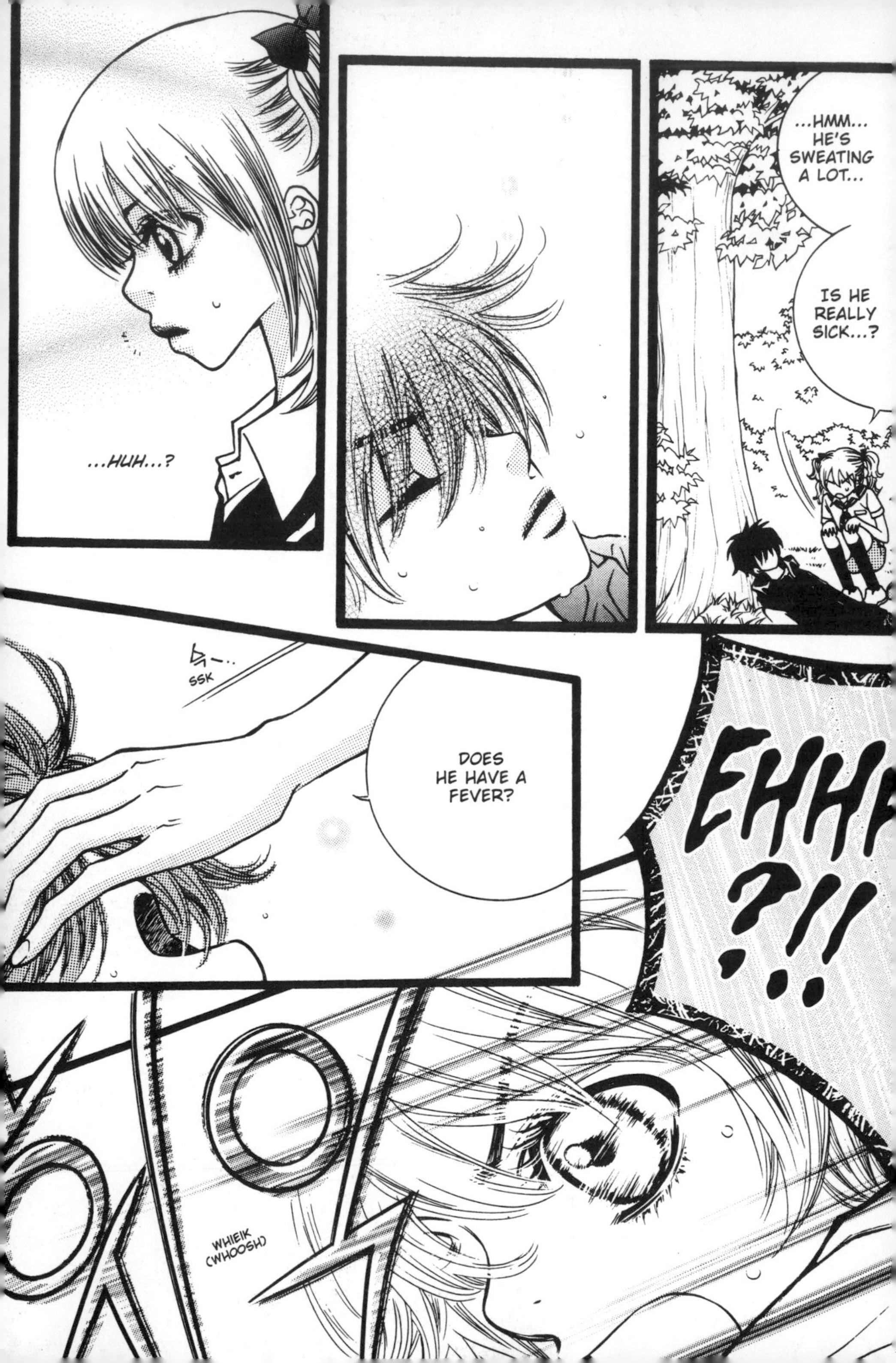
...HUH...?
...HMM... HE'S SWEATING A LOT...
IS HE REALLY SICK...?
SSK
DOES HE HAVE A FEVER?
EHH ?!!
WHIEIK (WHOOSH)

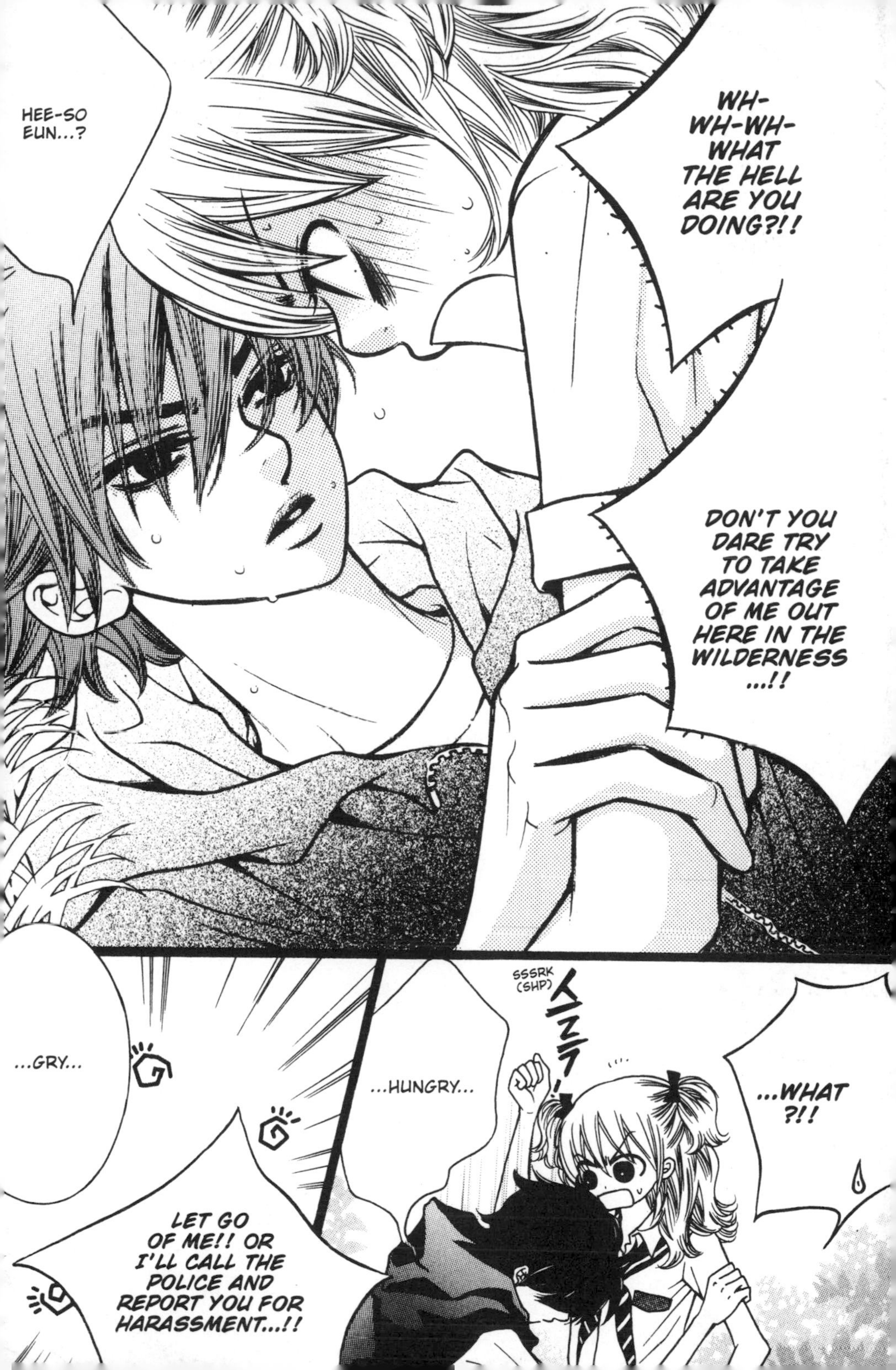
HEE-SO EUN...?
WH-WH-WH-WHAT THE HELL ARE YOU DOING?!!
DON'T YOU DARE TRY TO TAKE ADVANTAGE OF ME OUT HERE IN THE WILDERNESS ...!!
...GRY...
LET GO OF ME!! OR I'LL CALL THE POLICE AND REPORT YOU FOR HARASSMENT...!!
...HUNGRY...
SSSRK (SHP)
...WHAT ?!!

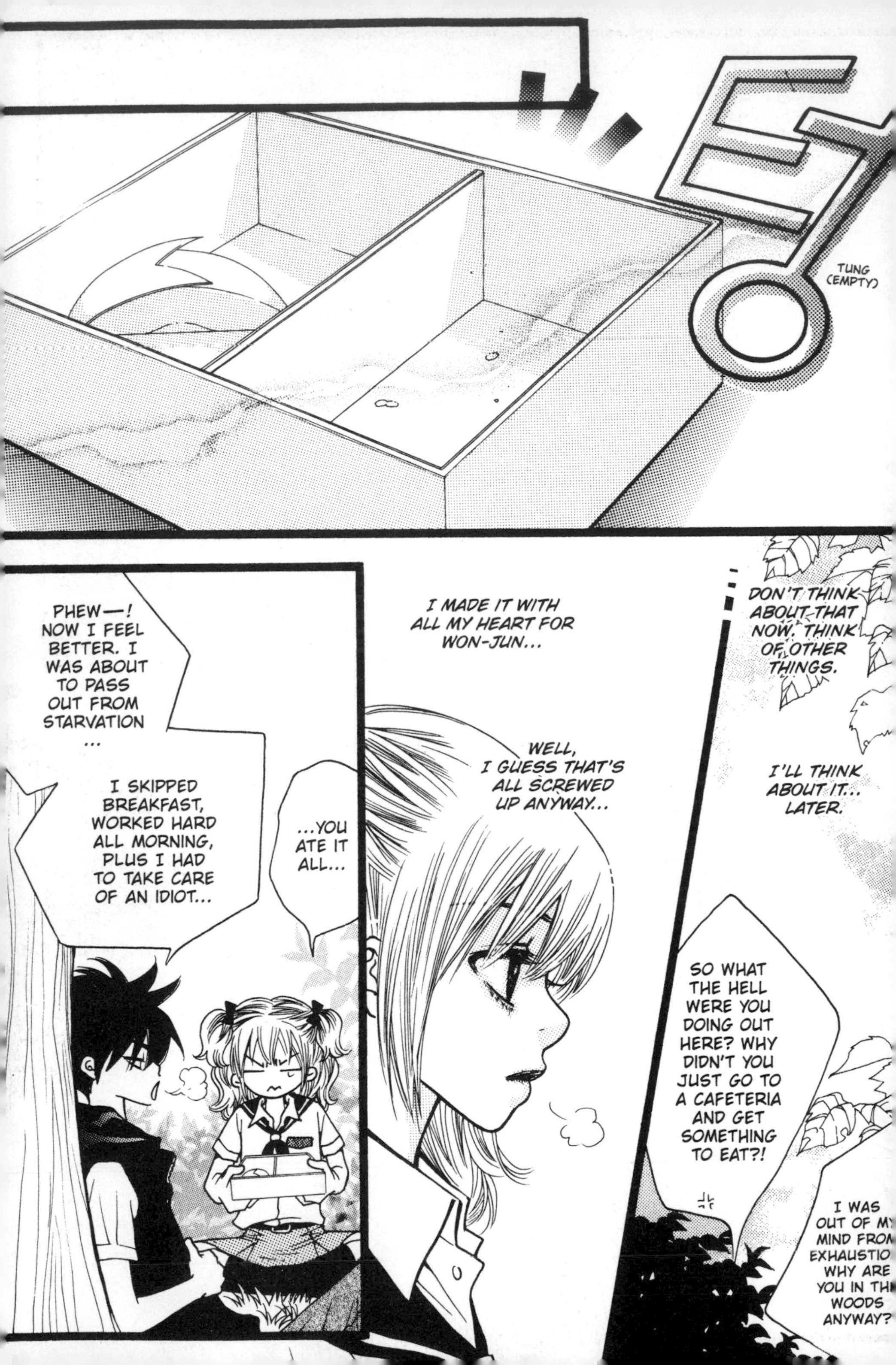
TUNG (EMPTY)
PHEW—! NOW I FEEL BETTER. I WAS ABOUT TO PASS OUT FROM STARVATION ...
I SKIPPED BREAKFAST, WORKED HARD ALL MORNING, PLUS I HAD TO TAKE CARE OF AN IDIOT...
...YOU ATE IT ALL...
I MADE IT WITH ALL MY HEART FOR WON-JUN...
WELL, I GUESS THAT'S ALL SCREWED UP ANYWAY...
DON'T THINK ABOUT THAT NOW. THINK OF OTHER THINGS.
I'LL THINK ABOUT IT... LATER.
SO WHAT THE HELL WERE YOU DOING OUT HERE? WHY DIDN'T YOU JUST GO TO A CAFETERIA AND GET SOMETHING TO EAT?!
I WAS OUT OF MY MIND FROM EXHAUSTIO WHY ARE YOU IN TH WOODS ANYWAY?

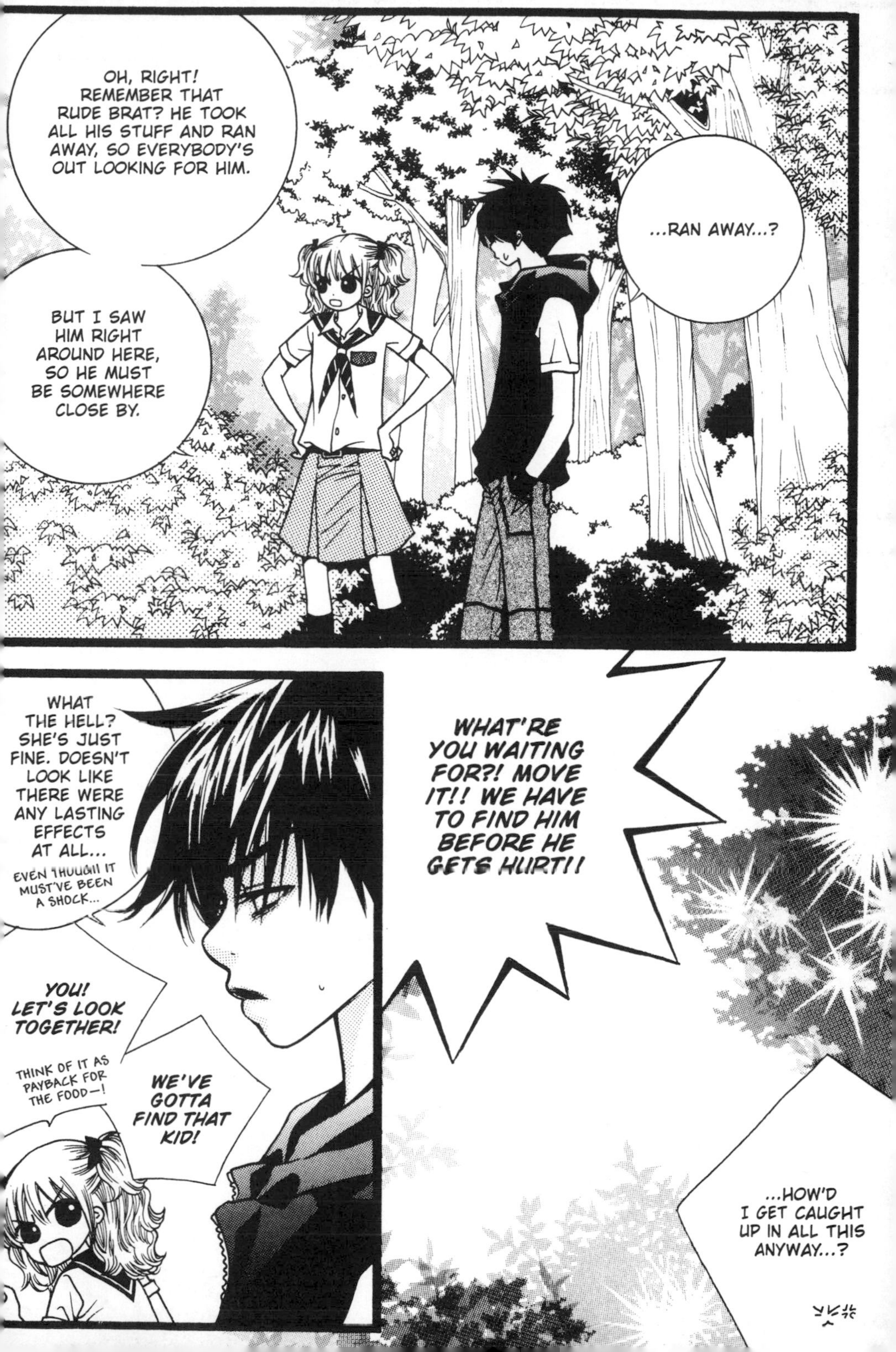

OH, RIGHT! REMEMBER THAT RUDE BRAT? HE TOOK ALL HIS STUFF AND RAN AWAY, SO EVERYBODY'S OUT LOOKING FOR HIM.
BUT I SAW HIM RIGHT AROUND HERE, SO HE MUST BE SOMEWHERE CLOSE BY.
...RAN AWAY...?
WHAT THE HELL? SHE'S JUST FINE. DOESN'T LOOK LIKE THERE WERE ANY LASTING EFFECTS AT ALL...
EVEN THOUGH IT MUST'VE BEEN A SHOCK...
YOU! LET'S LOOK TOGETHER!
THINK OF IT AS PAYBACK FOR THE FOOD—!
WE'VE GOTTA FIND THAT KID!
WHAT'RE YOU WAITING FOR?! MOVE IT!! WE HAVE TO FIND HIM BEFORE HE GETS HURT!!
...HOW'D I GET CAUGHT UP IN ALL THIS ANYWAY...?

STEP 10. GIANT SNOWFLAKES IN MIDSUMMER

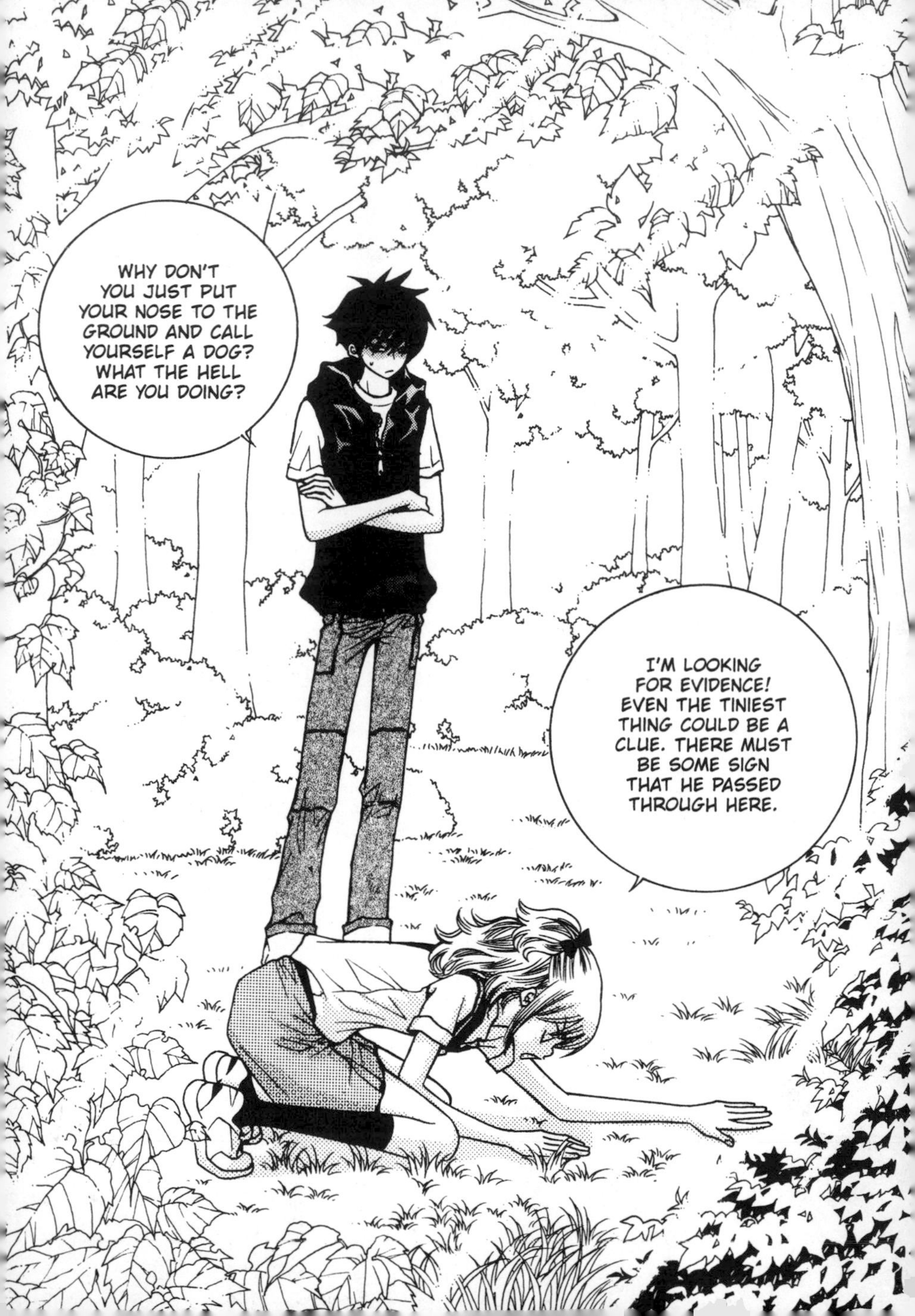
WHY DON'T YOU JUST PUT YOUR NOSE TO THE GROUND AND CALL YOURSELF A DOG? WHAT THE HELL ARE YOU DOING?
I'M LOOKING FOR EVIDENCE! EVEN THE TINIEST THING COULD BE A CLUE. THERE MUST BE SOME SIGN THAT HE PASSED THROUGH HERE.

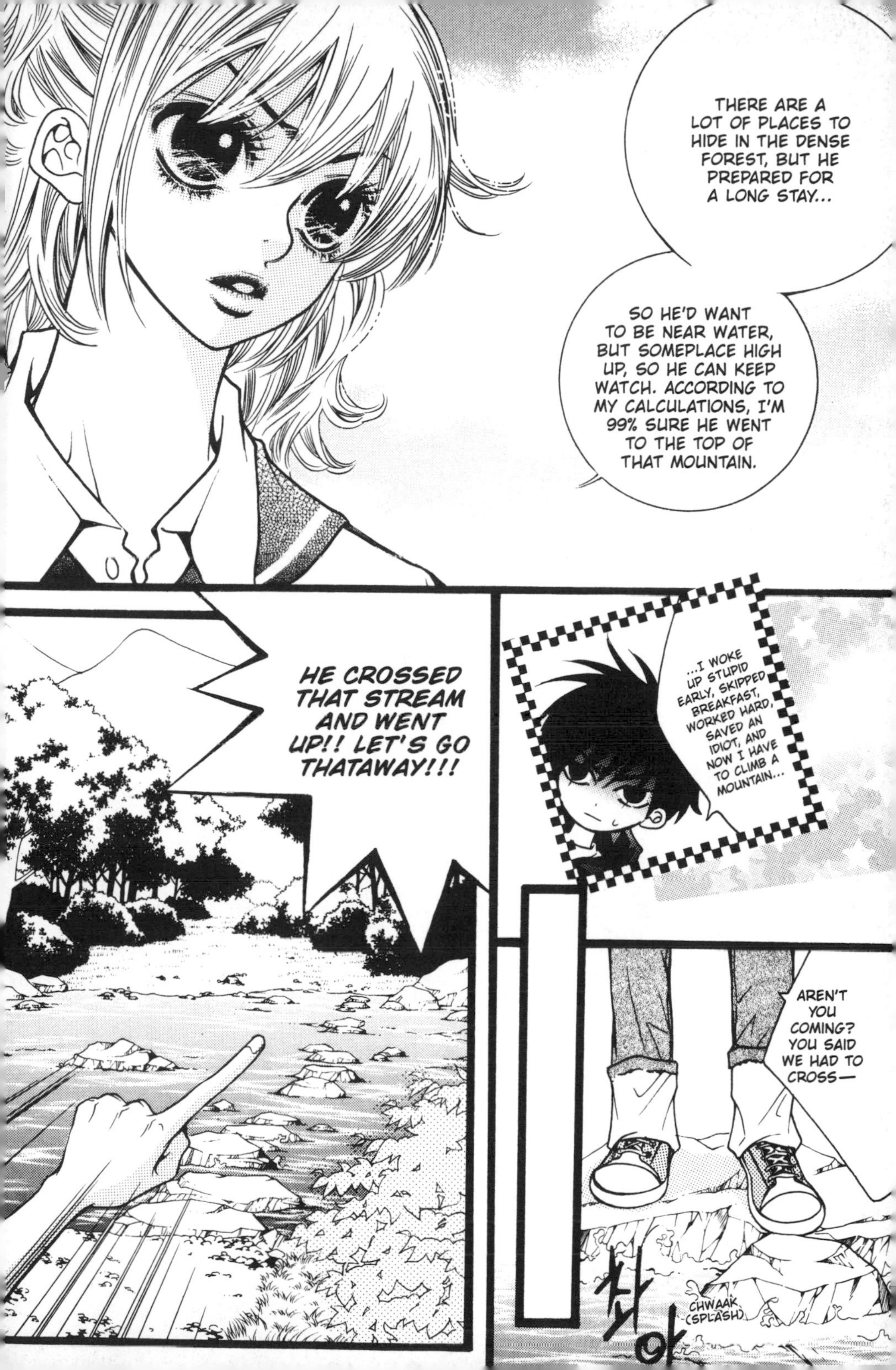
THERE ARE A LOT OF PLACES TO HIDE IN THE DENSE FOREST, BUT HE PREPARED FOR A LONG STAY...
SO HE'D WANT TO BE NEAR WATER, BUT SOMEPLACE HIGH UP, SO HE CAN KEEP WATCH. ACCORDING TO MY CALCULATIONS, I'M 99% SURE HE WENT TO THE TOP OF THAT MOUNTAIN.
HE CROSSED THAT STREAM AND WENT UP!! LET'S GO THATAWAY!!!
...I WOKE UP STUPID EARLY, SKIPPED BREAKFAST, WORKED HARD, SAVED AN IDIOT, AND NOW I HAVE TO CLIMB A MOUNTAIN...
AREN'T YOU COMING? YOU SAID WE HAD TO CROSS—
CHWAAK (SPLASH)

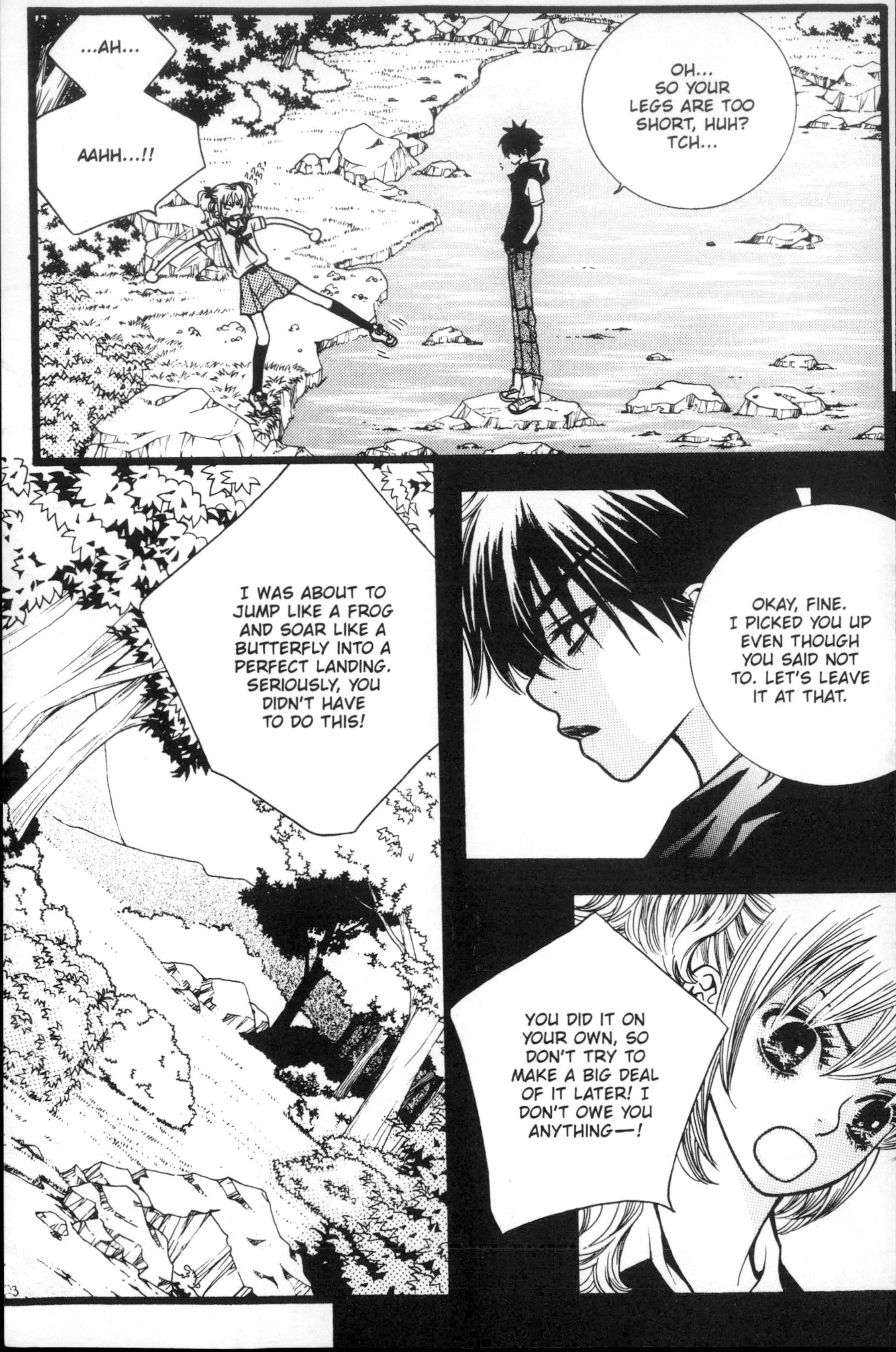
...AH...
AAHH...!!
OH...
SO YOUR
LEGS ARE TOO
SHORT, HUH?
TCH...
I WAS ABOUT TO
JUMP LIKE A FROG
AND SOAR LIKE A
BUTTERFLY INTO A
PERFECT LANDING.
SERIOUSLY, YOU
DIDN'T HAVE
TO DO THIS!
OKAY, FINE.
I PICKED YOU UP
EVEN THOUGH
YOU SAID NOT
TO. LET'S LEAVE
IT AT THAT.
YOU DID IT ON
YOUR OWN, SO
DON'T TRY TO
MAKE A BIG DEAL
OF IT LATER! I
DON'T OWE YOU
ANYTHING—!

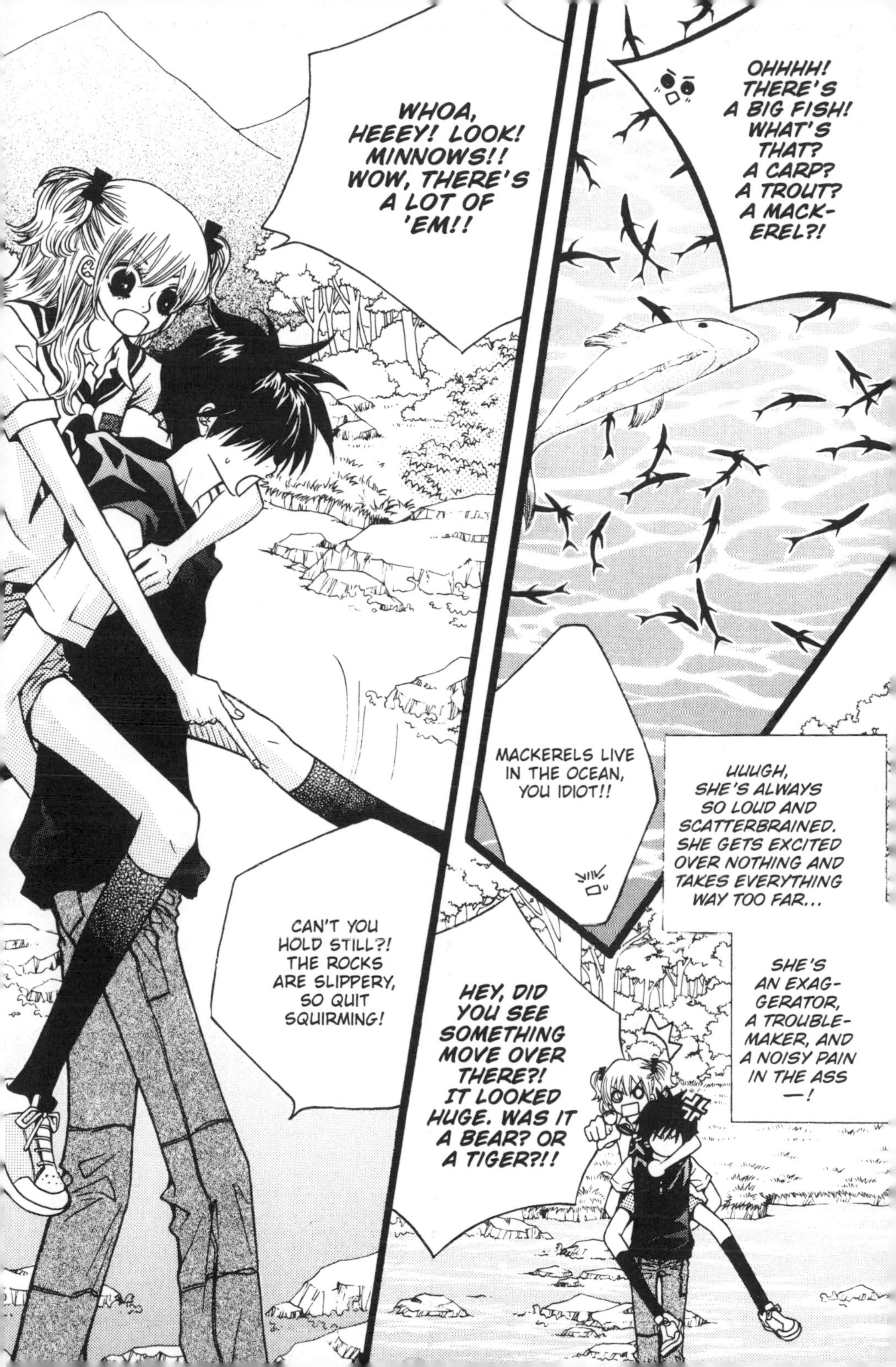
WHOA, HEEEY! LOOK! MINNOWS!! WOW, THERE'S A LOT OF 'EM!!
CAN'T YOU HOLD STILL?! THE ROCKS ARE SLIPPERY, SO QUIT SQUIRMING!
OHHHH! THERE'S A BIG FISH! WHAT'S THAT? A CARP? A TROUT? A MACK-EREL?!
MACKERELS LIVE IN THE OCEAN, YOU IDIOT!!
UUUGH, SHE'S ALWAYS SO LOUD AND SCATTERBRAINED. SHE GETS EXCITED OVER NOTHING AND TAKES EVERYTHING WAY TOO FAR...
HEY, DID YOU SEE SOMETHING MOVE OVER THERE?! IT LOOKED HUGE. WAS IT A BEAR? OR A TIGER?!!
SHE'S AN EXAG-GERATOR, A TROUBLE-MAKER, AND A NOISY PAIN IN THE ASS—!

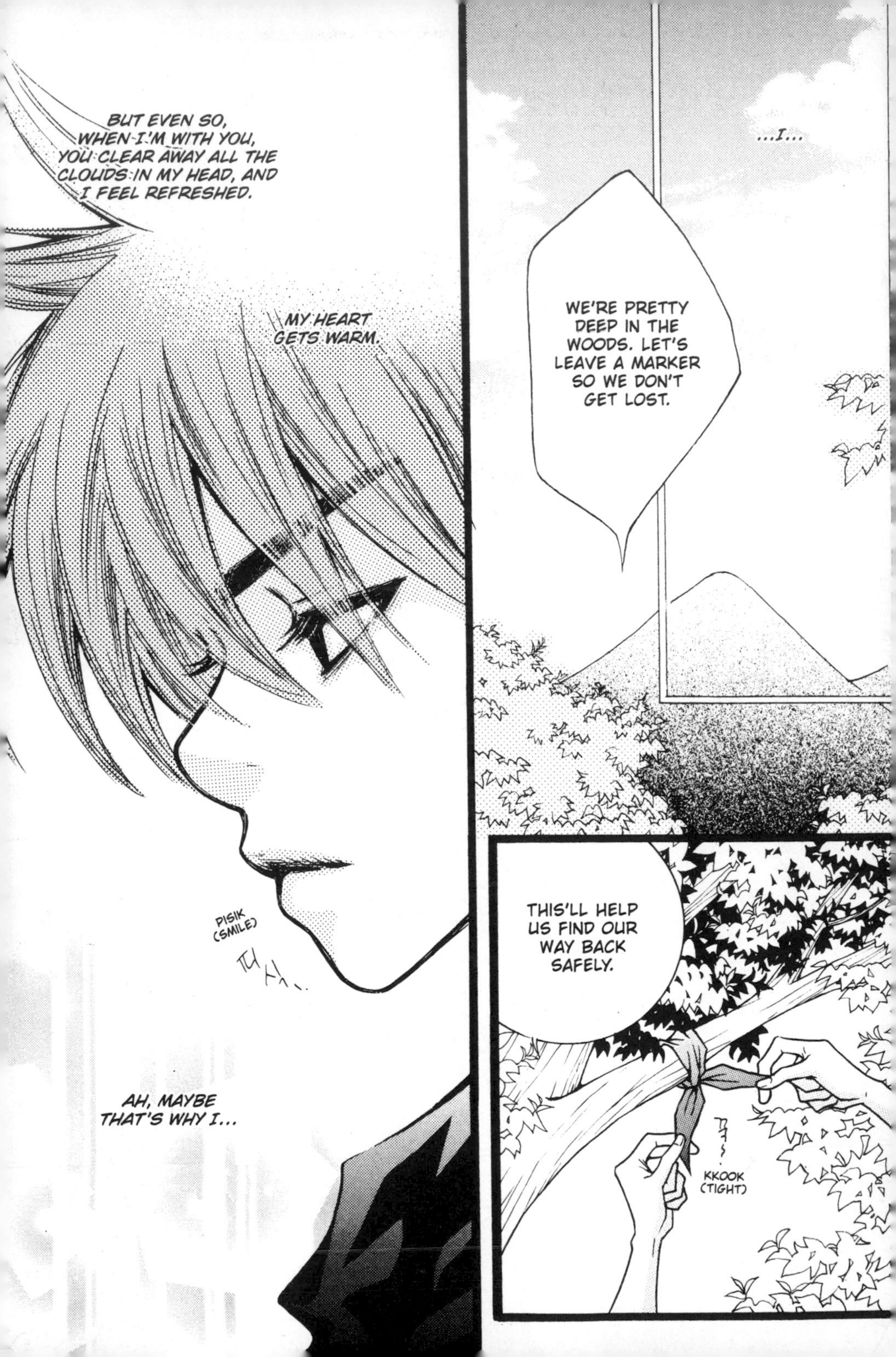
BUT EVEN SO, WHEN I'M WITH YOU, YOU CLEAR AWAY ALL THE CLOUDS IN MY HEAD, AND I FEEL REFRESHED.
MY HEART GETS WARM.
PISIK (SMILE)
AH, MAYBE THAT'S WHY I...
...I...
WE'RE PRETTY DEEP IN THE WOODS. LET'S LEAVE A MARKER SO WE DON'T GET LOST.
THIS'LL HELP US FIND OUR WAY BACK SAFELY.
KKOOK (TIGHT)

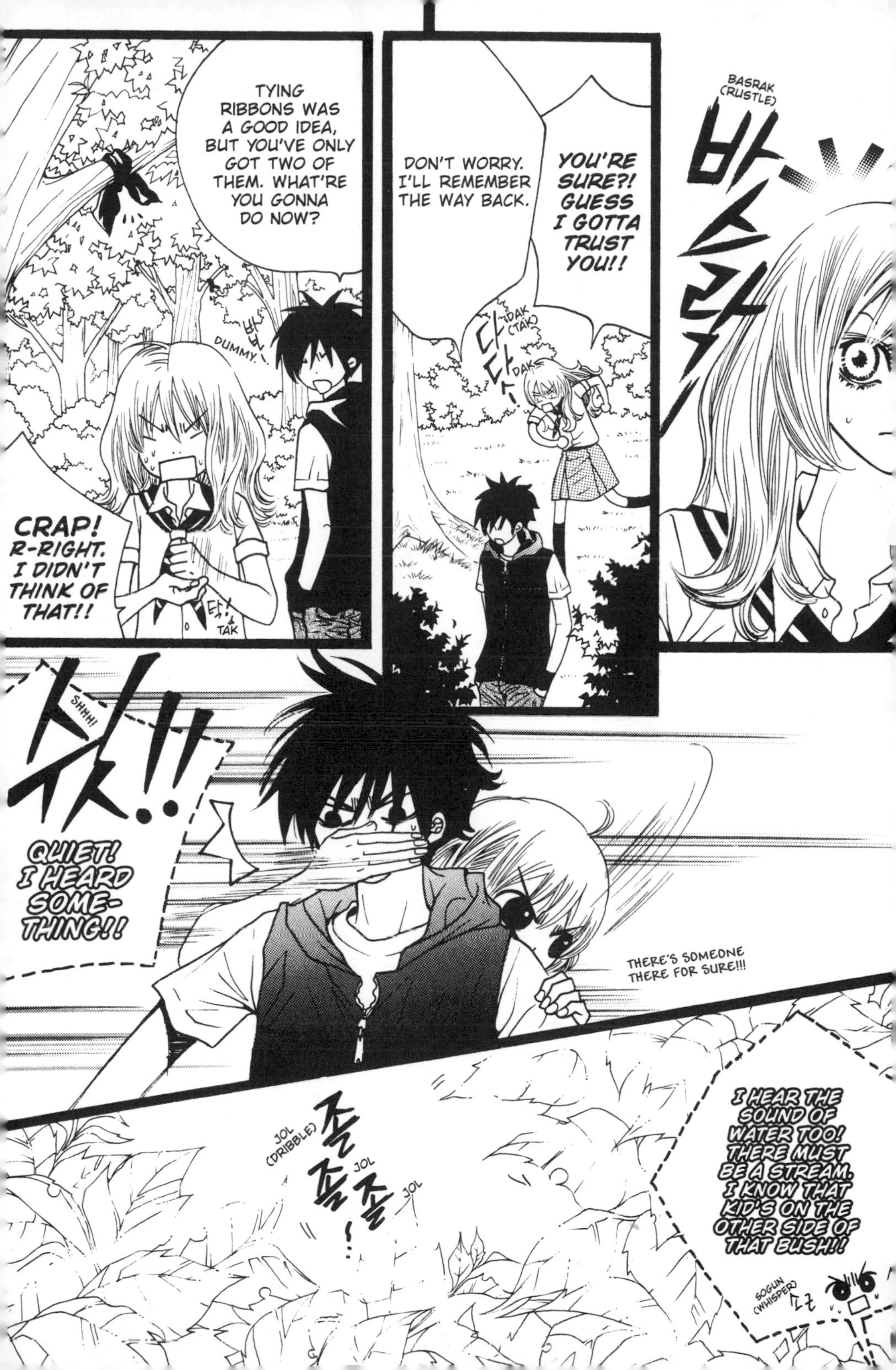

TYING RIBBONS WAS A GOOD IDEA, BUT YOU'VE ONLY GOT TWO OF THEM. WHAT'RE YOU GONNA DO NOW?
바보
DUMMY.
CRAP! R-RIGHT. I DIDN'T THINK OF THAT!!
탁!
TAK
DON'T WORRY. I'LL REMEMBER THE WAY BACK.
YOU'RE SURE?! GUESS I GOTTA TRUST YOU!!
다닥!
DAK (TAK) DAK
바스락
BASRAK (RUSTLE)
쉬잇!!
SHHH!
QUIET! I HEARD SOME-THING!!
THERE'S SOMEONE THERE FOR SURE!!!
졸졸졸
JOL (DRIBBLE) JOL JOL
I HEAR THE SOUND OF WATER TOO! THERE MUST BE A STREAM. I KNOW THAT KID'S ON THE OTHER SIDE OF THAT BUSH!!
소곤
SOGUN (WHISPER)

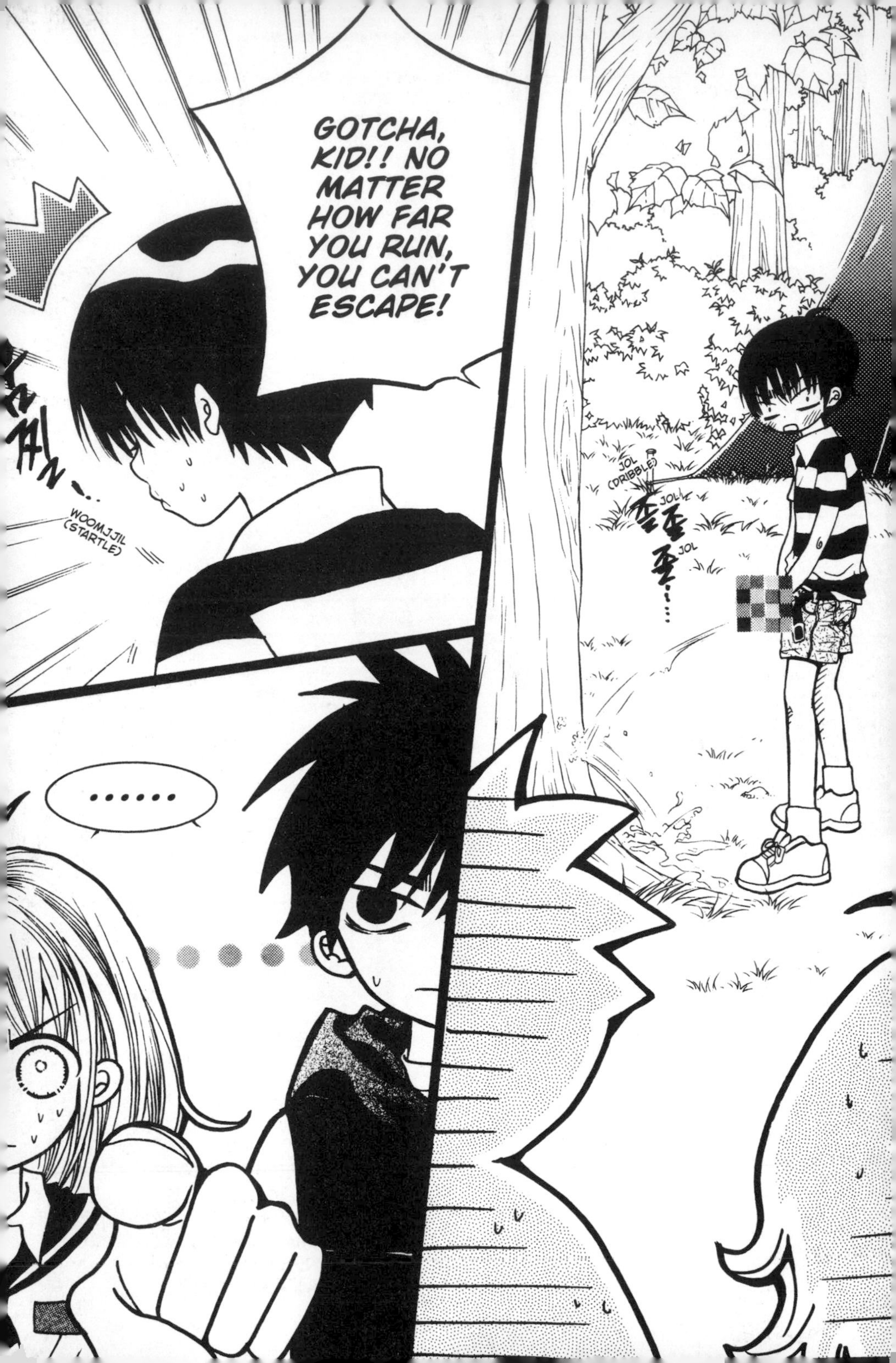
GOTCHA, KID!! NO MATTER HOW FAR YOU RUN, YOU CAN'T ESCAPE!
WOOMJJIL (STARTLE)
......
JOL (DRIBBLE)
JOL
JOL

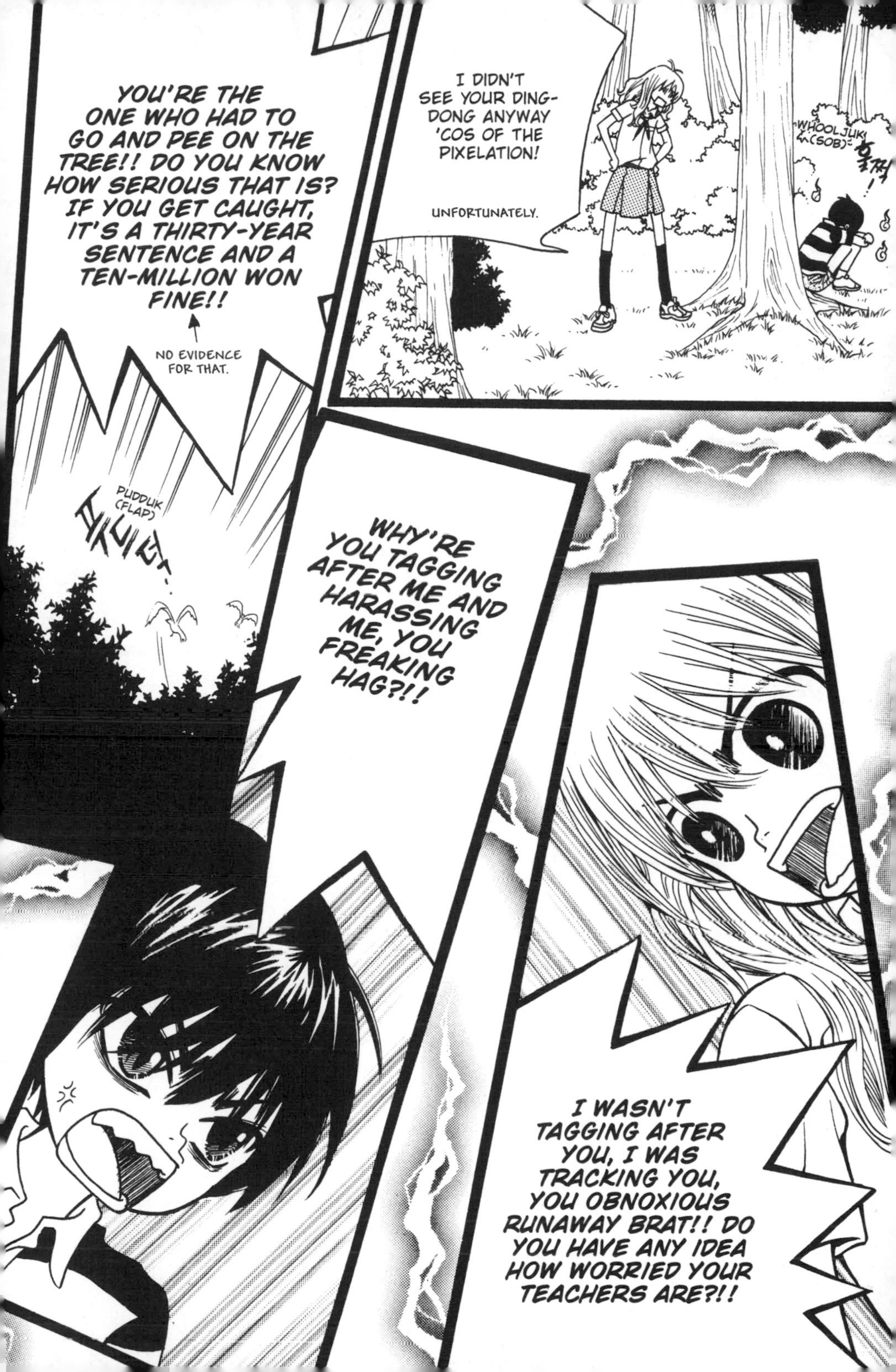

YOU'RE THE ONE WHO HAD TO GO AND PEE ON THE TREE!! DO YOU KNOW HOW SERIOUS THAT IS? IF YOU GET CAUGHT, IT'S A THIRTY-YEAR SENTENCE AND A TEN-MILLION WON FINE!!
NO EVIDENCE FOR THAT.
I DIDN'T SEE YOUR DING-DONG ANYWAY 'COS OF THE PIXELATION!
UNFORTUNATELY.
WHOOLJUK (SOB)
PUDDUK (FLAP)
WHY'RE YOU TAGGING AFTER ME AND HARASSING ME, YOU FREAKING HAG?!!
I WASN'T TAGGING AFTER YOU, I WAS TRACKING YOU, YOU OBNOXIOUS RUNAWAY BRAT!! DO YOU HAVE ANY IDEA HOW WORRIED YOUR TEACHERS ARE?!!

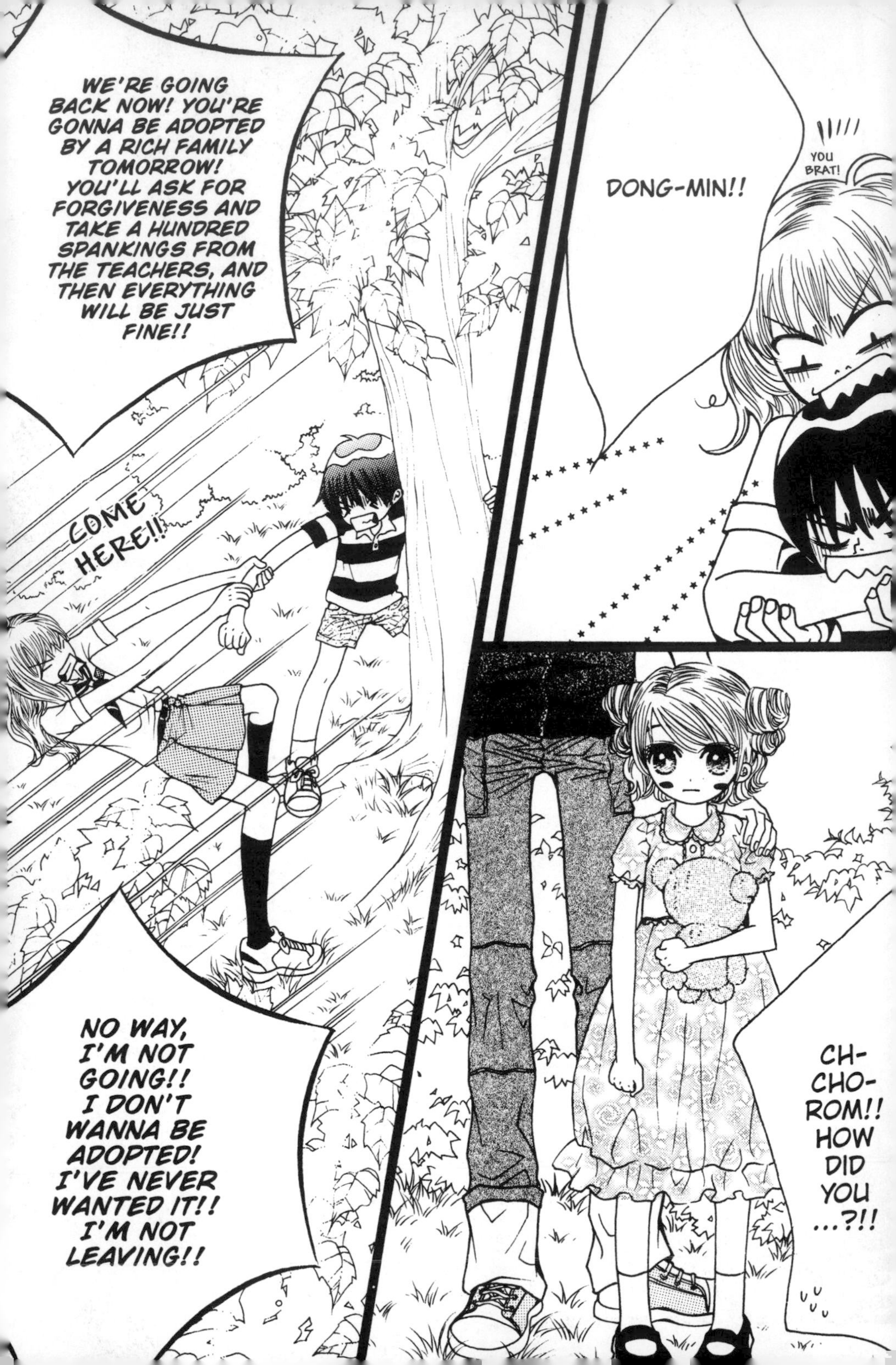
WE'RE GOING BACK NOW! YOU'RE GONNA BE ADOPTED BY A RICH FAMILY TOMORROW! YOU'LL ASK FOR FORGIVENESS AND TAKE A HUNDRED SPANKINGS FROM THE TEACHERS, AND THEN EVERYTHING WILL BE JUST FINE!!
COME HERE!!
NO WAY, I'M NOT GOING!! I DON'T WANNA BE ADOPTED! I'VE NEVER WANTED IT!! I'M NOT LEAVING!!
DONG-MIN!!
YOU BRAT!
CH-CHO-ROM!! HOW DID YOU ...?!!

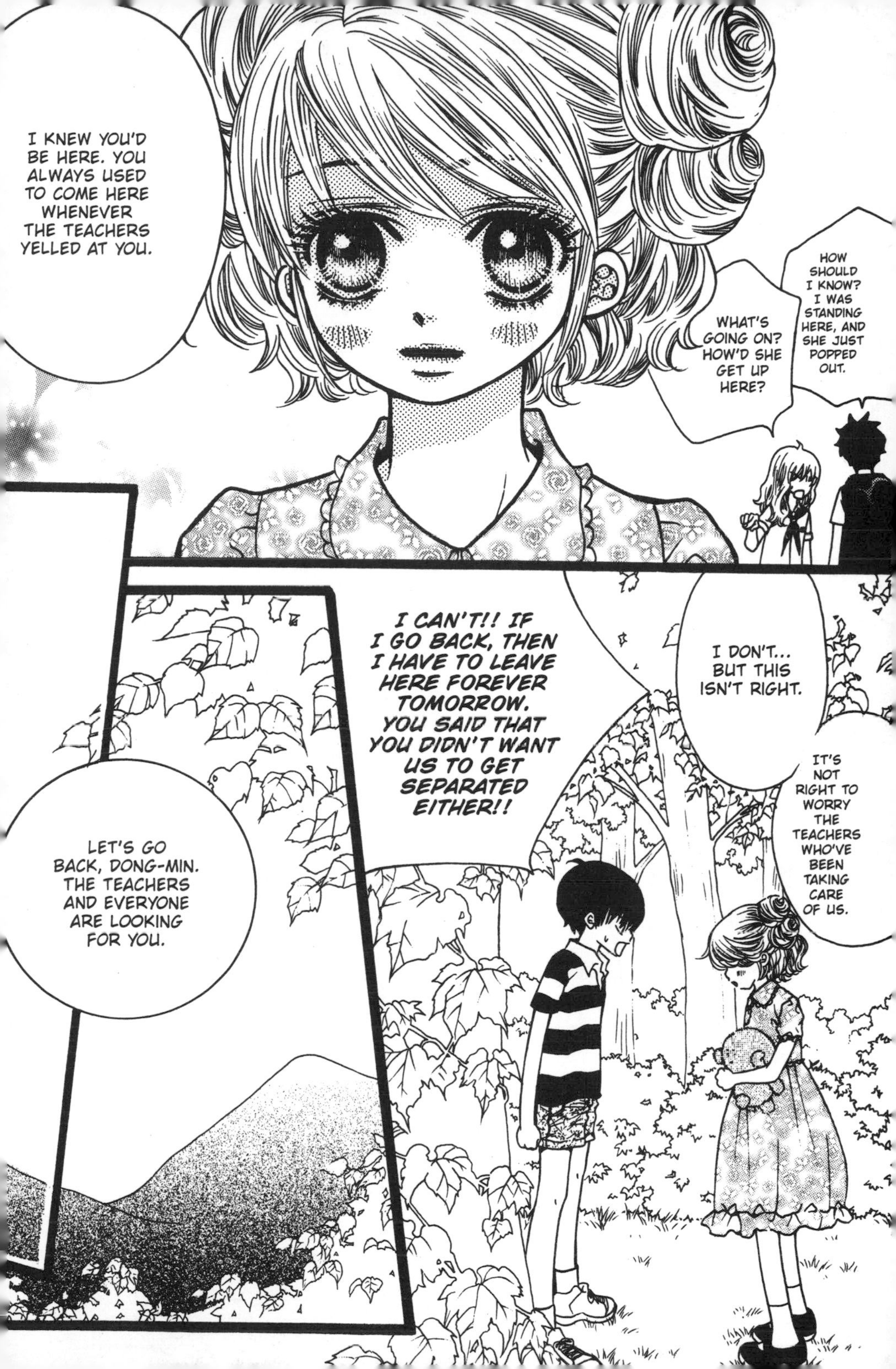
I KNEW YOU'D BE HERE. YOU ALWAYS USED TO COME HERE WHENEVER THE TEACHERS YELLED AT YOU.
WHAT'S GOING ON? HOW'D SHE GET UP HERE?
HOW SHOULD I KNOW? I WAS STANDING HERE, AND SHE JUST POPPED OUT.
LET'S GO BACK, DONG-MIN. THE TEACHERS AND EVERYONE ARE LOOKING FOR YOU.
I CAN'T!! IF I GO BACK, THEN I HAVE TO LEAVE HERE FOREVER TOMORROW. YOU SAID THAT YOU DIDN'T WANT US TO GET SEPARATED EITHER!!
I DON'T... BUT THIS ISN'T RIGHT.
IT'S NOT RIGHT TO WORRY THE TEACHERS WHO'VE BEEN TAKING CARE OF US.

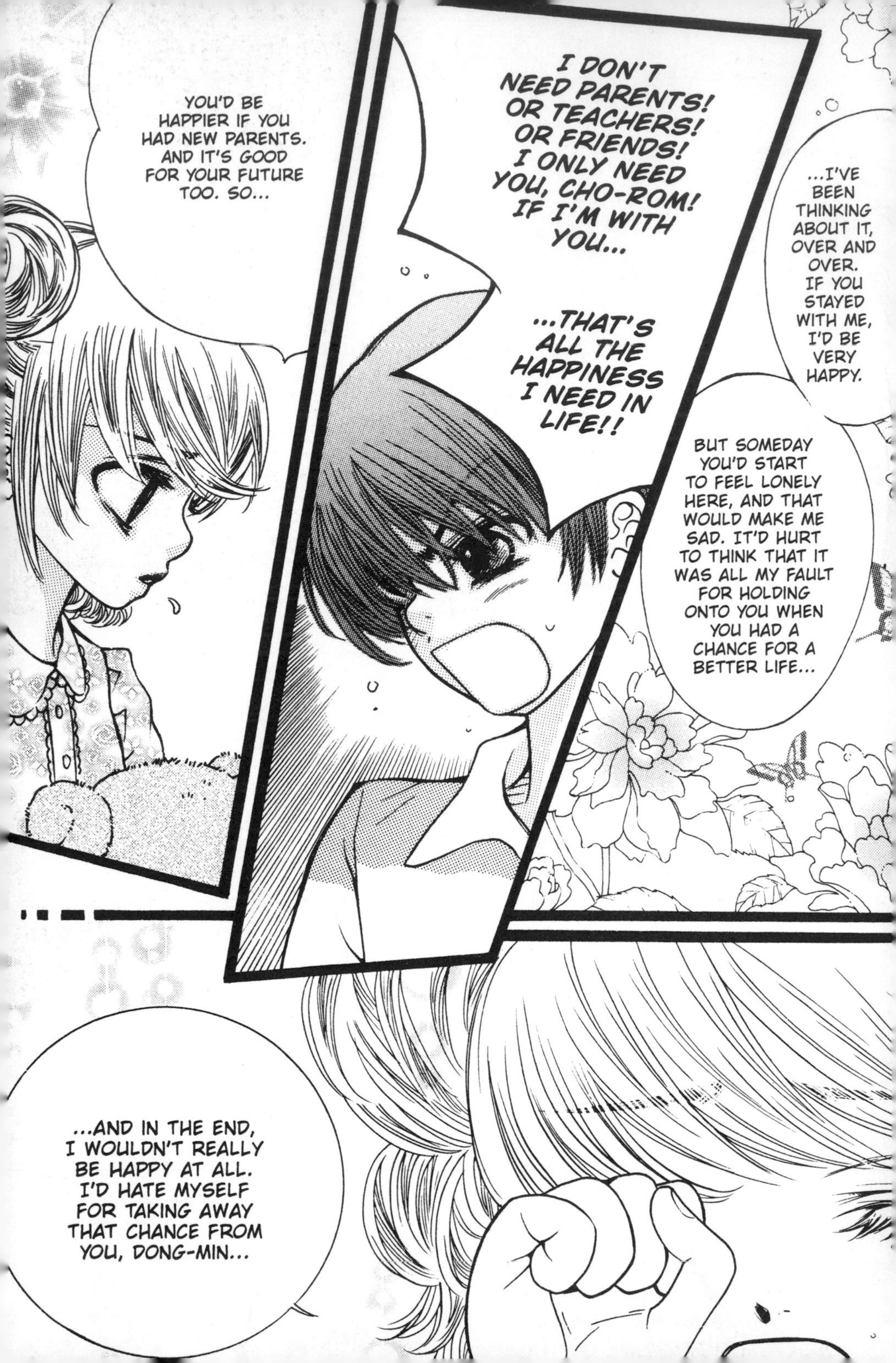
YOU'D BE HAPPIER IF YOU HAD NEW PARENTS. AND IT'S GOOD FOR YOUR FUTURE TOO. SO...
I DON'T NEED PARENTS! OR TEACHERS! OR FRIENDS! I ONLY NEED YOU, CHO-ROM! IF I'M WITH YOU...
...THAT'S ALL THE HAPPINESS I NEED IN LIFE!!
...I'VE BEEN THINKING ABOUT IT, OVER AND OVER. IF YOU STAYED WITH ME, I'D BE VERY HAPPY.
BUT SOMEDAY YOU'D START TO FEEL LONELY HERE, AND THAT WOULD MAKE ME SAD. IT'D HURT TO THINK THAT IT WAS ALL MY FAULT FOR HOLDING ONTO YOU WHEN YOU HAD A CHANCE FOR A BETTER LIFE...
...AND IN THE END, I WOULDN'T REALLY BE HAPPY AT ALL. I'D HATE MYSELF FOR TAKING AWAY THAT CHANCE FROM YOU, DONG-MIN...

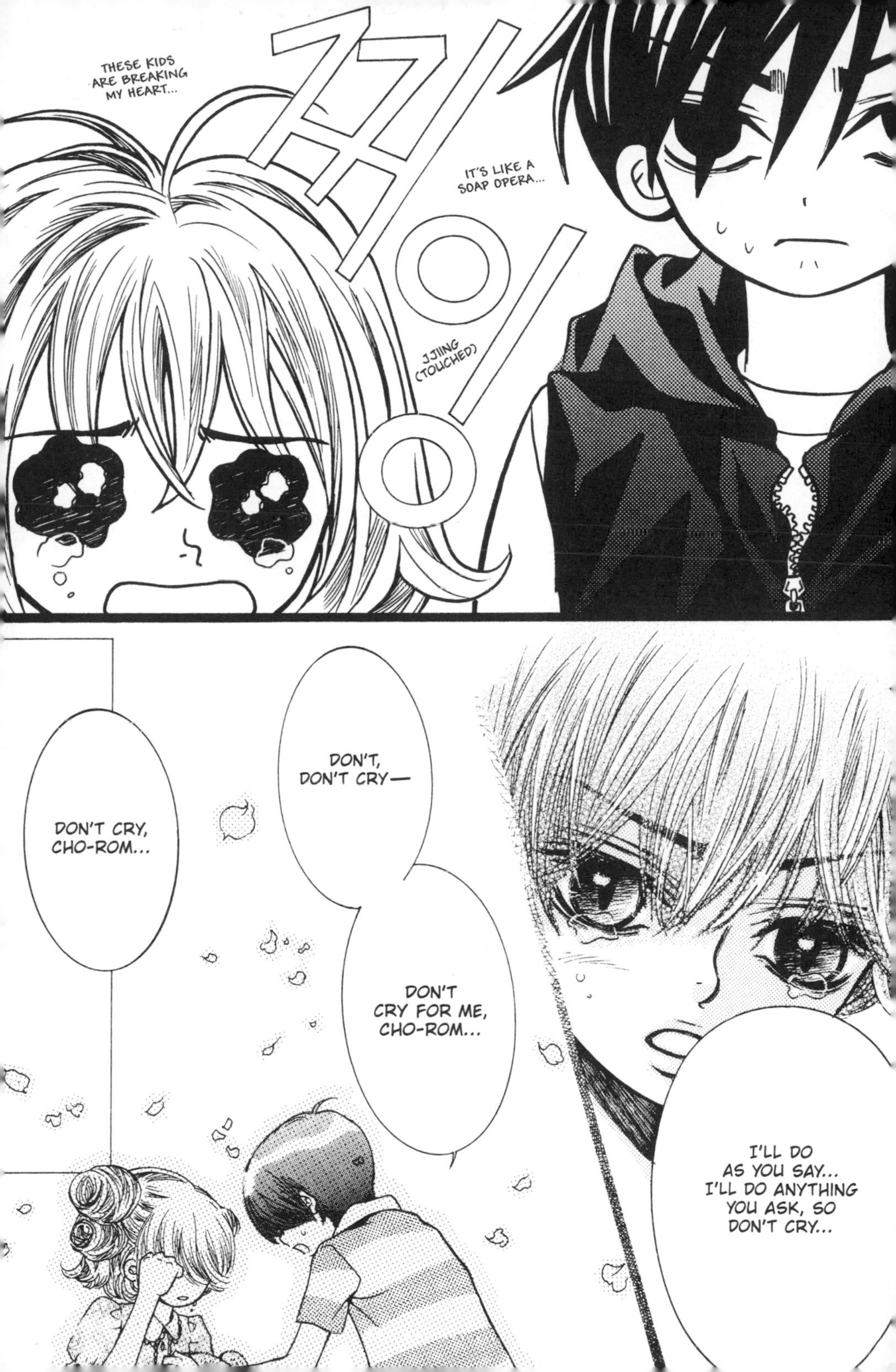
THESE KIDS ARE BREAKING MY HEART...
JJIING (TOUCHED)
IT'S LIKE A SOAP OPERA...
DON'T CRY, CHO-ROM...
DON'T, DON'T CRY—
DON'T CRY FOR ME, CHO-ROM...
I'LL DO AS YOU SAY... I'LL DO ANYTHING YOU ASK, SO DON'T CRY...

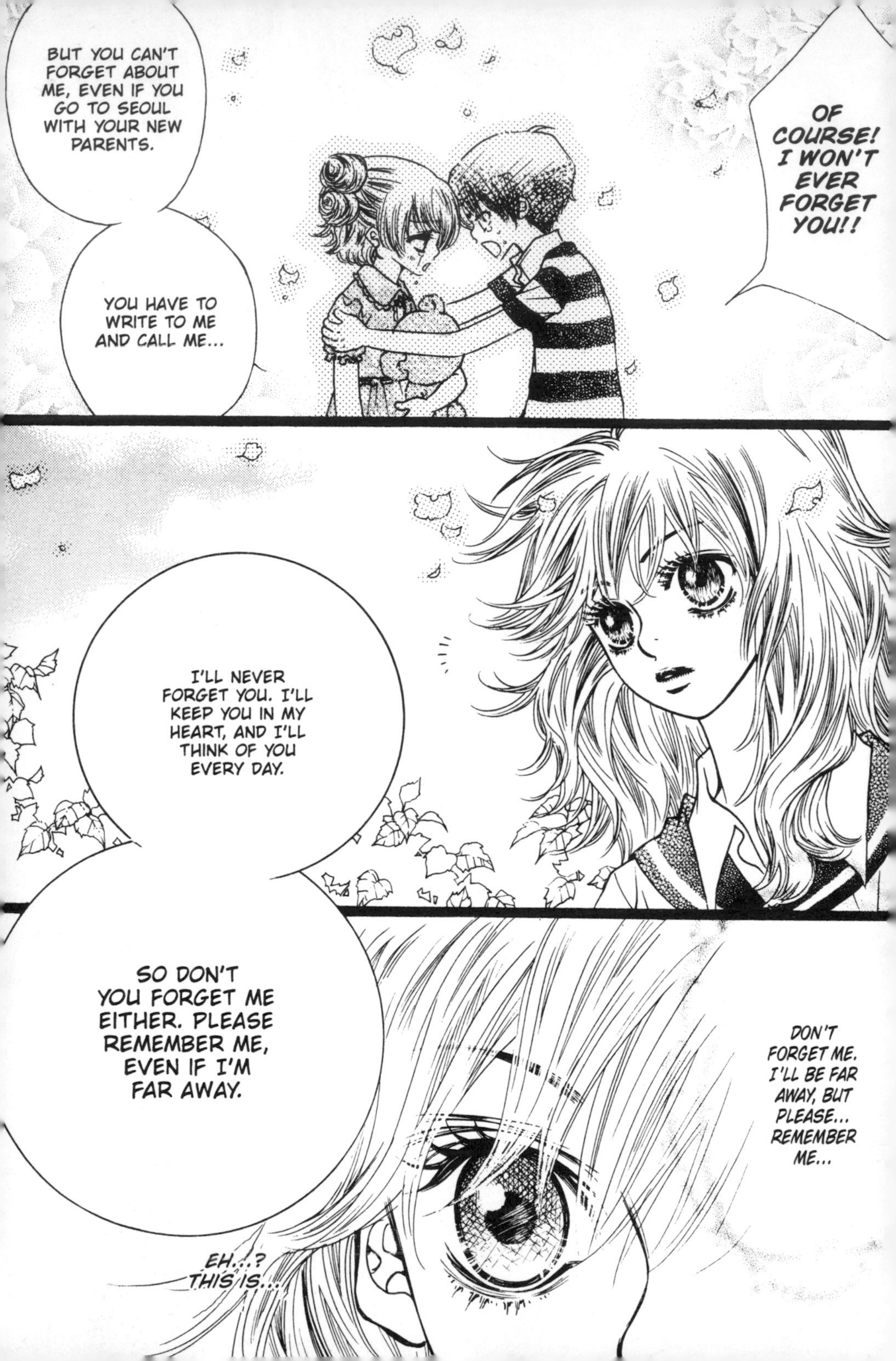
BUT YOU CAN'T FORGET ABOUT ME, EVEN IF YOU GO TO SEOUL WITH YOUR NEW PARENTS.
YOU HAVE TO WRITE TO ME AND CALL ME...
OF COURSE! I WON'T EVER FORGET YOU!!
I'LL NEVER FORGET YOU. I'LL KEEP YOU IN MY HEART, AND I'LL THINK OF YOU EVERY DAY.
SO DON'T YOU FORGET ME EITHER. PLEASE REMEMBER ME, EVEN IF I'M FAR AWAY.
DON'T FORGET ME. I'LL BE FAR AWAY, BUT PLEASE... REMEMBER ME...
EH...? THIS IS...

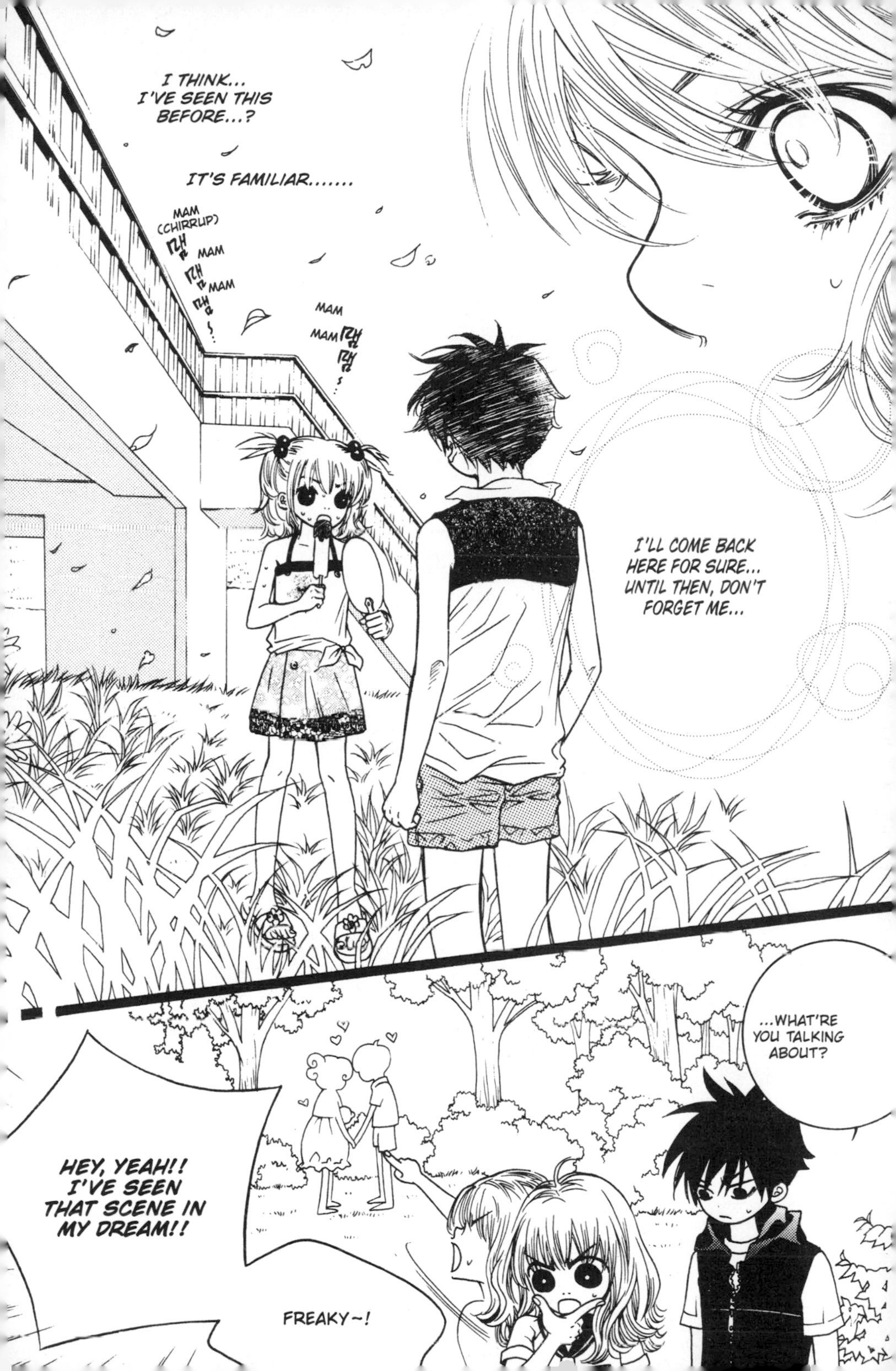
I THINK... I'VE SEEN THIS BEFORE...?
IT'S FAMILIAR.......
MAM (CHIRRUP)
MAM
MAM
MAM
MAM
I'LL COME BACK HERE FOR SURE... UNTIL THEN, DON'T FORGET ME...
HEY, YEAH!! I'VE SEEN THAT SCENE IN MY DREAM!!
FREAKY~!
...WHAT'RE YOU TALKING ABOUT?

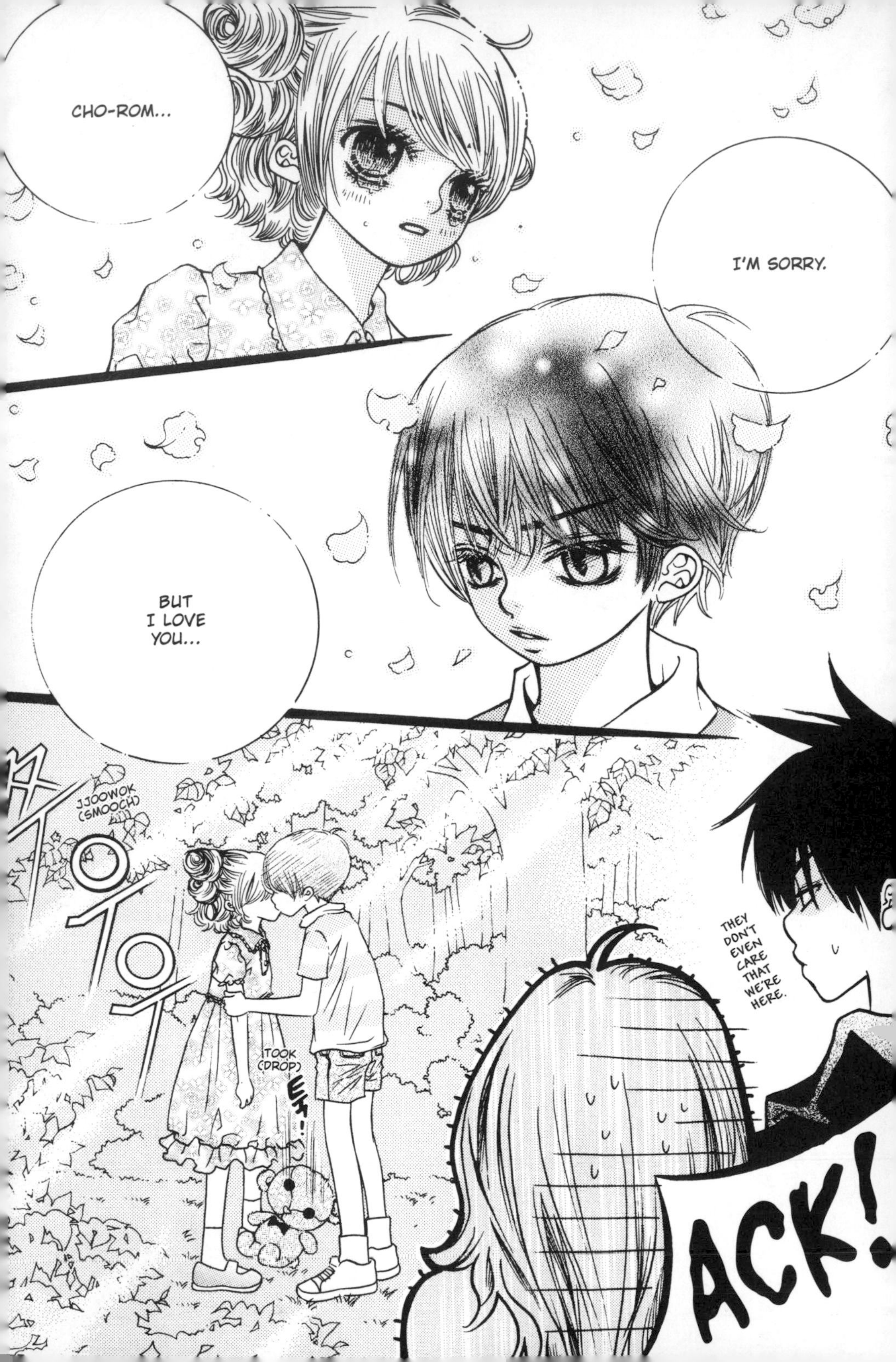
CHO-ROM...
I'M SORRY.
BUT I LOVE YOU...
JJOOWOK (SMOOCH)
TOOK (DROP)
THEY DON'T EVEN CARE THAT WE'RE HERE.
ACK!

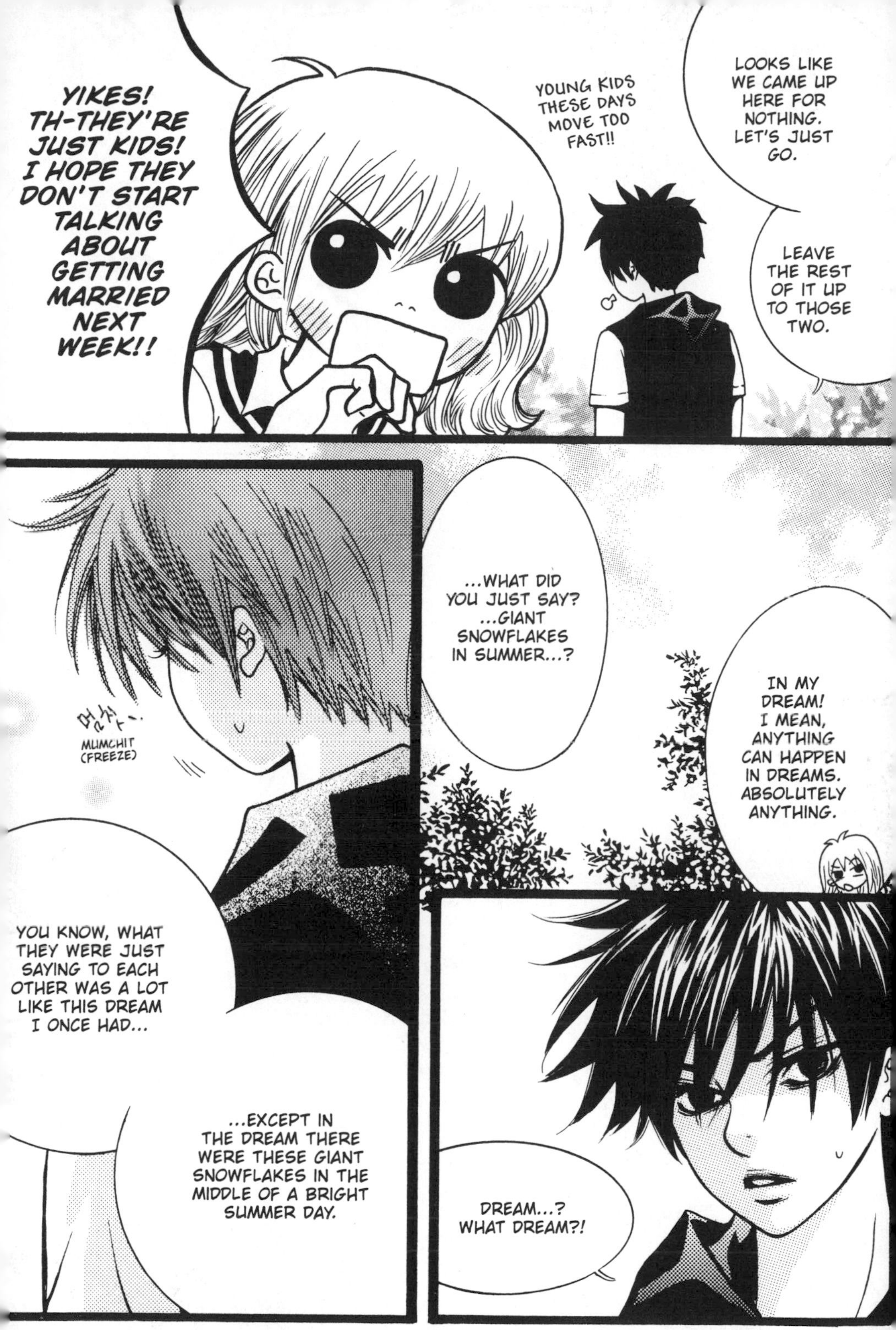
YIKES! TH-THEY'RE JUST KIDS! I HOPE THEY DON'T START TALKING ABOUT GETTING MARRIED NEXT WEEK!!
YOUNG KIDS THESE DAYS MOVE TOO FAST!!
LOOKS LIKE WE CAME UP HERE FOR NOTHING. LET'S JUST GO.
LEAVE THE REST OF IT UP TO THOSE TWO.
멈칫
MUMCHIT (FREEZE)
YOU KNOW, WHAT THEY WERE JUST SAYING TO EACH OTHER WAS A LOT LIKE THIS DREAM I ONCE HAD...
...EXCEPT IN THE DREAM THERE WERE THESE GIANT SNOWFLAKES IN THE MIDDLE OF A BRIGHT SUMMER DAY.
...WHAT DID YOU JUST SAY? ...GIANT SNOWFLAKES IN SUMMER...?
IN MY DREAM! I MEAN, ANYTHING CAN HAPPEN IN DREAMS. ABSOLUTELY ANYTHING.
DREAM...? WHAT DREAM?!

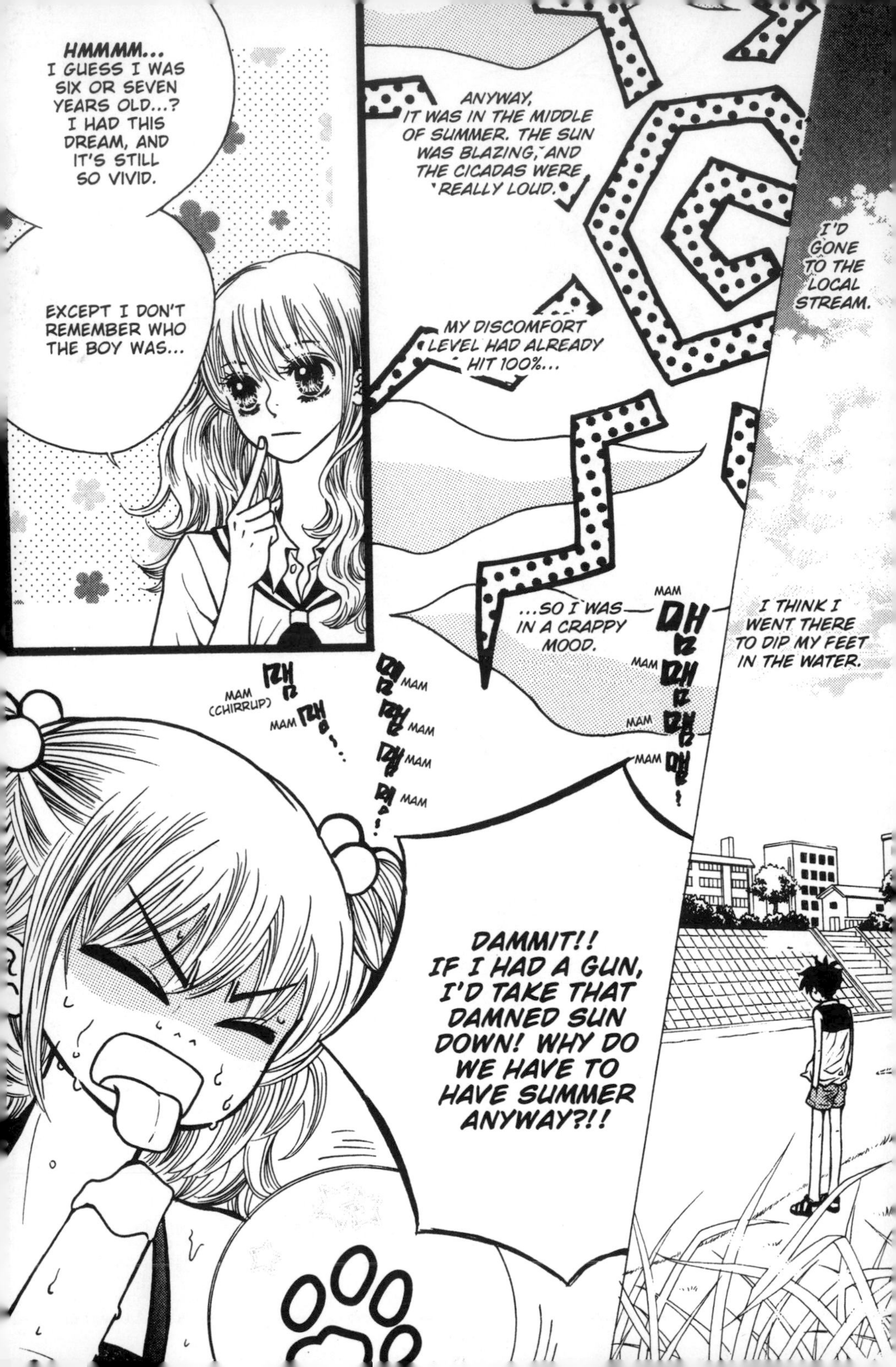
HMMMM... I GUESS I WAS SIX OR SEVEN YEARS OLD...? I HAD THIS DREAM, AND IT'S STILL SO VIVID.
EXCEPT I DON'T REMEMBER WHO THE BOY WAS...
ANYWAY, IT WAS IN THE MIDDLE OF SUMMER. THE SUN WAS BLAZING, AND THE CICADAS WERE REALLY LOUD.
MY DISCOMFORT LEVEL HAD ALREADY HIT 100%...
...SO I WAS IN A CRAPPY MOOD.
MAM
MAM
MAM
MAM
I'D GONE TO THE LOCAL STREAM.
I THINK I WENT THERE TO DIP MY FEET IN THE WATER.
MAM (CHIRRUP)
MAM
MAM
MAM
MAM
MAM
DAMMIT!! IF I HAD A GUN, I'D TAKE THAT DAMNED SUN DOWN! WHY DO WE HAVE TO HAVE SUMMER ANYWAY?!!

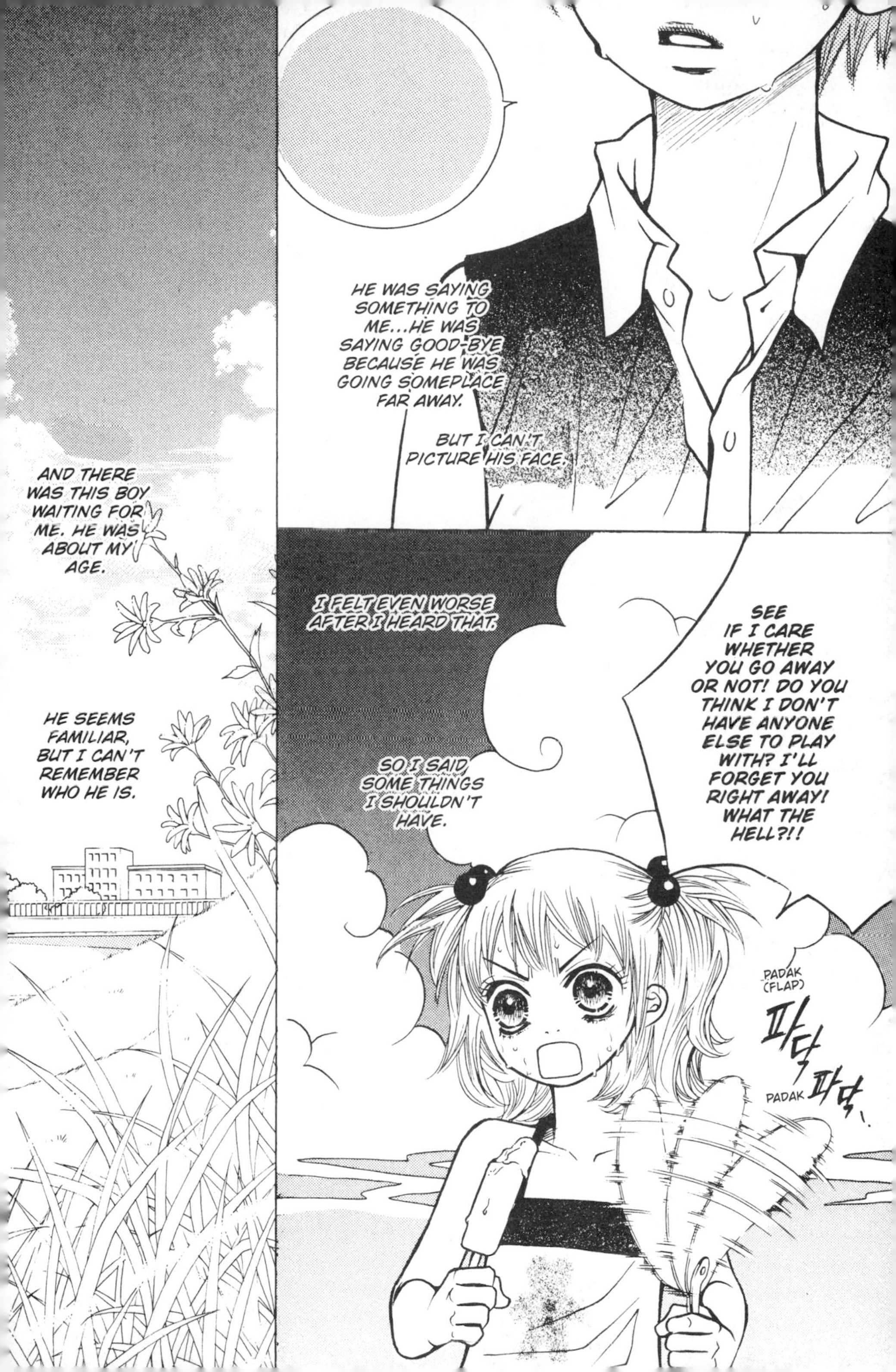
AND THERE WAS THIS BOY WAITING FOR ME. HE WAS ABOUT MY AGE.
HE SEEMS FAMILIAR, BUT I CAN'T REMEMBER WHO HE IS.
HE WAS SAYING SOMETHING TO ME...HE WAS SAYING GOOD-BYE BECAUSE HE WAS GOING SOMEPLACE FAR AWAY.
BUT I CAN'T PICTURE HIS FACE.
I FELT EVEN WORSE AFTER I HEARD THAT.
SO I SAID SOME THINGS I SHOULDN'T HAVE.
SEE IF I CARE WHETHER YOU GO AWAY OR NOT! DO YOU THINK I DON'T HAVE ANYONE ELSE TO PLAY WITH? I'LL FORGET YOU RIGHT AWAY! WHAT THE HELL?!!
PADAK (FLAP)
파닥
PADAK
파닥

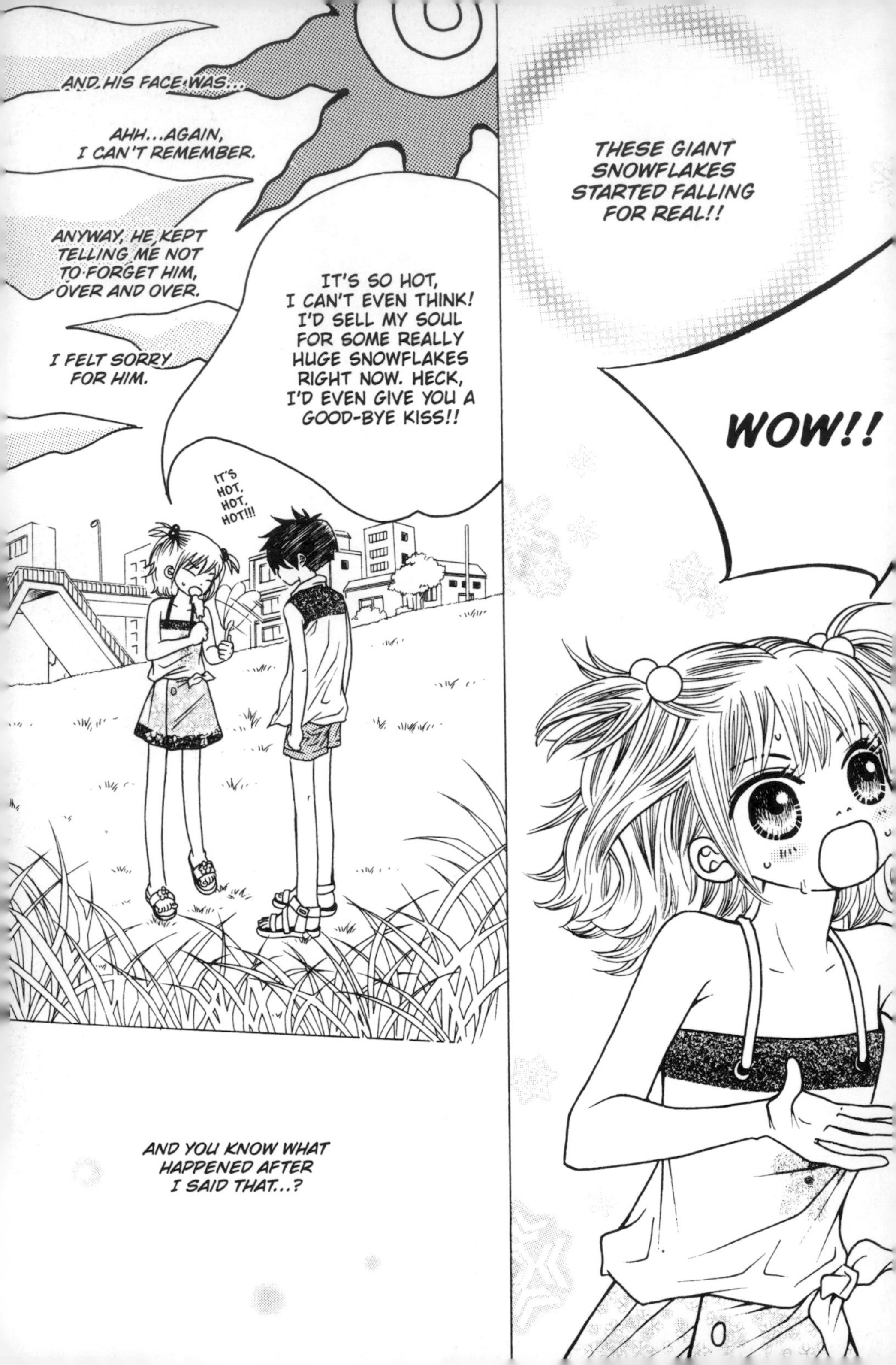
AND HIS FACE WAS...
AHH...AGAIN, I CAN'T REMEMBER.
ANYWAY, HE KEPT TELLING ME NOT TO FORGET HIM, OVER AND OVER.
I FELT SORRY FOR HIM.
IT'S SO HOT, I CAN'T EVEN THINK! I'D SELL MY SOUL FOR SOME REALLY HUGE SNOWFLAKES RIGHT NOW. HECK, I'D EVEN GIVE YOU A GOOD-BYE KISS!!
IT'S HOT, HOT, HOT!!!
AND YOU KNOW WHAT HAPPENED AFTER I SAID THAT...?
THESE GIANT SNOWFLAKES STARTED FALLING FOR REAL!!
WOW!!

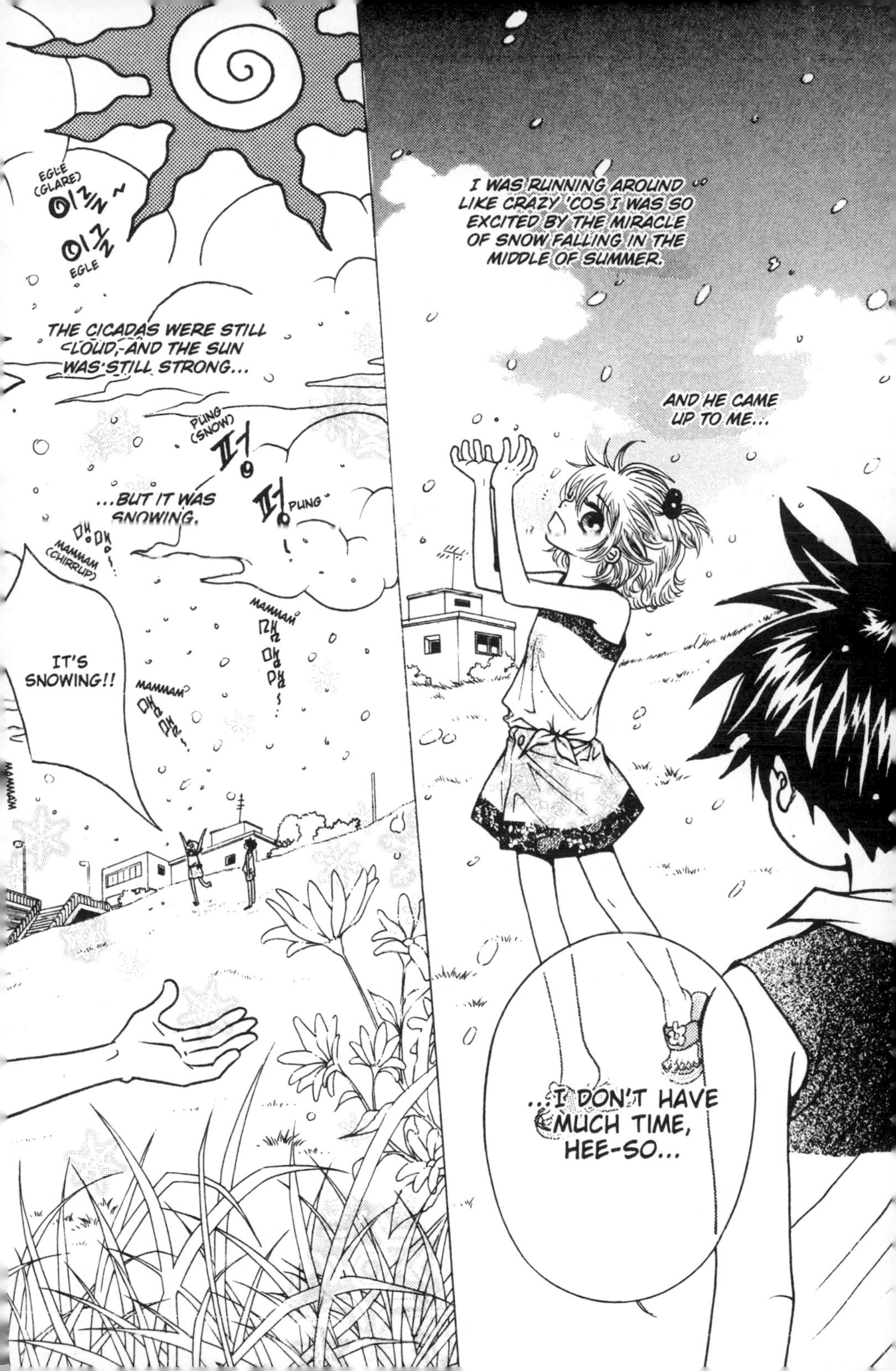
EGLE (GLARE)
EGLE
THE CICADAS WERE STILL LOUD, AND THE SUN WAS STILL STRONG...
PUNG (SNOW)
...BUT IT WAS SNOWING.
PUNG
MAMMAM (CHIRRUP)
MAMMAM
IT'S SNOWING!!
MAMMAM
MAMMAM
I WAS RUNNING AROUND LIKE CRAZY 'COS I WAS SO EXCITED BY THE MIRACLE OF SNOW FALLING IN THE MIDDLE OF SUMMER.
AND HE CAME UP TO ME...
...I DON'T HAVE MUCH TIME, HEE-SO...

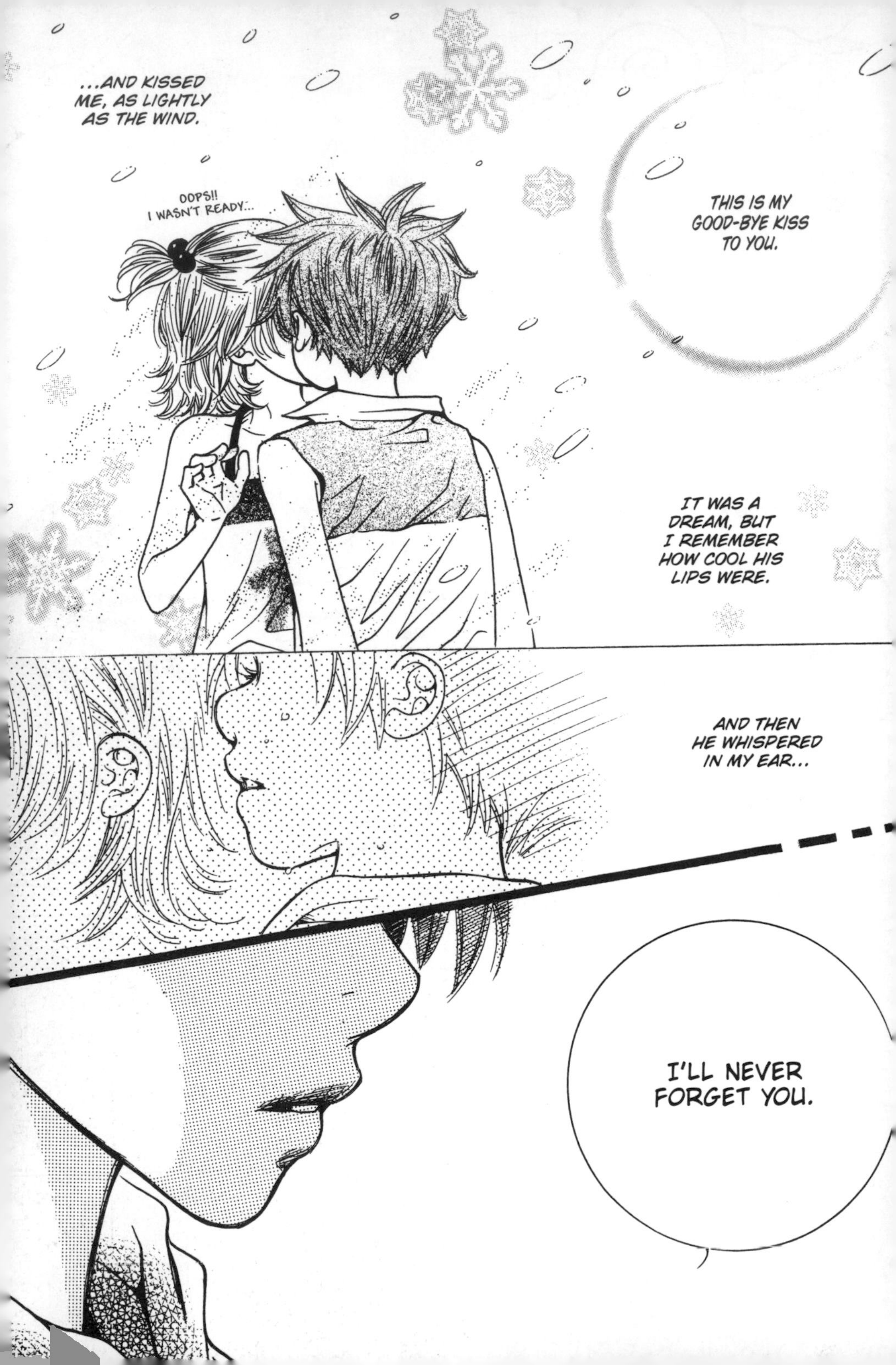

THIS IS MY GOOD-BYE KISS TO YOU.
...AND KISSED ME, AS LIGHTLY AS THE WIND.
OOPS!! I WASN'T READY...
IT WAS A DREAM, BUT I REMEMBER HOW COOL HIS LIPS WERE.
AND THEN HE WHISPERED IN MY EAR...
I'LL NEVER FORGET YOU.

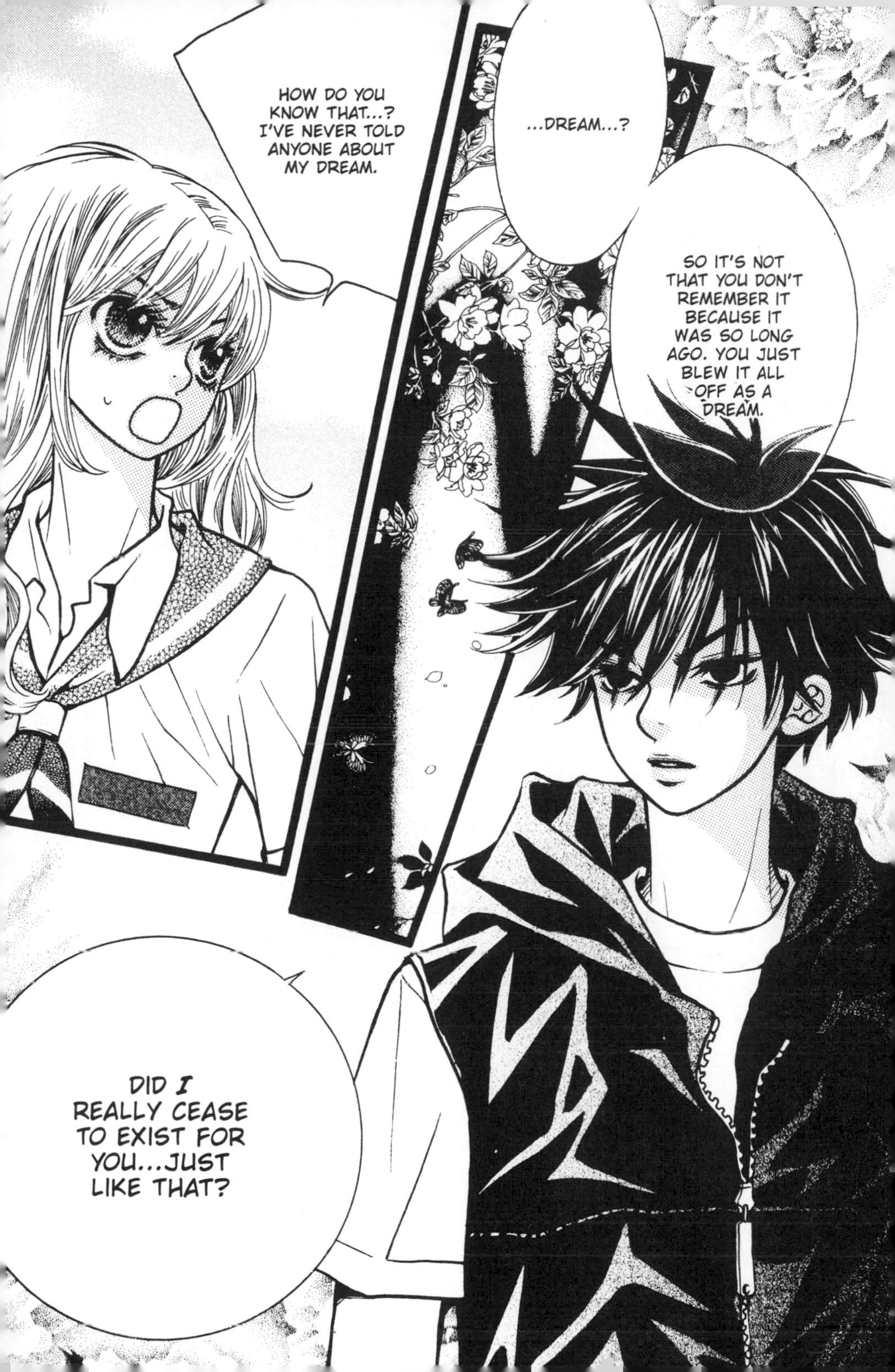
HOW DO YOU KNOW THAT...? I'VE NEVER TOLD ANYONE ABOUT MY DREAM.
...DREAM...?
SO IT'S NOT THAT YOU DON'T REMEMBER IT BECAUSE IT WAS SO LONG AGO. YOU JUST BLEW IT ALL OFF AS A DREAM.
DID *I* REALLY CEASE TO EXIST FOR YOU...JUST LIKE THAT?

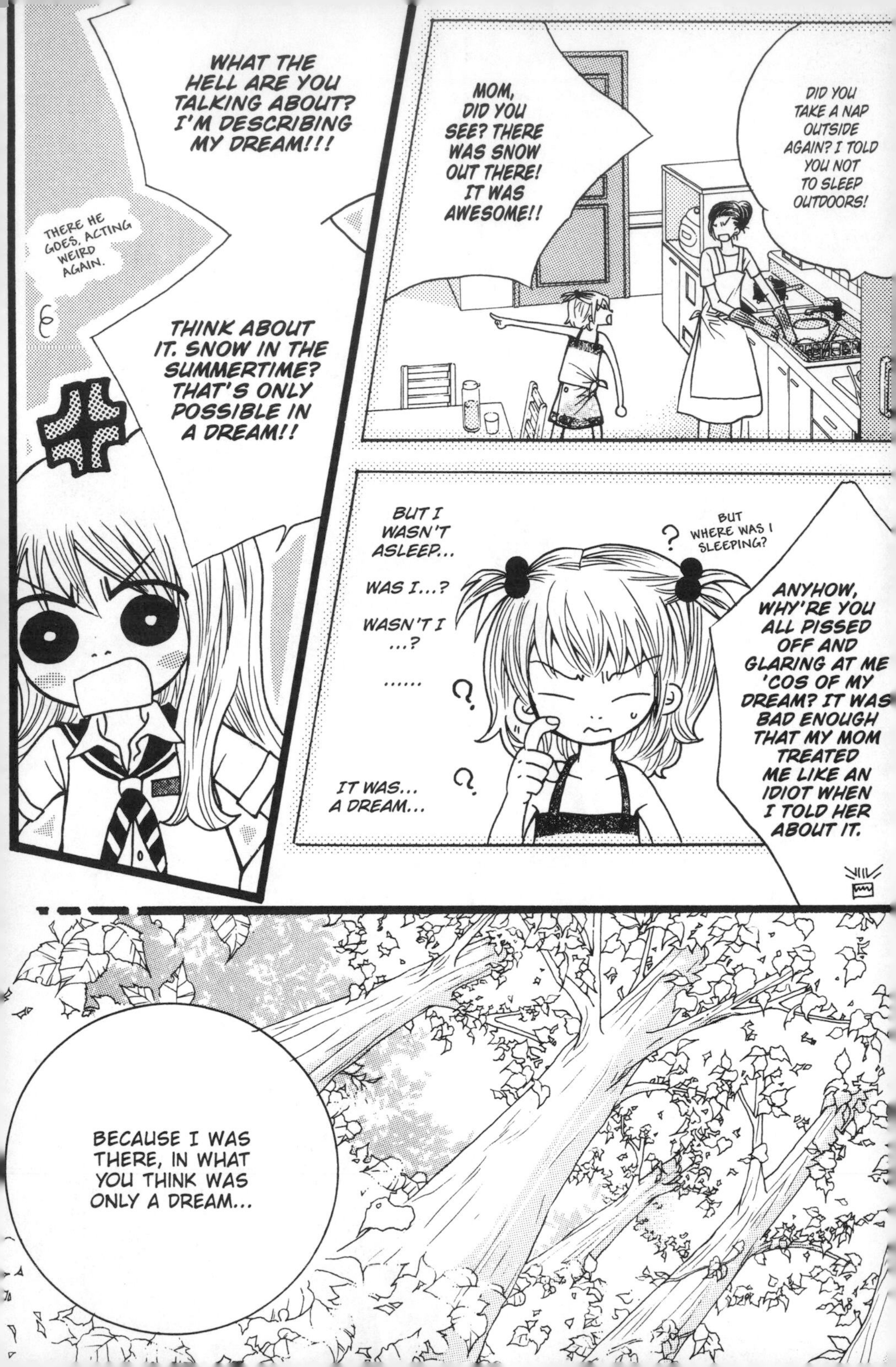
WHAT THE HELL ARE YOU TALKING ABOUT? I'M DESCRIBING MY DREAM!!!
THERE HE GOES, ACTING WEIRD AGAIN.
THINK ABOUT IT. SNOW IN THE SUMMERTIME? THAT'S ONLY POSSIBLE IN A DREAM!!
MOM, DID YOU SEE? THERE WAS SNOW OUT THERE! IT WAS AWESOME!!
DID YOU TAKE A NAP OUTSIDE AGAIN? I TOLD YOU NOT TO SLEEP OUTDOORS!
BUT I WASN'T ASLEEP...
WAS I...?
WASN'T I ...?
......
BUT WHERE WAS I SLEEPING?
IT WAS... A DREAM...
ANYHOW, WHY'RE YOU ALL PISSED OFF AND GLARING AT ME 'COS OF MY DREAM? IT WAS BAD ENOUGH THAT MY MOM TREATED ME LIKE AN IDIOT WHEN I TOLD HER ABOUT IT.
BECAUSE I WAS THERE, IN WHAT YOU THINK WAS ONLY A DREAM...

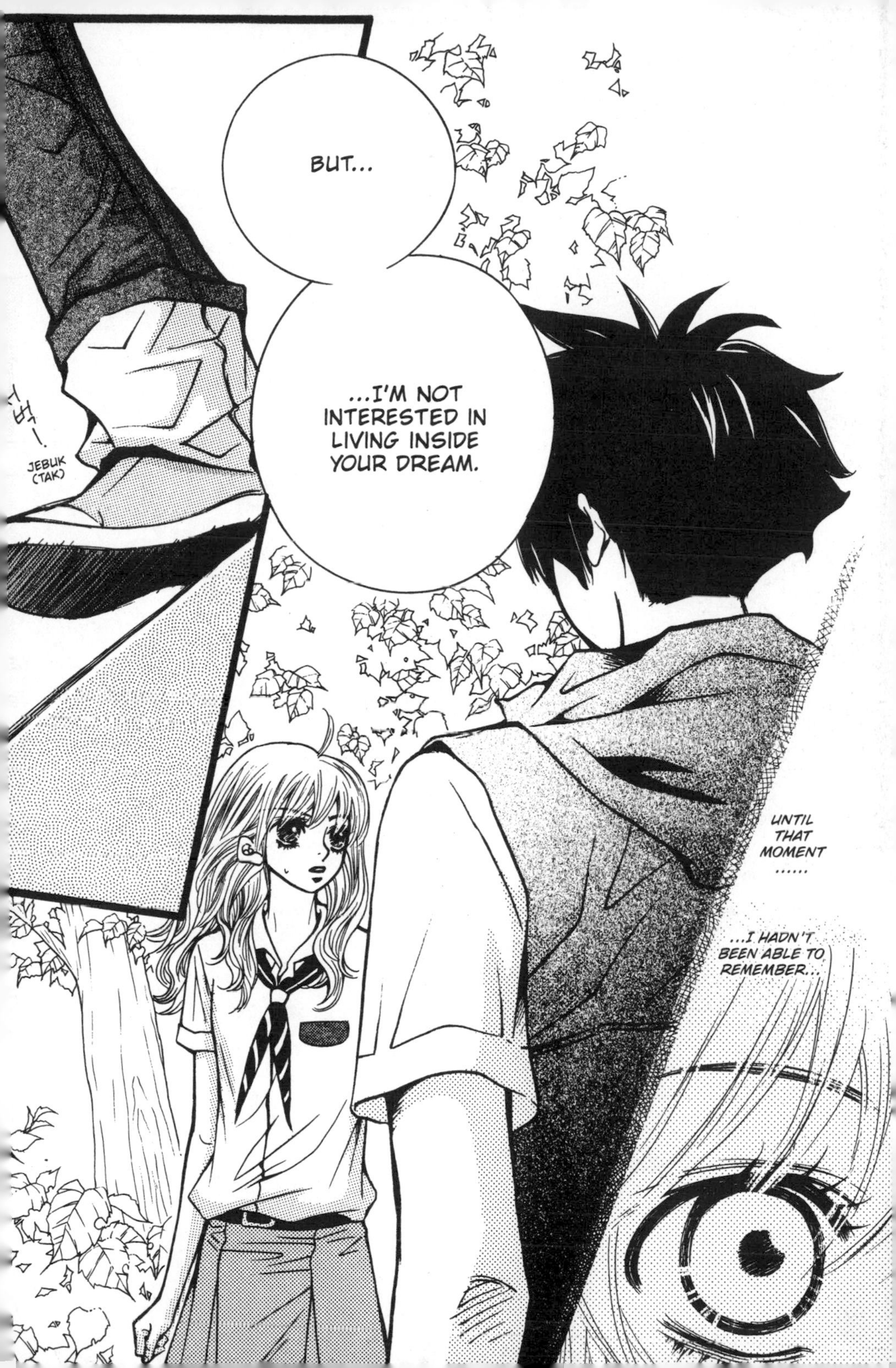
JEBUK (TAK)
BUT...
...I'M NOT INTERESTED IN LIVING INSIDE YOUR DREAM.
UNTIL THAT MOMENT ......
...I HADN'T BEEN ABLE TO REMEMBER...

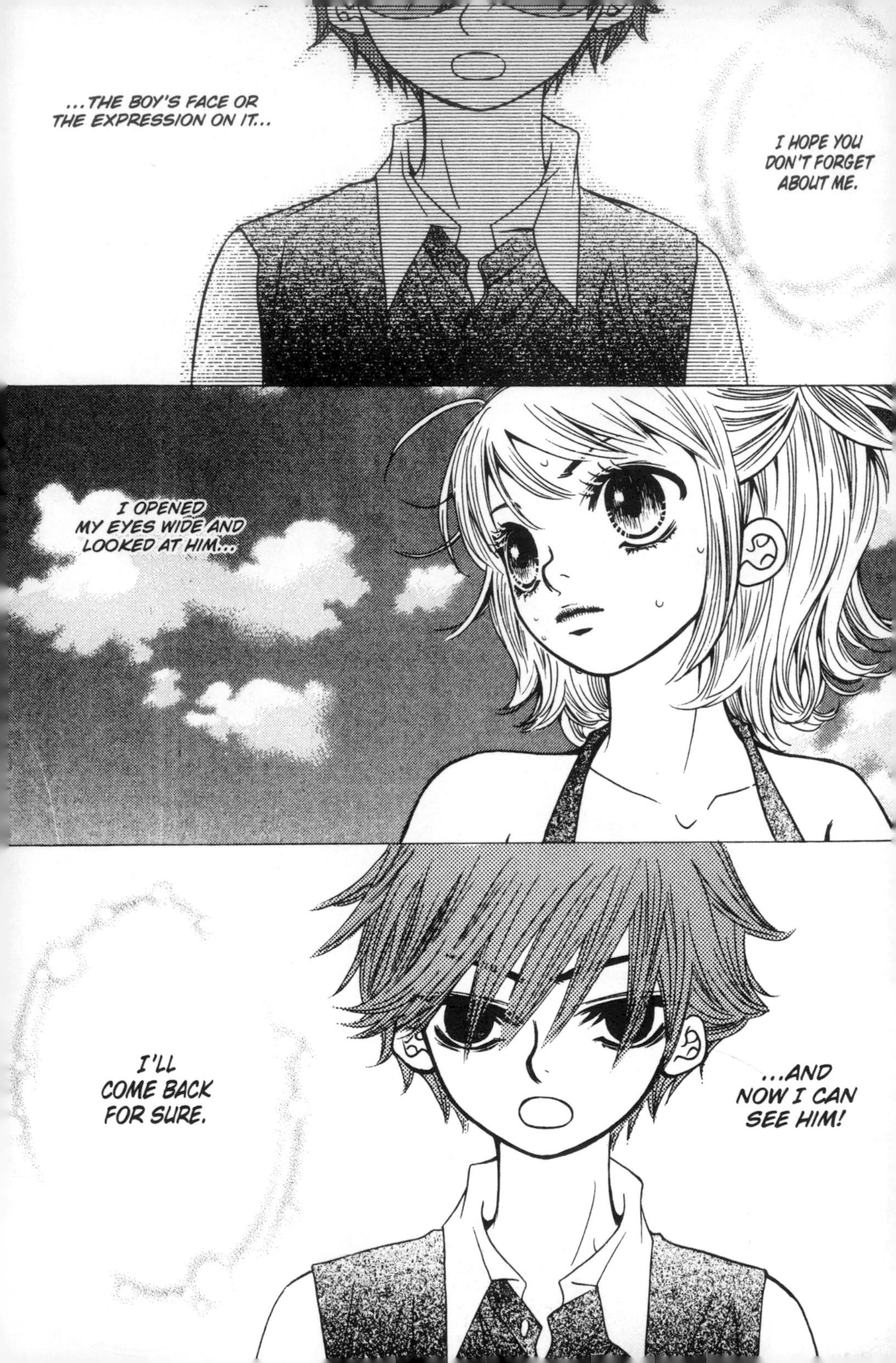
...THE BOY'S FACE OR THE EXPRESSION ON IT...
I HOPE YOU DON'T FORGET ABOUT ME.
I OPENED MY EYES WIDE AND LOOKED AT HIM...
I'LL COME BACK FOR SURE.
...AND NOW I CAN SEE HIM!

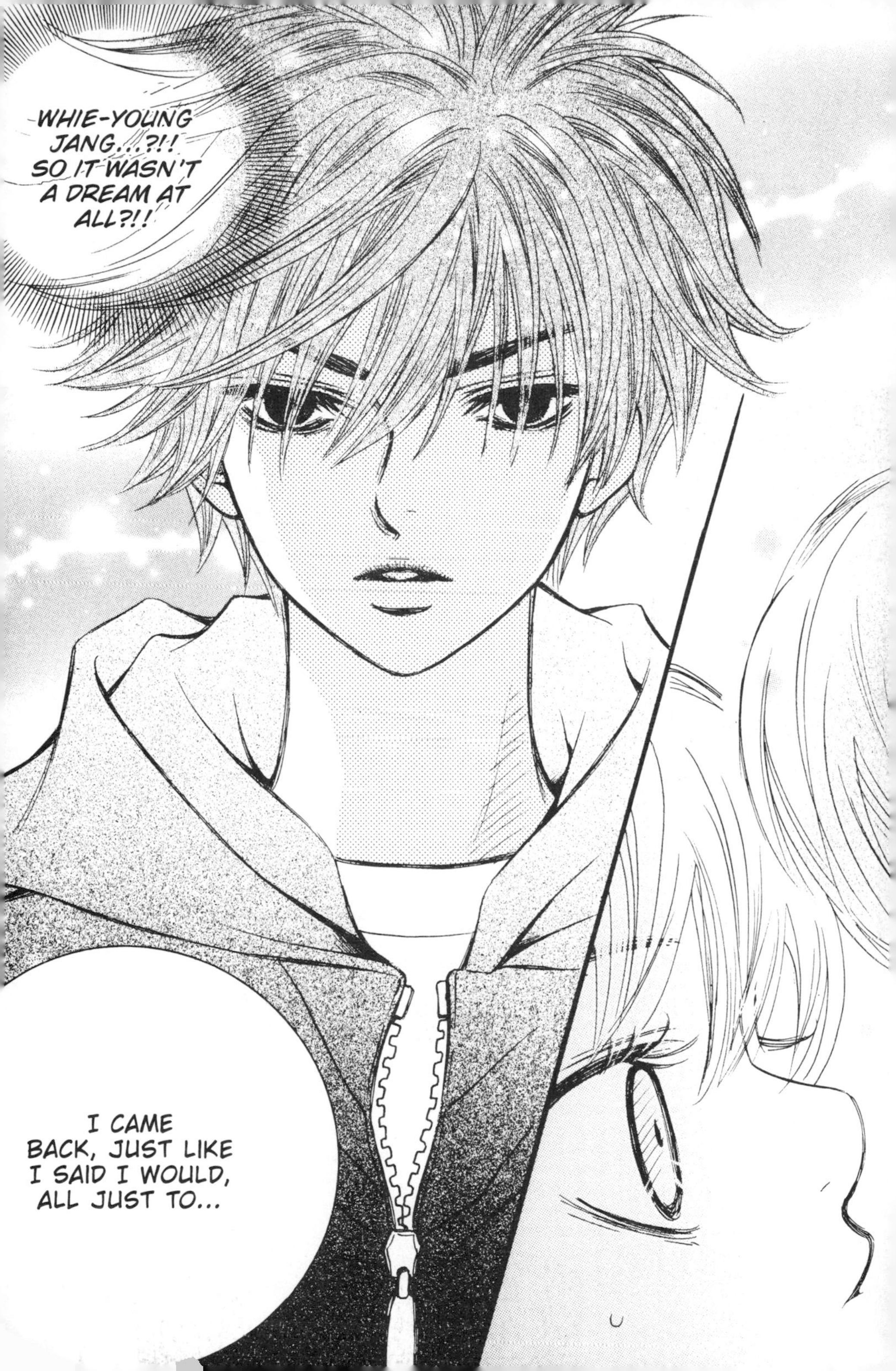
WHIE-YOUNG JANG...?!! SO IT WASN'T A DREAM AT ALL?!!
I CAME BACK, JUST LIKE I SAID I WOULD, ALL JUST TO...

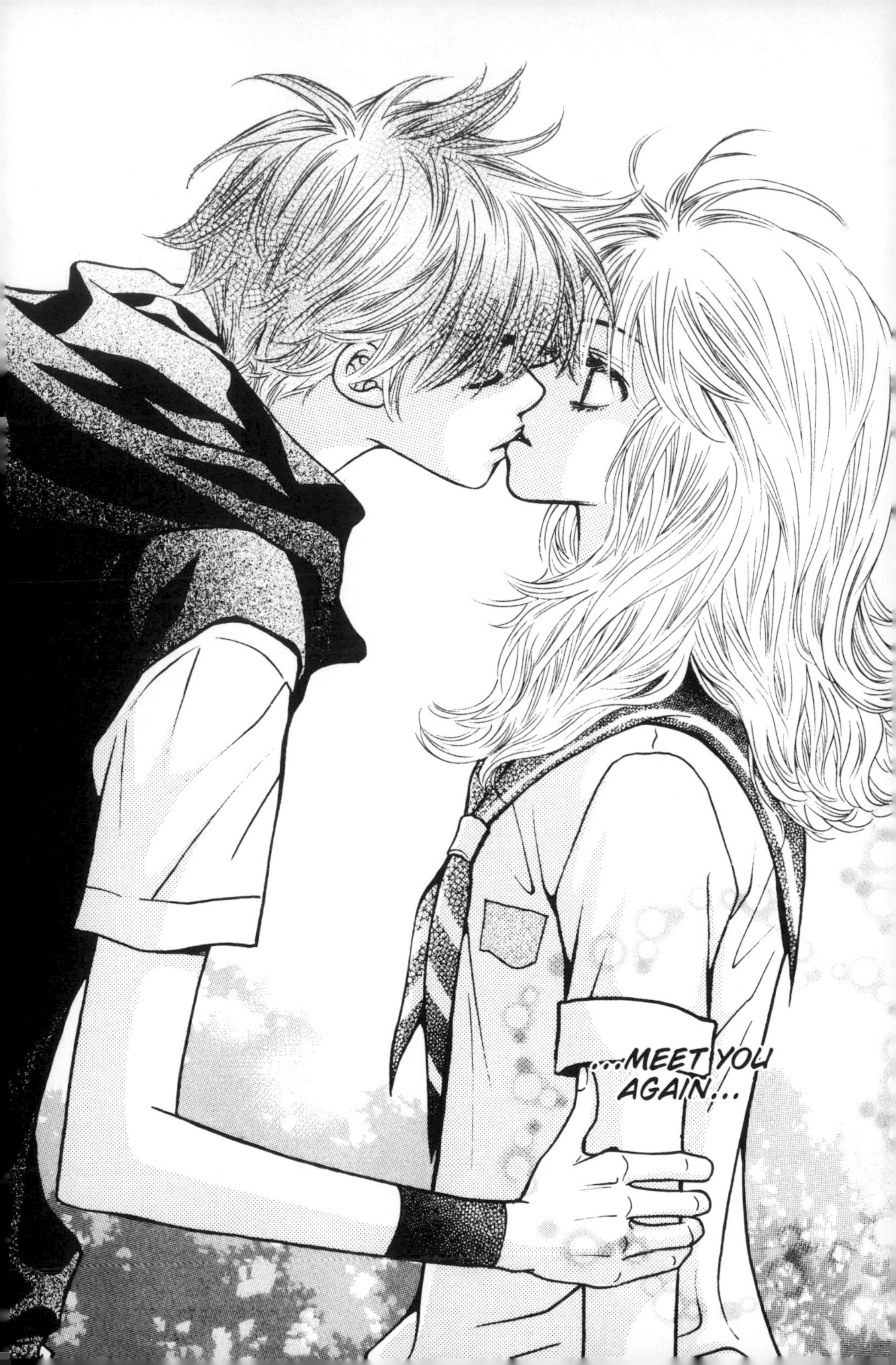
...MEET YOU AGAIN...

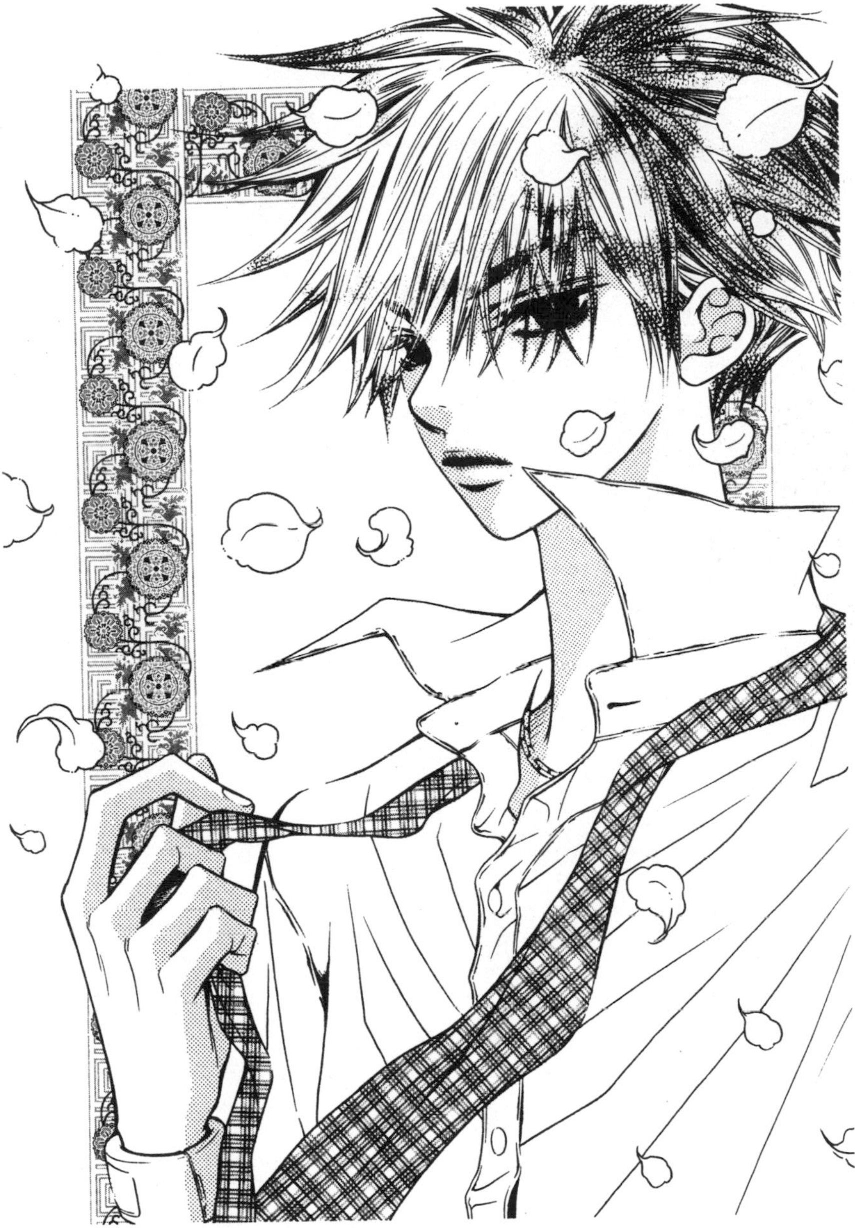

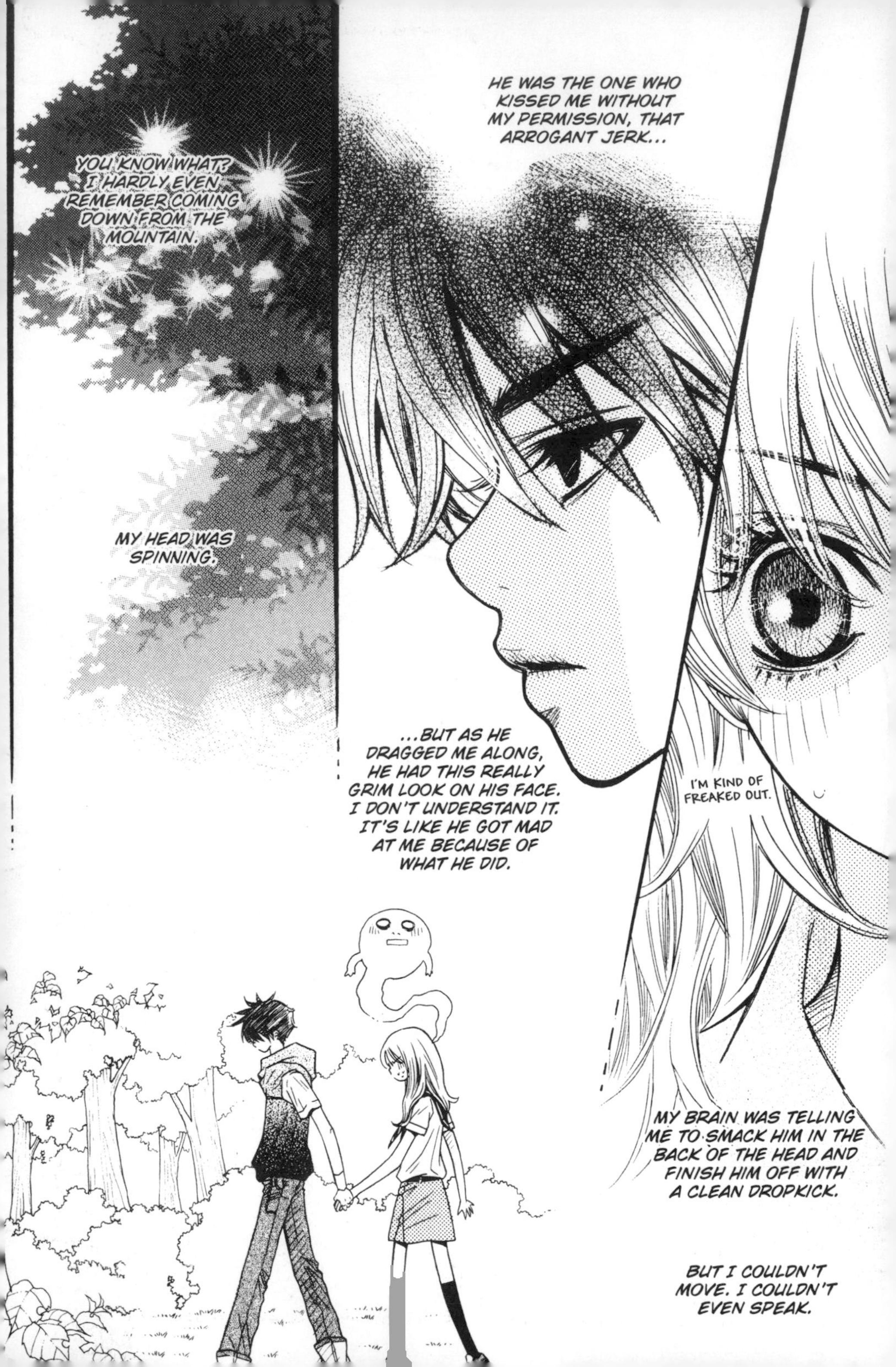
YOU KNOW WHAT? I HARDLY EVEN REMEMBER COMING DOWN FROM THE MOUNTAIN.
MY HEAD WAS SPINNING.
HE WAS THE ONE WHO KISSED ME WITHOUT MY PERMISSION, THAT ARROGANT JERK...
...BUT AS HE DRAGGED ME ALONG, HE HAD THIS REALLY GRIM LOOK ON HIS FACE. I DON'T UNDERSTAND IT. IT'S LIKE HE GOT MAD AT ME BECAUSE OF WHAT HE DID.
I'M KIND OF FREAKED OUT.
MY BRAIN WAS TELLING ME TO SMACK HIM IN THE BACK OF THE HEAD AND FINISH HIM OFF WITH A CLEAN DROPKICK.
BUT I COULDN'T MOVE. I COULDN'T EVEN SPEAK.

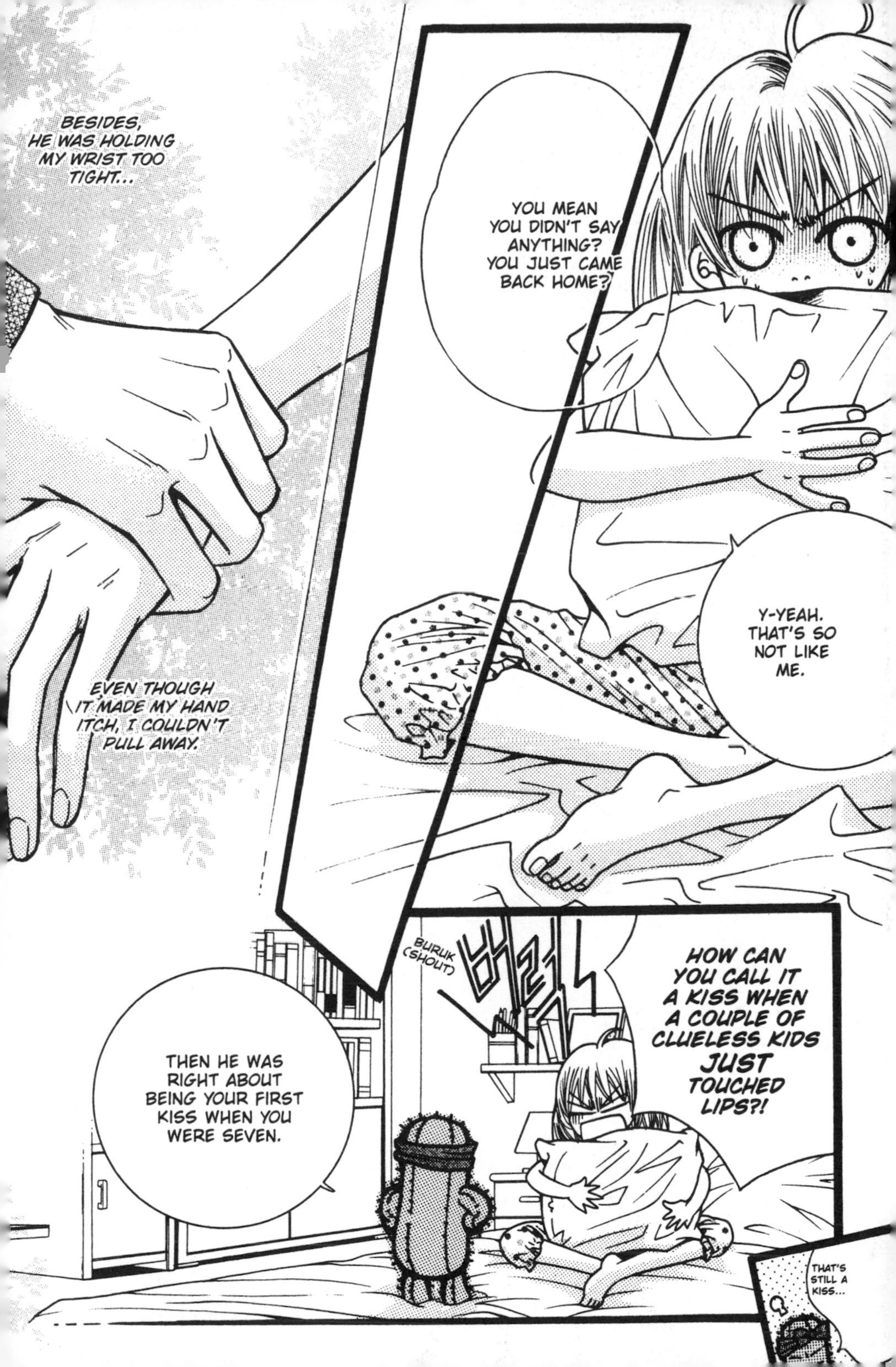
BESIDES, HE WAS HOLDING MY WRIST TOO TIGHT...
EVEN THOUGH IT MADE MY HAND ITCH, I COULDN'T PULL AWAY.
YOU MEAN YOU DIDN'T SAY ANYTHING? YOU JUST CAME BACK HOME?
Y-YEAH. THAT'S SO NOT LIKE ME.
THEN HE WAS RIGHT ABOUT BEING YOUR FIRST KISS WHEN YOU WERE SEVEN.
BURUK (SHOUT)
HOW CAN YOU CALL IT A KISS WHEN A COUPLE OF CLUELESS KIDS JUST TOUCHED LIPS?!
THAT'S STILL A KISS...

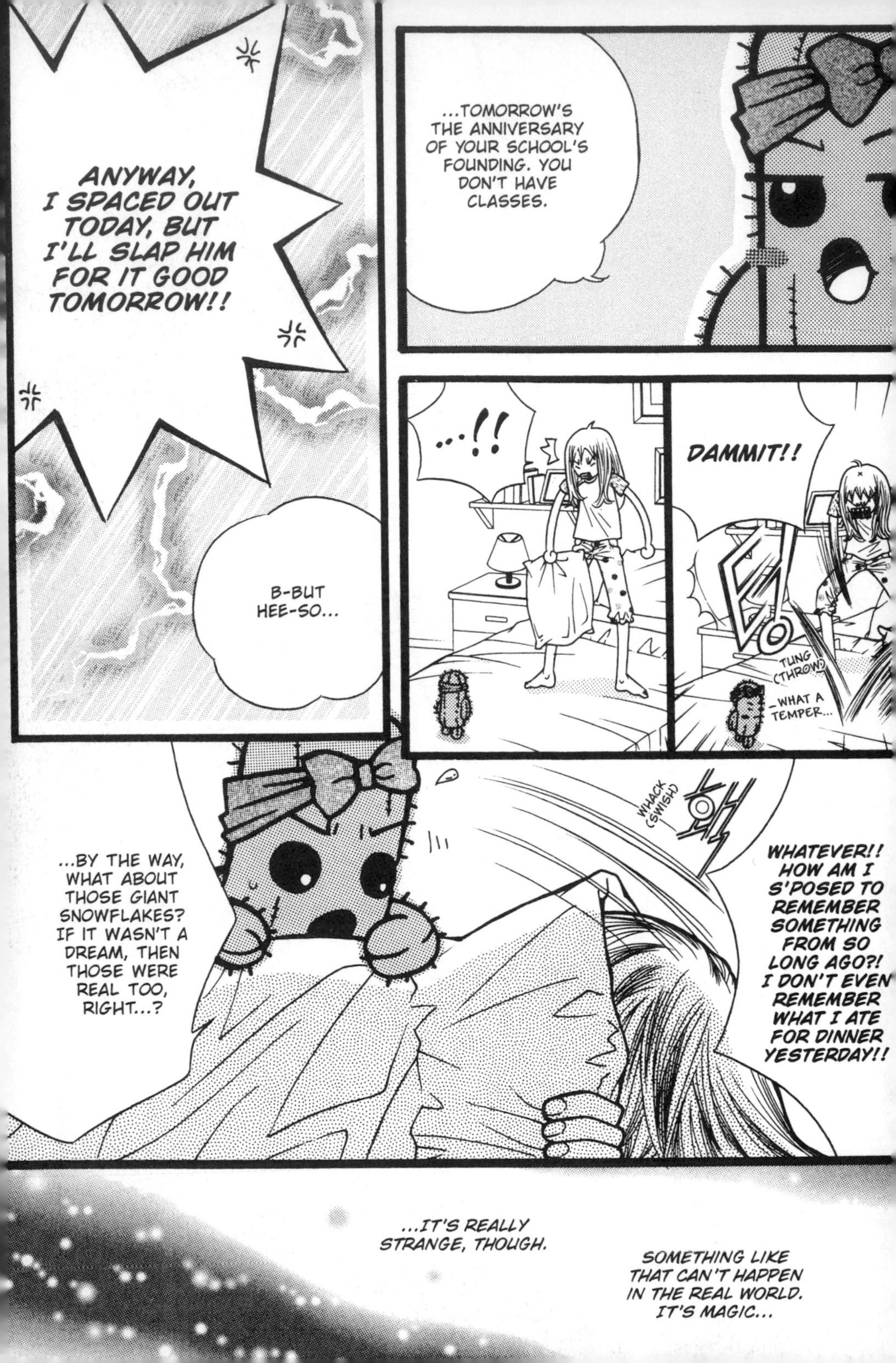

ANYWAY, I SPACED OUT TODAY, BUT I'LL SLAP HIM FOR IT GOOD TOMORROW!!
B-BUT HEE-SO...
...TOMORROW'S THE ANNIVERSARY OF YOUR SCHOOL'S FOUNDING. YOU DON'T HAVE CLASSES.
...!!
DAMMIT!!
TUNG (THROW)
WHAT A TEMPER...
...BY THE WAY, WHAT ABOUT THOSE GIANT SNOWFLAKES? IF IT WASN'T A DREAM, THEN THOSE WERE REAL TOO, RIGHT...?
WHACK (SWISH)
WHATEVER!! HOW AM I S'POSED TO REMEMBER SOMETHING FROM SO LONG AGO?! I DON'T EVEN REMEMBER WHAT I ATE FOR DINNER YESTERDAY!!
...IT'S REALLY STRANGE, THOUGH.
SOMETHING LIKE THAT CAN'T HAPPEN IN THE REAL WORLD. IT'S MAGIC...

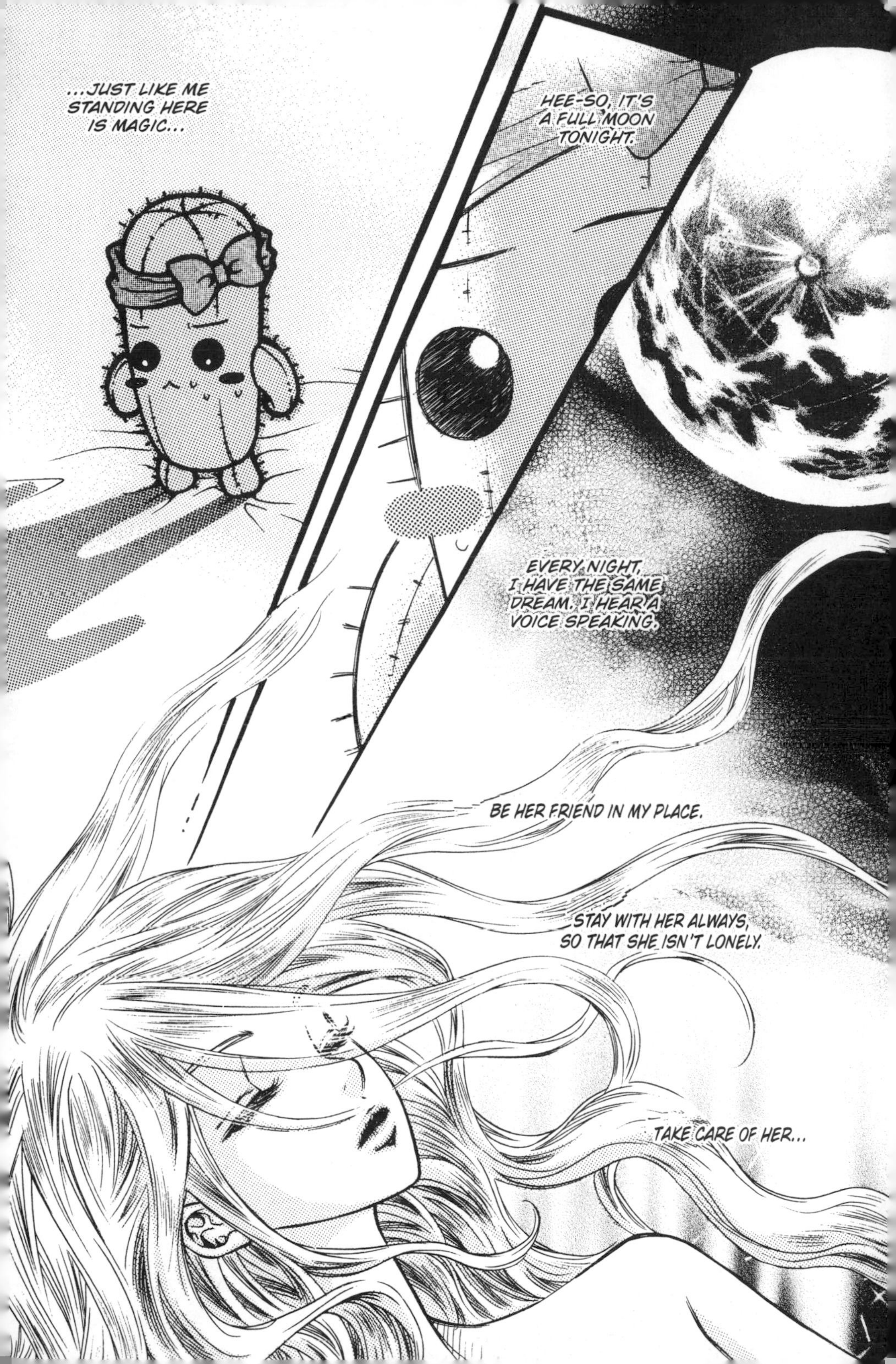
...JUST LIKE ME STANDING HERE IS MAGIC...
HEE-SO, IT'S A FULL MOON TONIGHT.
EVERY NIGHT, I HAVE THE SAME DREAM. I HEAR A VOICE SPEAKING.
BE HER FRIEND IN MY PLACE.
STAY WITH HER ALWAYS, SO THAT SHE ISN'T LONELY.
TAKE CARE OF HER...

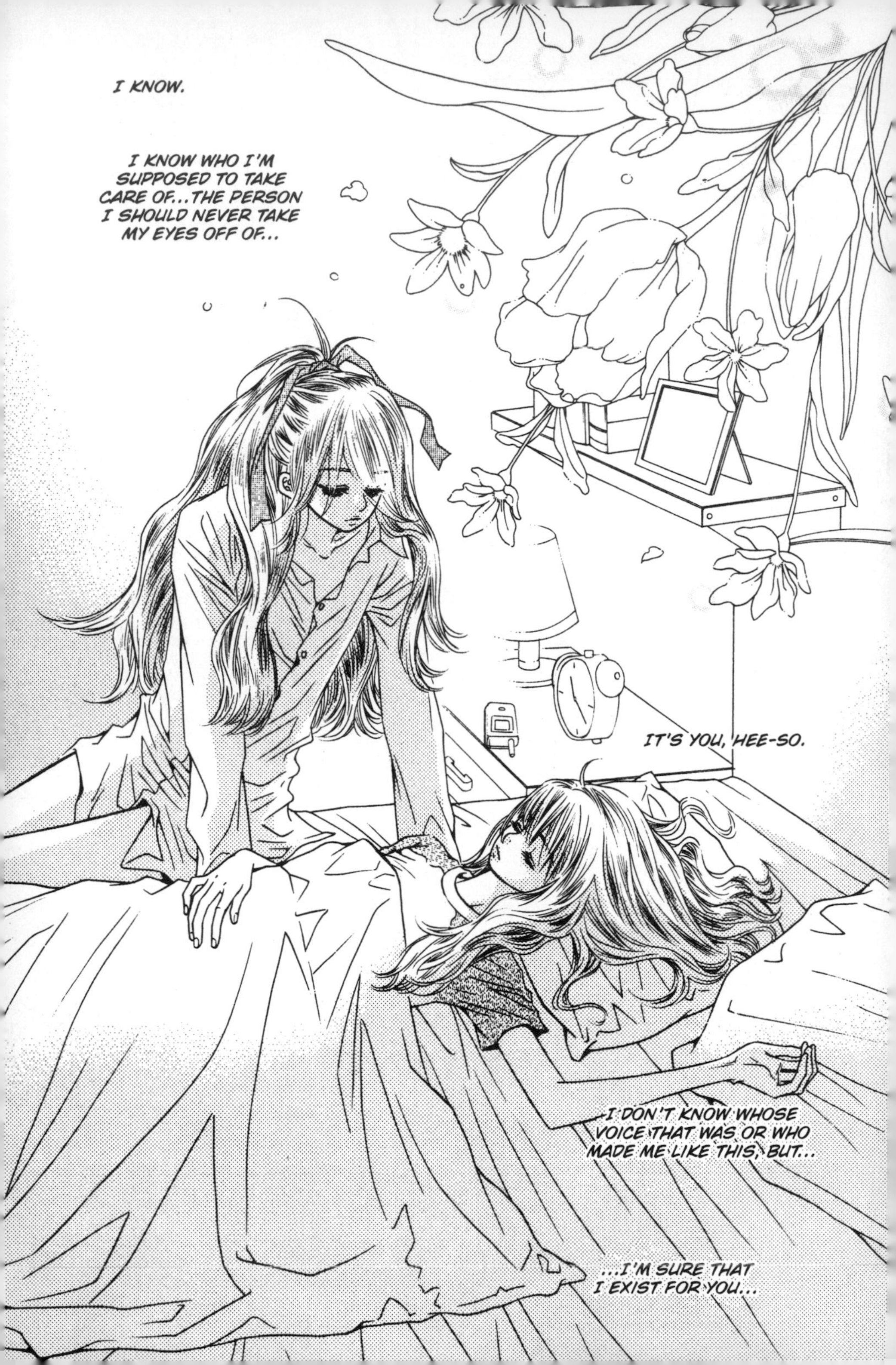
I KNOW.
I KNOW WHO I'M SUPPOSED TO TAKE CARE OF...THE PERSON I SHOULD NEVER TAKE MY EYES OFF OF...
IT'S YOU, HEE-SO.
I DON'T KNOW WHOSE VOICE THAT WAS OR WHO MADE ME LIKE THIS, BUT...
...I'M SURE THAT I EXIST FOR YOU...

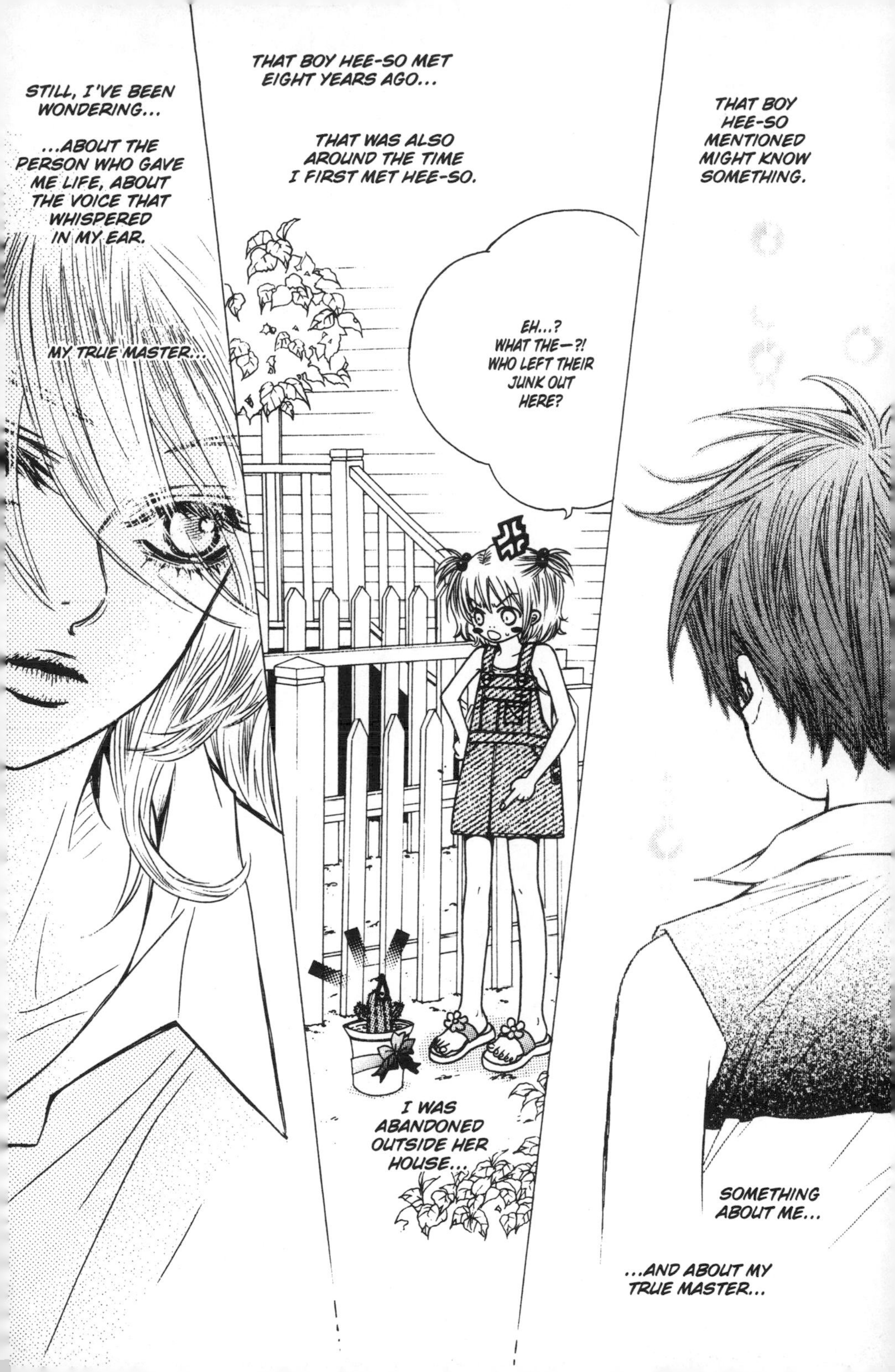
STILL, I'VE BEEN WONDERING...
...ABOUT THE PERSON WHO GAVE ME LIFE, ABOUT THE VOICE THAT WHISPERED IN MY EAR.
MY TRUE MASTER...
THAT BOY HEE-SO MET EIGHT YEARS AGO...
THAT WAS ALSO AROUND THE TIME I FIRST MET HEE-SO.
EH...? WHAT THE—?! WHO LEFT THEIR JUNK OUT HERE?
I WAS ABANDONED OUTSIDE HER HOUSE...
THAT BOY HEE-SO MENTIONED MIGHT KNOW SOMETHING.
SOMETHING ABOUT ME...
...AND ABOUT MY TRUE MASTER...

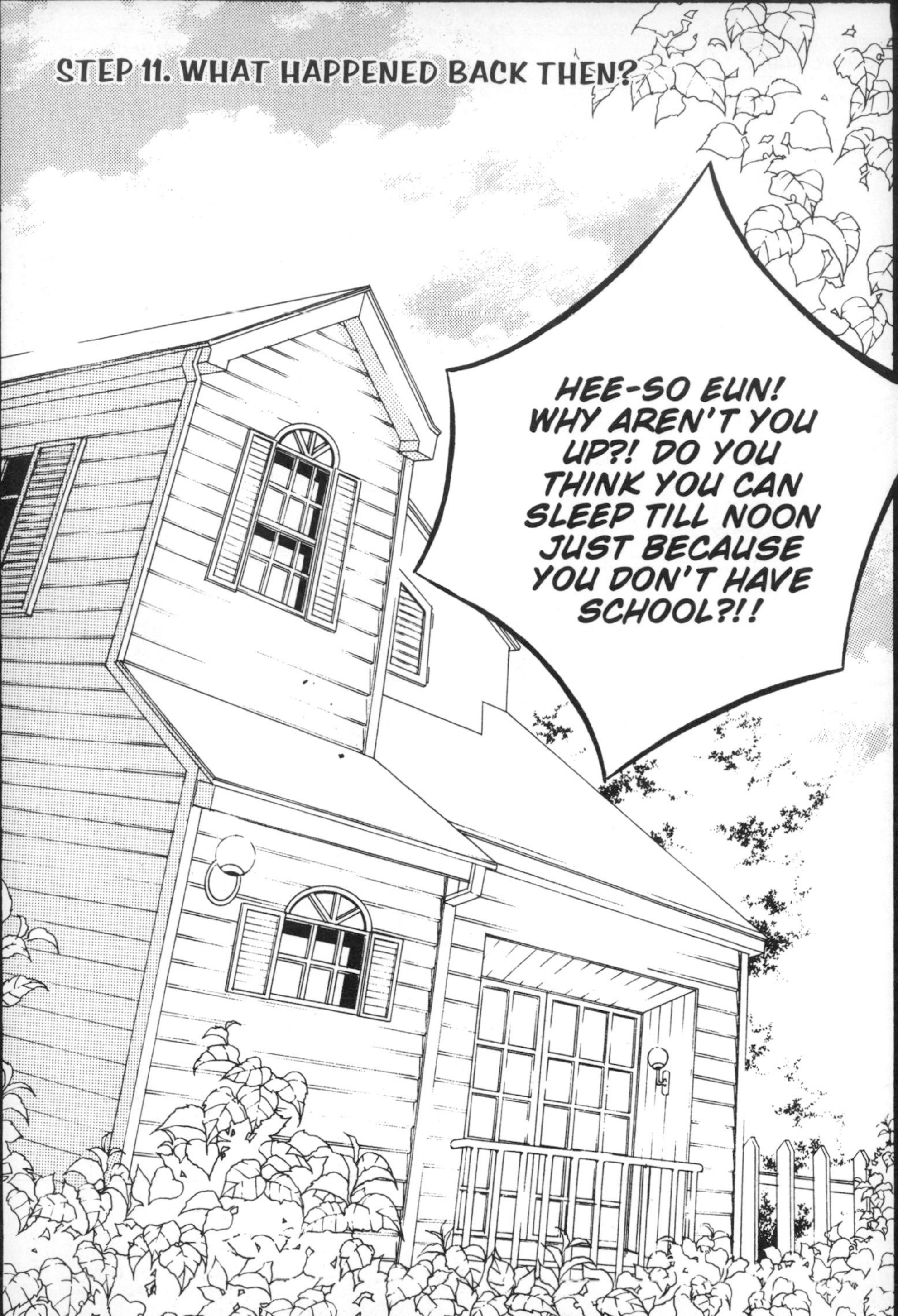
STEP 11. WHAT HAPPENED BACK THEN?
HEE-SO EUN! WHY AREN'T YOU UP?! DO YOU THINK YOU CAN SLEEP TILL NOON JUST BECAUSE YOU DON'T HAVE SCHOOL?!!

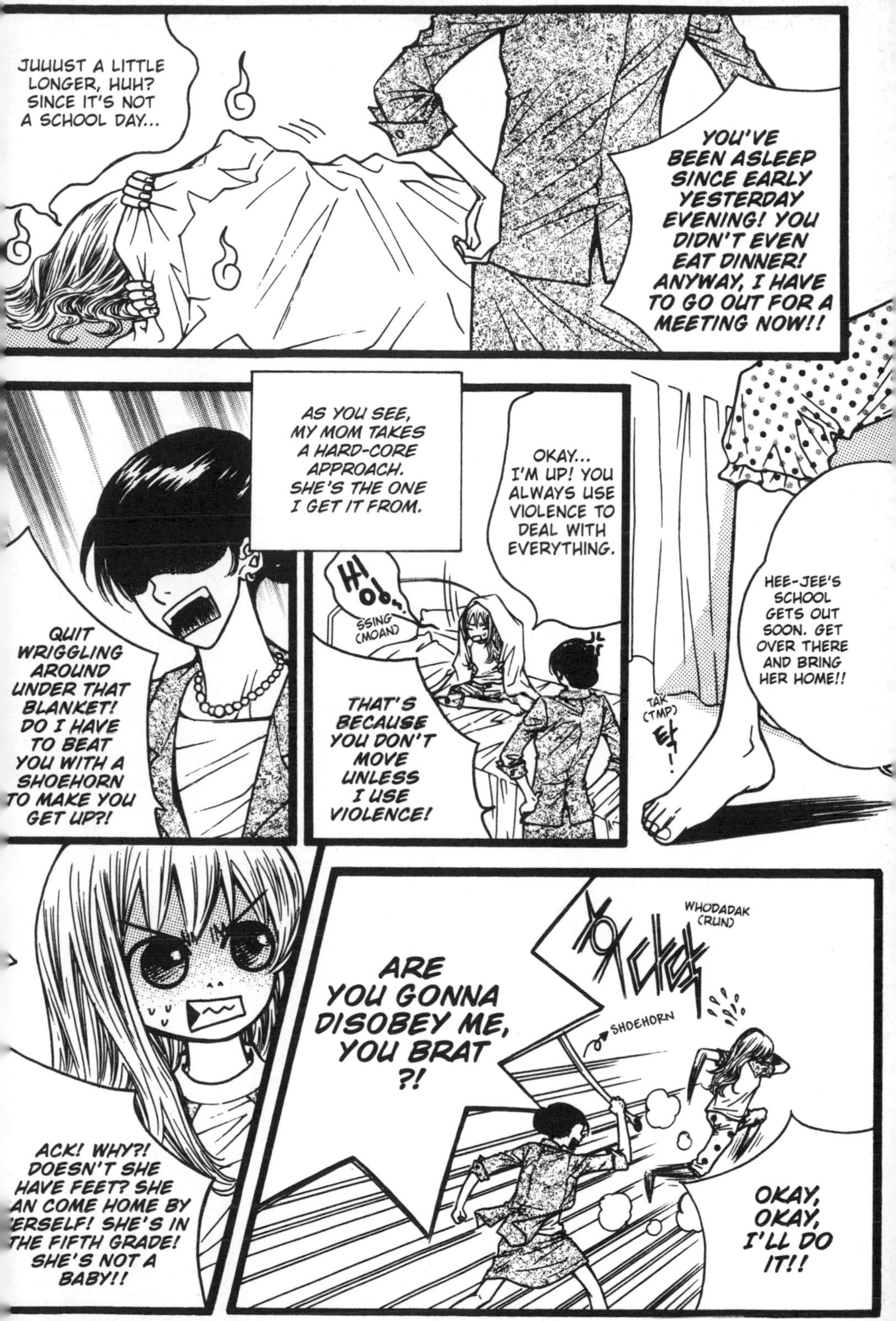
JUUUST A LITTLE LONGER, HUH? SINCE IT'S NOT A SCHOOL DAY...
YOU'VE BEEN ASLEEP SINCE EARLY YESTERDAY EVENING! YOU DIDN'T EVEN EAT DINNER! ANYWAY, I HAVE TO GO OUT FOR A MEETING NOW!!
QUIT WRIGGLING AROUND UNDER THAT BLANKET! DO I HAVE TO BEAT YOU WITH A SHOEHORN TO MAKE YOU GET UP?!
AS YOU SEE, MY MOM TAKES A HARD-CORE APPROACH. SHE'S THE ONE I GET IT FROM.
OKAY... I'M UP! YOU ALWAYS USE VIOLENCE TO DEAL WITH EVERYTHING.
SSING (MOAN)
THAT'S BECAUSE YOU DON'T MOVE UNLESS I USE VIOLENCE!
HEE-JEE'S SCHOOL GETS OUT SOON. GET OVER THERE AND BRING HER HOME!!
TAK (TMP)
ACK! WHY?! DOESN'T SHE HAVE FEET? SHE AN COME HOME BY ERSELF! SHE'S IN THE FIFTH GRADE! SHE'S NOT A BABY!!
ARE YOU GONNA DISOBEY ME, YOU BRAT ?!
WHODADAK (RUN)
SHOEHORN
OKAY, OKAY, I'LL DO IT!!

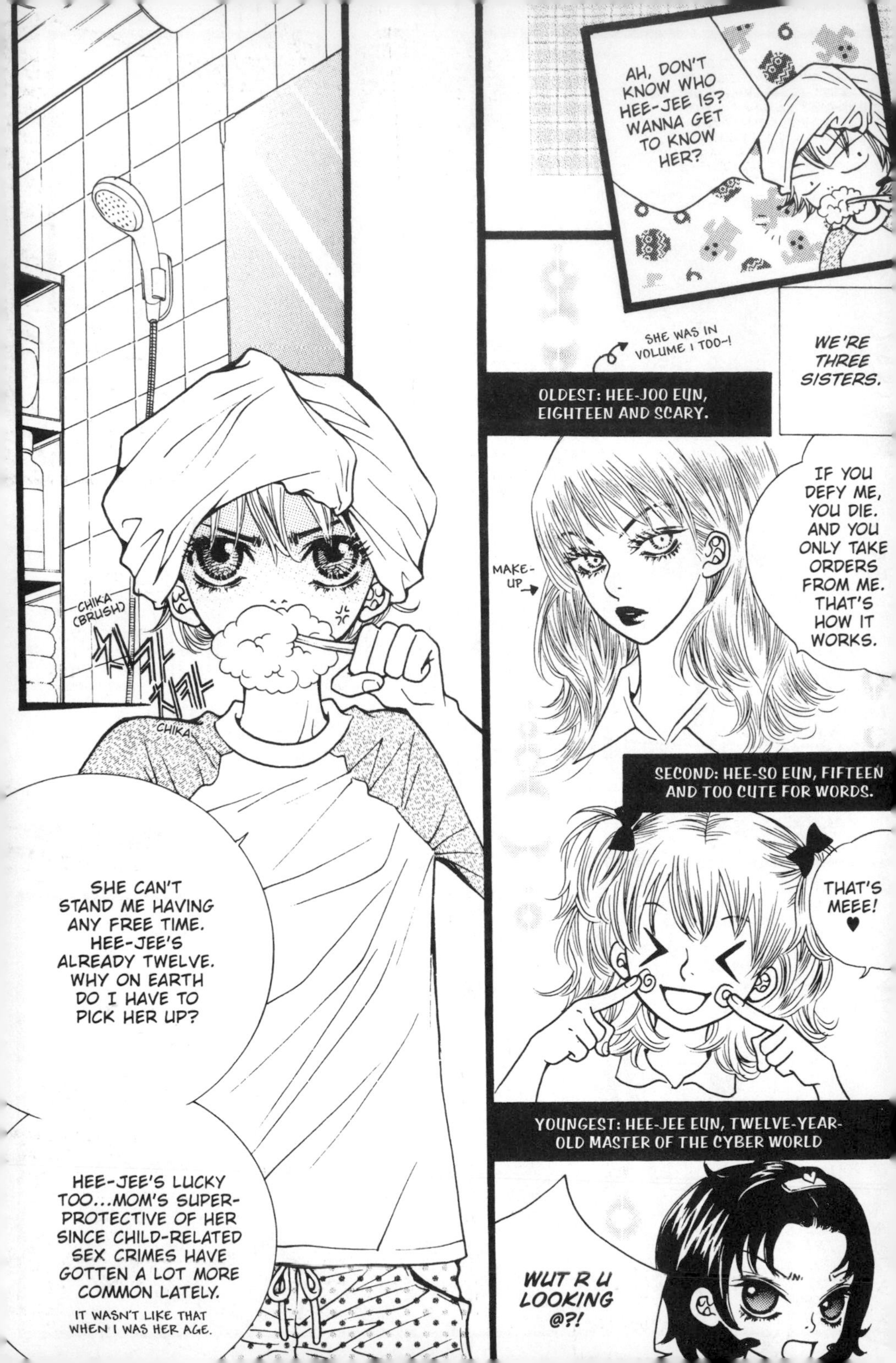

CHIKA (BRUSH)
CHIKA
SHE CAN'T STAND ME HAVING ANY FREE TIME. HEE-JEE'S ALREADY TWELVE. WHY ON EARTH DO I HAVE TO PICK HER UP?
HEE-JEE'S LUCKY TOO...MOM'S SUPER-PROTECTIVE OF HER SINCE CHILD-RELATED SEX CRIMES HAVE GOTTEN A LOT MORE COMMON LATELY.
IT WASN'T LIKE THAT WHEN I WAS HER AGE.
AH, DON'T KNOW WHO HEE-JEE IS? WANNA GET TO KNOW HER?
WE'RE THREE SISTERS.
SHE WAS IN VOLUME 1 TOO~!
OLDEST: HEE-JOO EUN, EIGHTEEN AND SCARY.
MAKE-UP
IF YOU DEFY ME, YOU DIE. AND YOU ONLY TAKE ORDERS FROM ME. THAT'S HOW IT WORKS.
SECOND: HEE-SO EUN, FIFTEEN AND TOO CUTE FOR WORDS.
THAT'S MEEE! ♥
YOUNGEST: HEE-JEE EUN, TWELVE-YEAR-OLD MASTER OF THE CYBER WORLD
WUT R U LOOKING @?!

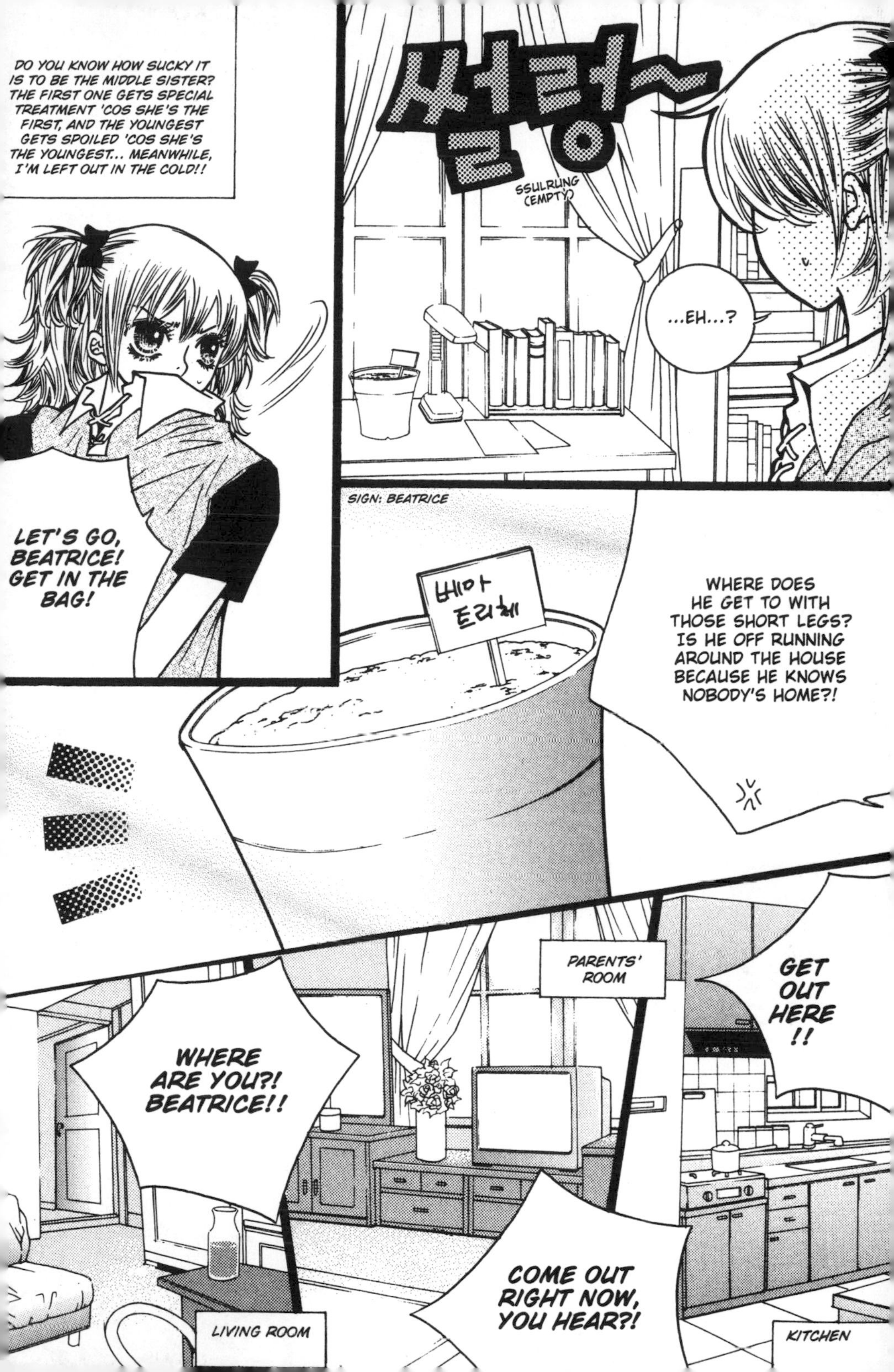
DO YOU KNOW HOW SUCKY IT IS TO BE THE MIDDLE SISTER? THE FIRST ONE GETS SPECIAL TREATMENT 'COS SHE'S THE FIRST, AND THE YOUNGEST GETS SPOILED 'COS SHE'S THE YOUNGEST... MEANWHILE, I'M LEFT OUT IN THE COLD!!
LET'S GO, BEATRICE! GET IN THE BAG!
썰렁~
SSULRUNG (EMPTY)
...EH...?
SIGN: BEATRICE
베아 트리체
WHERE DOES HE GET TO WITH THOSE SHORT LEGS? IS HE OFF RUNNING AROUND THE HOUSE BECAUSE HE KNOWS NOBODY'S HOME?!
WHERE ARE YOU?! BEATRICE!!
PARENTS' ROOM
GET OUT HERE !!
COME OUT RIGHT NOW, YOU HEAR?!
LIVING ROOM
KITCHEN

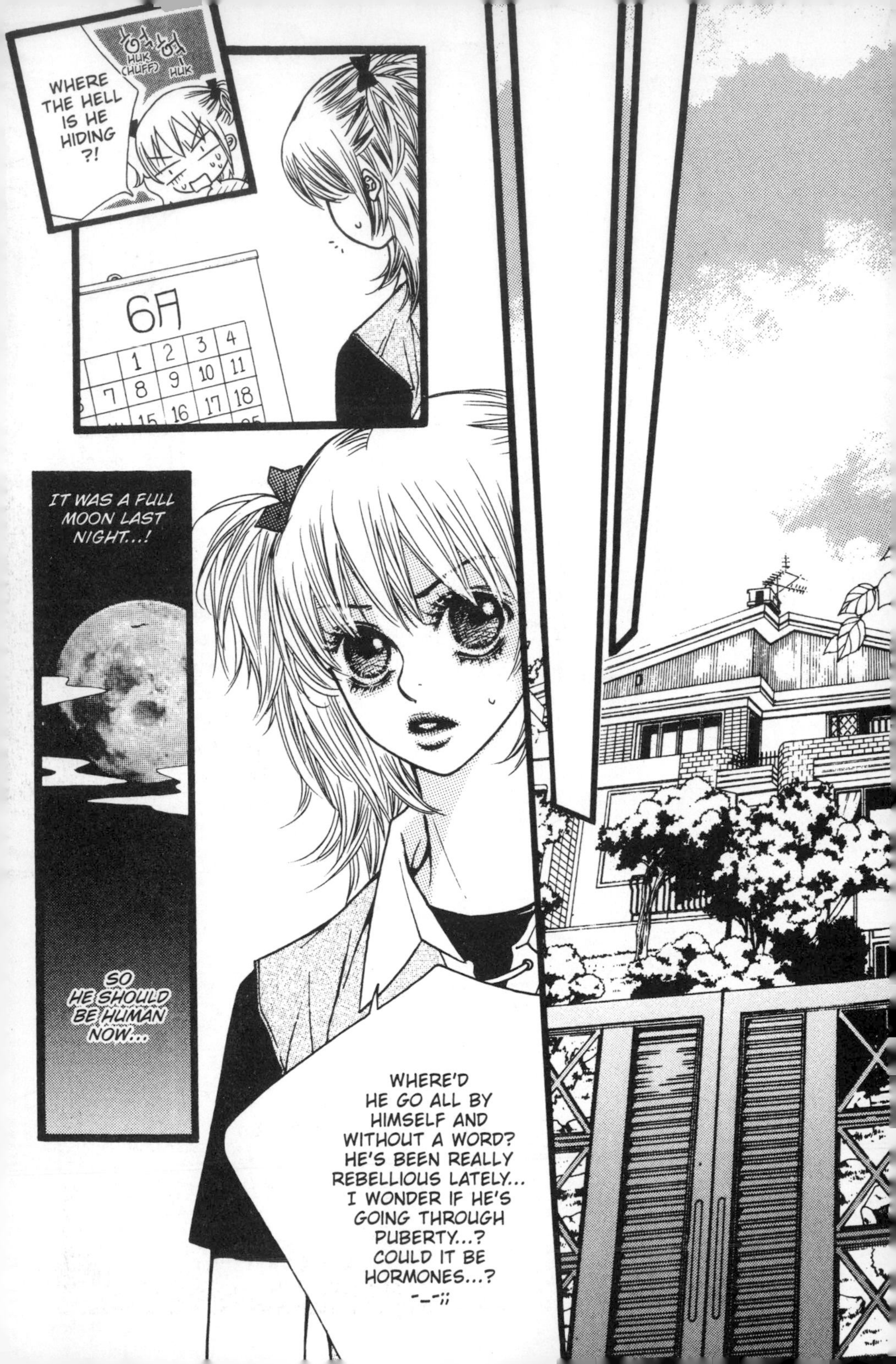
헉헉
HUK (CHUFF) HUK
WHERE THE HELL IS HE HIDING ?!
6月
1 2 3 4
7 8 9 10 11
15 16 17 18
IT WAS A FULL MOON LAST NIGHT...!
SO HE SHOULD BE HUMAN NOW...
WHERE'D HE GO ALL BY HIMSELF AND WITHOUT A WORD? HE'S BEEN REALLY REBELLIOUS LATELY... I WONDER IF HE'S GOING THROUGH PUBERTY...? COULD IT BE HORMONES...?
-_-;;

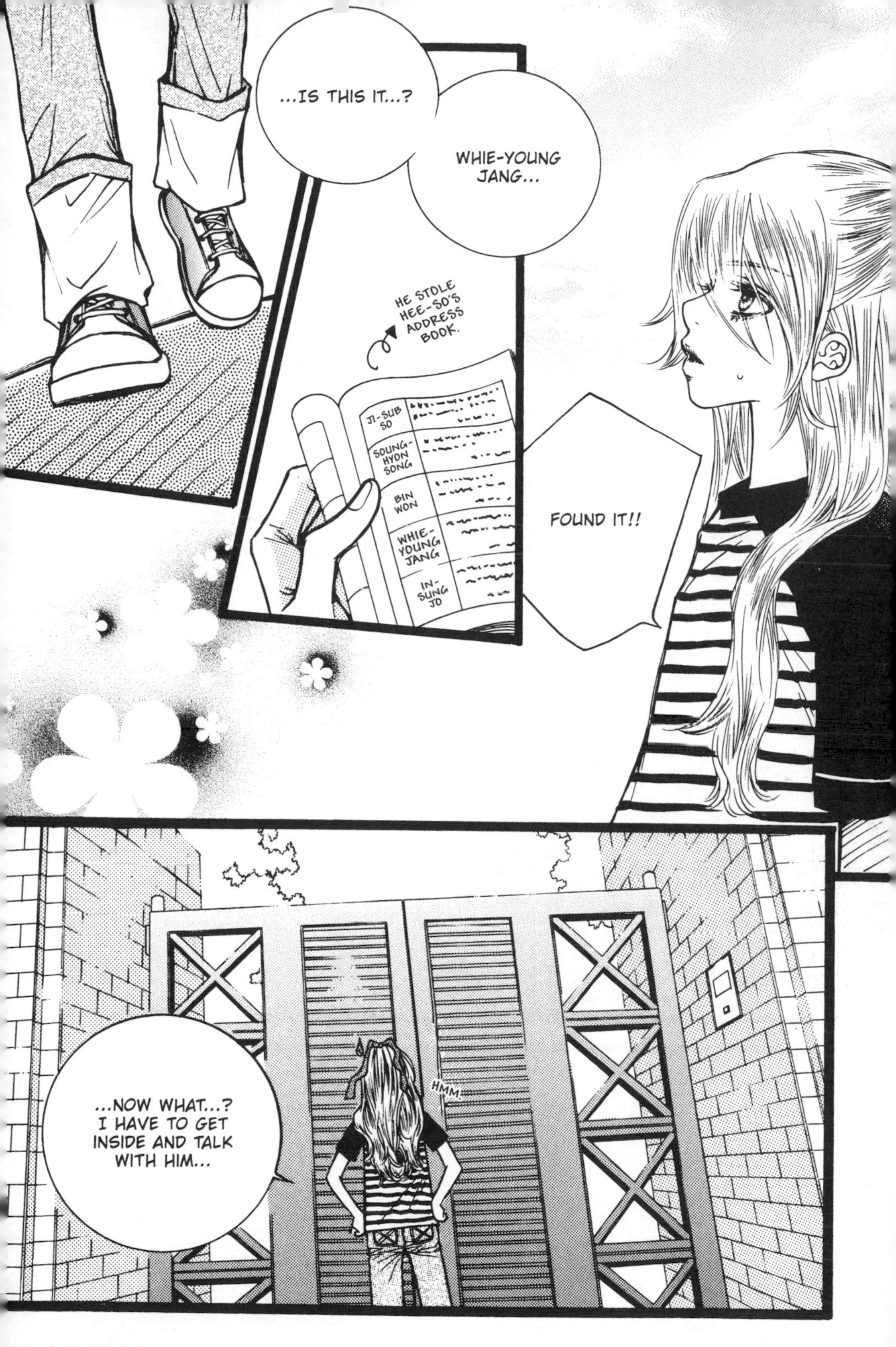
...IS THIS IT...?
WHIE-YOUNG JANG...
HE STOLE HEE-SO'S ADDRESS BOOK.
JI-SUB SO
SOUNG-HYON SONG
BIN WON
WHIE-YOUNG JANG
IN-SUNG JO
FOUND IT!!
...NOW WHAT...? I HAVE TO GET INSIDE AND TALK WITH HIM...
HMM.

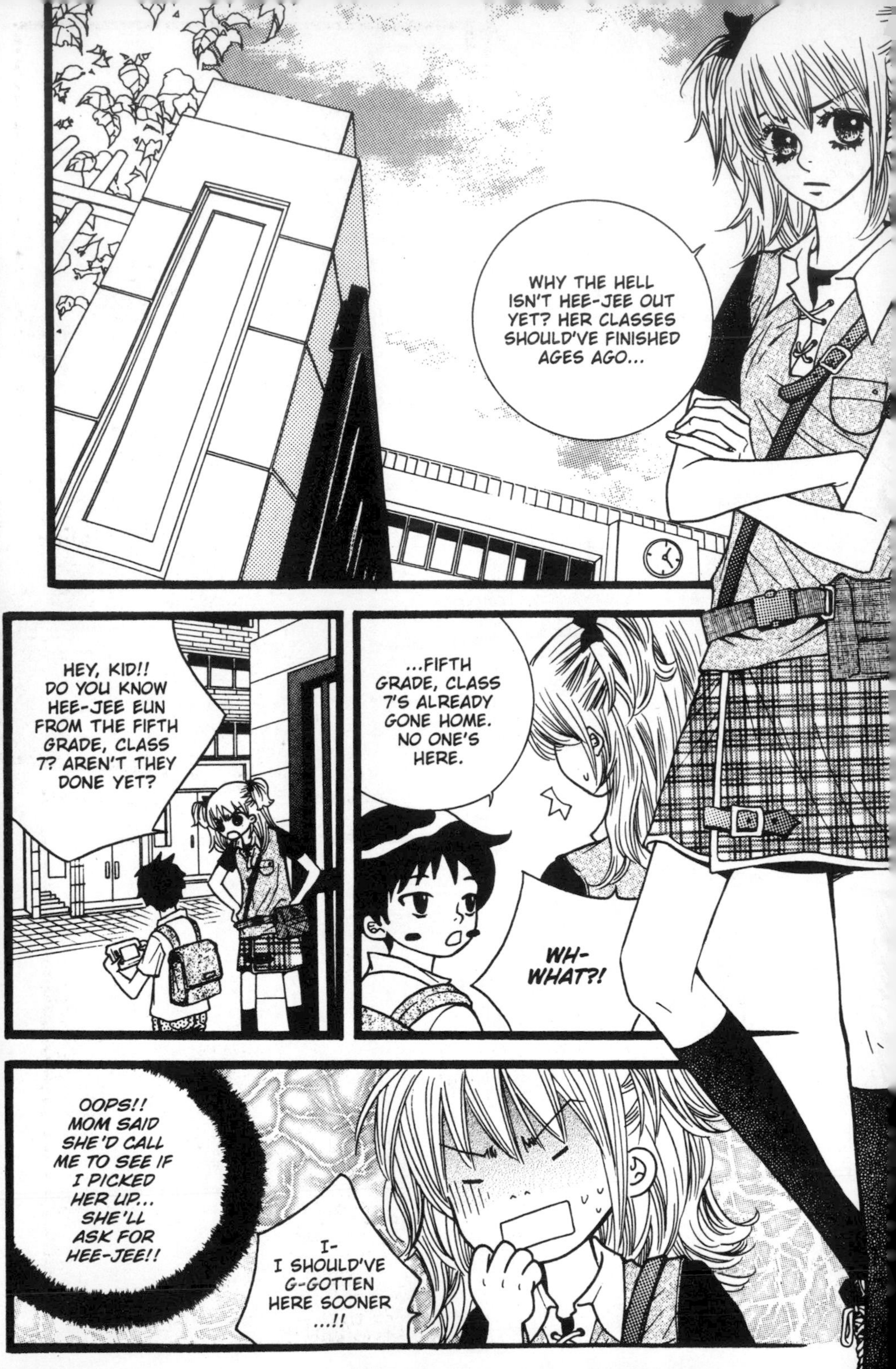
WHY THE HELL ISN'T HEE-JEE OUT YET? HER CLASSES SHOULD'VE FINISHED AGES AGO...
HEY, KID!! DO YOU KNOW HEE-JEE EUN FROM THE FIFTH GRADE, CLASS 7? AREN'T THEY DONE YET?
...FIFTH GRADE, CLASS 7'S ALREADY GONE HOME. NO ONE'S HERE.
WH-WHAT?!
OOPS!! MOM SAID SHE'D CALL ME TO SEE IF I PICKED HER UP... SHE'LL ASK FOR HEE-JEE!!
I- I SHOULD'VE G-GOTTEN HERE SOONER ...!!

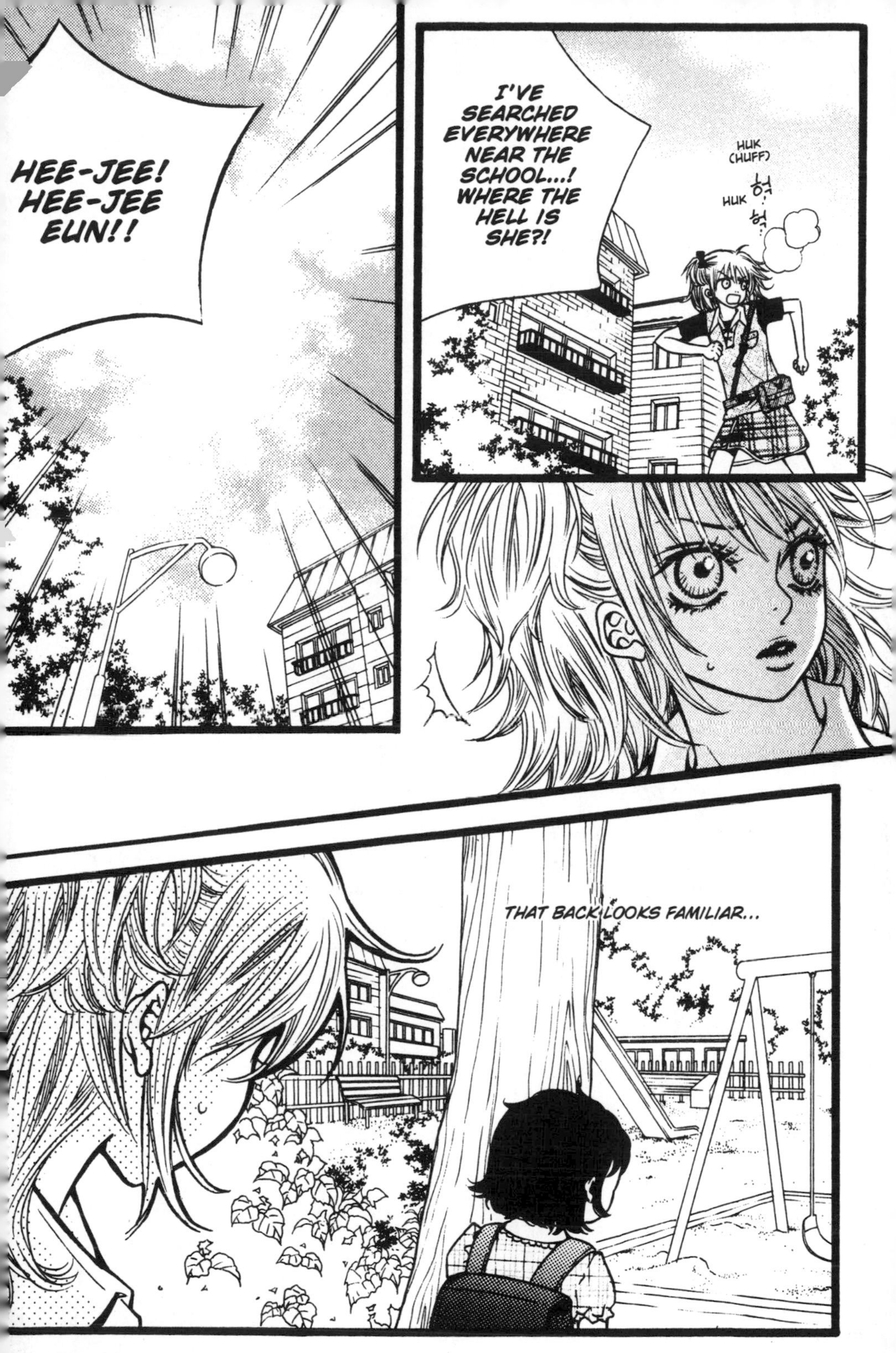
HEE-JEE! HEE-JEE EUN!!
I'VE SEARCHED EVERYWHERE NEAR THE SCHOOL...! WHERE THE HELL IS SHE?!
HUK (HUFF)
HUK
헉
헉
THAT BACK LOOKS FAMILIAR...

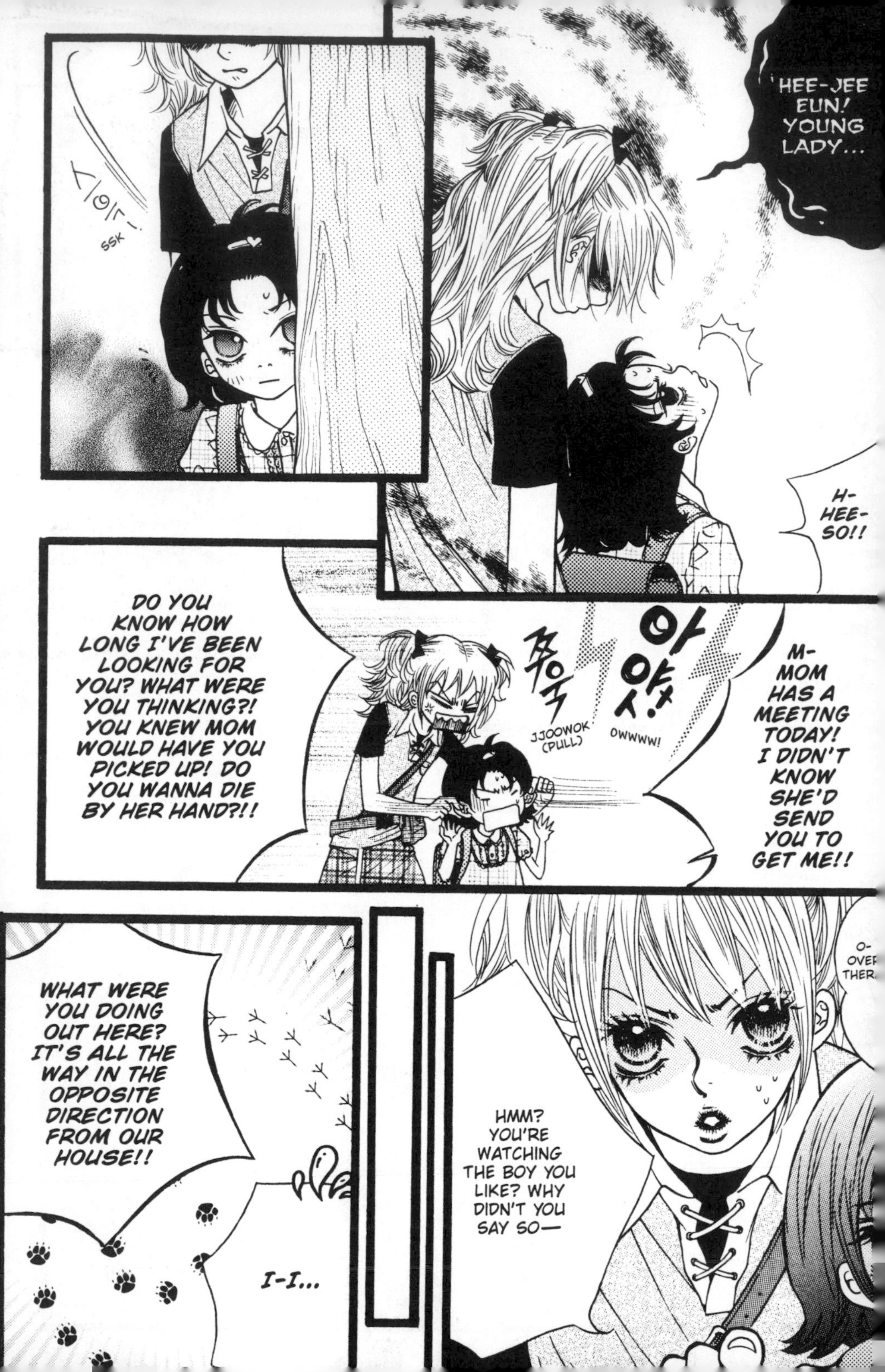
SSK
'HEE-JEE EUN! YOUNG LADY...
H- HEE- SO!!
DO YOU KNOW HOW LONG I'VE BEEN LOOKING FOR YOU? WHAT WERE YOU THINKING?! YOU KNEW MOM WOULD HAVE YOU PICKED UP! DO YOU WANNA DIE BY HER HAND?!!
쭈욱
JJOOWOK (PULL)
아얏!
OWWWW!
M- MOM HAS A MEETING TODAY! I DIDN'T KNOW SHE'D SEND YOU TO GET ME!!
WHAT WERE YOU DOING OUT HERE? IT'S ALL THE WAY IN THE OPPOSITE DIRECTION FROM OUR HOUSE!!
I-I...
HMM? YOU'RE WATCHING THE BOY YOU LIKE? WHY DIDN'T YOU SAY SO—
O- OVER THER

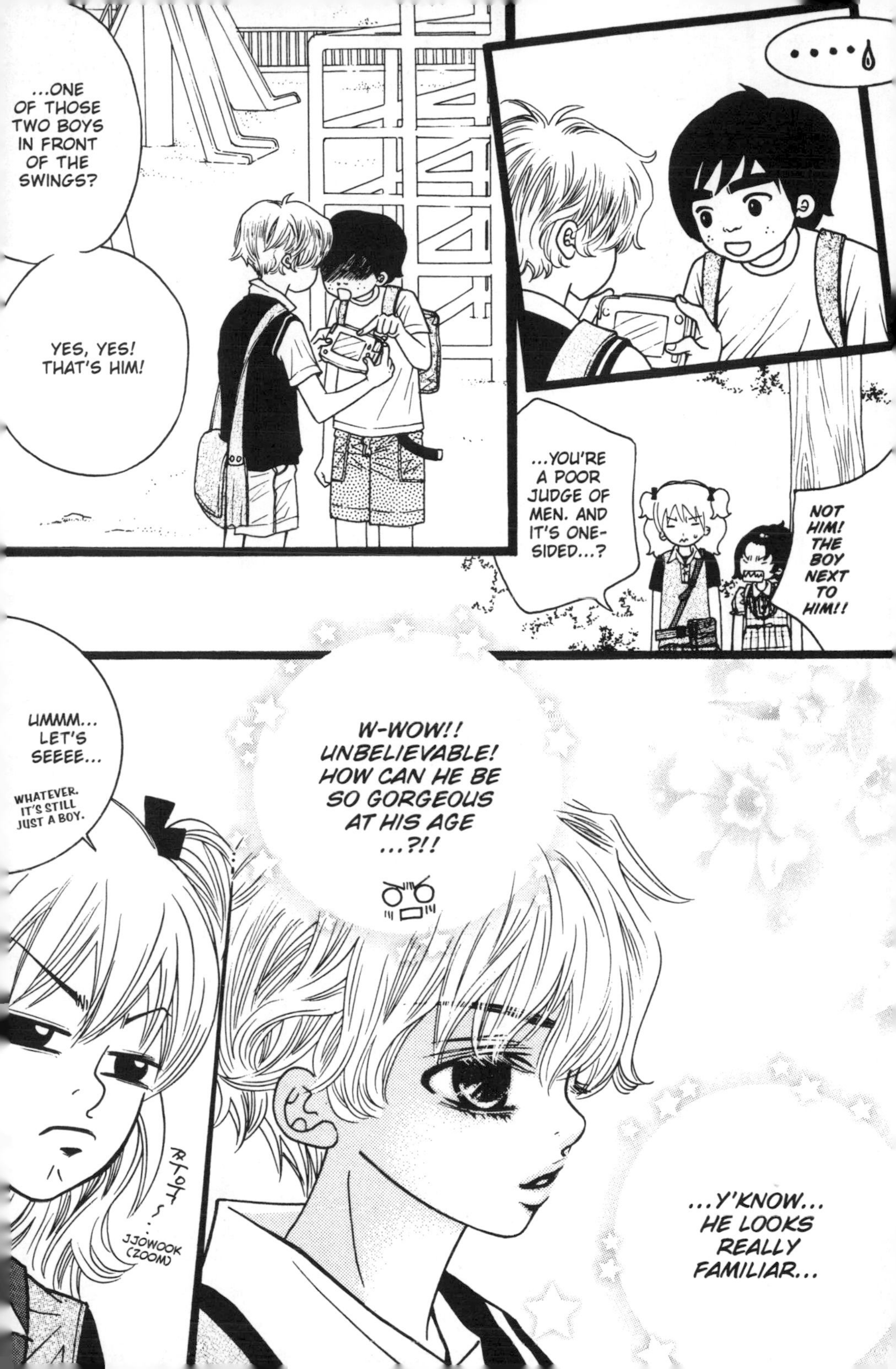
...ONE OF THOSE TWO BOYS IN FRONT OF THE SWINGS?
YES, YES! THAT'S HIM!
....
...YOU'RE A POOR JUDGE OF MEN. AND IT'S ONE-SIDED...?
NOT HIM! THE BOY NEXT TO HIM!!
UMMM... LET'S SEEEE...
WHATEVER. IT'S STILL JUST A BOY.
W-WOW!! UNBELIEVABLE! HOW CAN HE BE SO GORGEOUS AT HIS AGE ...?!!
JJOWOOK (ZOOM)
...Y'KNOW... HE LOOKS REALLY FAMILIAR...

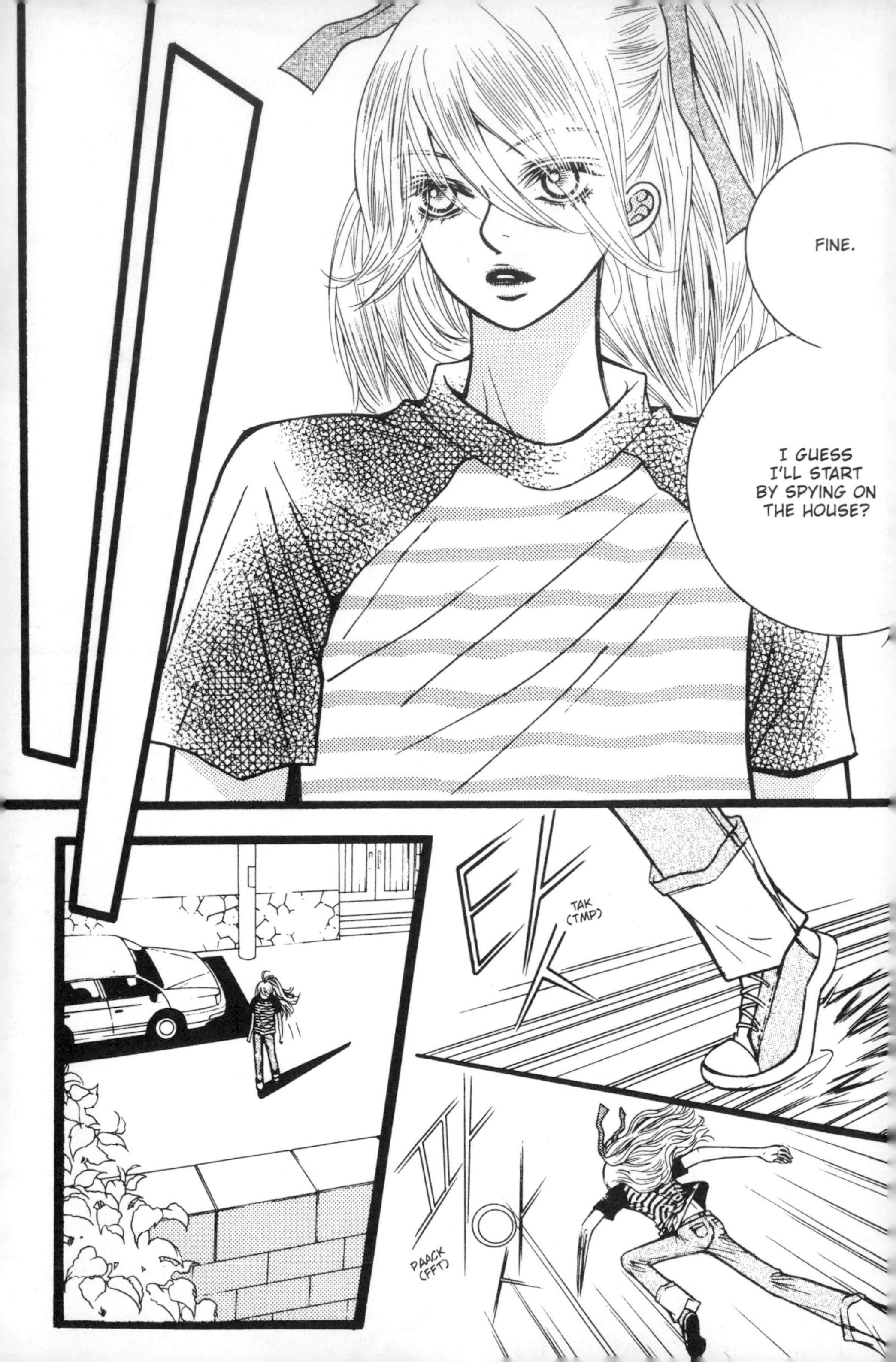
FINE.
I GUESS I'LL START BY SPYING ON THE HOUSE?
TAK (TMP)
PAACK (FFT)

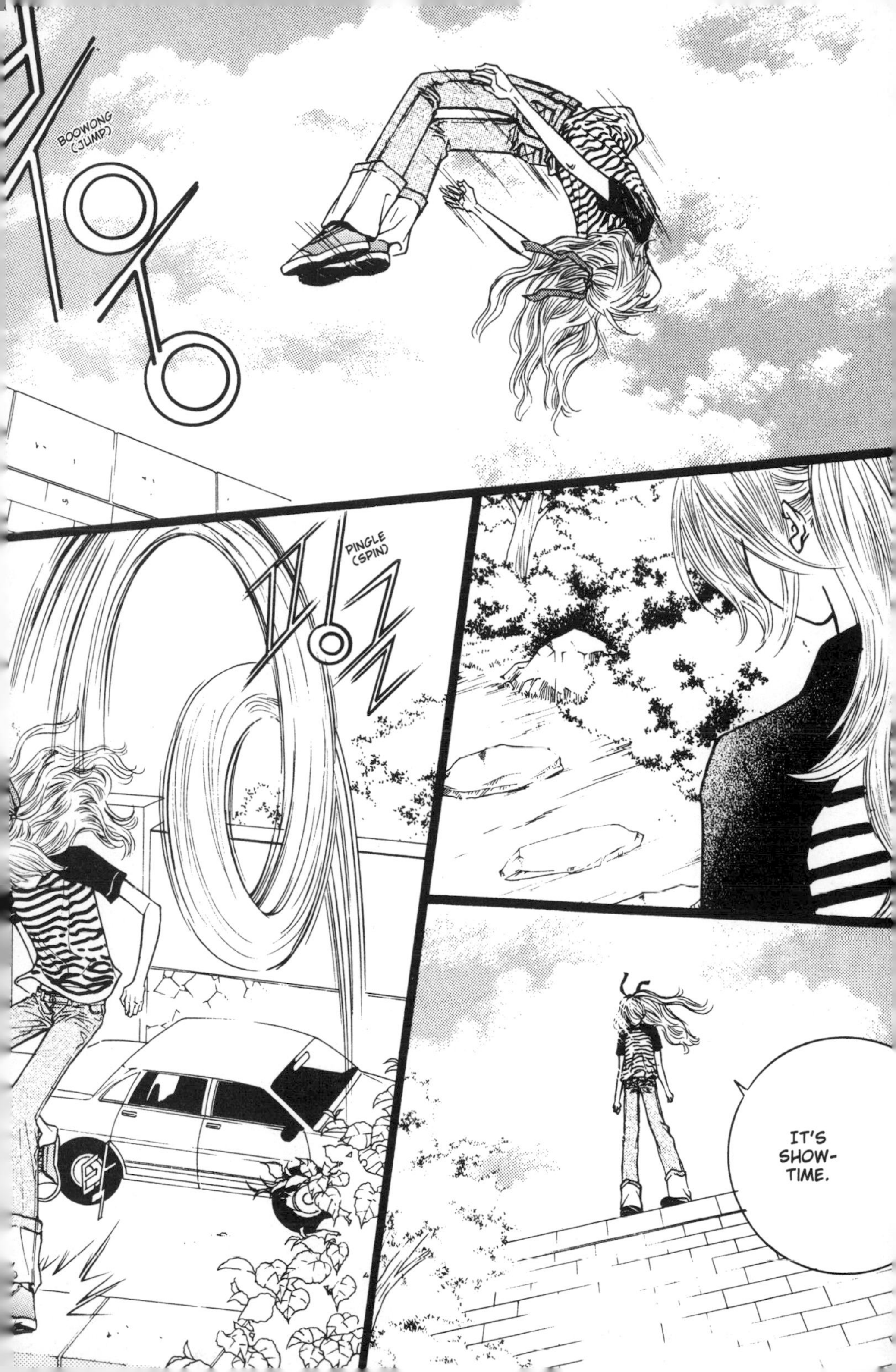
BOOWONG
(JUMP)
PINGLE
(SPIN)
IT'S SHOW-TIME.

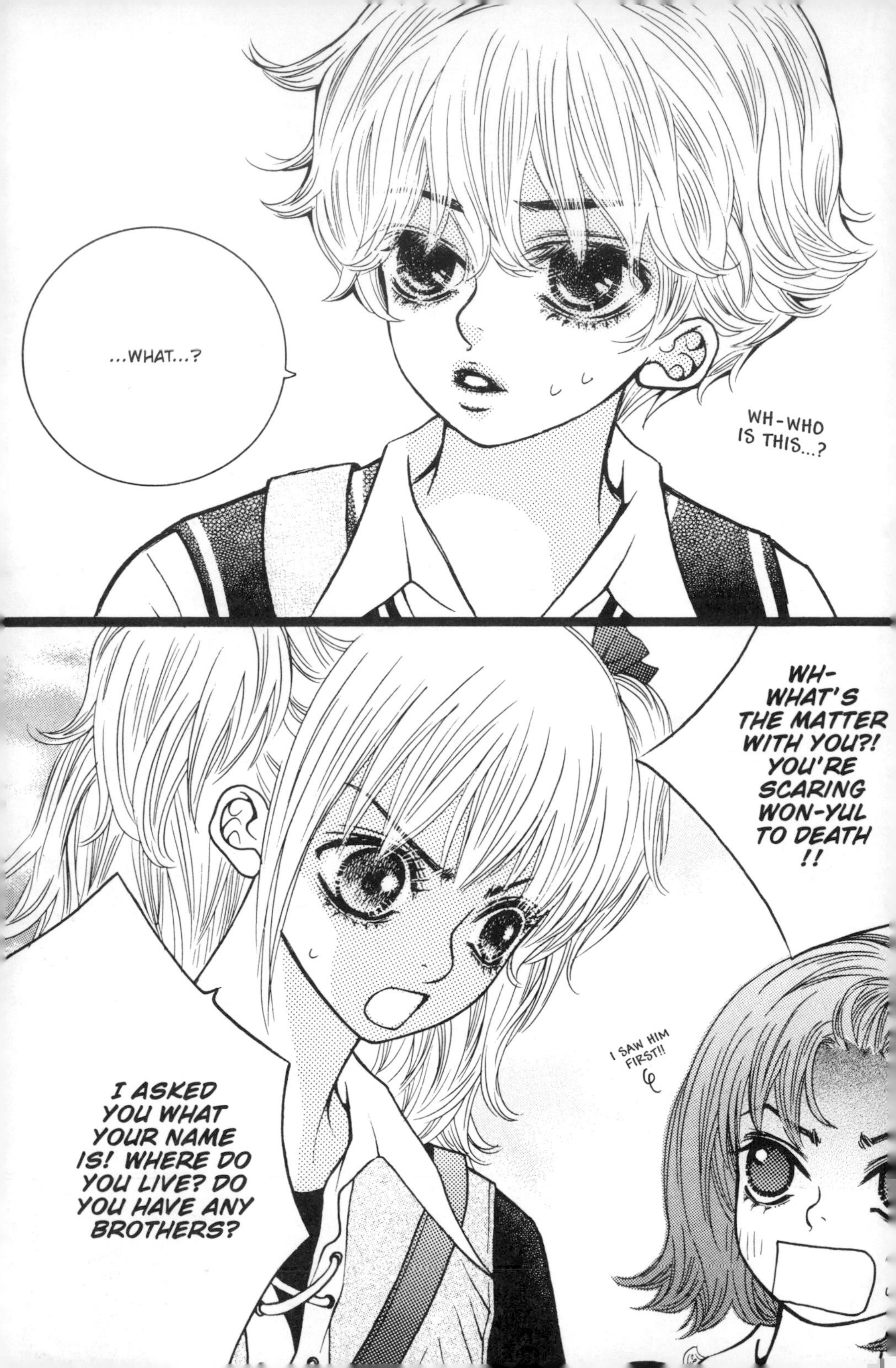
...WHAT...?
WH-WHO IS THIS...?
WH- WHAT'S THE MATTER WITH YOU?! YOU'RE SCARING WON-YUL TO DEATH !!
I SAW HIM FIRST!!
I ASKED YOU WHAT YOUR NAME IS! WHERE DO YOU LIVE? DO YOU HAVE ANY BROTHERS?

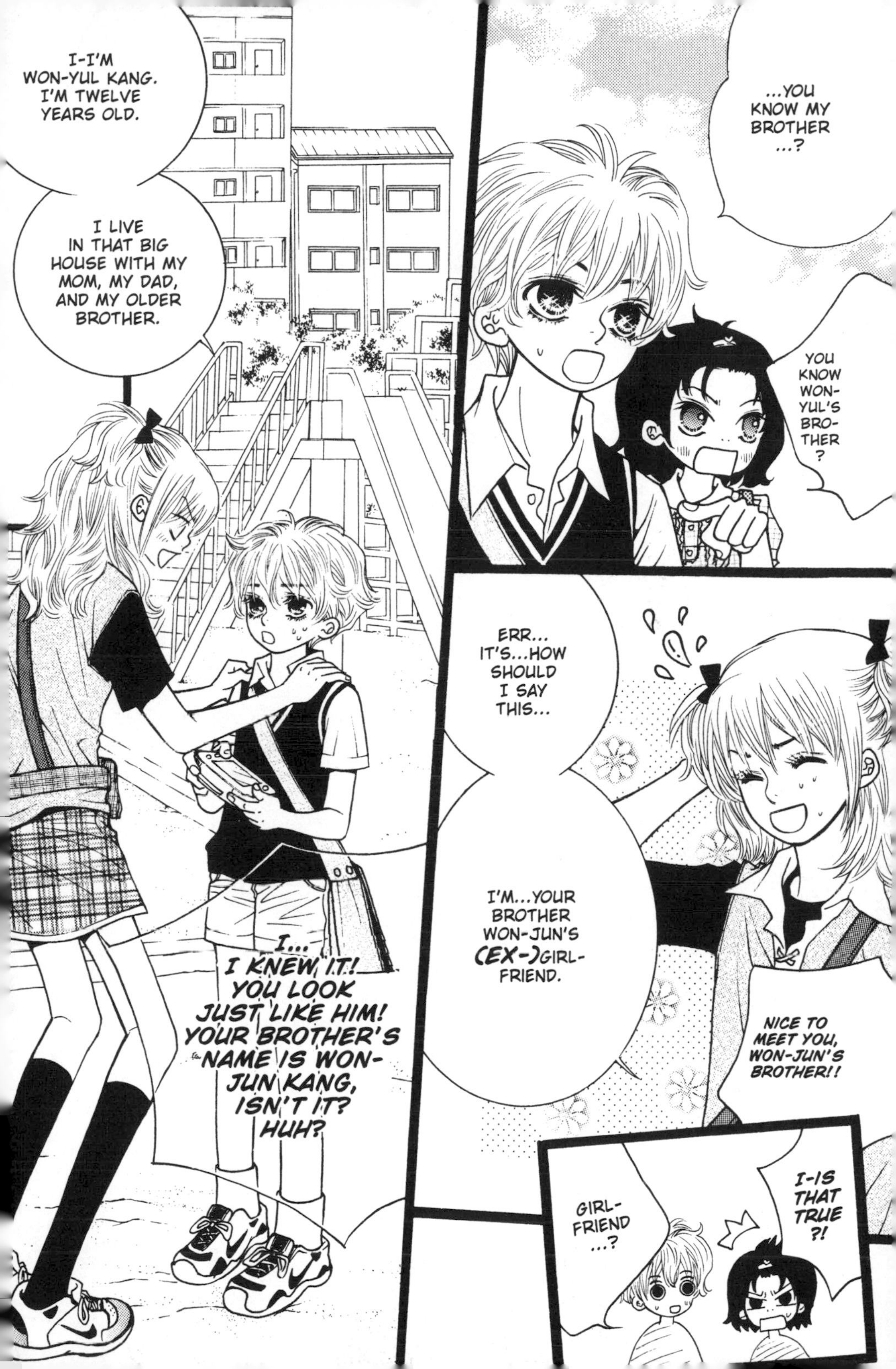
I-I'M WON-YUL KANG. I'M TWELVE YEARS OLD.
I LIVE IN THAT BIG HOUSE WITH MY MOM, MY DAD, AND MY OLDER BROTHER.
I... I KNEW IT! YOU LOOK JUST LIKE HIM! YOUR BROTHER'S NAME IS WON-JUN KANG, ISN'T IT? HUH?
...YOU KNOW MY BROTHER ...?
YOU KNOW WON-YUL'S BRO-THER ?
ERR... IT'S...HOW SHOULD I SAY THIS...
I'M...YOUR BROTHER WON-JUN'S (EX-)GIRL-FRIEND.
NICE TO MEET YOU, WON-JUN'S BROTHER!!
GIRL-FRIEND ...?
I-IS THAT TRUE ?!

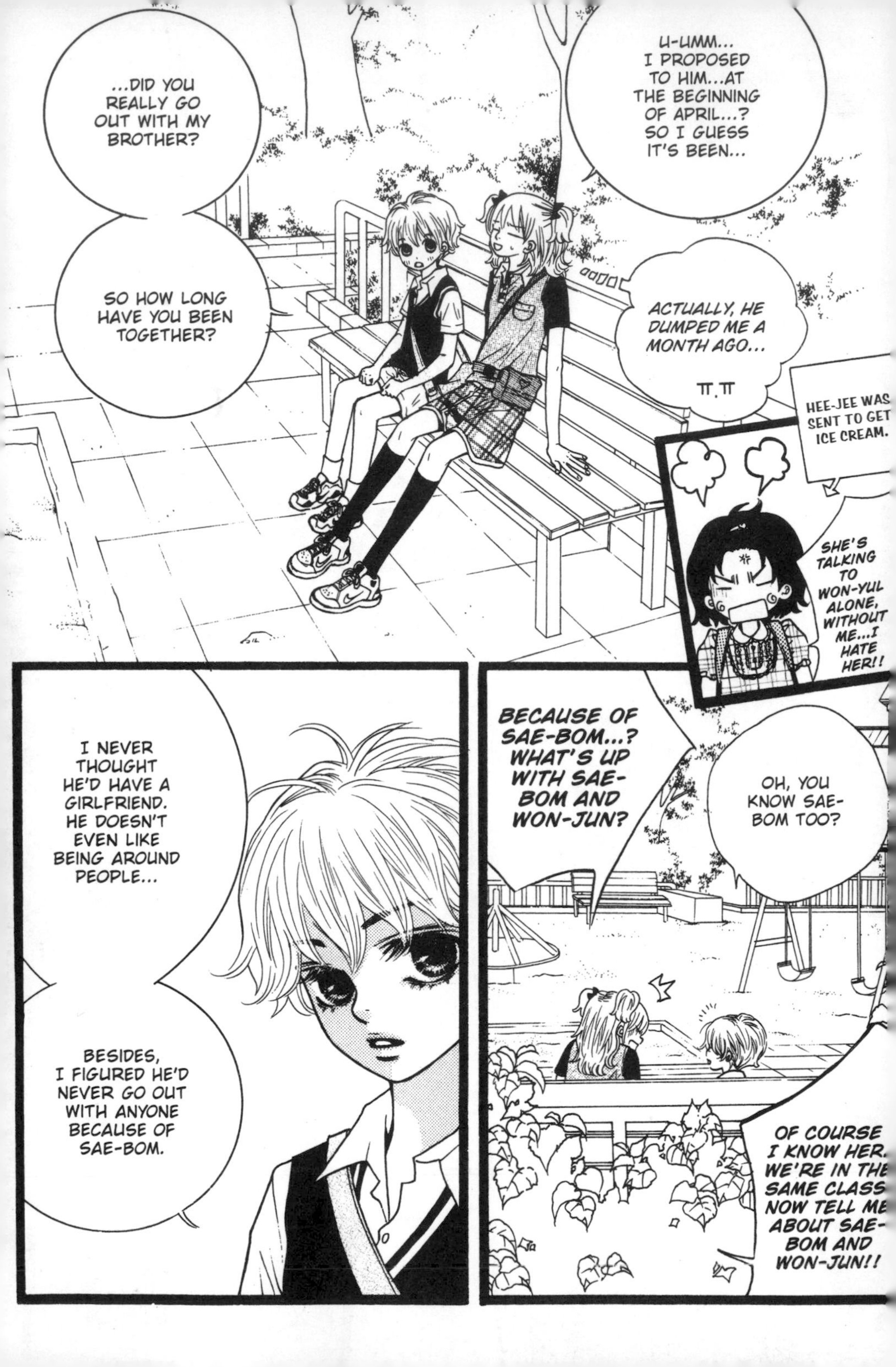
...DID YOU REALLY GO OUT WITH MY BROTHER?
SO HOW LONG HAVE YOU BEEN TOGETHER?
U-UMM... I PROPOSED TO HIM...AT THE BEGINNING OF APRIL...? SO I GUESS IT'S BEEN...
ACTUALLY, HE DUMPED ME A MONTH AGO...
ㅠ.ㅠ
HEE-JEE WAS SENT TO GET ICE CREAM.
SHE'S TALKING TO WON-YUL ALONE, WITHOUT ME...I HATE HER!!
I NEVER THOUGHT HE'D HAVE A GIRLFRIEND. HE DOESN'T EVEN LIKE BEING AROUND PEOPLE...
BESIDES, I FIGURED HE'D NEVER GO OUT WITH ANYONE BECAUSE OF SAE-BOM.
BECAUSE OF SAE-BOM...? WHAT'S UP WITH SAE-BOM AND WON-JUN?
OH, YOU KNOW SAE-BOM TOO?
OF COURSE I KNOW HER. WE'RE IN THE SAME CLASS NOW TELL ME ABOUT SAE-BOM AND WON-JUN!!

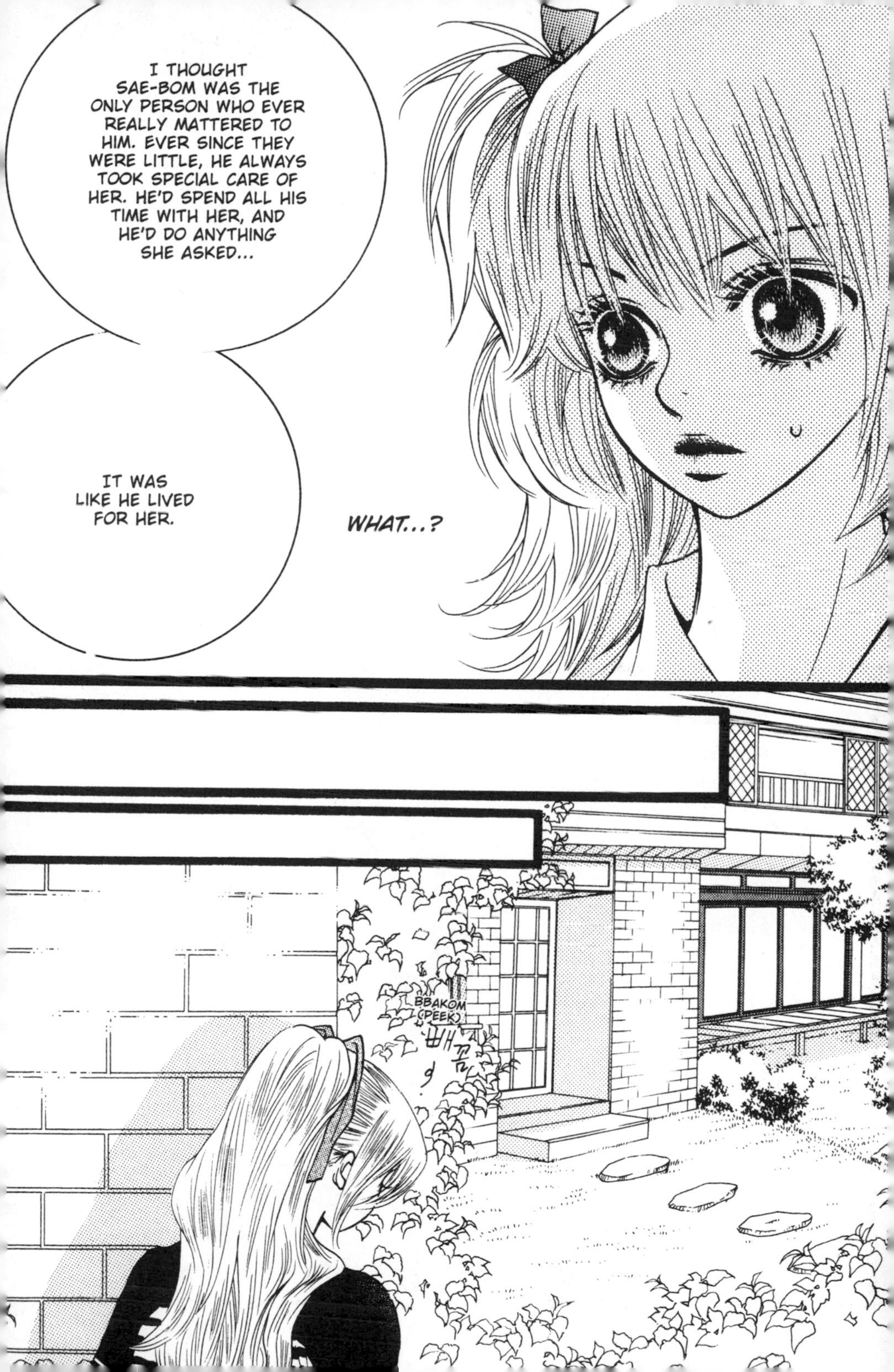
I THOUGHT SAE-BOM WAS THE ONLY PERSON WHO EVER REALLY MATTERED TO HIM. EVER SINCE THEY WERE LITTLE, HE ALWAYS TOOK SPECIAL CARE OF HER. HE'D SPEND ALL HIS TIME WITH HER, AND HE'D DO ANYTHING SHE ASKED...
IT WAS LIKE HE LIVED FOR HER.
WHAT...?
BBAKOM (PEEK)
빠꼼

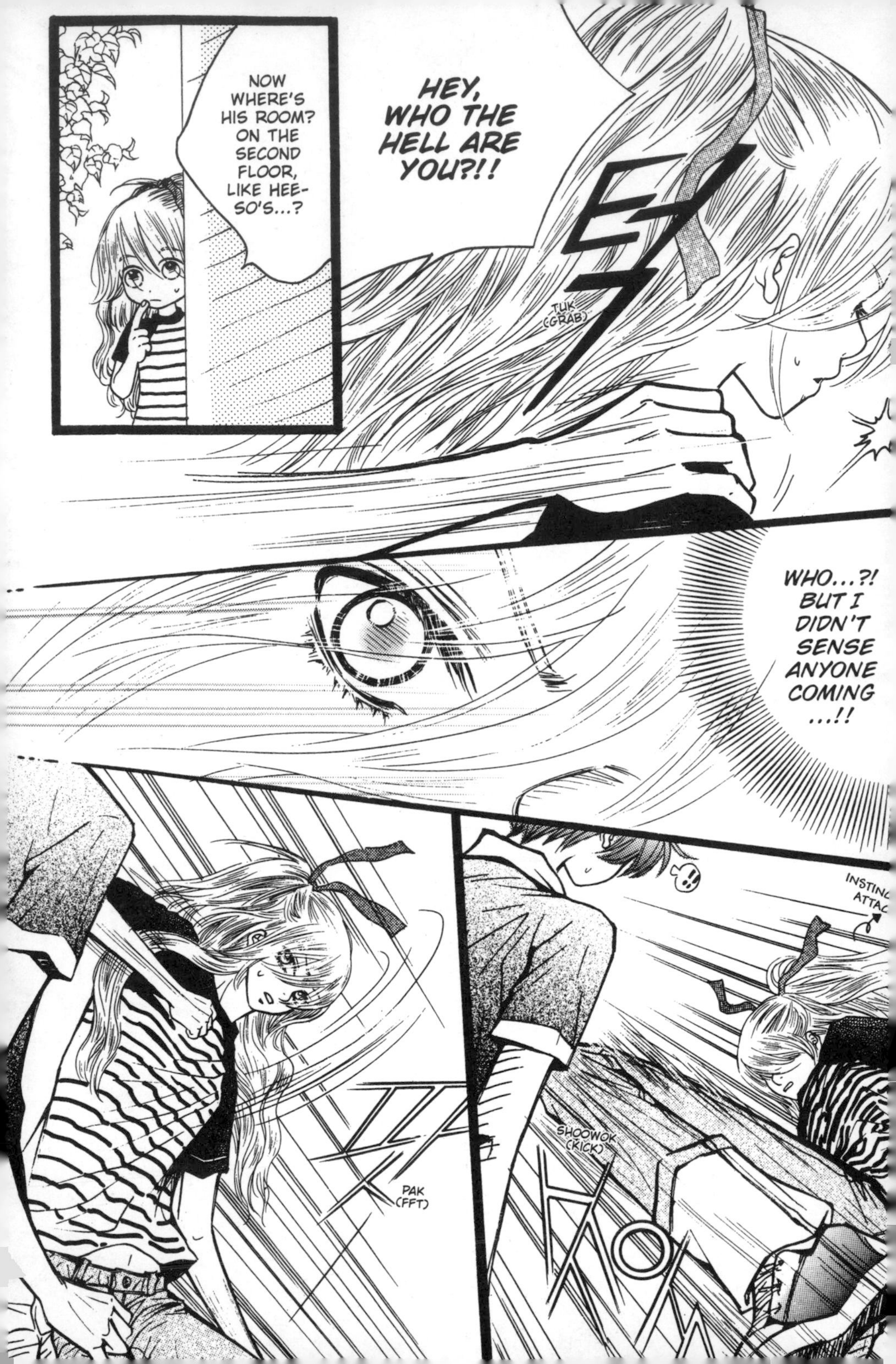
NOW WHERE'S HIS ROOM? ON THE SECOND FLOOR, LIKE HEE-SO'S...?
HEY, WHO THE HELL ARE YOU?!!
TUK (GRAB)
WHO...?! BUT I DIDN'T SENSE ANYONE COMING ...!!
PAK (FFT)
INSTINC ATTAC
SHOOWOK (KICK)

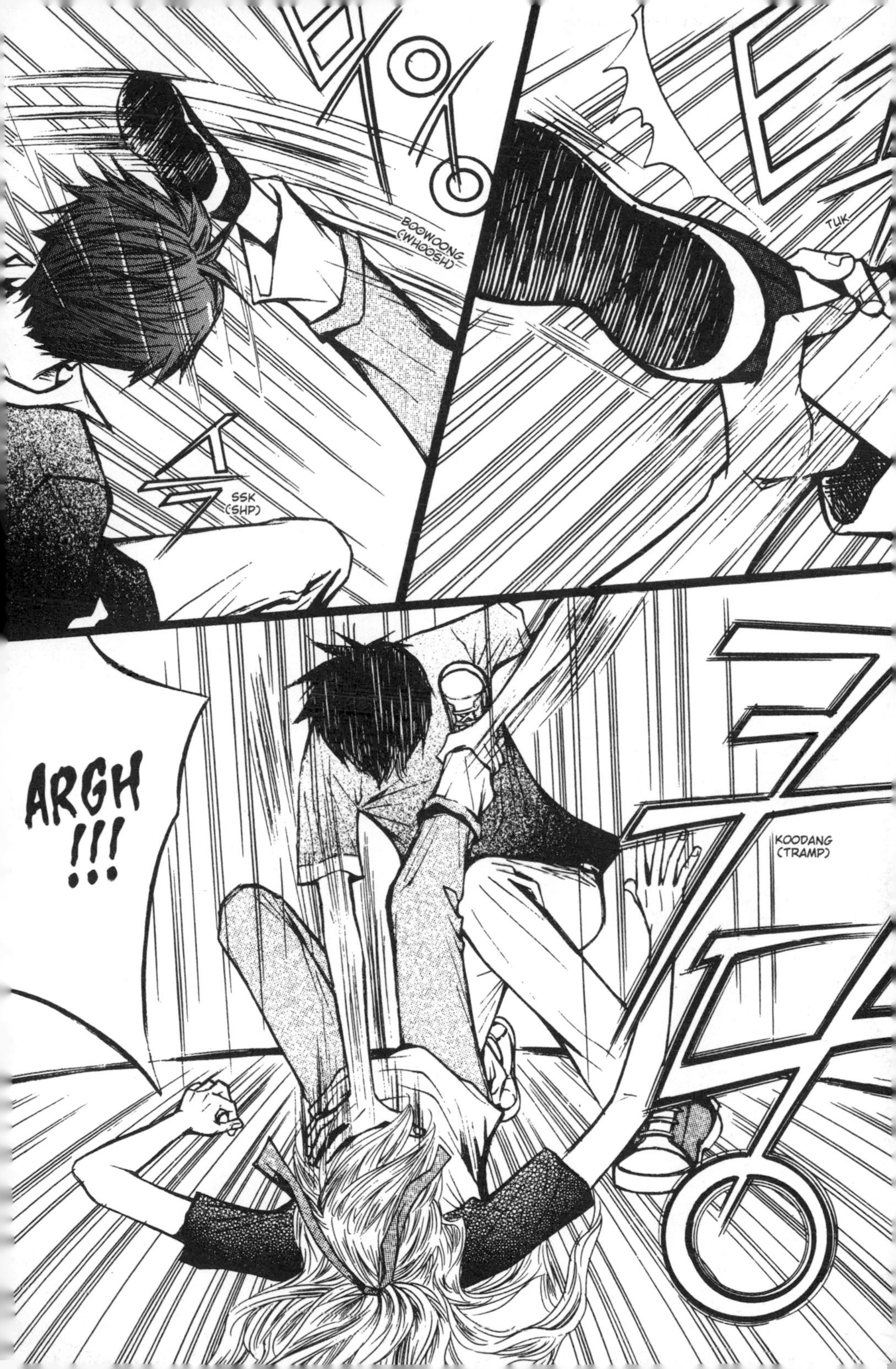

BOOWOONG (WHOOSH)
SSK (SHP)
TUK
ARGH !!!
KOODANG (TRAMP)

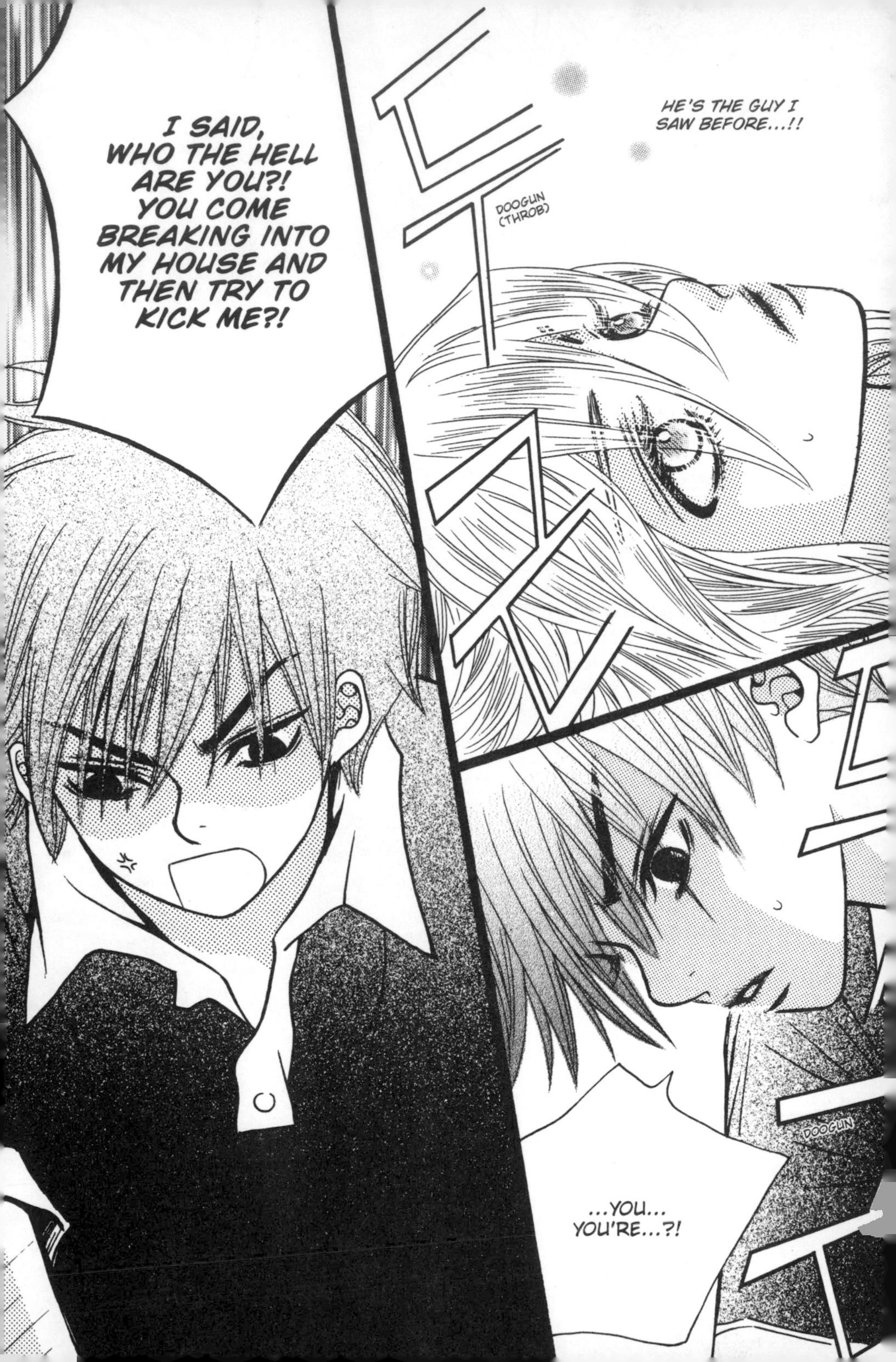
I SAID, WHO THE HELL ARE YOU?! YOU COME BREAKING INTO MY HOUSE AND THEN TRY TO KICK ME?!
HE'S THE GUY I SAW BEFORE...!!
DOOGUN (THROB)
DOOGUN
...YOU... YOU'RE...?!

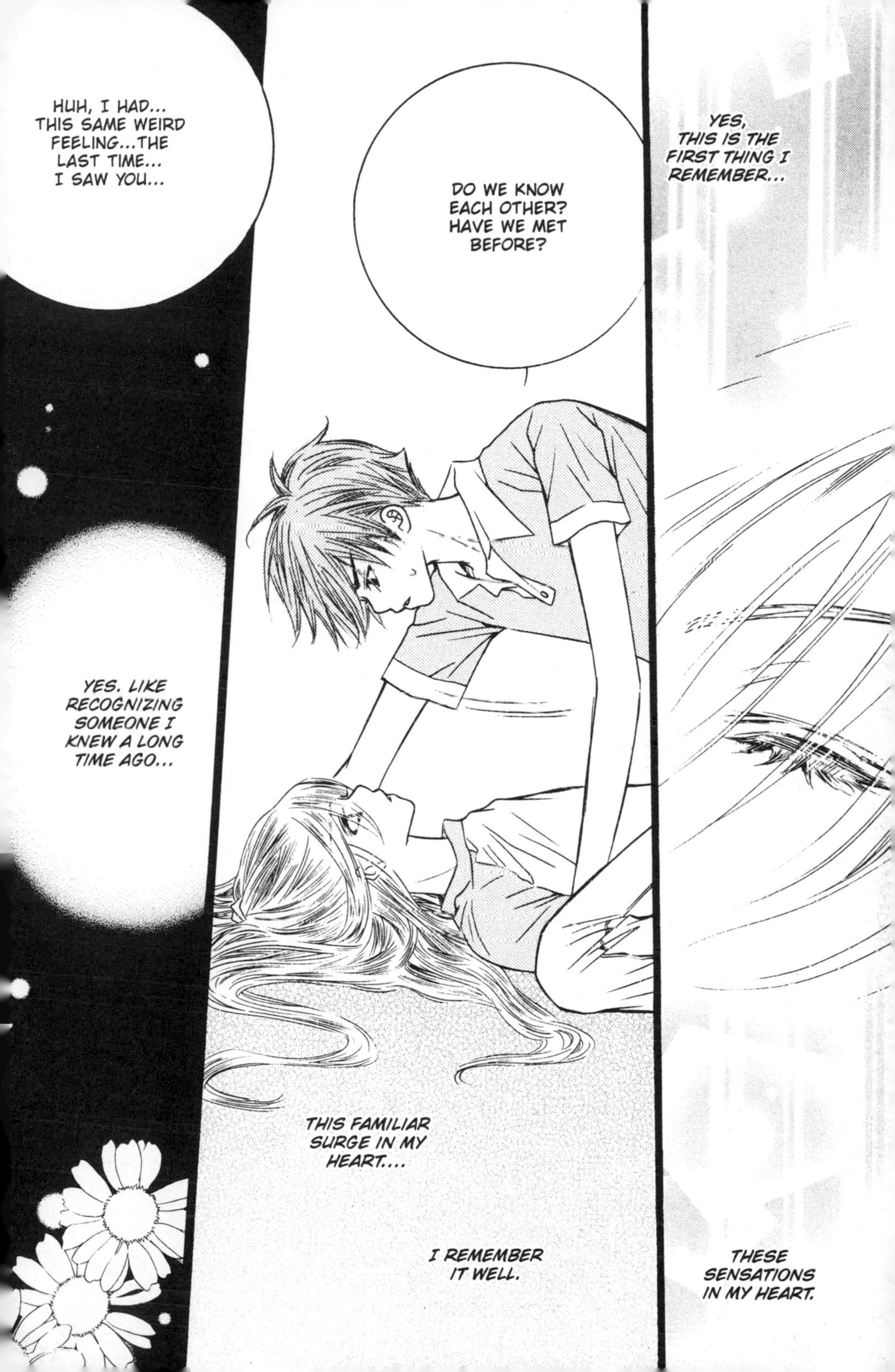
HUH, I HAD... THIS SAME WEIRD FEELING...THE LAST TIME... I SAW YOU...
YES. LIKE RECOGNIZING SOMEONE I KNEW A LONG TIME AGO...
DO WE KNOW EACH OTHER? HAVE WE MET BEFORE?
THIS FAMILIAR SURGE IN MY HEART....
I REMEMBER IT WELL.
YES, THIS IS THE FIRST THING I REMEMBER...
THESE SENSATIONS IN MY HEART.

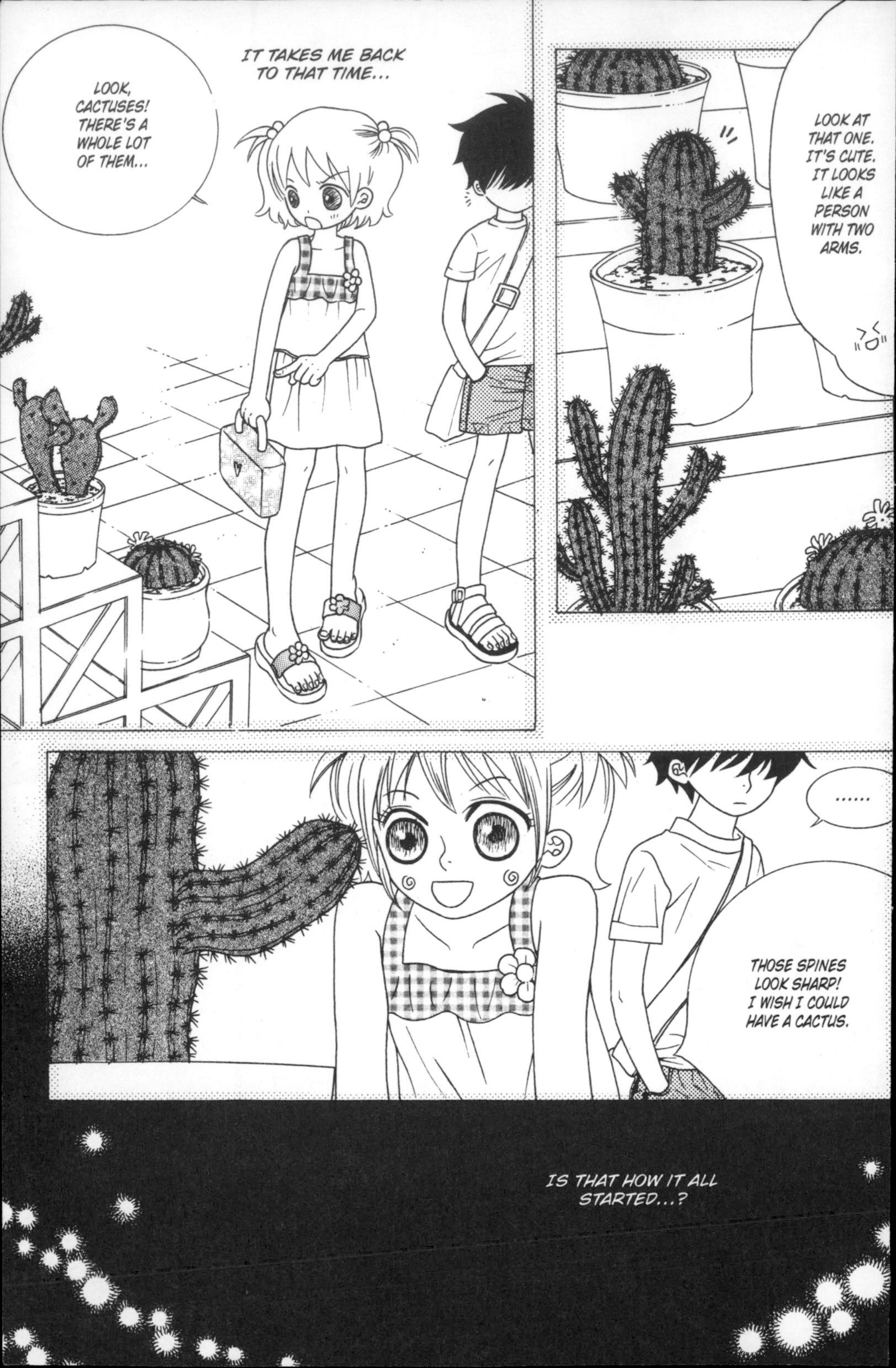

LOOK, CACTUSES! THERE'S A WHOLE LOT OF THEM...
IT TAKES ME BACK TO THAT TIME...
LOOK AT THAT ONE. IT'S CUTE. IT LOOKS LIKE A PERSON WITH TWO ARMS.
......
THOSE SPINES LOOK SHARP! I WISH I COULD HAVE A CACTUS.
IS THAT HOW IT ALL STARTED...?

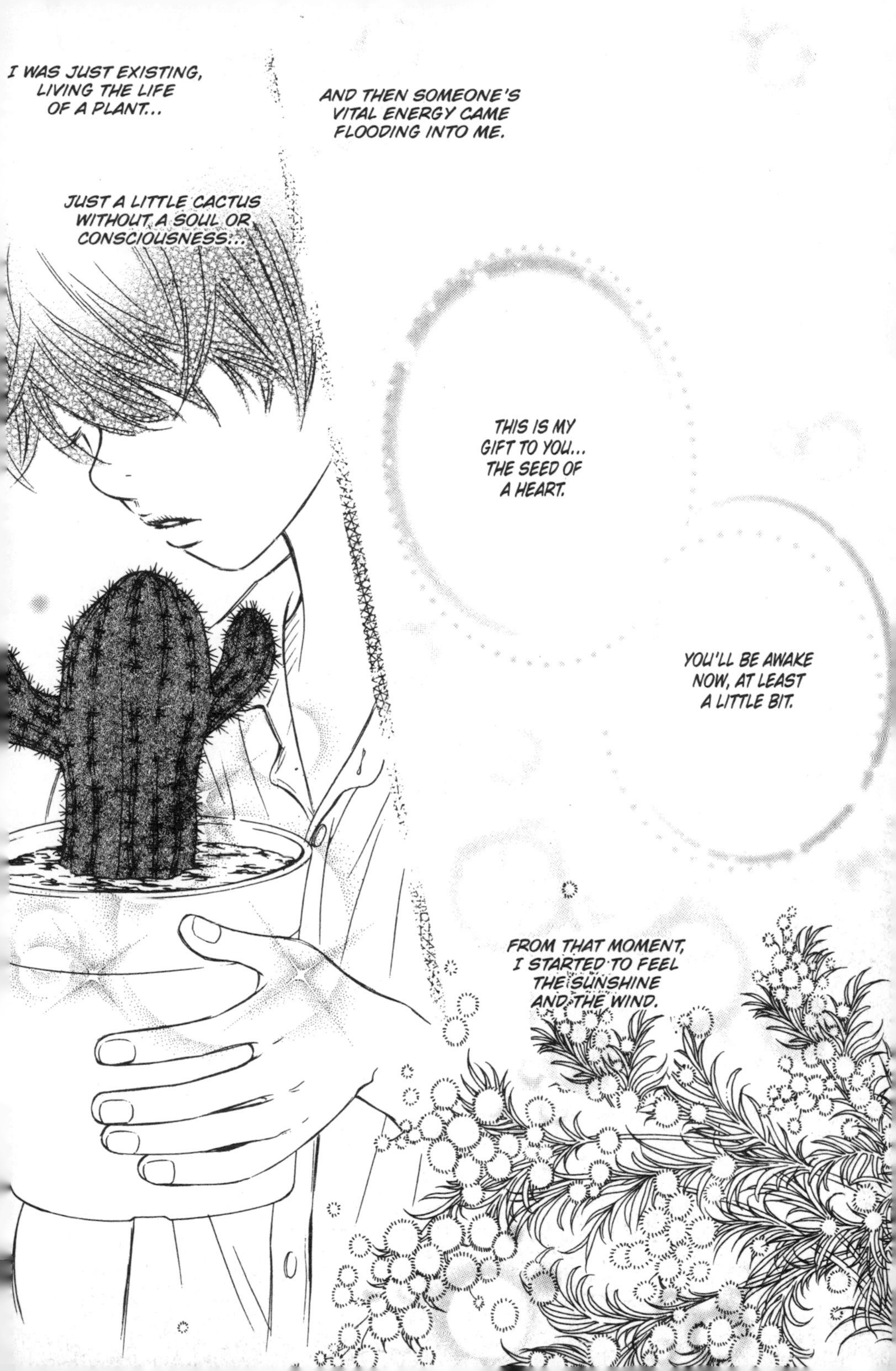
I WAS JUST EXISTING, LIVING THE LIFE OF A PLANT...
JUST A LITTLE CACTUS WITHOUT A SOUL OR CONSCIOUSNESS...
AND THEN SOMEONE'S VITAL ENERGY CAME FLOODING INTO ME.
THIS IS MY GIFT TO YOU... THE SEED OF A HEART.
YOU'LL BE AWAKE NOW, AT LEAST A LITTLE BIT.
FROM THAT MOMENT, I STARTED TO FEEL THE SUNSHINE AND THE WIND.

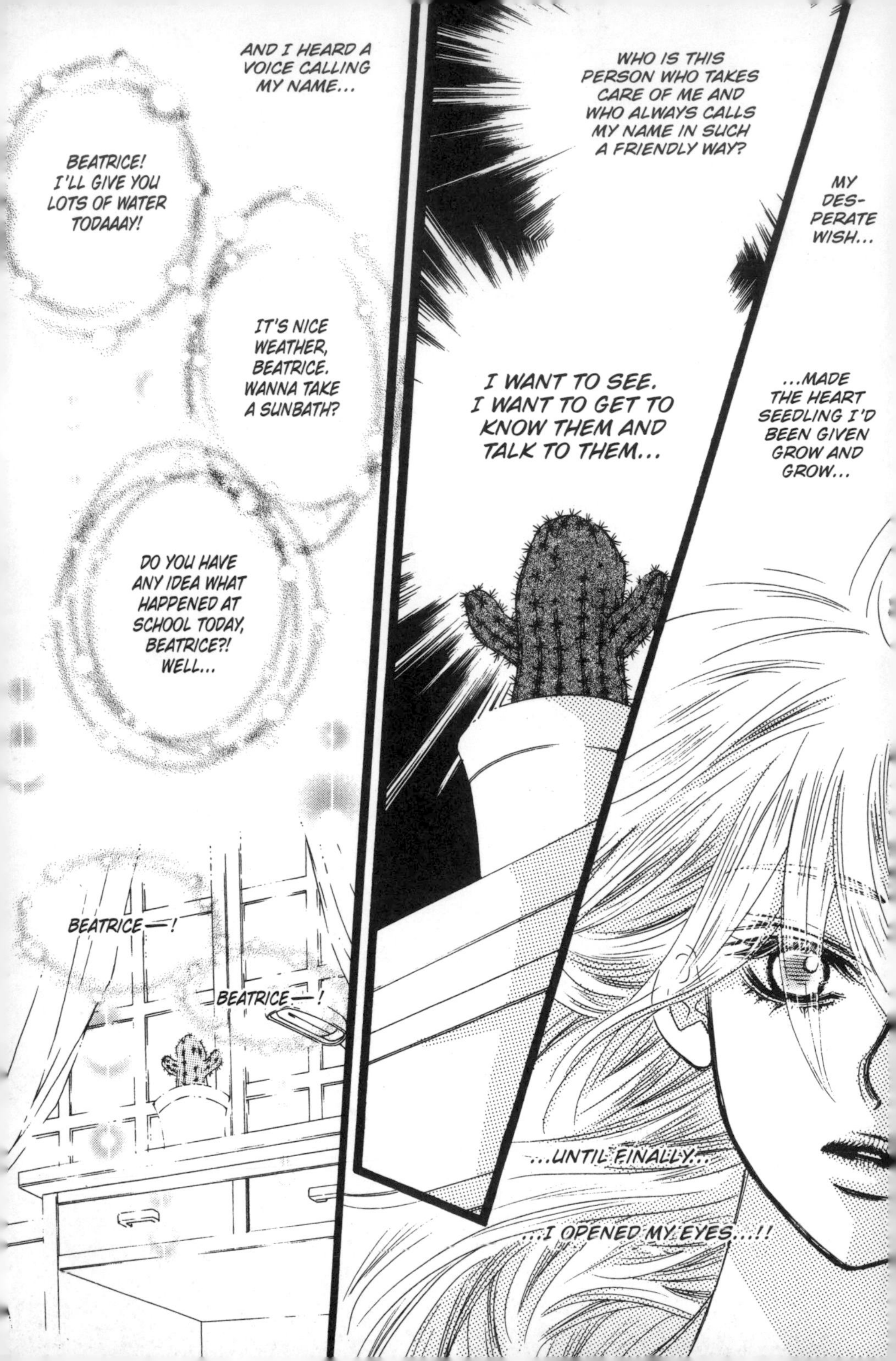
AND I HEARD A VOICE CALLING MY NAME...
BEATRICE! I'LL GIVE YOU LOTS OF WATER TODAAAY!
IT'S NICE WEATHER, BEATRICE. WANNA TAKE A SUNBATH?
DO YOU HAVE ANY IDEA WHAT HAPPENED AT SCHOOL TODAY, BEATRICE?! WELL...
BEATRICE—!
BEATRICE—!
WHO IS THIS PERSON WHO TAKES CARE OF ME AND WHO ALWAYS CALLS MY NAME IN SUCH A FRIENDLY WAY?
I WANT TO SEE. I WANT TO GET TO KNOW THEM AND TALK TO THEM...
MY DES-PERATE WISH...
...MADE THE HEART SEEDLING I'D BEEN GIVEN GROW AND GROW...
...UNTIL FINALLY...
...I OPENED MY EYES...!!

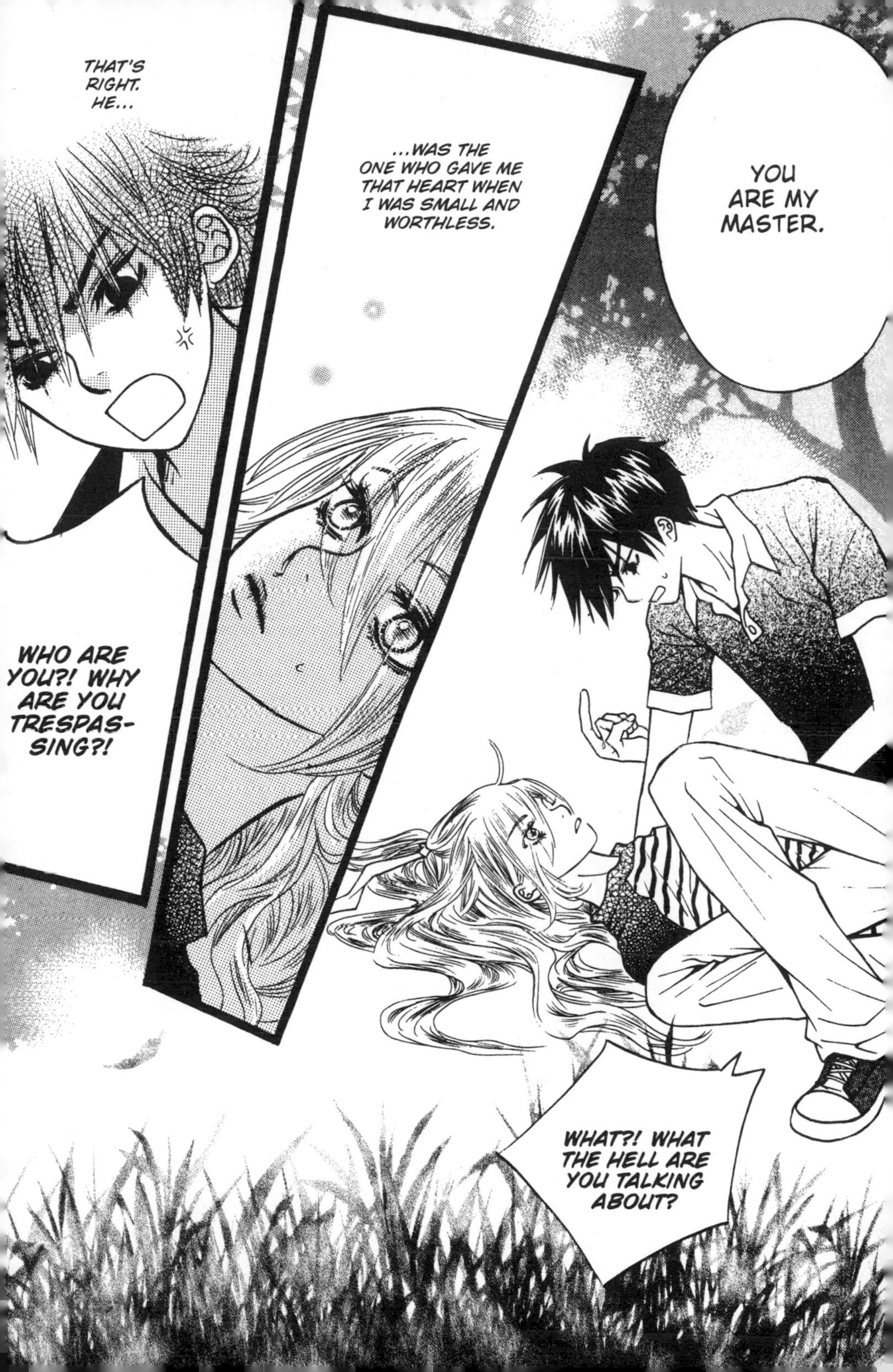
THAT'S RIGHT. HE...
WHO ARE YOU?! WHY ARE YOU TRESPAS-SING?!
...WAS THE ONE WHO GAVE ME THAT HEART WHEN I WAS SMALL AND WORTHLESS.
YOU ARE MY MASTER.
WHAT?! WHAT THE HELL ARE YOU TALKING ABOUT?

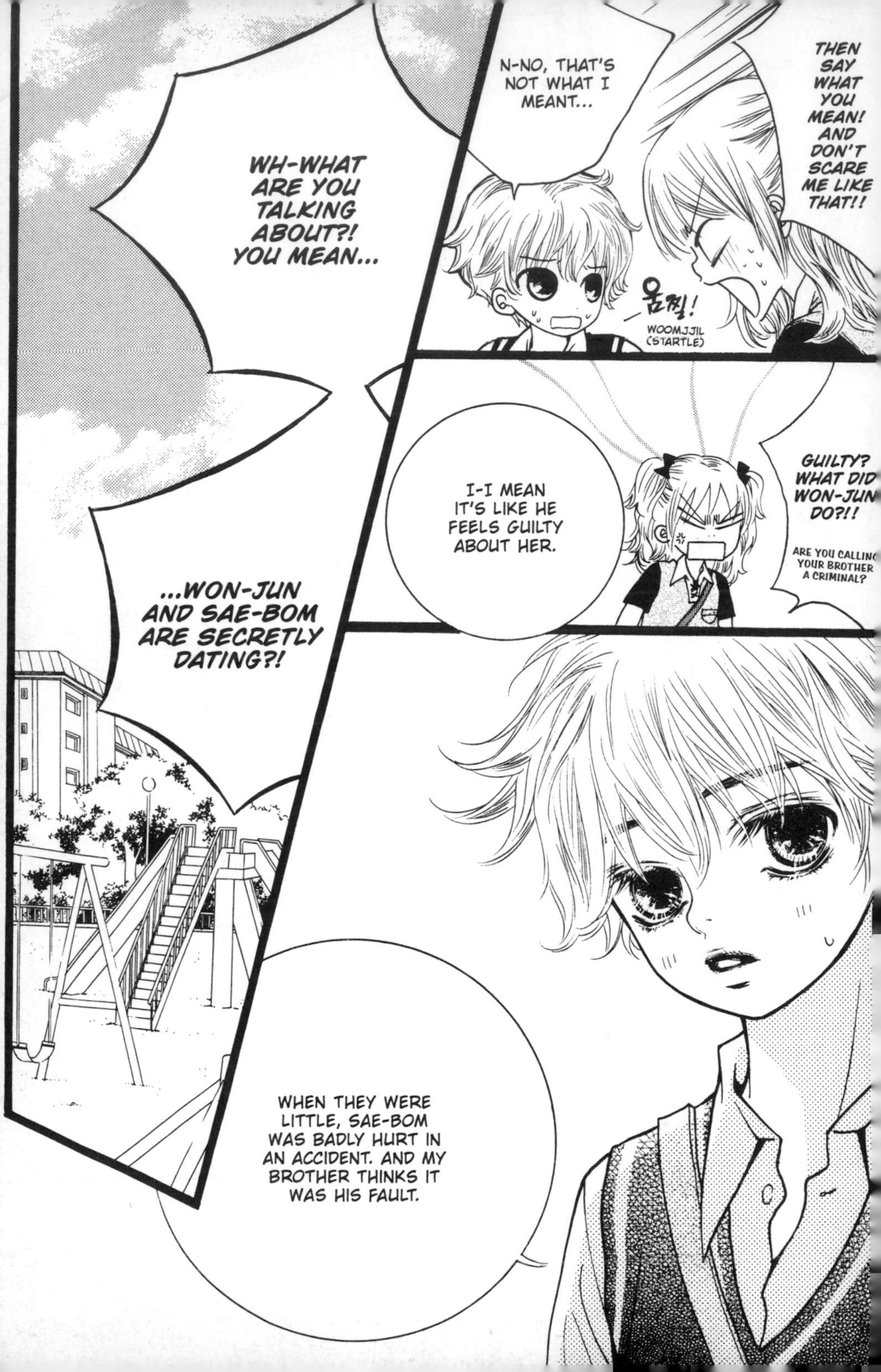
WH-WHAT ARE YOU TALKING ABOUT?! YOU MEAN...
...WON-JUN AND SAE-BOM ARE SECRETLY DATING?!
N-NO, THAT'S NOT WHAT I MEANT...
THEN SAY WHAT YOU MEAN! AND DON'T SCARE ME LIKE THAT!!
움찔!
WOOMJJIL (STARTLE)
I-I MEAN IT'S LIKE HE FEELS GUILTY ABOUT HER.
GUILTY? WHAT DID WON-JUN DO?!!
ARE YOU CALLING YOUR BROTHER A CRIMINAL?
WHEN THEY WERE LITTLE, SAE-BOM WAS BADLY HURT IN AN ACCIDENT. AND MY BROTHER THINKS IT WAS HIS FAULT.

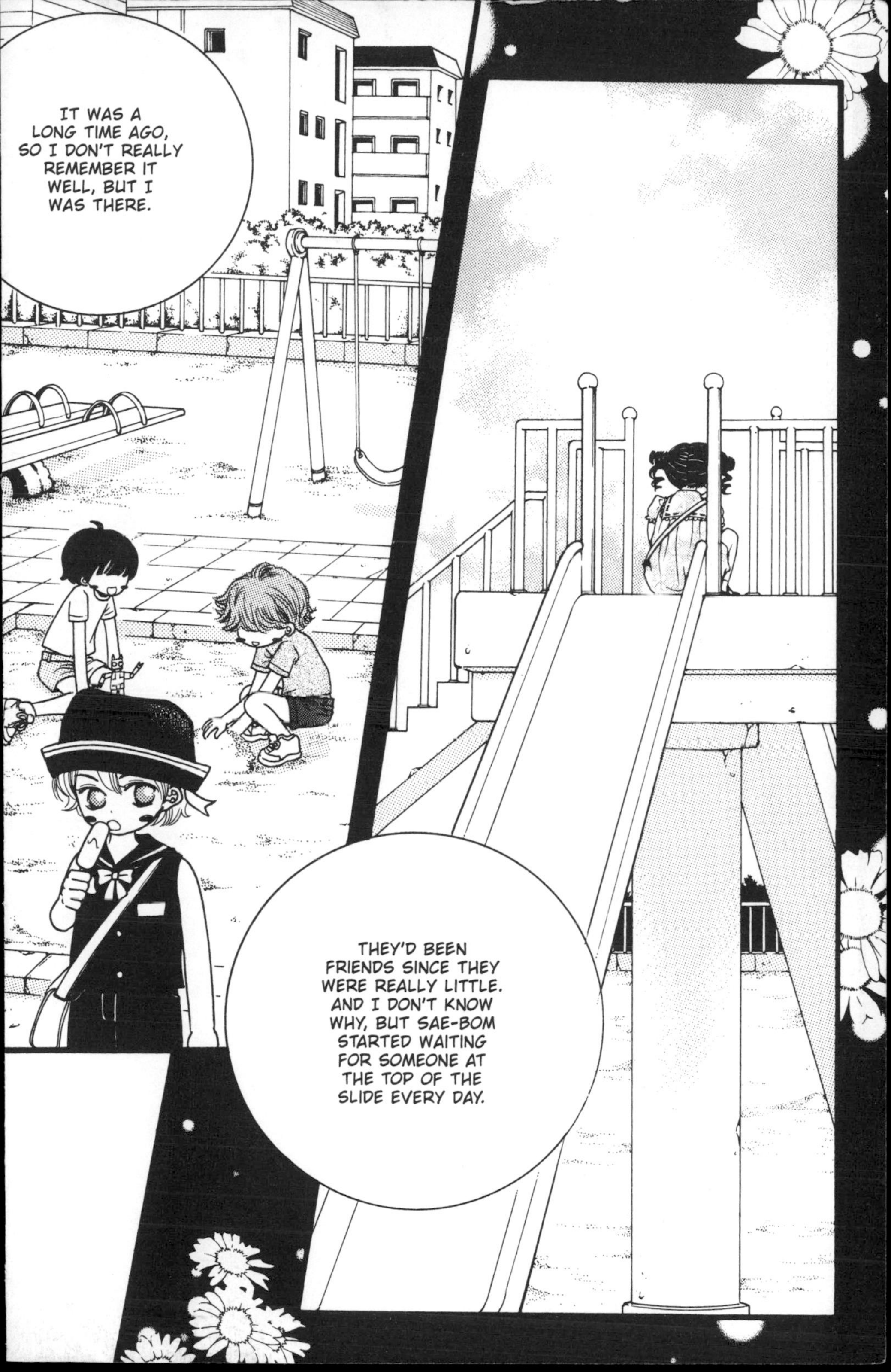
IT WAS A LONG TIME AGO, SO I DON'T REALLY REMEMBER IT WELL, BUT I WAS THERE.
THEY'D BEEN FRIENDS SINCE THEY WERE REALLY LITTLE. AND I DON'T KNOW WHY, BUT SAE-BOM STARTED WAITING FOR SOMEONE AT THE TOP OF THE SLIDE EVERY DAY.

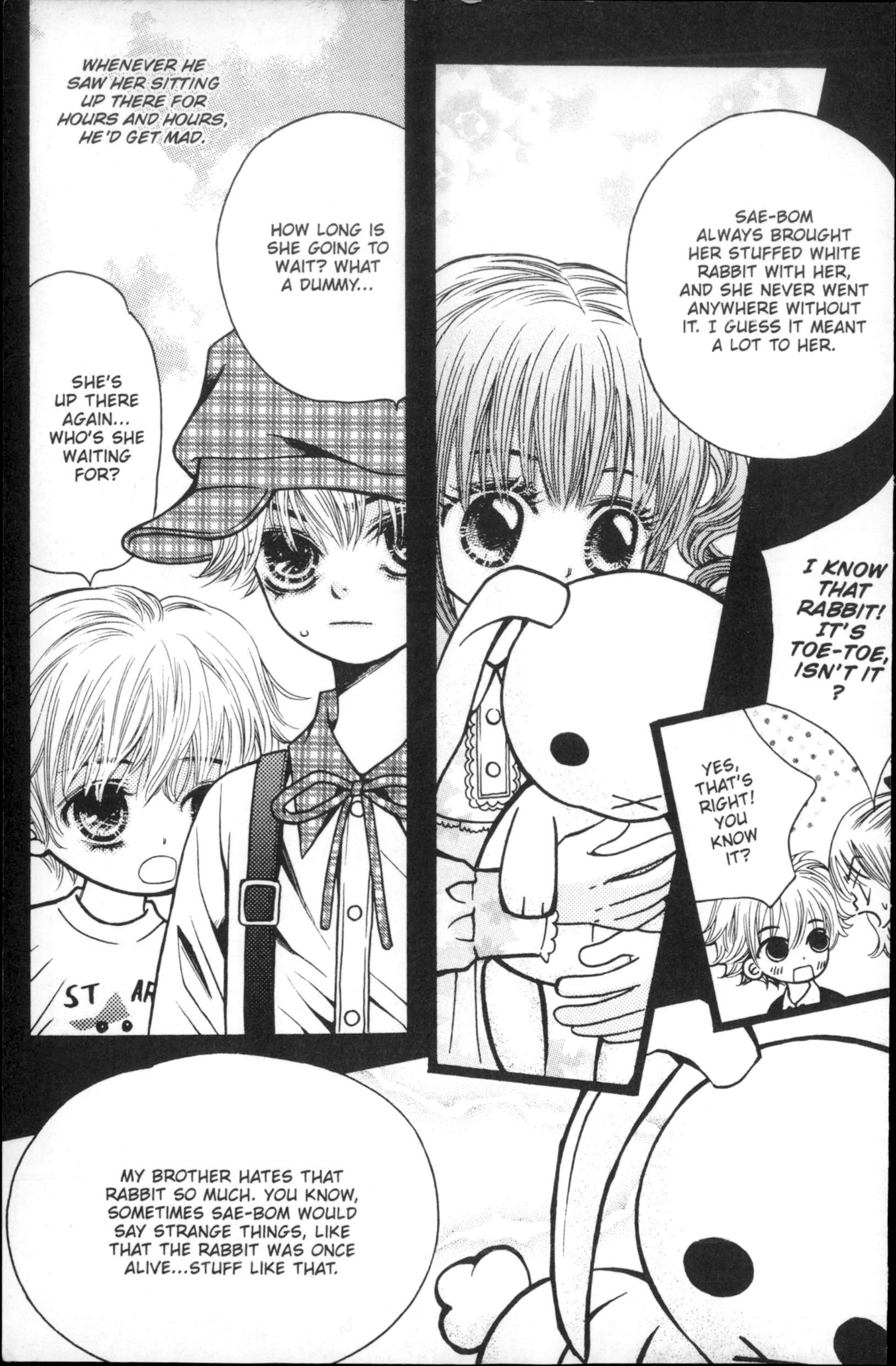
WHENEVER HE SAW HER SITTING UP THERE FOR HOURS AND HOURS, HE'D GET MAD.
HOW LONG IS SHE GOING TO WAIT? WHAT A DUMMY...
SHE'S UP THERE AGAIN... WHO'S SHE WAITING FOR?
SAE-BOM ALWAYS BROUGHT HER STUFFED WHITE RABBIT WITH HER, AND SHE NEVER WENT ANYWHERE WITHOUT IT. I GUESS IT MEANT A LOT TO HER.
I KNOW THAT RABBIT! IT'S TOE-TOE, ISN'T IT?
YES, THAT'S RIGHT! YOU KNOW IT?
MY BROTHER HATES THAT RABBIT SO MUCH. YOU KNOW, SOMETIMES SAE-BOM WOULD SAY STRANGE THINGS, LIKE THAT THE RABBIT WAS ONCE ALIVE...STUFF LIKE THAT.

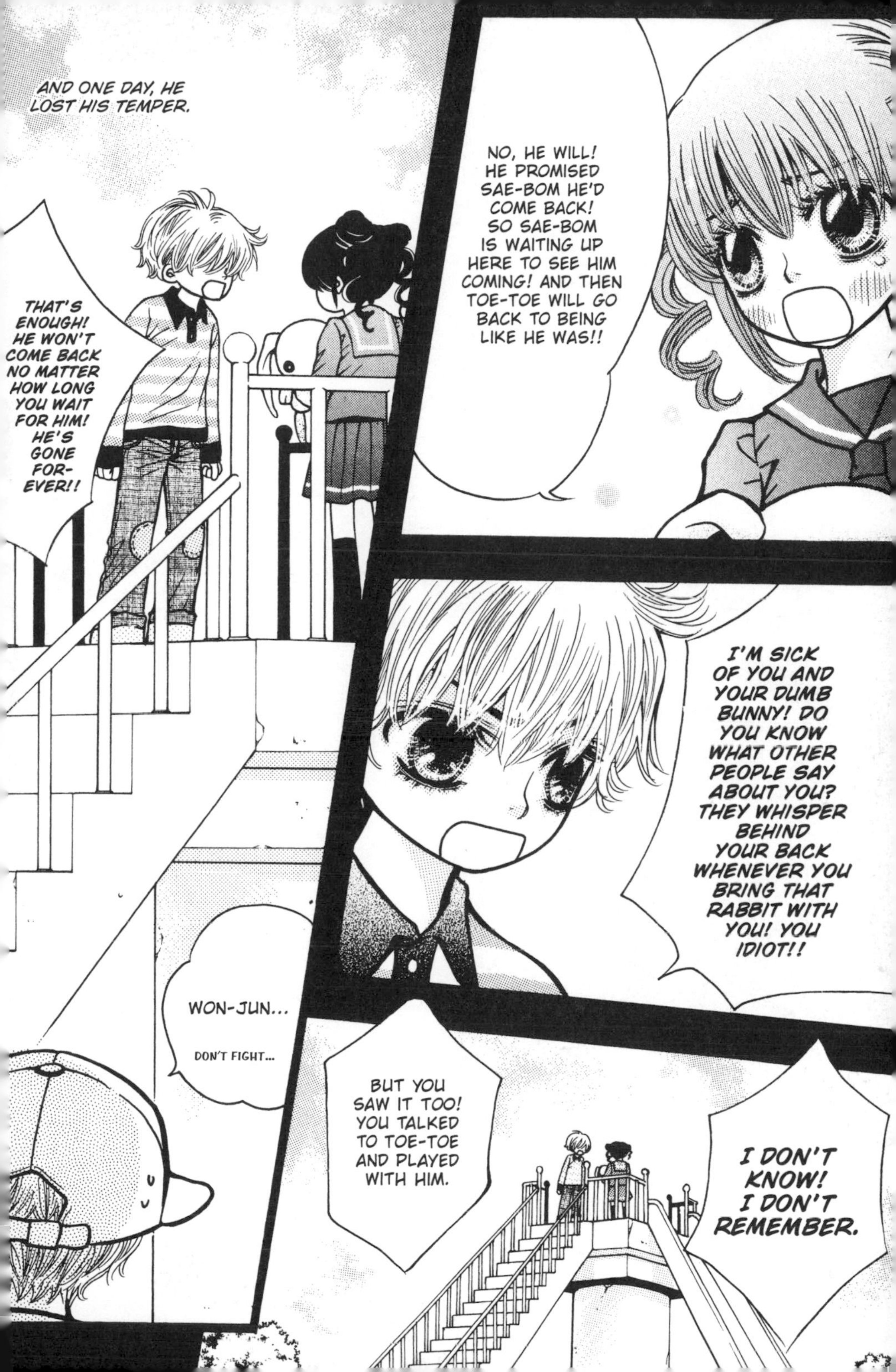

AND ONE DAY, HE LOST HIS TEMPER.
THAT'S ENOUGH! HE WON'T COME BACK NO MATTER HOW LONG YOU WAIT FOR HIM! HE'S GONE FOR-EVER!!
NO, HE WILL! HE PROMISED SAE-BOM HE'D COME BACK! SO SAE-BOM IS WAITING UP HERE TO SEE HIM COMING! AND THEN TOE-TOE WILL GO BACK TO BEING LIKE HE WAS!!
I'M SICK OF YOU AND YOUR DUMB BUNNY! DO YOU KNOW WHAT OTHER PEOPLE SAY ABOUT YOU? THEY WHISPER BEHIND YOUR BACK WHENEVER YOU BRING THAT RABBIT WITH YOU! YOU IDIOT!!
WON-JUN...
DON'T FIGHT...
BUT YOU SAW IT TOO! YOU TALKED TO TOE-TOE AND PLAYED WITH HIM.
I DON'T KNOW! I DON'T REMEMBER.

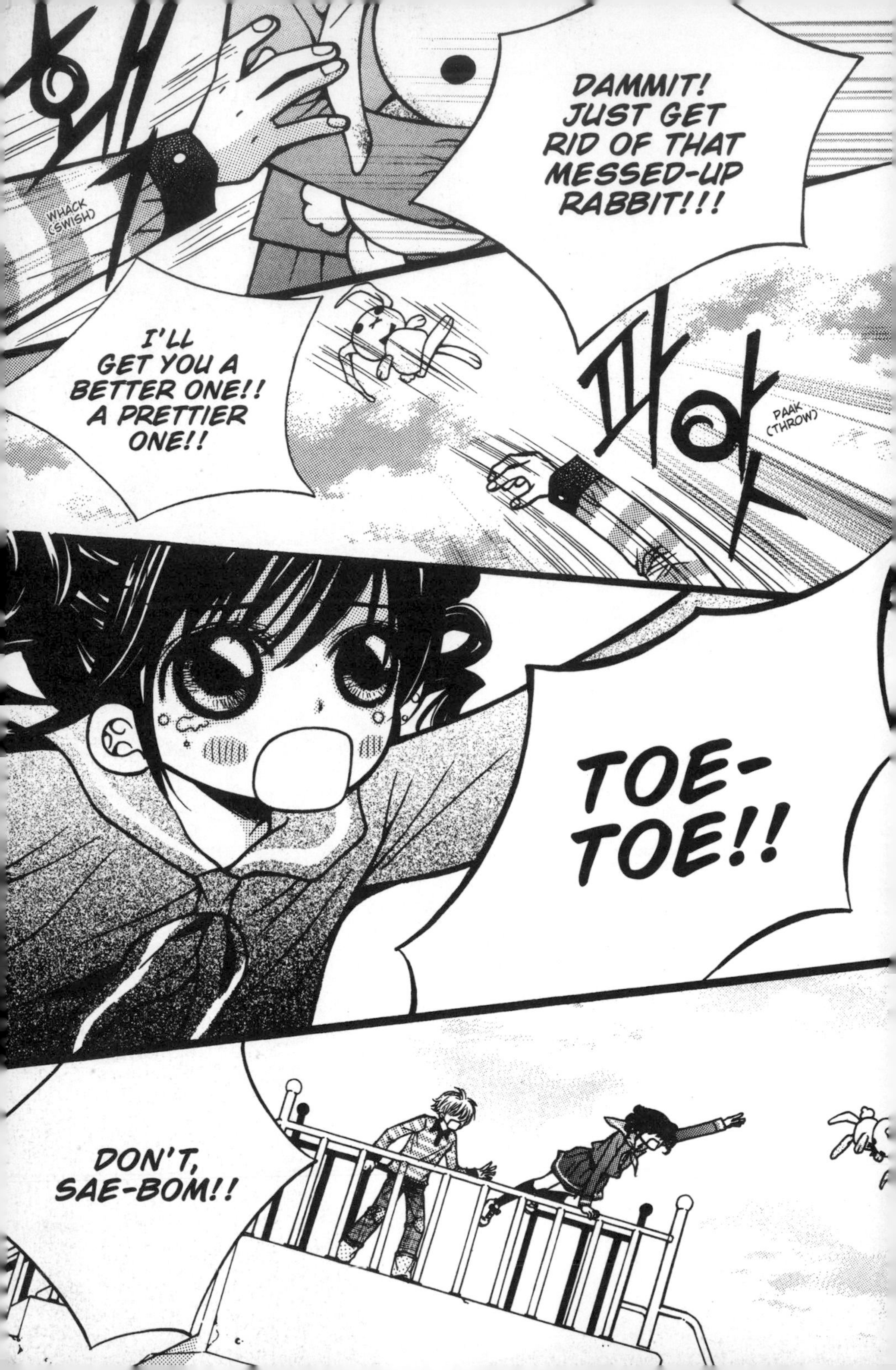

WHACK (SWISH)
DAMMIT! JUST GET RID OF THAT MESSED-UP RABBIT!!!
I'LL GET YOU A BETTER ONE!! A PRETTIER ONE!!
PAAK (THROW)
TOE-TOE!!
DON'T, SAE-BOM!!

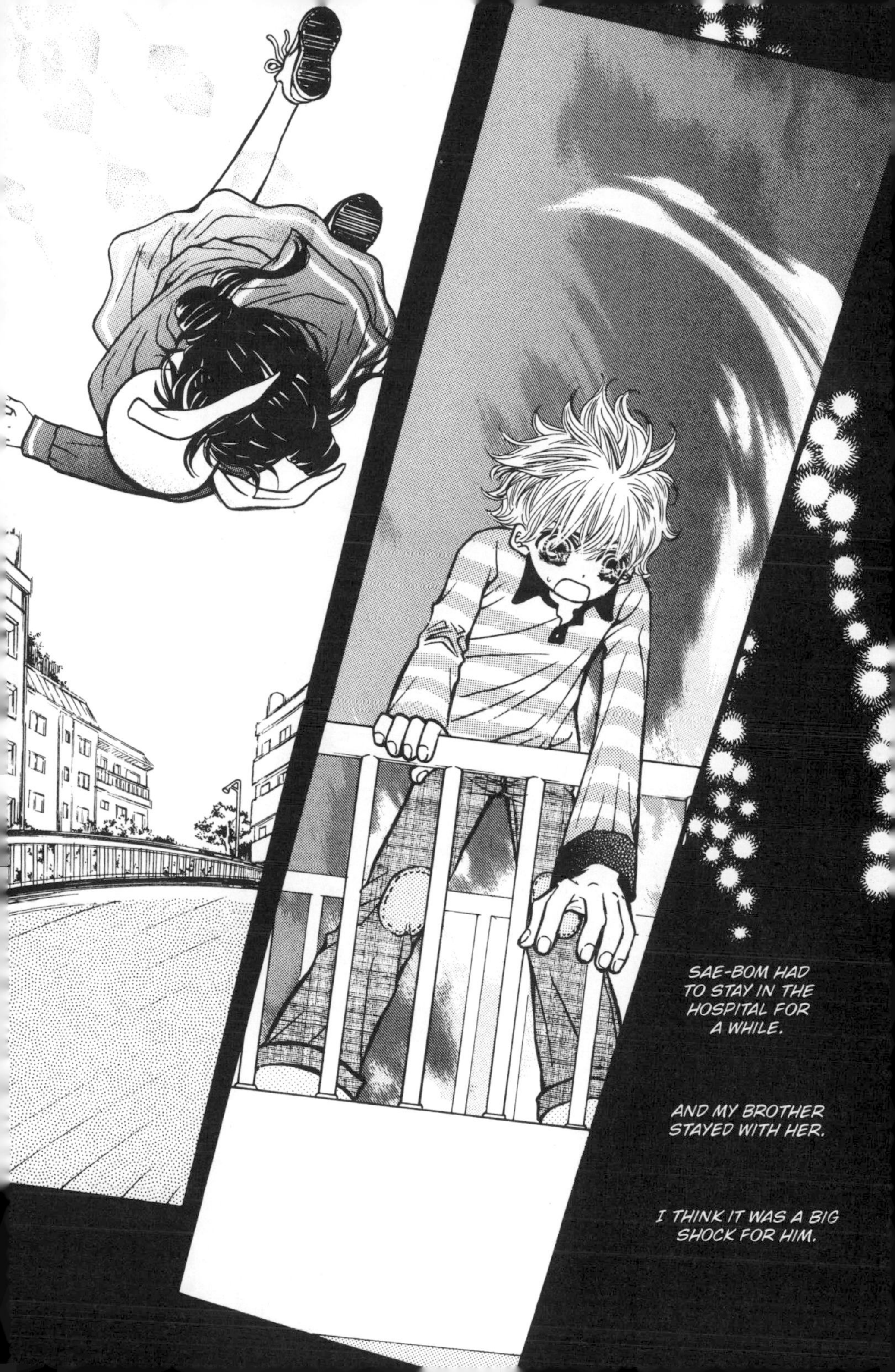
SAE-BOM HAD TO STAY IN THE HOSPITAL FOR A WHILE.
AND MY BROTHER STAYED WITH HER.
I THINK IT WAS A BIG SHOCK FOR HIM.

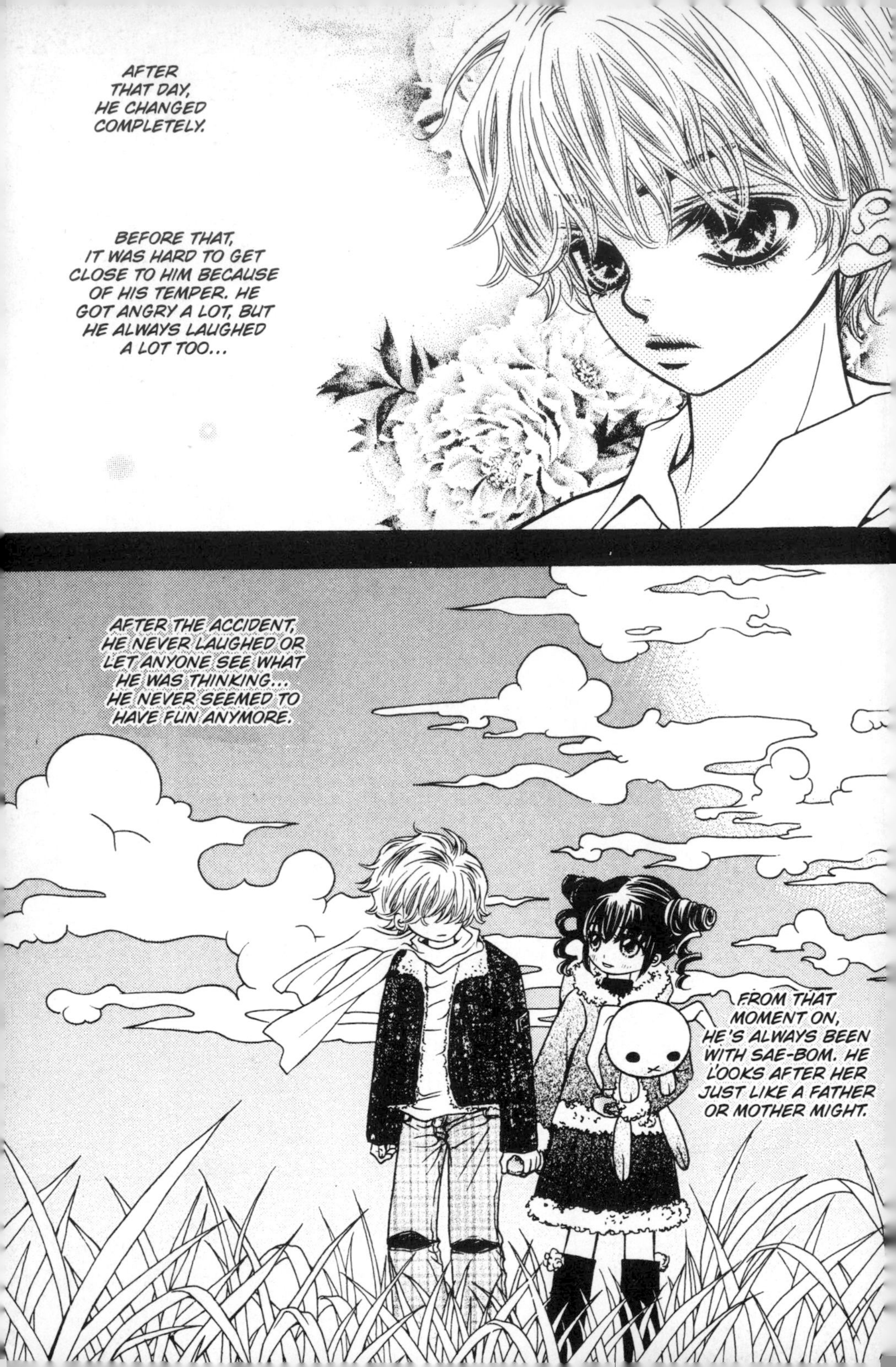
AFTER THAT DAY, HE CHANGED COMPLETELY.
BEFORE THAT, IT WAS HARD TO GET CLOSE TO HIM BECAUSE OF HIS TEMPER. HE GOT ANGRY A LOT, BUT HE ALWAYS LAUGHED A LOT TOO...
AFTER THE ACCIDENT, HE NEVER LAUGHED OR LET ANYONE SEE WHAT HE WAS THINKING... HE NEVER SEEMED TO HAVE FUN ANYMORE.
FROM THAT MOMENT ON, HE'S ALWAYS BEEN WITH SAE-BOM. HE LOOKS AFTER HER JUST LIKE A FATHER OR MOTHER MIGHT.

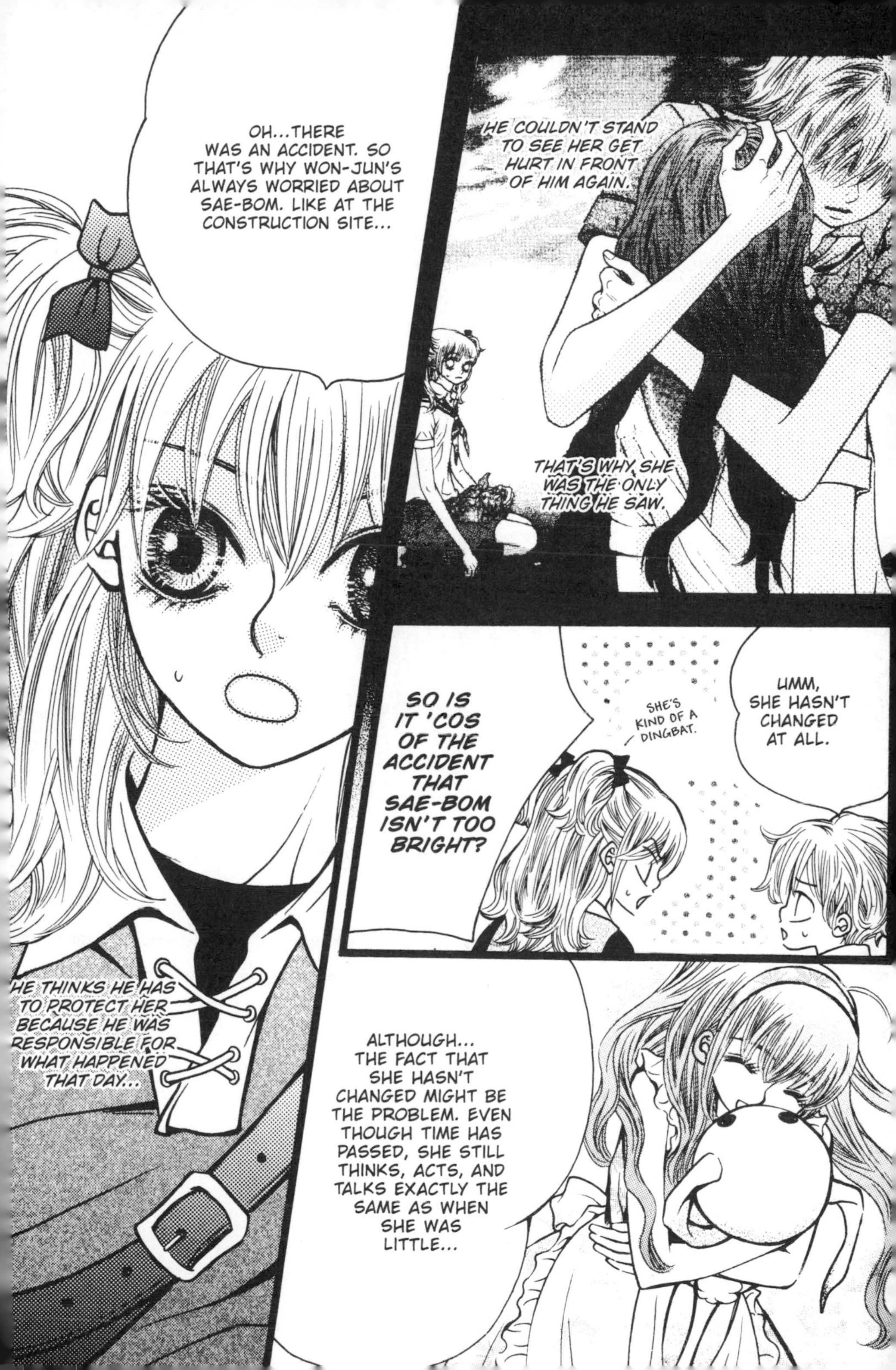
OH...THERE WAS AN ACCIDENT. SO THAT'S WHY WON-JUN'S ALWAYS WORRIED ABOUT SAE-BOM. LIKE AT THE CONSTRUCTION SITE...
HE THINKS HE HAS TO PROTECT HER BECAUSE HE WAS RESPONSIBLE FOR WHAT HAPPENED THAT DAY...
HE COULDN'T STAND TO SEE HER GET HURT IN FRONT OF HIM AGAIN.
THAT'S WHY SHE WAS THE ONLY THING HE SAW.
SO IS IT 'COS OF THE ACCIDENT THAT SAE-BOM ISN'T TOO BRIGHT?
SHE'S KIND OF A DINGBAT.
UMM, SHE HASN'T CHANGED AT ALL.
ALTHOUGH... THE FACT THAT SHE HASN'T CHANGED MIGHT BE THE PROBLEM. EVEN THOUGH TIME HAS PASSED, SHE STILL THINKS, ACTS, AND TALKS EXACTLY THE SAME AS WHEN SHE WAS LITTLE...

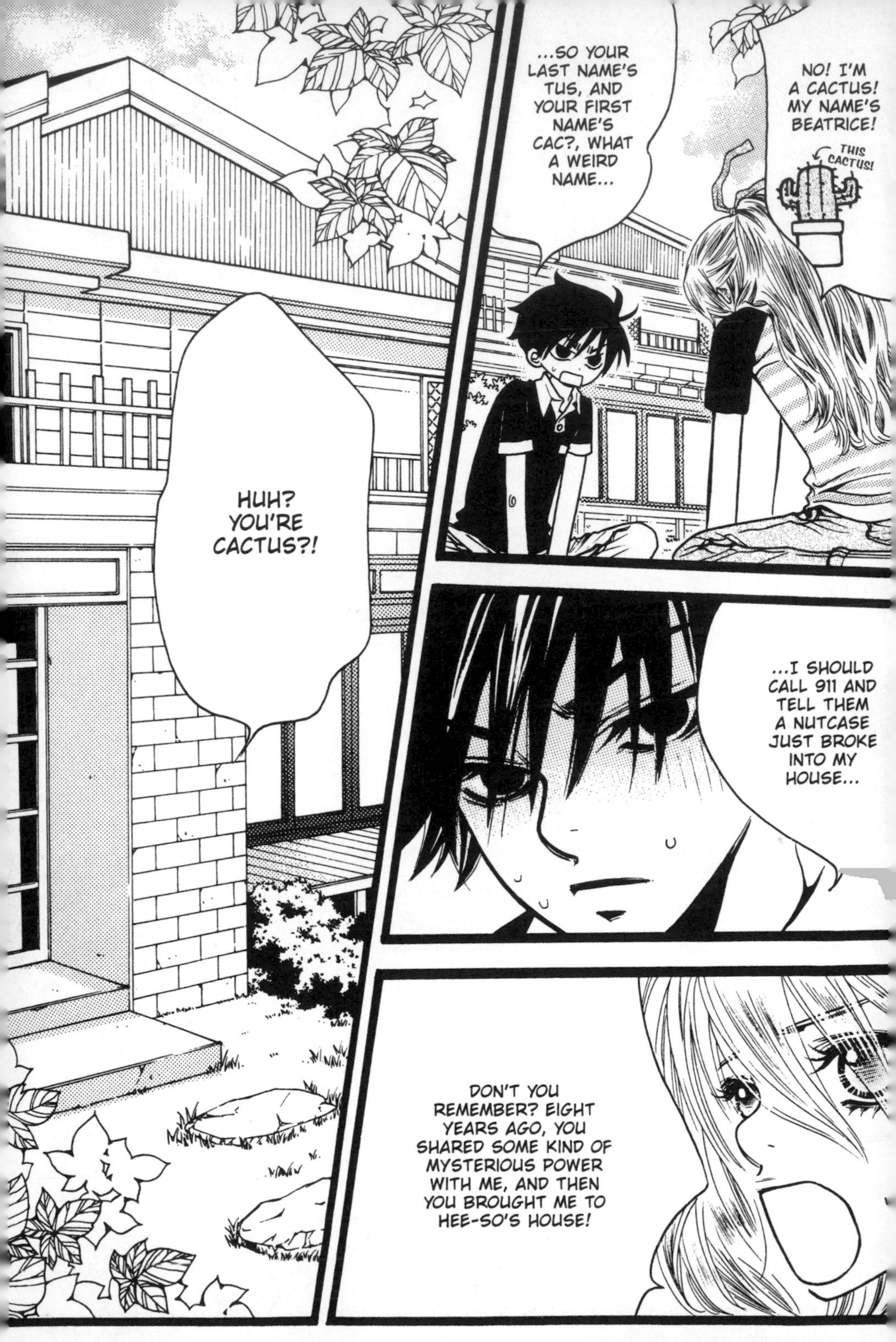
HUH? YOU'RE CACTUS?!
...SO YOUR LAST NAME'S TUS, AND YOUR FIRST NAME'S CAC?, WHAT A WEIRD NAME...
NO! I'M A CACTUS! MY NAME'S BEATRICE!
THIS CACTUS!
...I SHOULD CALL 911 AND TELL THEM A NUTCASE JUST BROKE INTO MY HOUSE...
DON'T YOU REMEMBER? EIGHT YEARS AGO, YOU SHARED SOME KIND OF MYSTERIOUS POWER WITH ME, AND THEN YOU BROUGHT ME TO HEE-SO'S HOUSE!

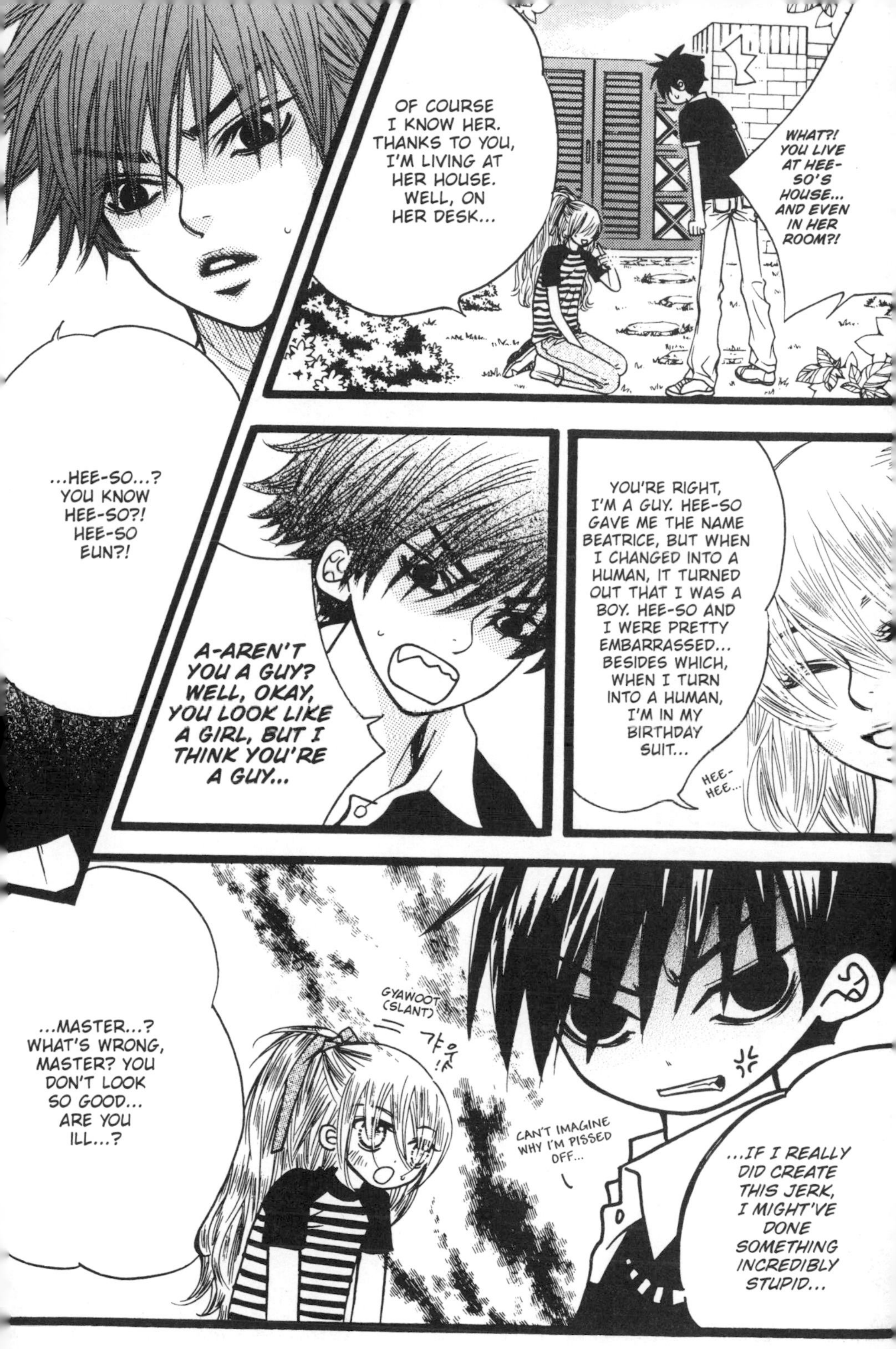
...HEE-SO...? YOU KNOW HEE-SO?! HEE-SO EUN?!
OF COURSE I KNOW HER. THANKS TO YOU, I'M LIVING AT HER HOUSE. WELL, ON HER DESK...
WHAT?! YOU LIVE AT HEE-SO'S HOUSE... AND EVEN IN HER ROOM?!
A-AREN'T YOU A GUY? WELL, OKAY, YOU LOOK LIKE A GIRL, BUT I THINK YOU'RE A GUY...
YOU'RE RIGHT, I'M A GUY. HEE-SO GAVE ME THE NAME BEATRICE, BUT WHEN I CHANGED INTO A HUMAN, IT TURNED OUT THAT I WAS A BOY. HEE-SO AND I WERE PRETTY EMBARRASSED... BESIDES WHICH, WHEN I TURN INTO A HUMAN, I'M IN MY BIRTHDAY SUIT...
HEE-HEE...
...MASTER...? WHAT'S WRONG, MASTER? YOU DON'T LOOK SO GOOD... ARE YOU ILL...?
GYAWOOT (SLANT)
갸웃
CAN'T IMAGINE WHY I'M PISSED OFF...
...IF I REALLY DID CREATE THIS JERK, I MIGHT'VE DONE SOMETHING INCREDIBLY STUPID...

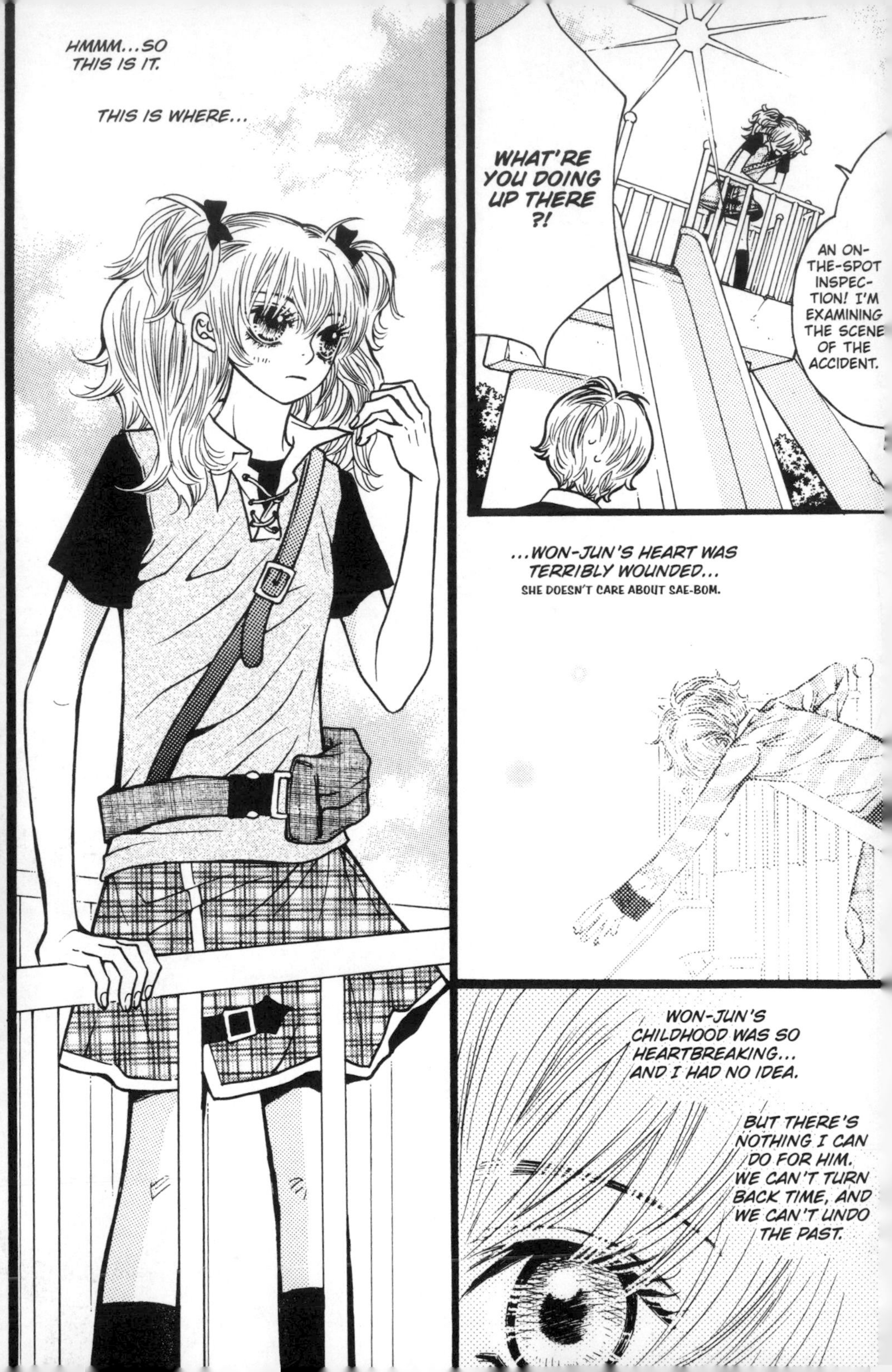
HMMM...SO THIS IS IT.
THIS IS WHERE...
WHAT'RE YOU DOING UP THERE ?!
AN ON-THE-SPOT INSPECTION! I'M EXAMINING THE SCENE OF THE ACCIDENT.
...WON-JUN'S HEART WAS TERRIBLY WOUNDED...
SHE DOESN'T CARE ABOUT SAE-BOM.
WON-JUN'S CHILDHOOD WAS SO HEARTBREAKING... AND I HAD NO IDEA.
BUT THERE'S NOTHING I CAN DO FOR HIM. WE CAN'T TURN BACK TIME, AND WE CAN'T UNDO THE PAST.

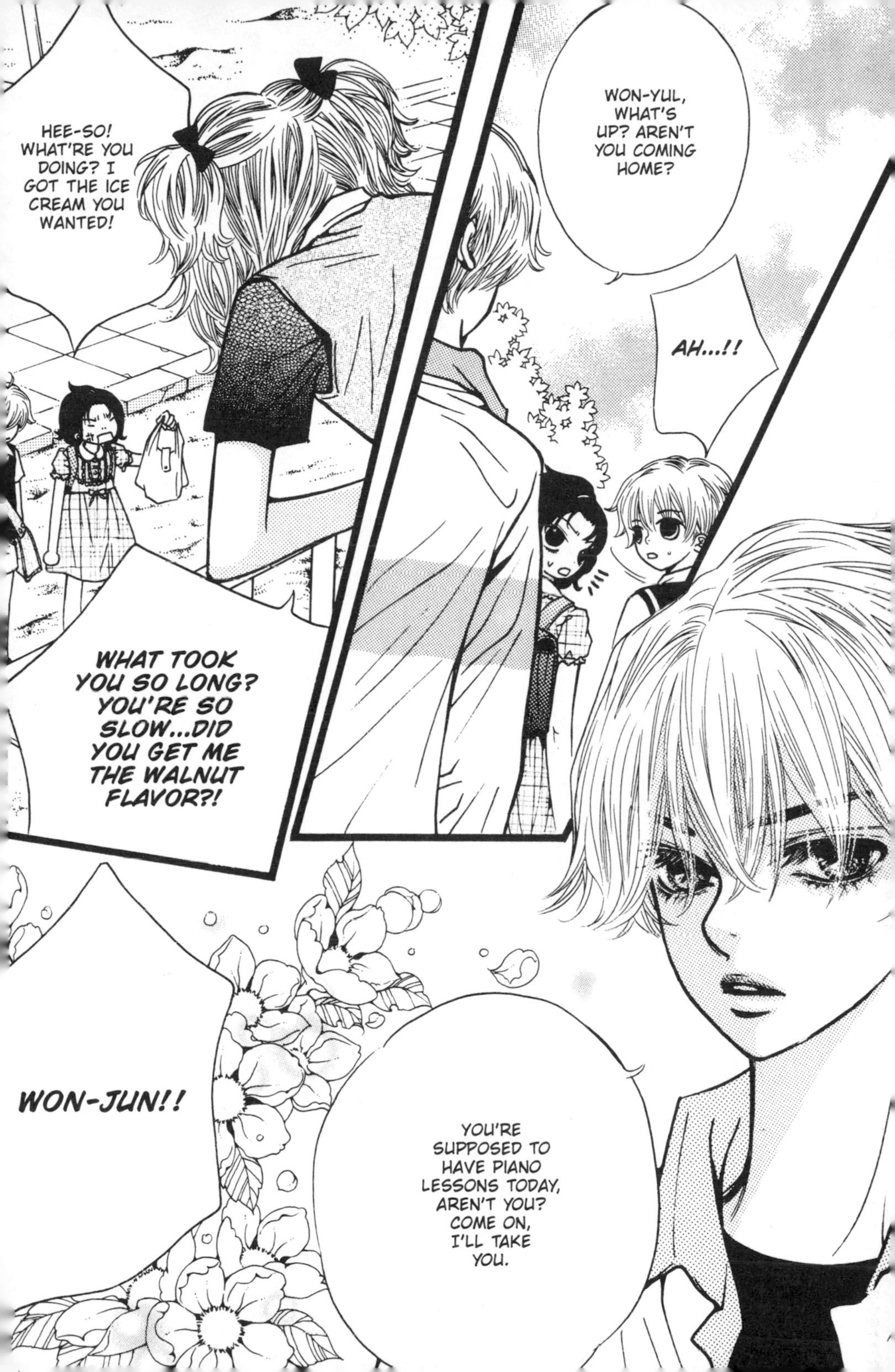
HEE-SO! WHAT'RE YOU DOING? I GOT THE ICE CREAM YOU WANTED!
WHAT TOOK YOU SO LONG? YOU'RE SO SLOW...DID YOU GET ME THE WALNUT FLAVOR?!
WON-YUL, WHAT'S UP? AREN'T YOU COMING HOME?
AH...!!
WON-JUN!!
YOU'RE SUPPOSED TO HAVE PIANO LESSONS TODAY, AREN'T YOU? COME ON, I'LL TAKE YOU.

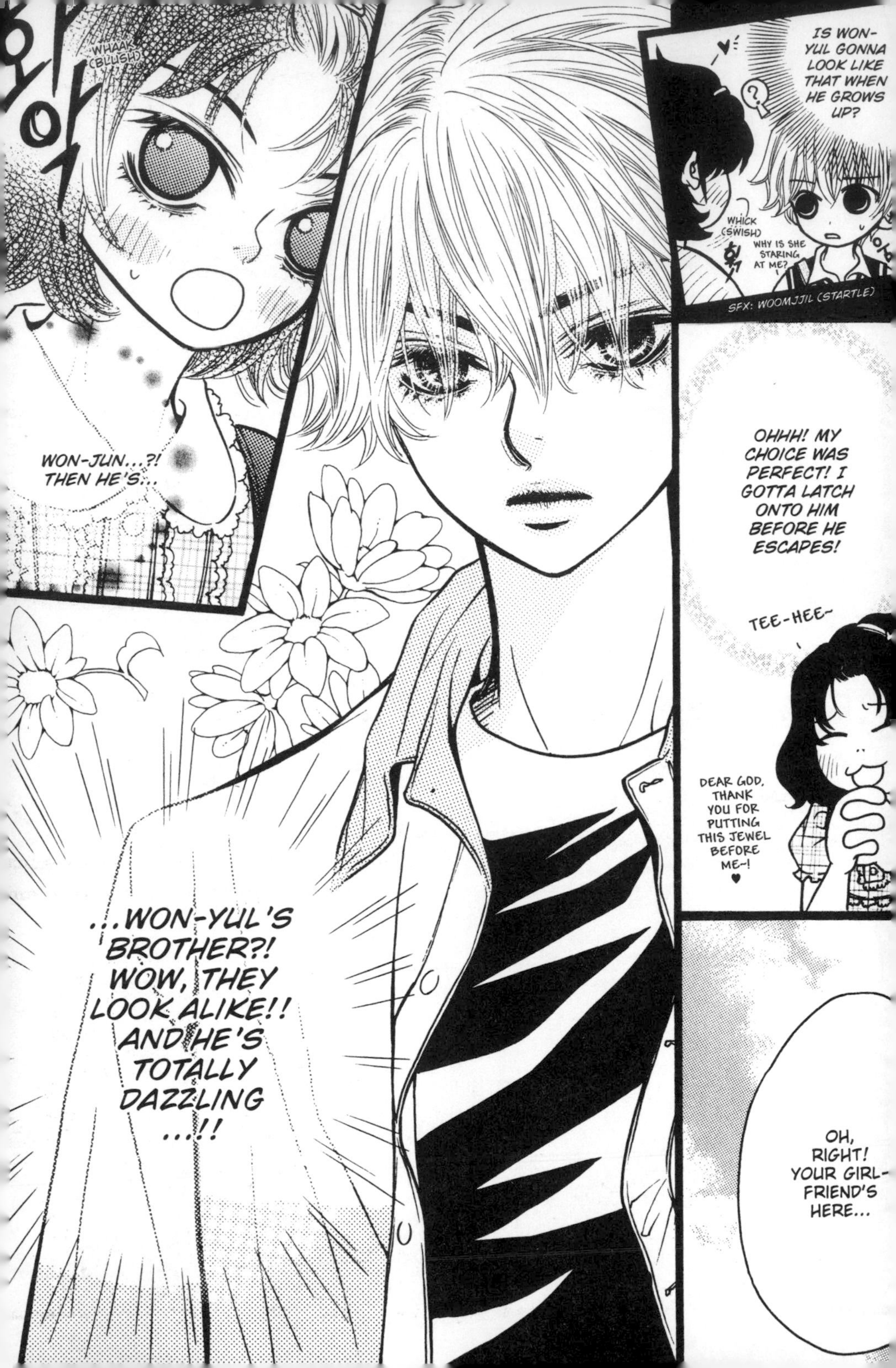
WHAAK (BLUSH)
WON-JUN...?! THEN HE'S...
...WON-YUL'S BROTHER?! WOW, THEY LOOK ALIKE!! AND HE'S TOTALLY DAZZLING ...!!
IS WON-YUL GONNA LOOK LIKE THAT WHEN HE GROWS UP?
WHICK (SWISH)
WHY IS SHE STARING AT ME?
SFX: WOOMJJIL (STARTLE)
OHHH! MY CHOICE WAS PERFECT! I GOTTA LATCH ONTO HIM BEFORE HE ESCAPES!
TEE-HEE~
DEAR GOD, THANK YOU FOR PUTTING THIS JEWEL BEFORE ME~! ♥
OH, RIGHT! YOUR GIRL-FRIEND'S HERE...

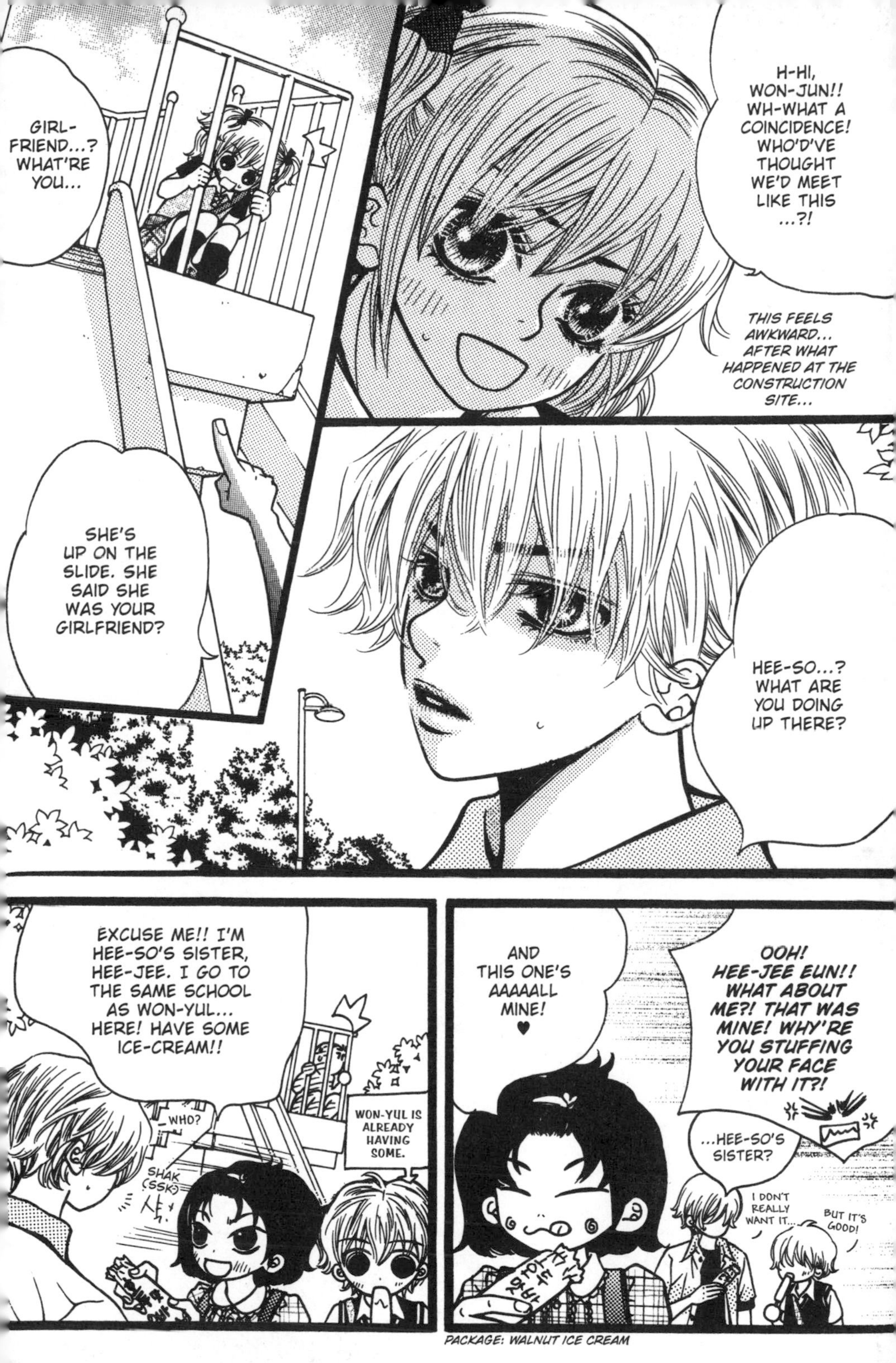
GIRL-FRIEND...? WHAT'RE YOU...
H-HI, WON-JUN!! WH-WHAT A COINCIDENCE! WHO'D'VE THOUGHT WE'D MEET LIKE THIS ...?!
THIS FEELS AWKWARD... AFTER WHAT HAPPENED AT THE CONSTRUCTION SITE...
SHE'S UP ON THE SLIDE. SHE SAID SHE WAS YOUR GIRLFRIEND?
HEE-SO...? WHAT ARE YOU DOING UP THERE?
EXCUSE ME!! I'M HEE-SO'S SISTER, HEE-JEE. I GO TO THE SAME SCHOOL AS WON-YUL... HERE! HAVE SOME ICE-CREAM!!
WHO?
SHAK (SSK)
샥
WON-YUL IS ALREADY HAVING SOME.
AND THIS ONE'S AAAAALL MINE! ♥
OOH! HEE-JEE EUN!! WHAT ABOUT ME?! THAT WAS MINE! WHY'RE YOU STUFFING YOUR FACE WITH IT?!
...HEE-SO'S SISTER?
I DON'T REALLY WANT IT...
BUT IT'S GOOD!
PACKAGE: WALNUT ICE CREAM

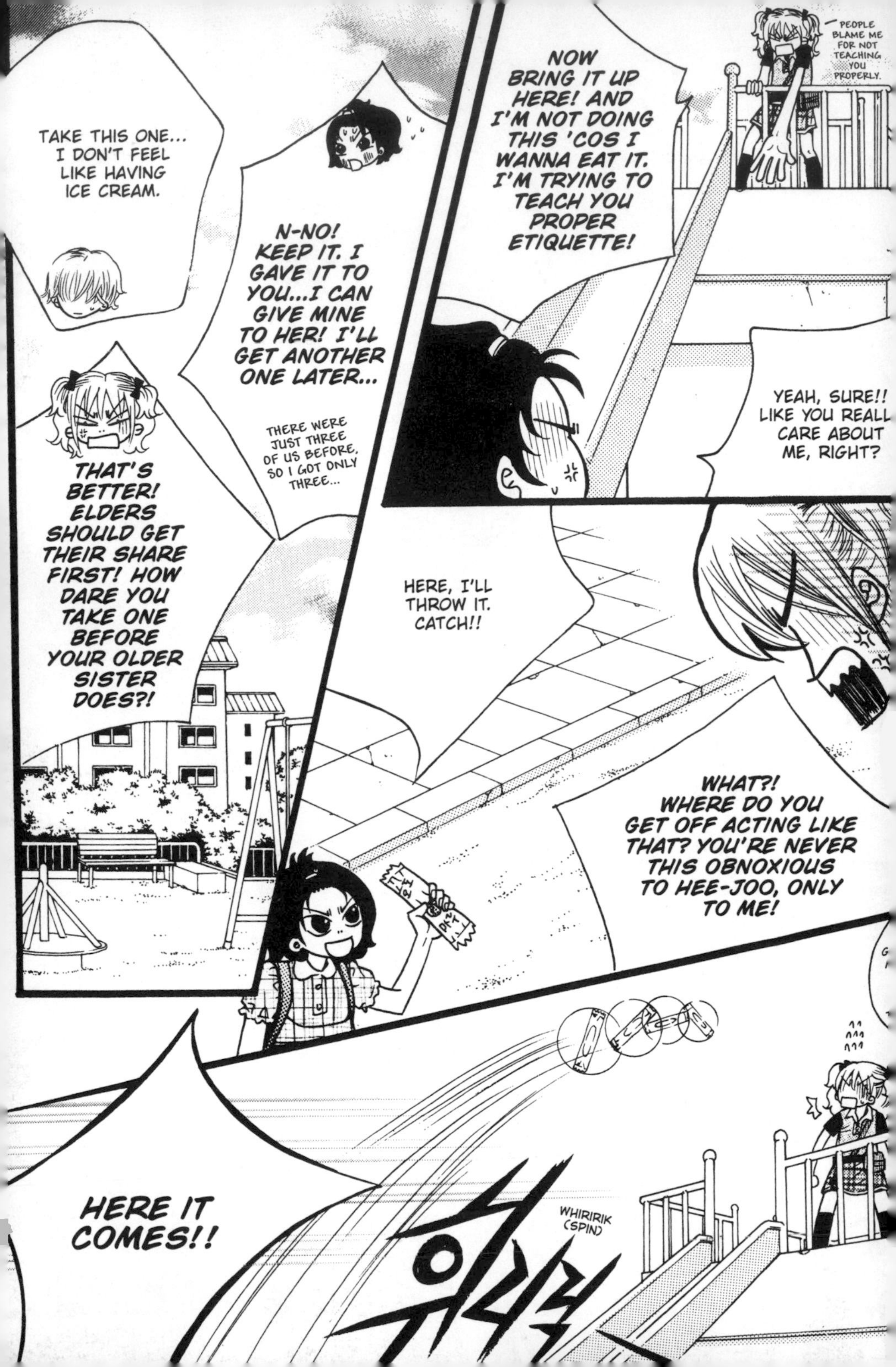
TAKE THIS ONE... I DON'T FEEL LIKE HAVING ICE CREAM.
N-NO! KEEP IT. I GAVE IT TO YOU...I CAN GIVE MINE TO HER! I'LL GET ANOTHER ONE LATER...
THERE WERE JUST THREE OF US BEFORE, SO I GOT ONLY THREE...
THAT'S BETTER! ELDERS SHOULD GET THEIR SHARE FIRST! HOW DARE YOU TAKE ONE BEFORE YOUR OLDER SISTER DOES?!
NOW BRING IT UP HERE! AND I'M NOT DOING THIS 'COS I WANNA EAT IT. I'M TRYING TO TEACH YOU PROPER ETIQUETTE!
PEOPLE BLAME ME FOR NOT TEACHING YOU PROPERLY.
YEAH, SURE!! LIKE YOU REALL CARE ABOUT ME, RIGHT?
HERE, I'LL THROW IT. CATCH!!
WHAT?! WHERE DO YOU GET OFF ACTING LIKE THAT? YOU'RE NEVER THIS OBNOXIOUS TO HEE-JOO, ONLY TO ME!
HERE IT COMES!!
WHIRIRIK (SPIN)

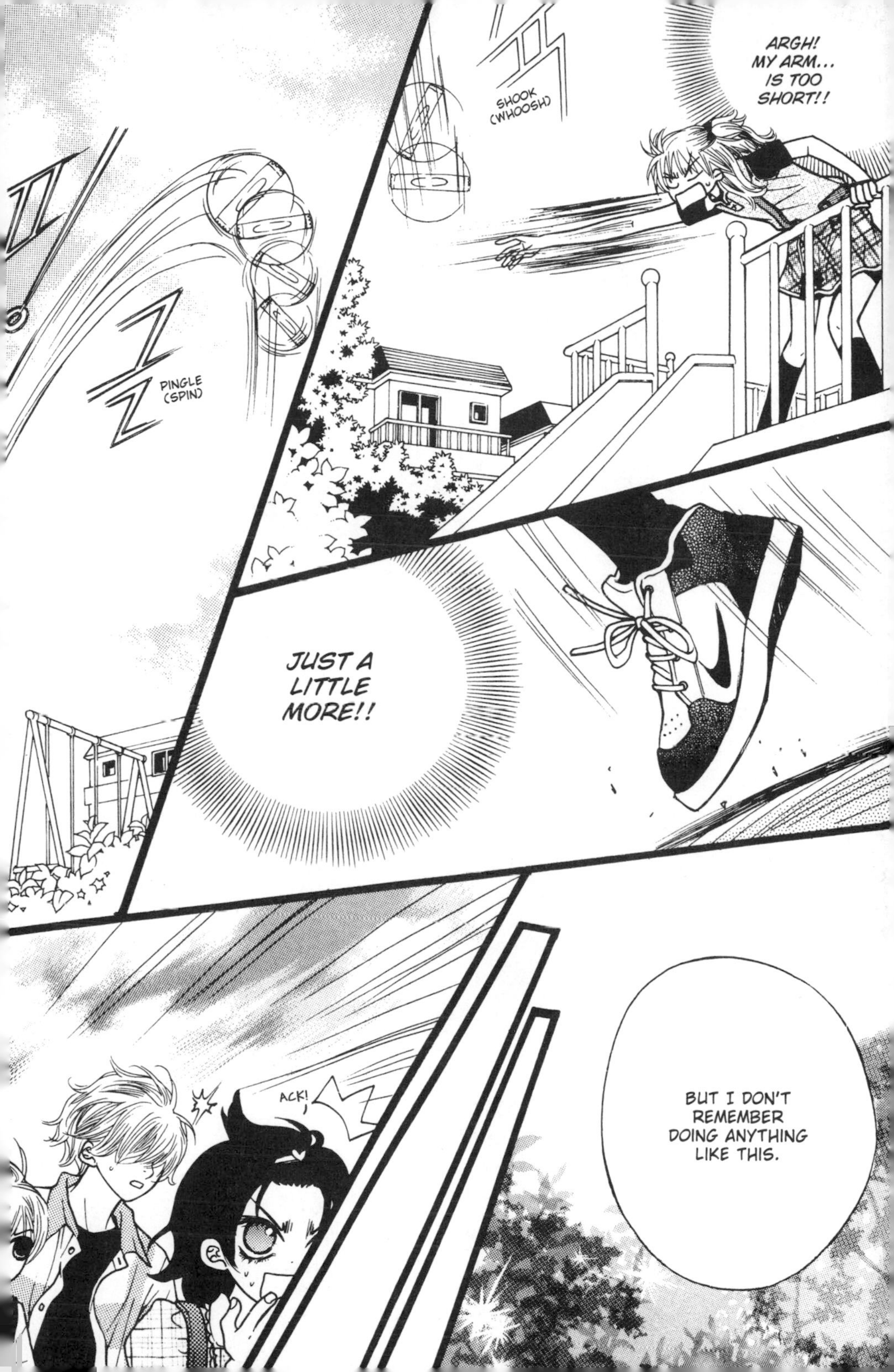
PINGLE
(SPIN)
SHOOK
(WHOOSH)
ARGH!
MY ARM...
IS TOO
SHORT!!
JUST A
LITTLE
MORE!!
ACK!
BUT I DON'T
REMEMBER
DOING ANYTHING
LIKE THIS.

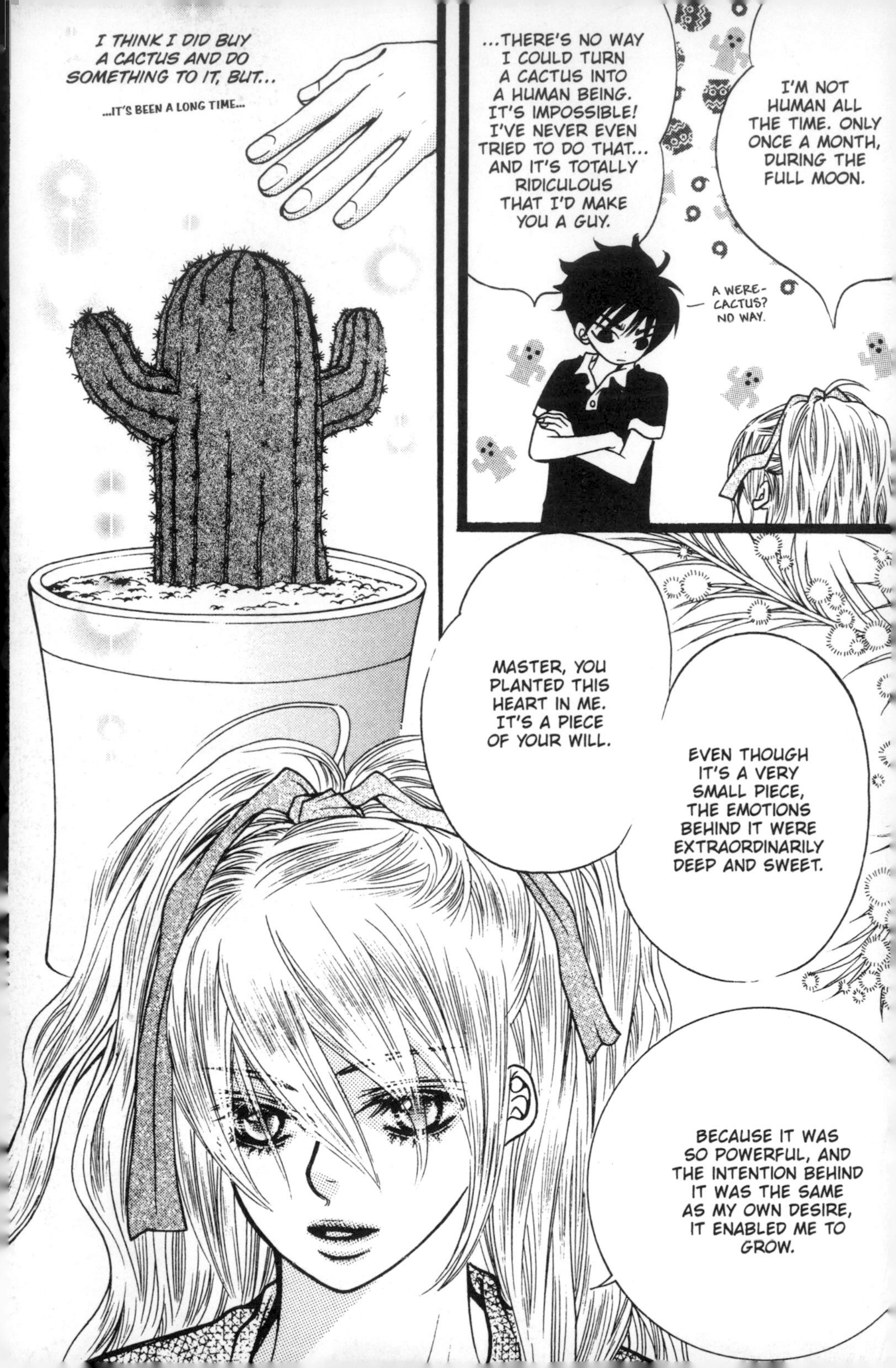
I THINK I DID BUY A CACTUS AND DO SOMETHING TO IT, BUT...
...IT'S BEEN A LONG TIME...
...THERE'S NO WAY I COULD TURN A CACTUS INTO A HUMAN BEING. IT'S IMPOSSIBLE! I'VE NEVER EVEN TRIED TO DO THAT... AND IT'S TOTALLY RIDICULOUS THAT I'D MAKE YOU A GUY.
I'M NOT HUMAN ALL THE TIME. ONLY ONCE A MONTH, DURING THE FULL MOON.
A WERE-CACTUS? NO WAY.
MASTER, YOU PLANTED THIS HEART IN ME. IT'S A PIECE OF YOUR WILL.
EVEN THOUGH IT'S A VERY SMALL PIECE, THE EMOTIONS BEHIND IT WERE EXTRAORDINARILY DEEP AND SWEET.
BECAUSE IT WAS SO POWERFUL, AND THE INTENTION BEHIND IT WAS THE SAME AS MY OWN DESIRE, IT ENABLED ME TO GROW.

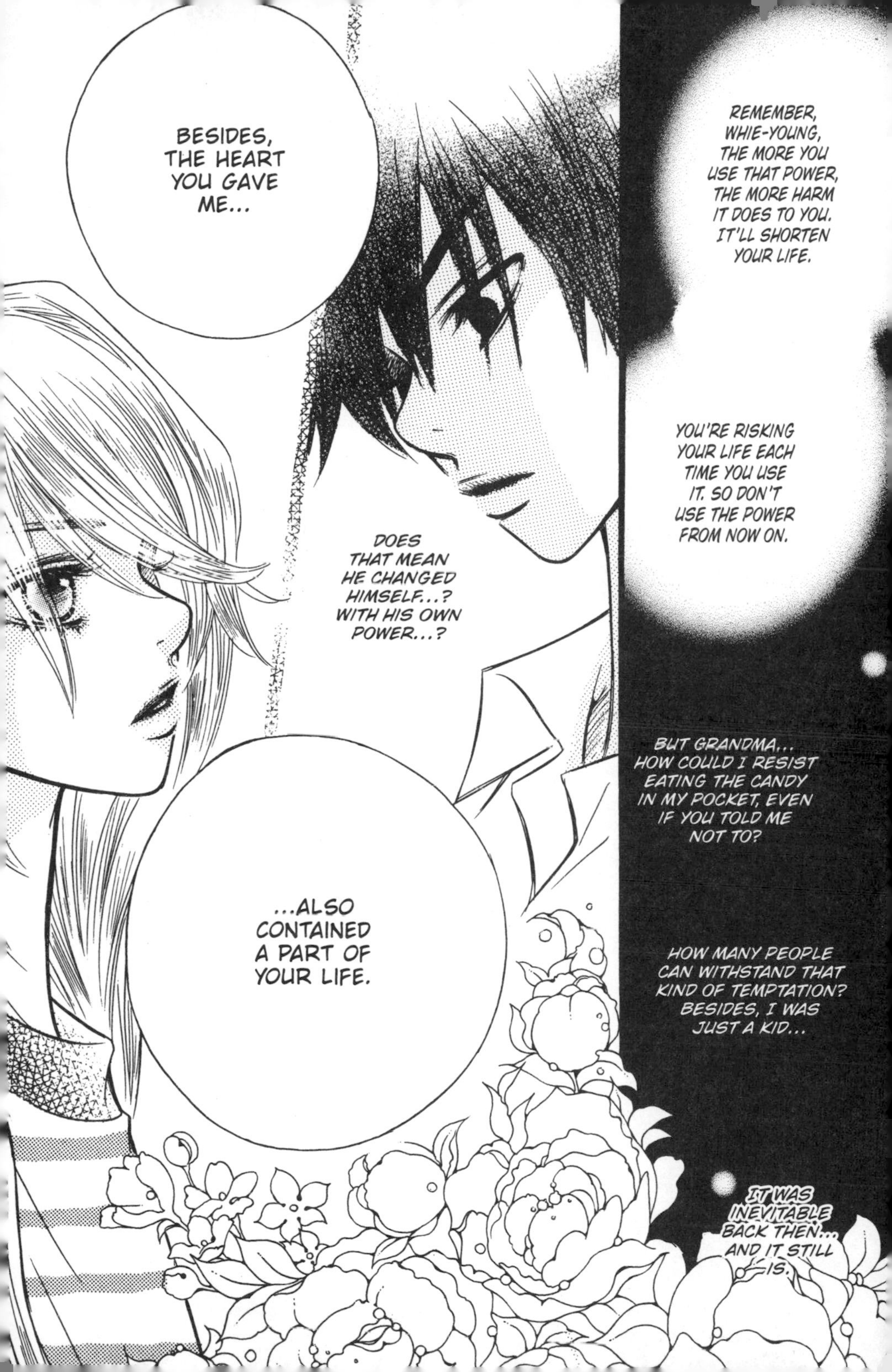
BESIDES, THE HEART YOU GAVE ME...
DOES THAT MEAN HE CHANGED HIMSELF...? WITH HIS OWN POWER...?
...ALSO CONTAINED A PART OF YOUR LIFE.
REMEMBER, WHIE-YOUNG, THE MORE YOU USE THAT POWER, THE MORE HARM IT DOES TO YOU. IT'LL SHORTEN YOUR LIFE.
YOU'RE RISKING YOUR LIFE EACH TIME YOU USE IT. SO DON'T USE THE POWER FROM NOW ON.
BUT GRANDMA... HOW COULD I RESIST EATING THE CANDY IN MY POCKET, EVEN IF YOU TOLD ME NOT TO?
HOW MANY PEOPLE CAN WITHSTAND THAT KIND OF TEMPTATION? BESIDES, I WAS JUST A KID...
IT WAS INEVITABLE BACK THEN... AND IT STILL IS.

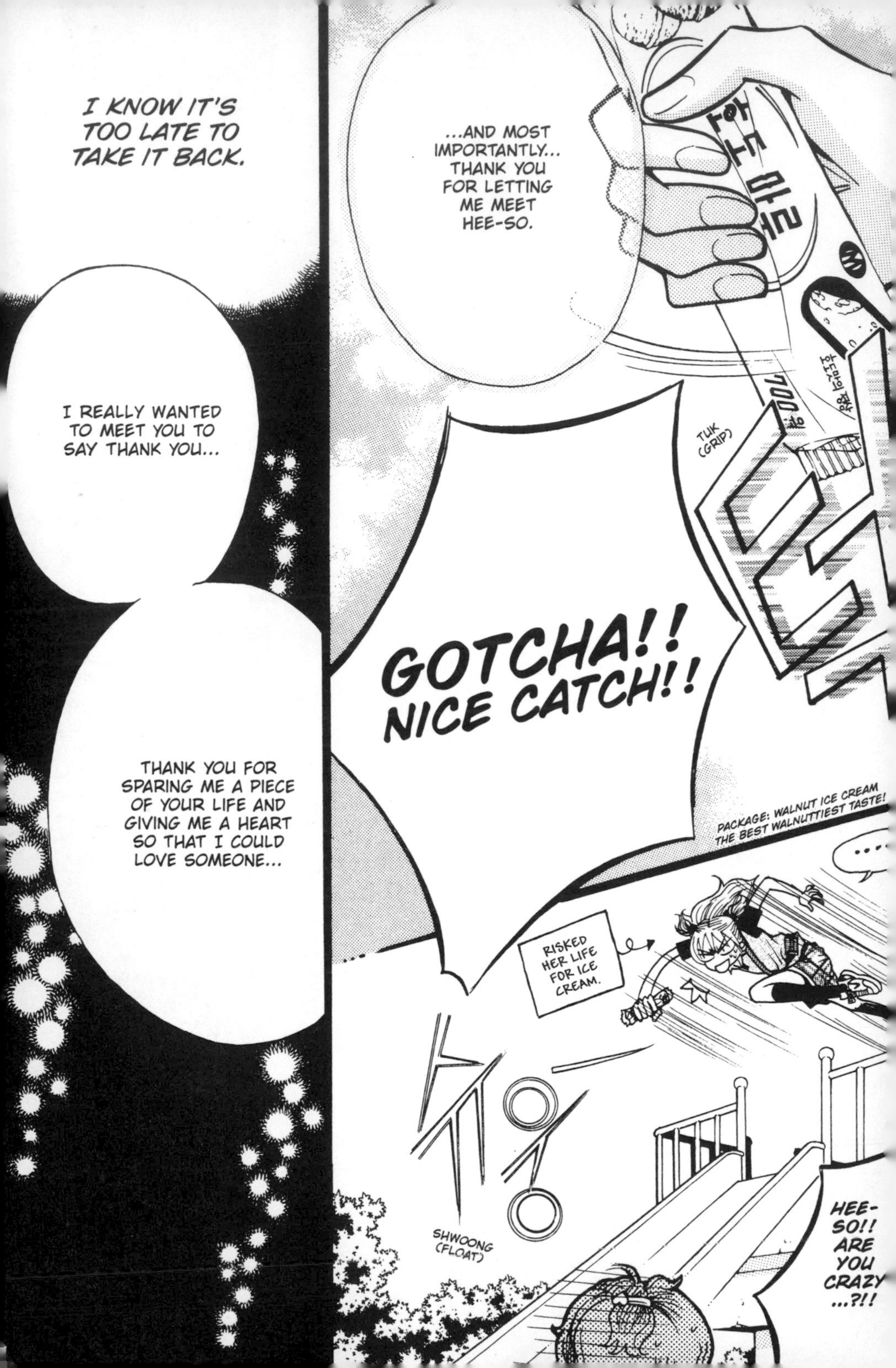

I KNOW IT'S TOO LATE TO TAKE IT BACK.
I REALLY WANTED TO MEET YOU TO SAY THANK YOU...
THANK YOU FOR SPARING ME A PIECE OF YOUR LIFE AND GIVING ME A HEART SO THAT I COULD LOVE SOMEONE...
...AND MOST IMPORTANTLY... THANK YOU FOR LETTING ME MEET HEE-SO.
TUK (GRIP)
GOTCHA!! NICE CATCH!!
PACKAGE: WALNUT ICE CREAM THE BEST WALNUTTIEST TASTE!
....
RISKED HER LIFE FOR ICE CREAM.
SHWOONG (FLOAT)
HEE-SO!! ARE YOU CRAZY...?!!

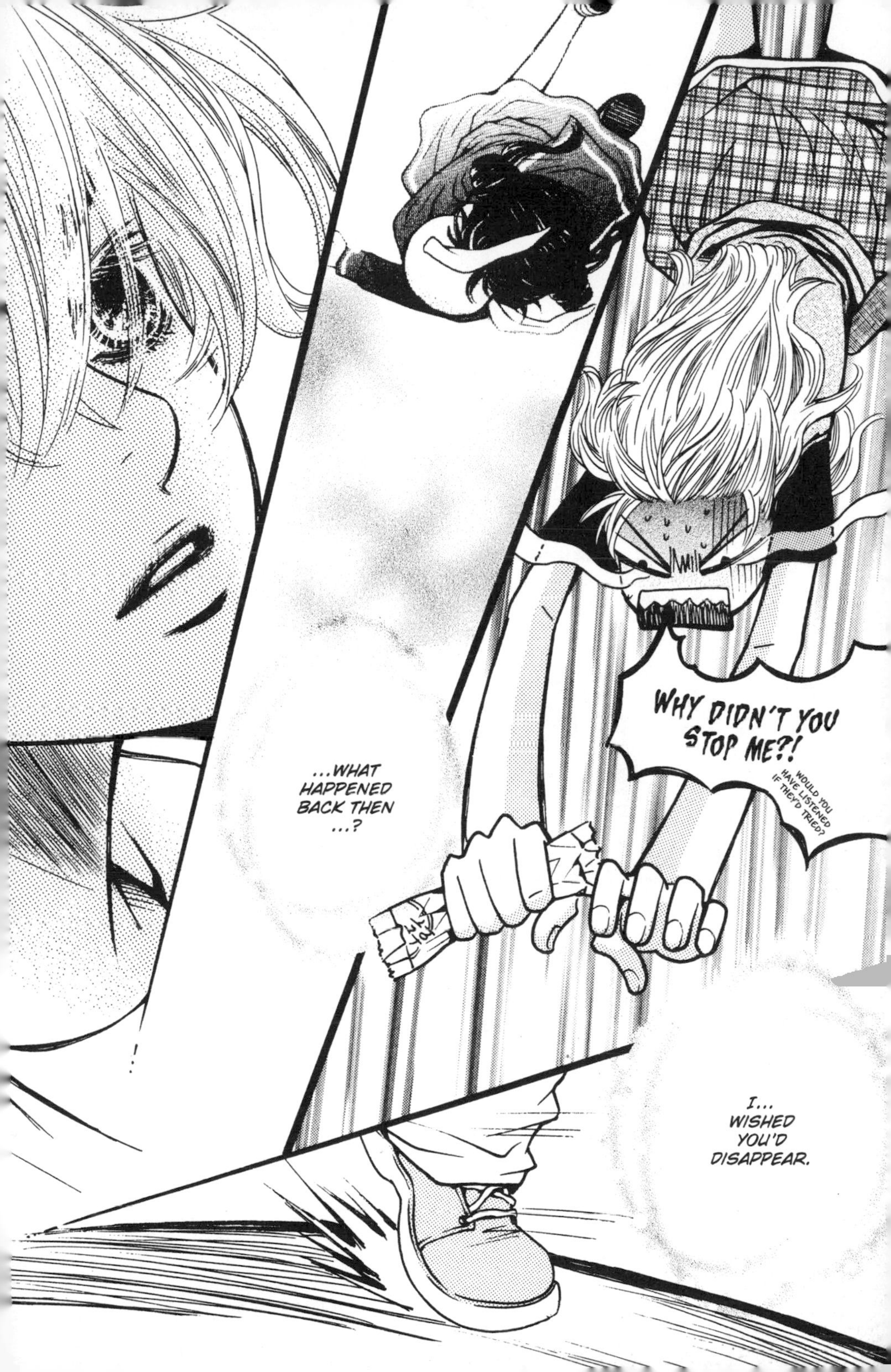
!
...WHAT HAPPENED BACK THEN ...?
WHY DIDN'T YOU STOP ME?!
WOULD YOU HAVE LISTENED IF THEY'D TRIED?
I... WISHED YOU'D DISAPPEAR.

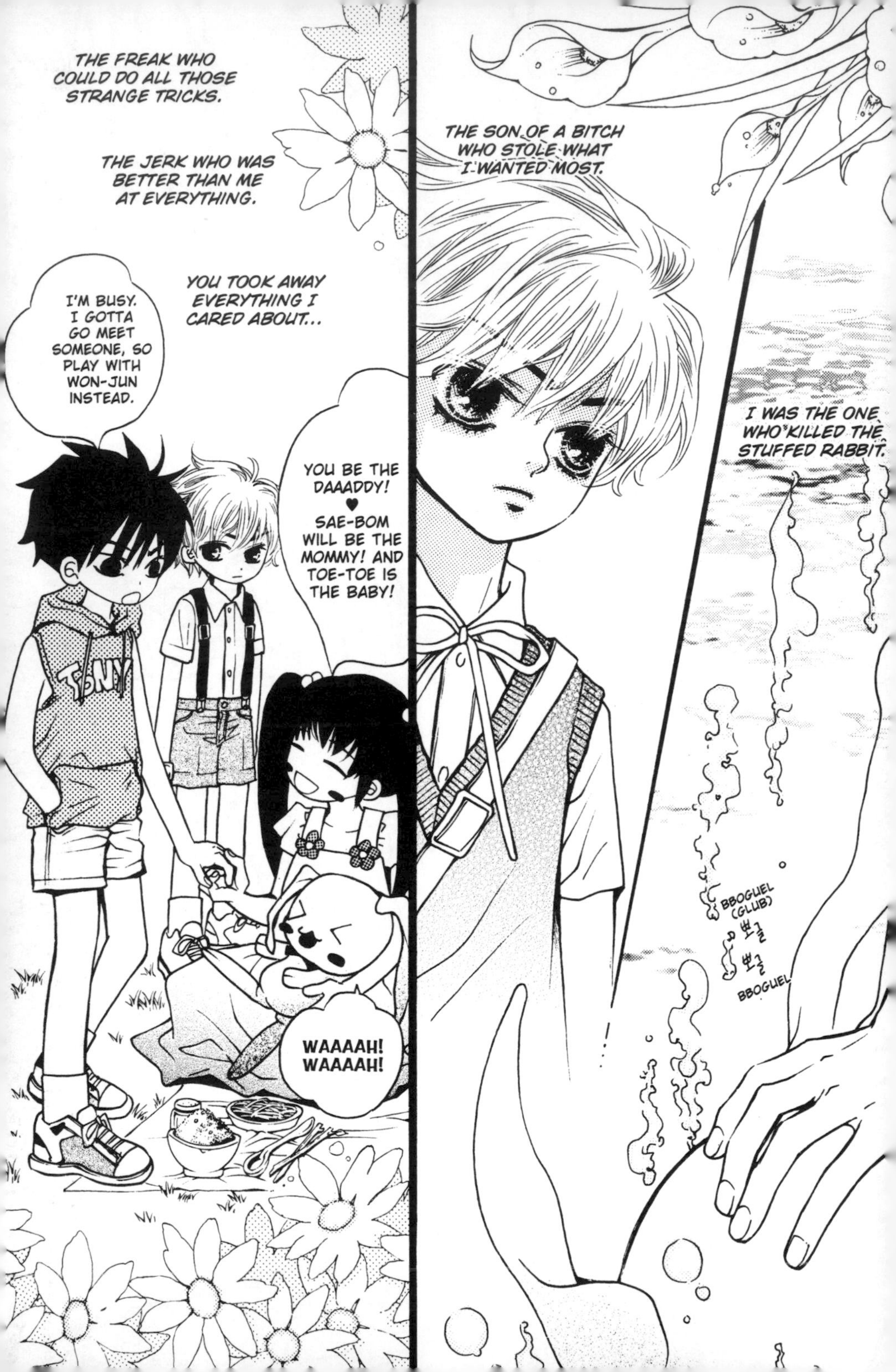
THE FREAK WHO COULD DO ALL THOSE STRANGE TRICKS.
THE JERK WHO WAS BETTER THAN ME AT EVERYTHING.
I'M BUSY. I GOTTA GO MEET SOMEONE, SO PLAY WITH WON-JUN INSTEAD.
YOU TOOK AWAY EVERYTHING I CARED ABOUT...
YOU BE THE DAAADDY! ♥ SAE-BOM WILL BE THE MOMMY! AND TOE-TOE IS THE BABY!
WAAAAH! WAAAAH!
THE SON OF A BITCH WHO STOLE WHAT I WANTED MOST.
I WAS THE ONE WHO KILLED THE STUFFED RABBIT.
BBOGUEL (GLUB)
뽀글
뽀글
BBOGUEL

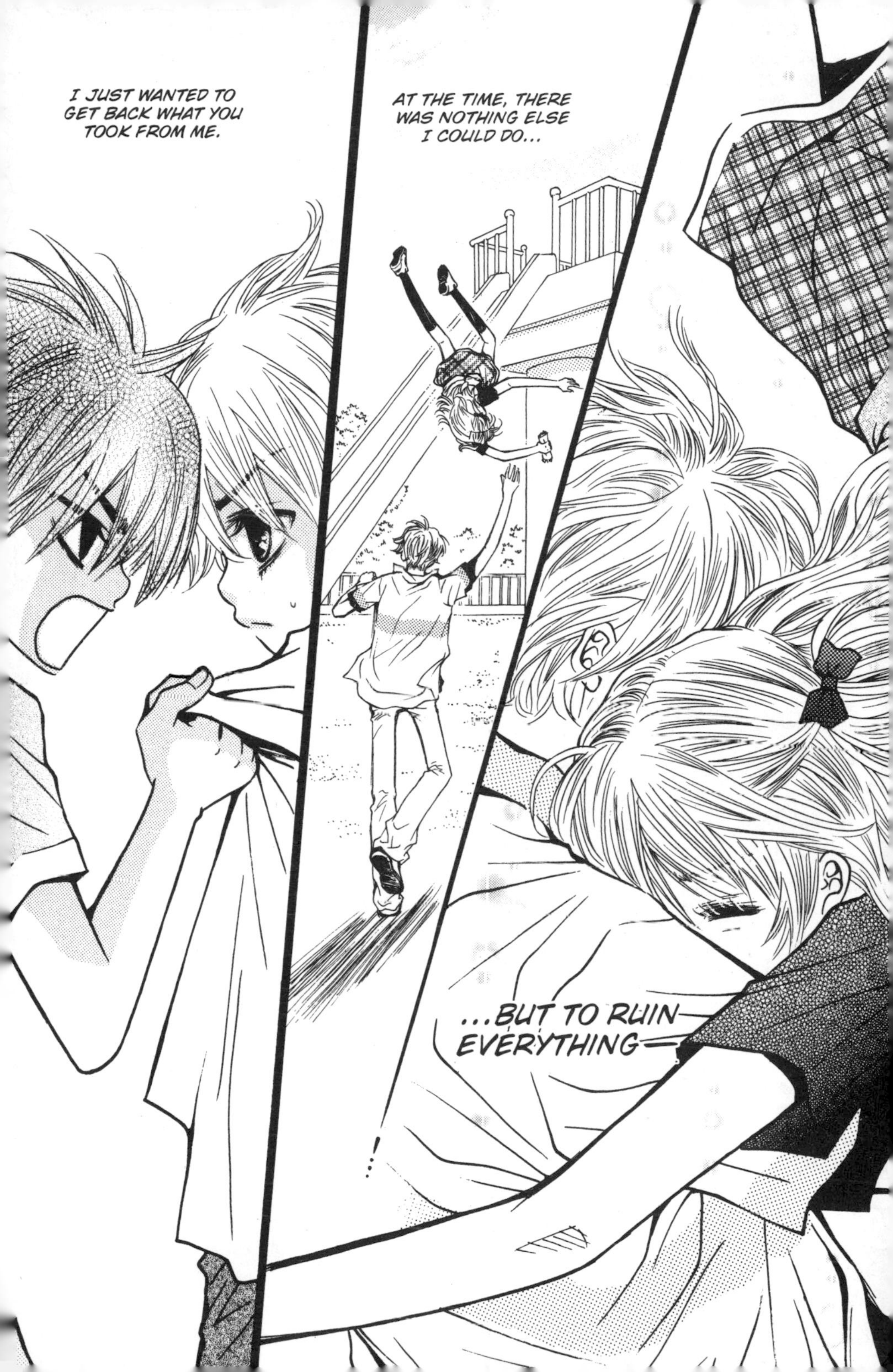
I JUST WANTED TO GET BACK WHAT YOU TOOK FROM ME.
AT THE TIME, THERE WAS NOTHING ELSE I COULD DO...
...BUT TO RUIN EVERYTHING

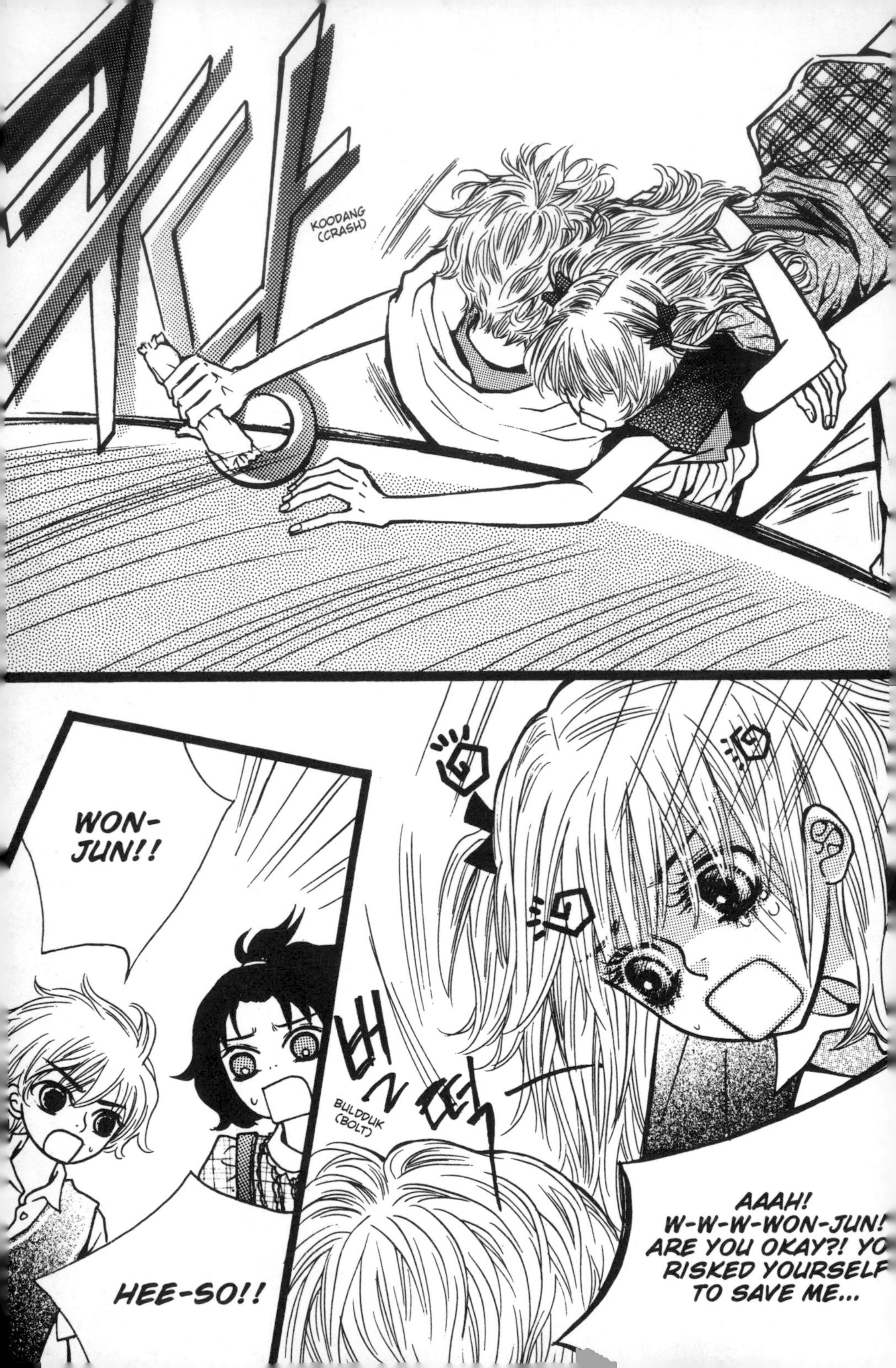
KOODANG (CRASH)
WON-JUN!!
HEE-SO!!
BULDDUK (BOLT)
AAAH! W-W-W-WON-JUN! ARE YOU OKAY?! YO RISKED YOURSELF TO SAVE ME...

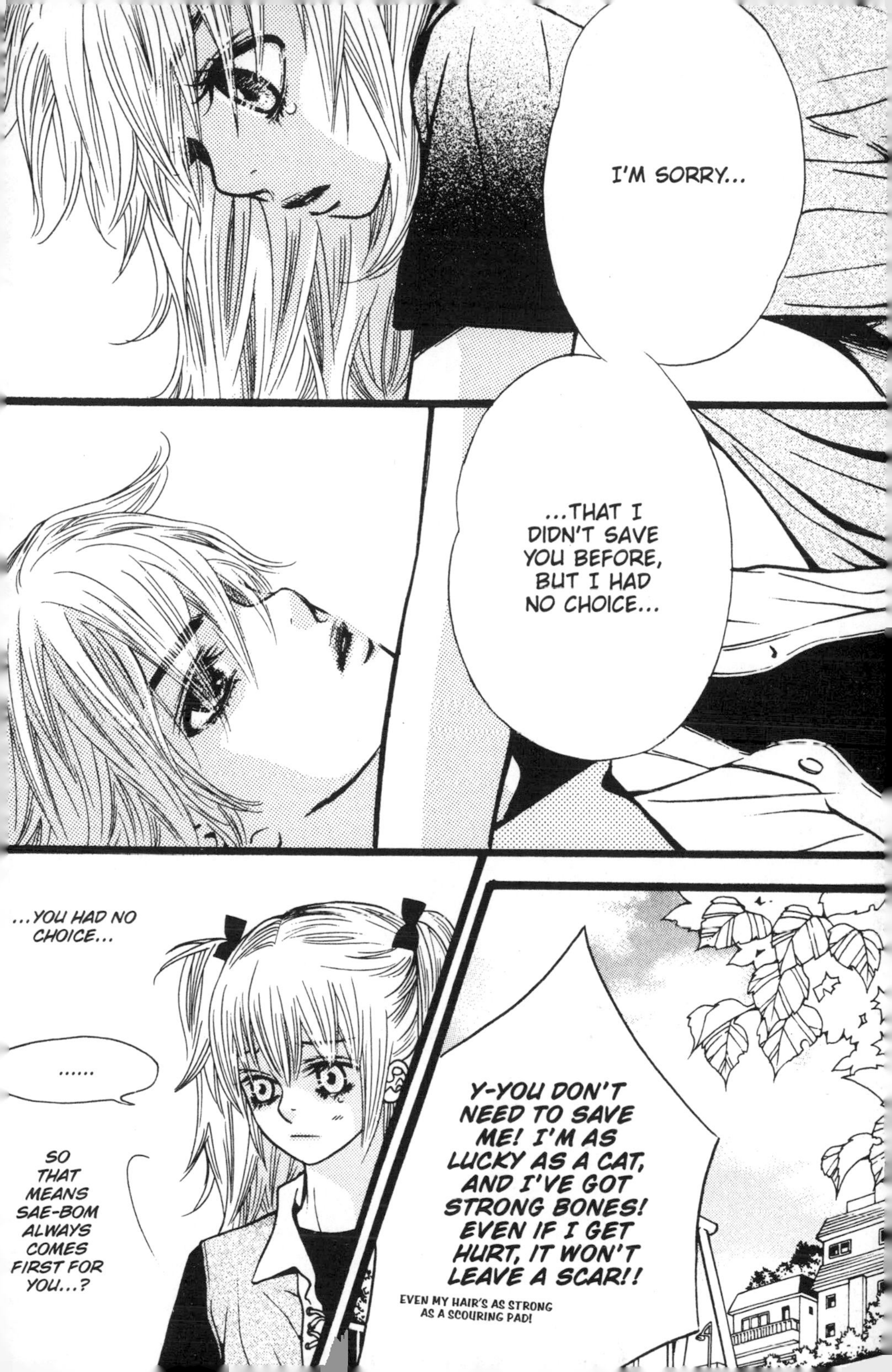
I'M SORRY...
...THAT I DIDN'T SAVE YOU BEFORE, BUT I HAD NO CHOICE...
...YOU HAD NO CHOICE...
......
SO THAT MEANS SAE-BOM ALWAYS COMES FIRST FOR YOU...?
Y-YOU DON'T NEED TO SAVE ME! I'M AS LUCKY AS A CAT, AND I'VE GOT STRONG BONES! EVEN IF I GET HURT, IT WON'T LEAVE A SCAR!!
EVEN MY HAIR'S AS STRONG AS A SCOURING PAD!

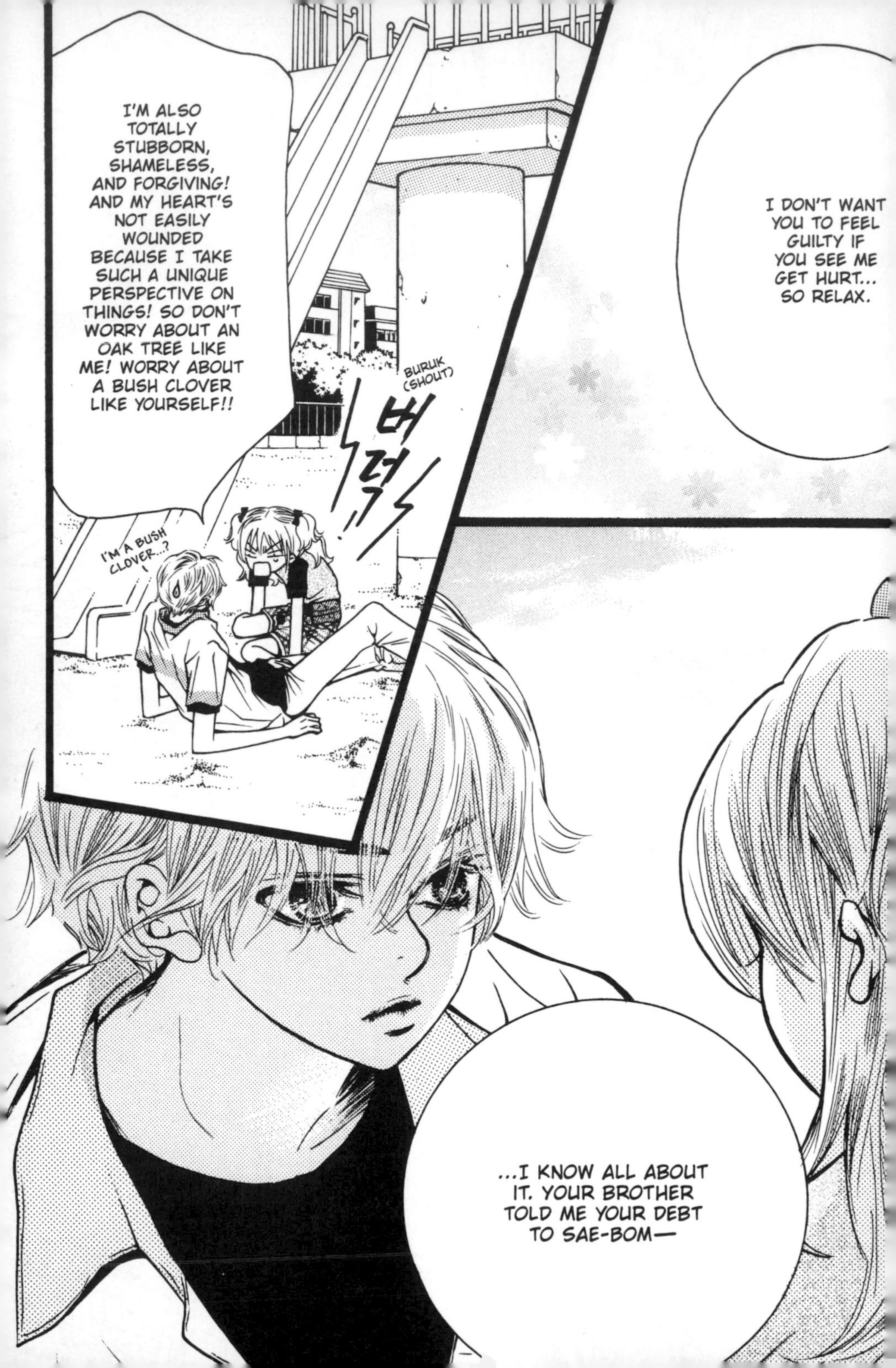

I'M ALSO TOTALLY STUBBORN, SHAMELESS, AND FORGIVING! AND MY HEART'S NOT EASILY WOUNDED BECAUSE I TAKE SUCH A UNIQUE PERSPECTIVE ON THINGS! SO DON'T WORRY ABOUT AN OAK TREE LIKE ME! WORRY ABOUT A BUSH CLOVER LIKE YOURSELF!!
BURUK (SHOUT)
버럭!!
I'M A BUSH CLOVER...?
I DON'T WANT YOU TO FEEL GUILTY IF YOU SEE ME GET HURT... SO RELAX.
...I KNOW ALL ABOUT IT. YOUR BROTHER TOLD ME YOUR DEBT TO SAE-BOM—

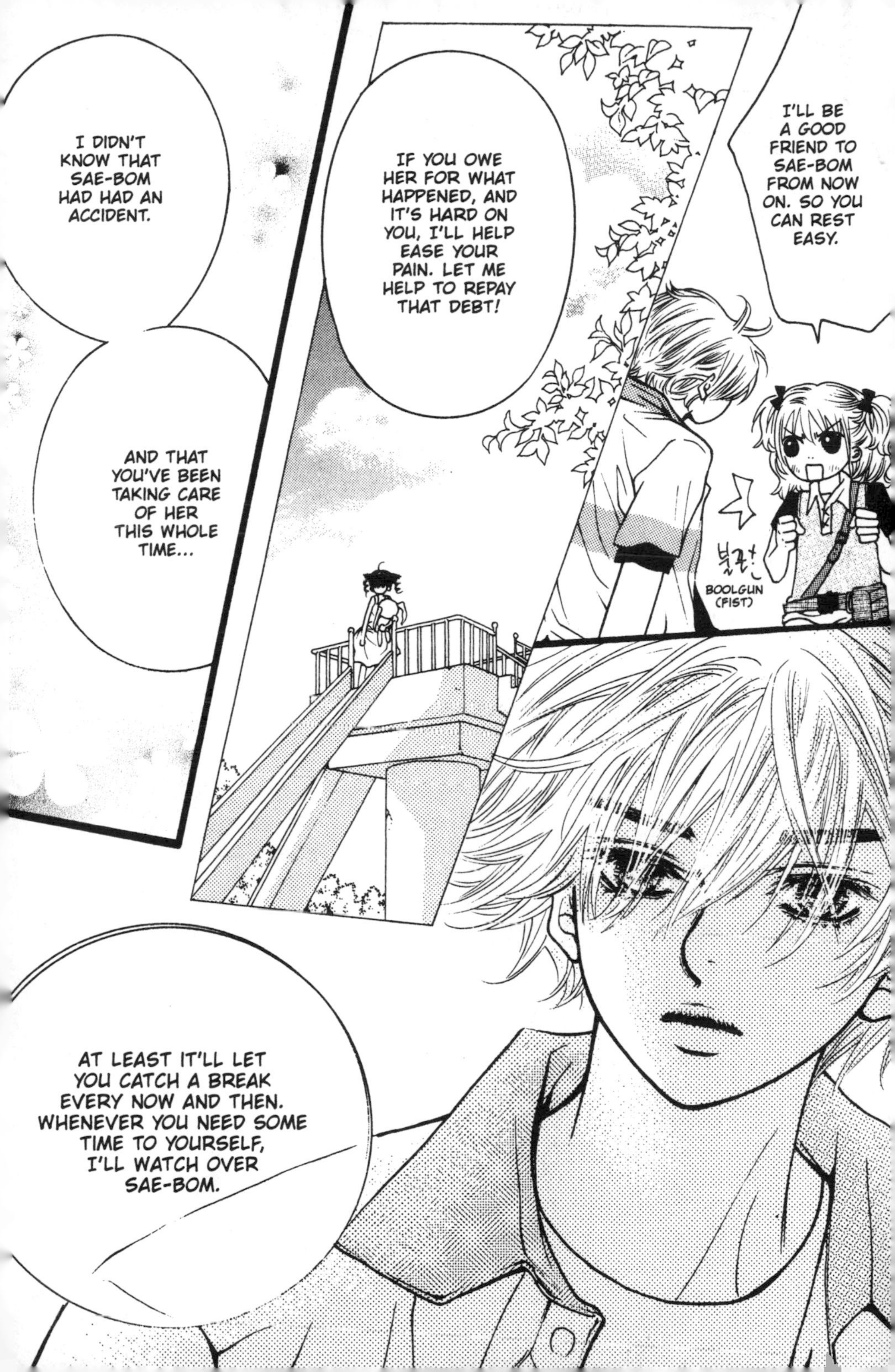

I DIDN'T KNOW THAT SAE-BOM HAD HAD AN ACCIDENT.
AND THAT YOU'VE BEEN TAKING CARE OF HER THIS WHOLE TIME...
IF YOU OWE HER FOR WHAT HAPPENED, AND IT'S HARD ON YOU, I'LL HELP EASE YOUR PAIN. LET ME HELP TO REPAY THAT DEBT!
I'LL BE A GOOD FRIEND TO SAE-BOM FROM NOW ON. SO YOU CAN REST EASY.
불끈
BOOLGUN (FIST)
AT LEAST IT'LL LET YOU CATCH A BREAK EVERY NOW AND THEN. WHENEVER YOU NEED SOME TIME TO YOURSELF, I'LL WATCH OVER SAE-BOM.

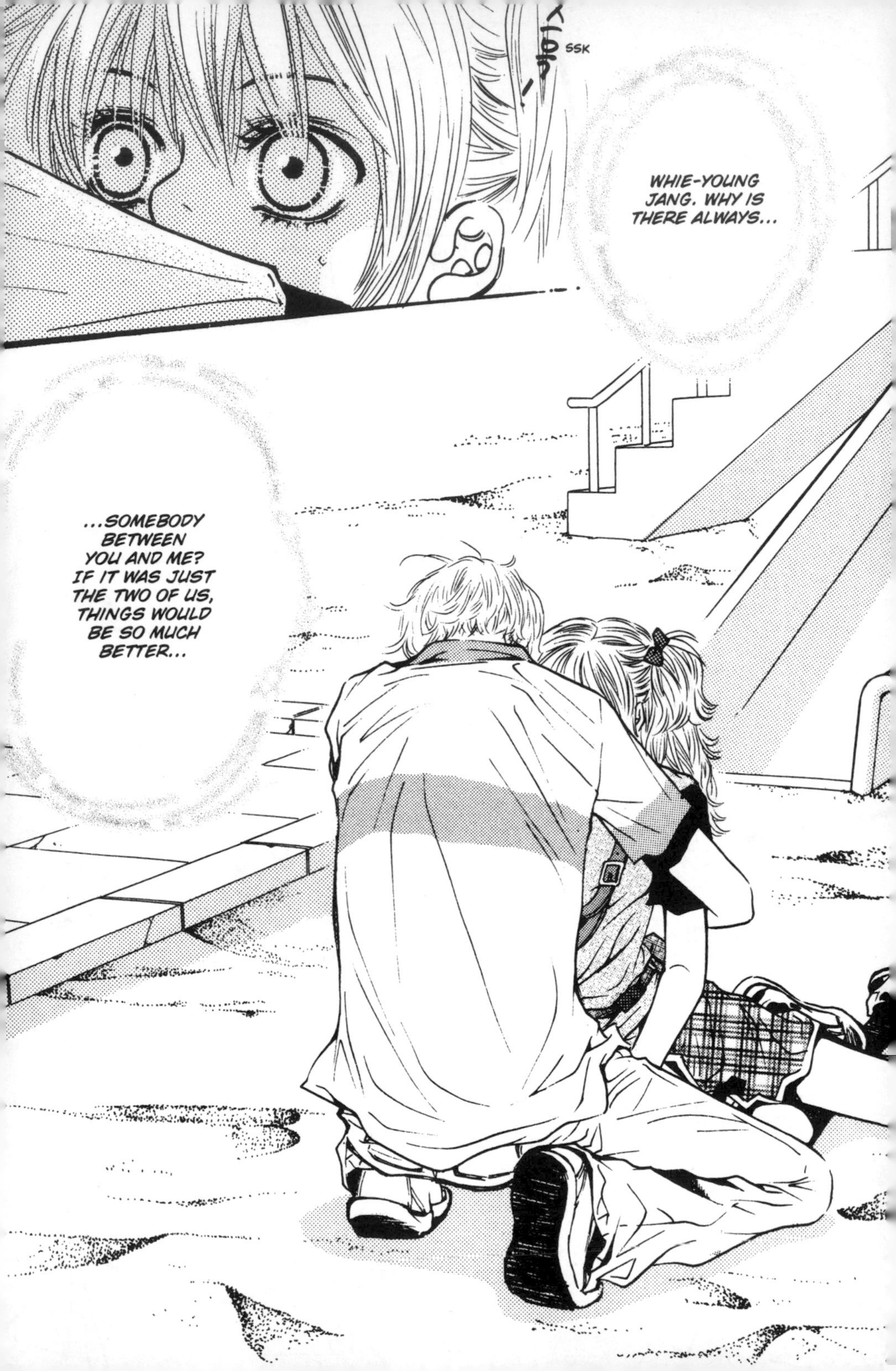
SSK
WHIE-YOUNG JANG. WHY IS THERE ALWAYS...
...SOMEBODY BETWEEN YOU AND ME? IF IT WAS JUST THE TWO OF US, THINGS WOULD BE SO MUCH BETTER...

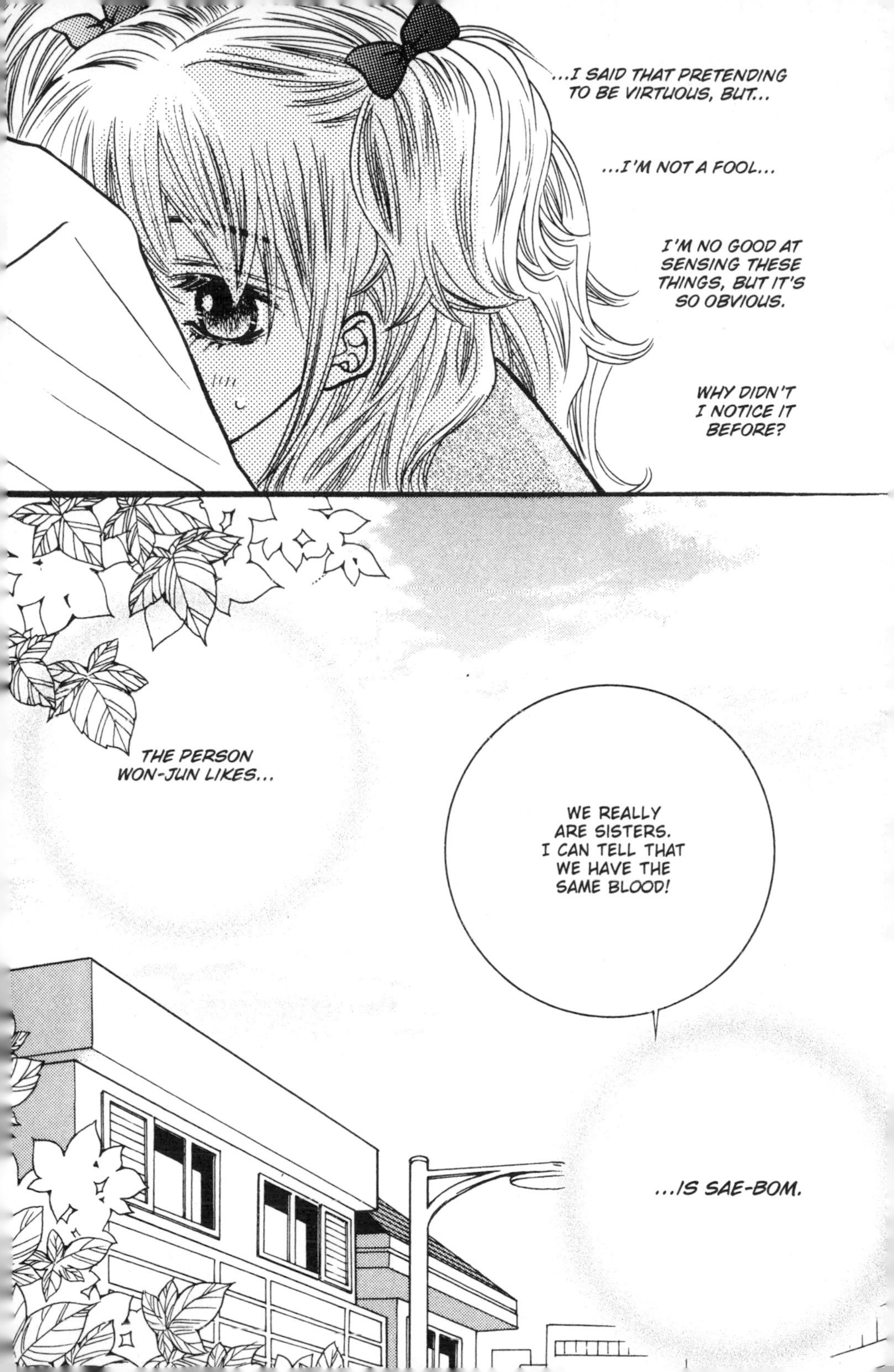
...I SAID THAT PRETENDING TO BE VIRTUOUS, BUT...
...I'M NOT A FOOL...
I'M NO GOOD AT SENSING THESE THINGS, BUT IT'S SO OBVIOUS.
WHY DIDN'T I NOTICE IT BEFORE?
THE PERSON WON-JUN LIKES...
WE REALLY ARE SISTERS. I CAN TELL THAT WE HAVE THE SAME BLOOD!
...IS SAE-BOM.

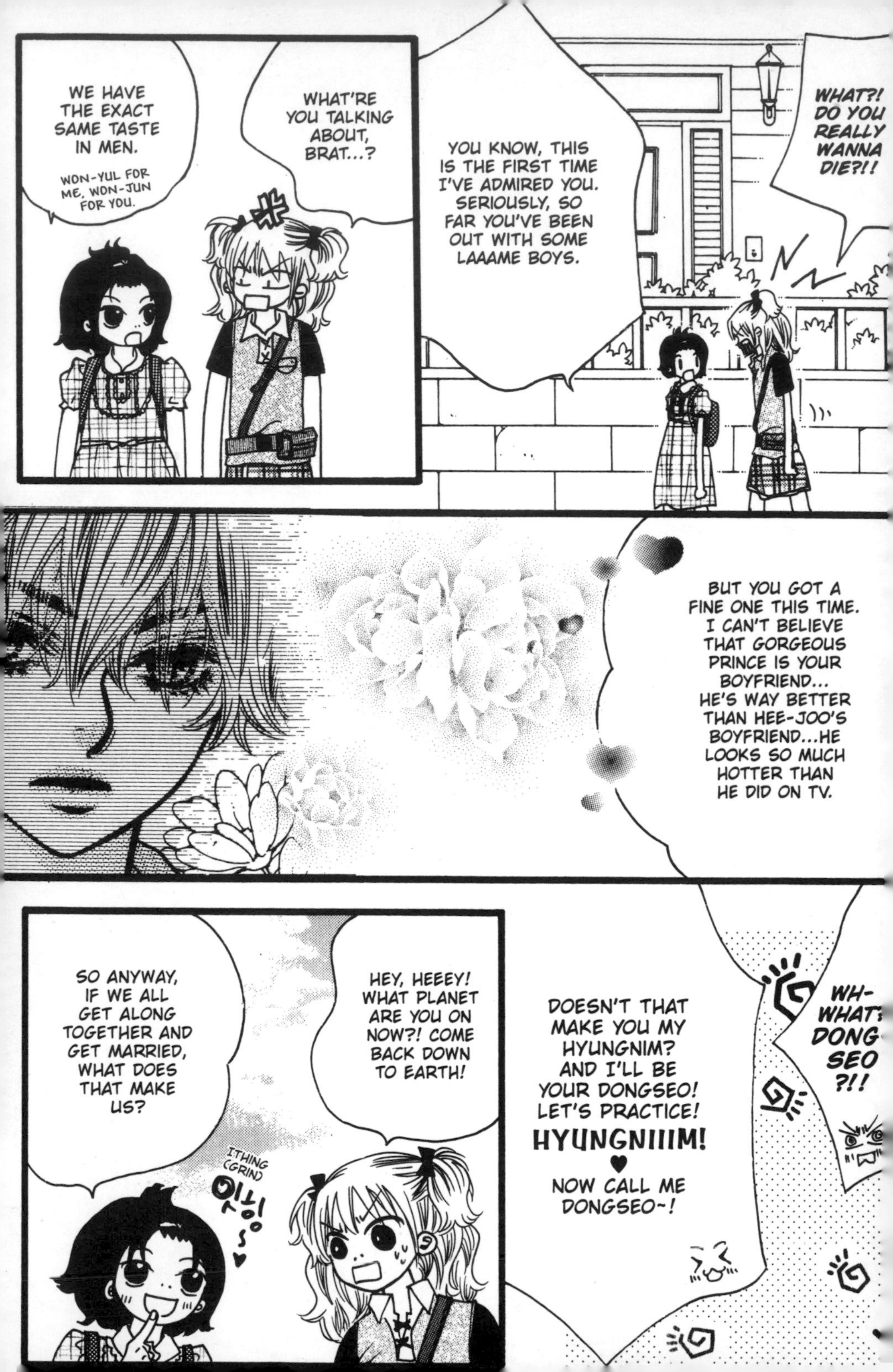
WE HAVE THE EXACT SAME TASTE IN MEN.
WON-YUL FOR ME, WON-JUN FOR YOU.
WHAT'RE YOU TALKING ABOUT, BRAT...?
YOU KNOW, THIS IS THE FIRST TIME I'VE ADMIRED YOU. SERIOUSLY, SO FAR YOU'VE BEEN OUT WITH SOME LAAAME BOYS.
WHAT?! DO YOU REALLY WANNA DIE?!!
BUT YOU GOT A FINE ONE THIS TIME. I CAN'T BELIEVE THAT GORGEOUS PRINCE IS YOUR BOYFRIEND... HE'S WAY BETTER THAN HEE-JOO'S BOYFRIEND...HE LOOKS SO MUCH HOTTER THAN HE DID ON TV.
SO ANYWAY, IF WE ALL GET ALONG TOGETHER AND GET MARRIED, WHAT DOES THAT MAKE US?
HEY, HEEEY! WHAT PLANET ARE YOU ON NOW?! COME BACK DOWN TO EARTH!
ITHING (GRIN)
DOESN'T THAT MAKE YOU MY HYUNGNIM? AND I'LL BE YOUR DONGSEO! LET'S PRACTICE! HYUNGNIIIM! ♥ NOW CALL ME DONGSEO~!
WH-WHAT: DONG SEO ?!!

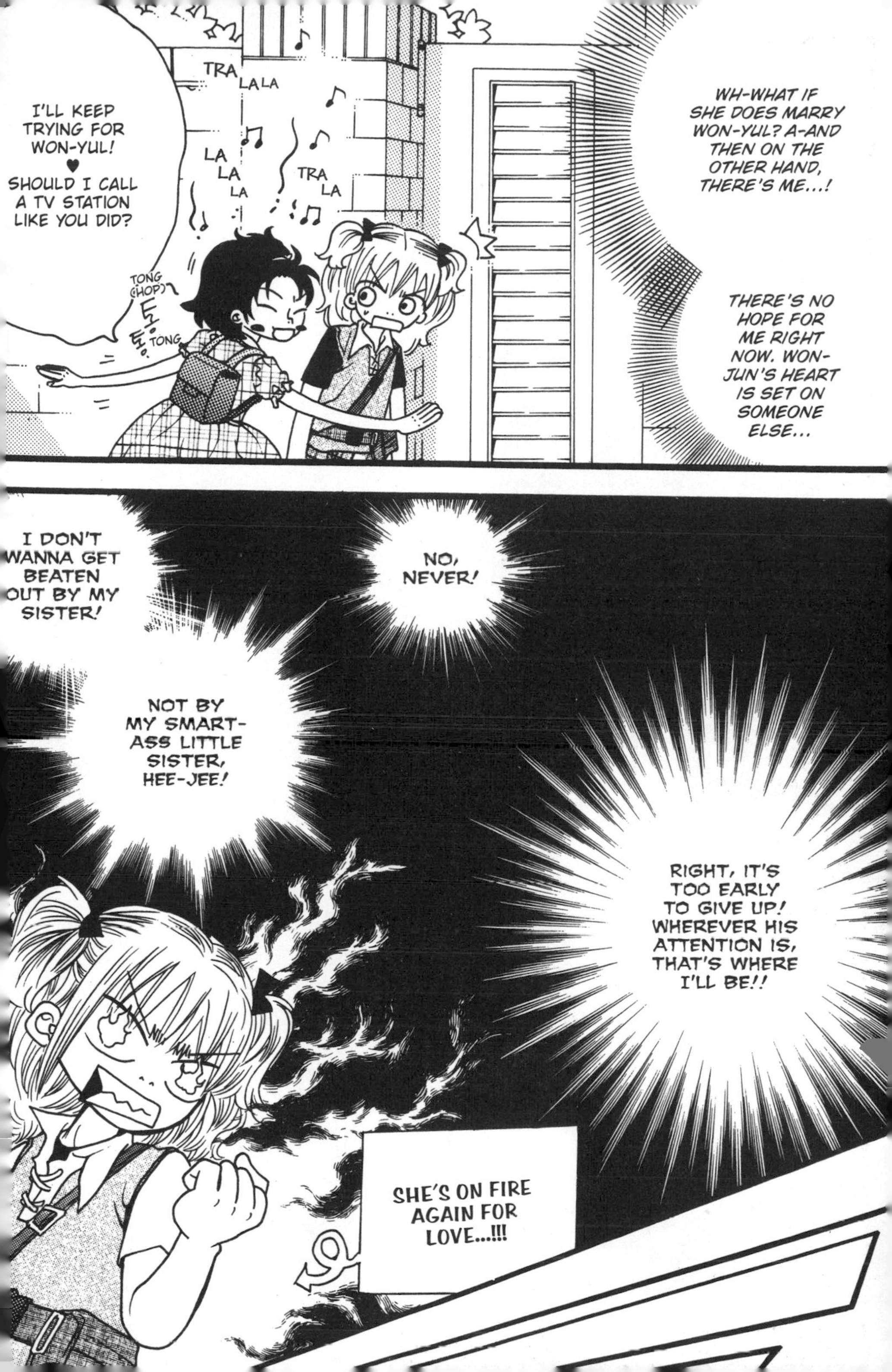
I'LL KEEP TRYING FOR WON-YUL! ♥ SHOULD I CALL A TV STATION LIKE YOU DID?
TRA LALA
LA LA LA
TRA LA
TONG (HOP)
TONG
WH-WHAT IF SHE DOES MARRY WON-YUL? A-AND THEN ON THE OTHER HAND, THERE'S ME...!
THERE'S NO HOPE FOR ME RIGHT NOW. WON-JUN'S HEART IS SET ON SOMEONE ELSE...
I DON'T WANNA GET BEATEN OUT BY MY SISTER!
NO, NEVER!
NOT BY MY SMART-ASS LITTLE SISTER, HEE-JEE!
RIGHT, IT'S TOO EARLY TO GIVE UP! WHEREVER HIS ATTENTION IS, THAT'S WHERE I'LL BE!!
SHE'S ON FIRE AGAIN FOR LOVE...!!!

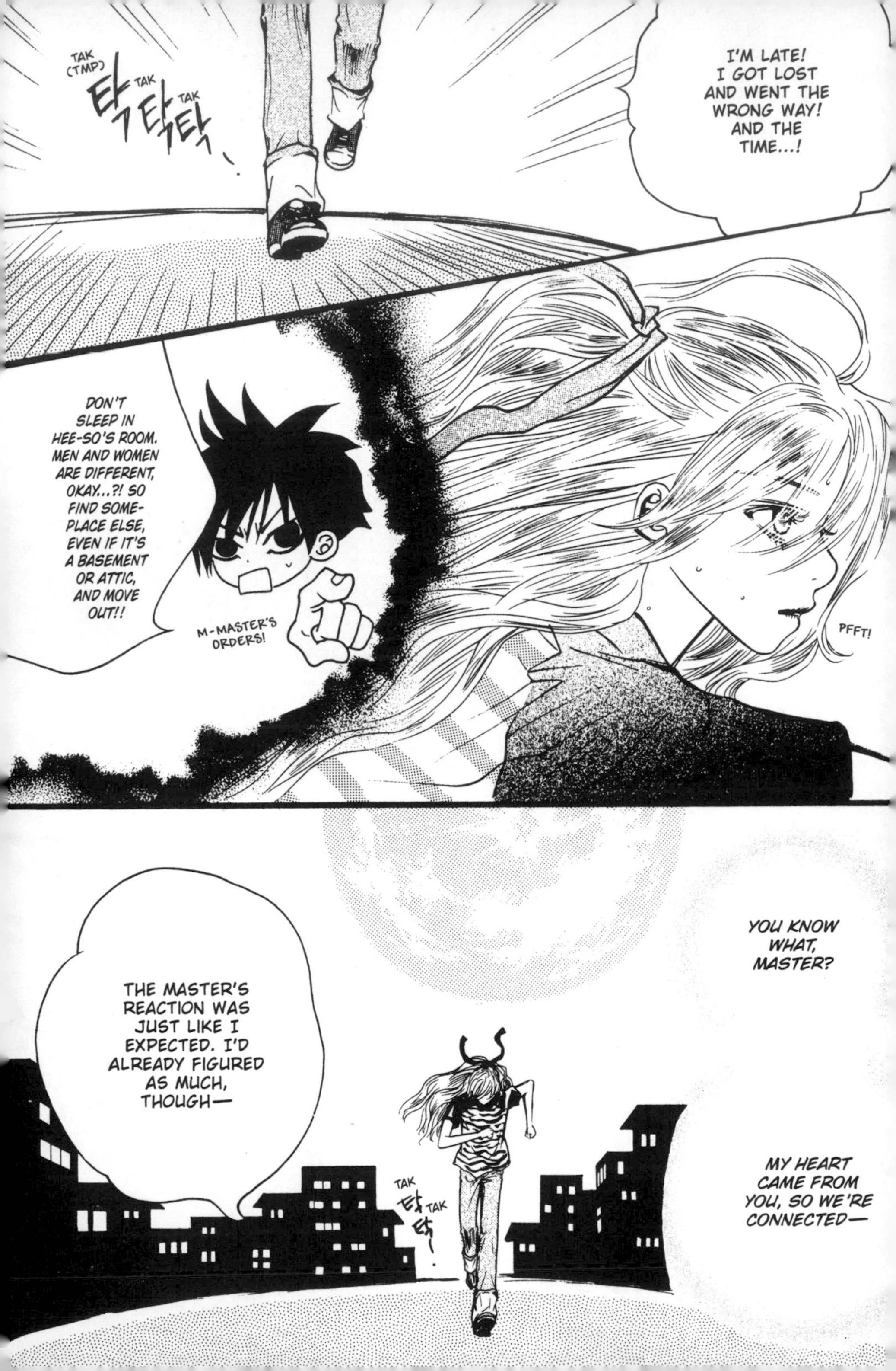
TAK (TMP)
TAK
TAK
I'M LATE! I GOT LOST AND WENT THE WRONG WAY! AND THE TIME...!
DON'T SLEEP IN HEE-SO'S ROOM. MEN AND WOMEN ARE DIFFERENT, OKAY...?! SO FIND SOME-PLACE ELSE, EVEN IF IT'S A BASEMENT OR ATTIC, AND MOVE OUT!!
M-MASTER'S ORDERS!
PFFT!
THE MASTER'S REACTION WAS JUST LIKE I EXPECTED. I'D ALREADY FIGURED AS MUCH, THOUGH—
TAK
TAK
YOU KNOW WHAT, MASTER?
MY HEART CAME FROM YOU, SO WE'RE CONNECTED—

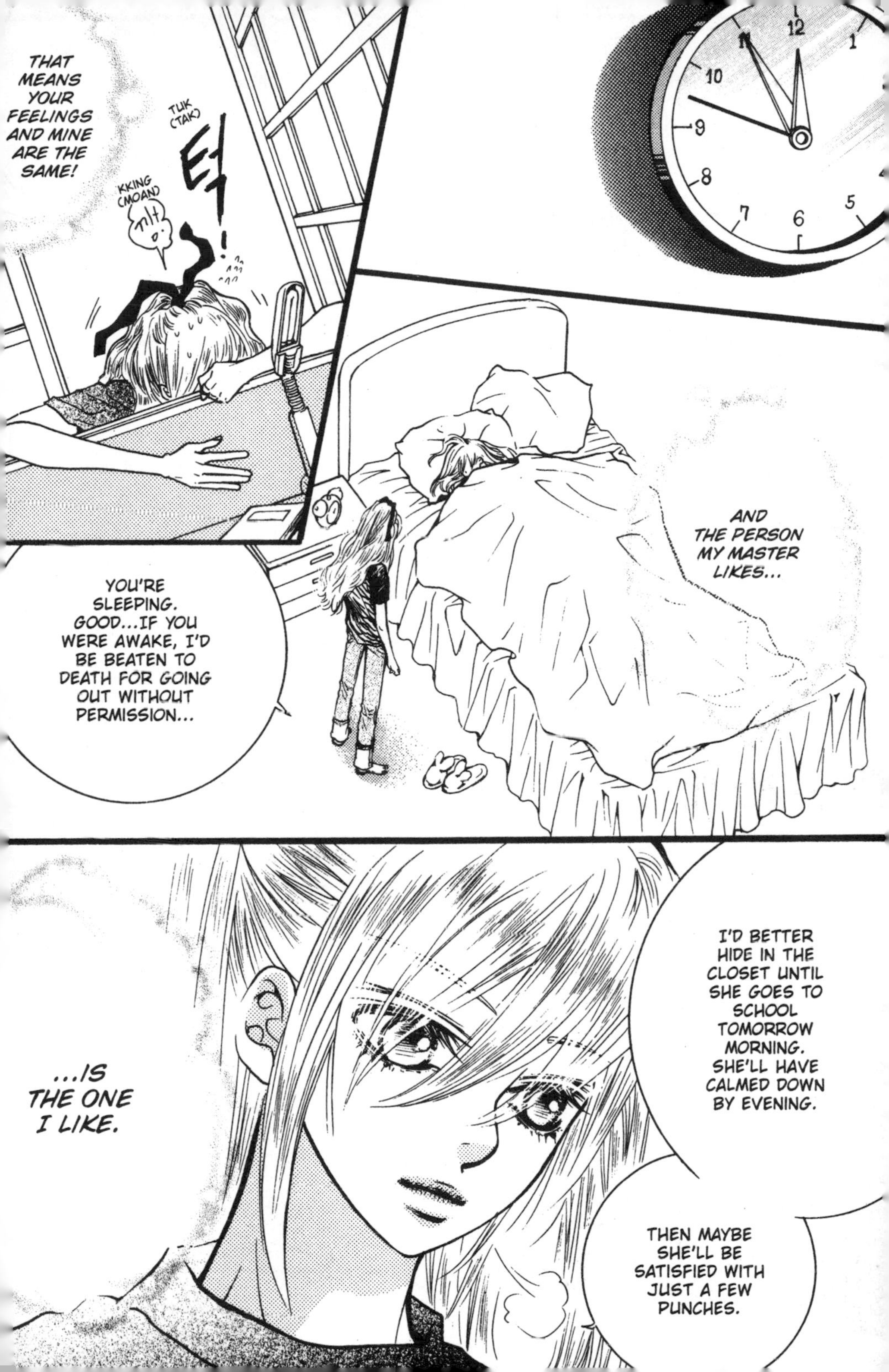
THAT MEANS YOUR FEELINGS AND MINE ARE THE SAME!
TUK (TAK)
KKING (MOAN)
YOU'RE SLEEPING. GOOD...IF YOU WERE AWAKE, I'D BE BEATEN TO DEATH FOR GOING OUT WITHOUT PERMISSION...
AND THE PERSON MY MASTER LIKES...
...IS THE ONE I LIKE.
I'D BETTER HIDE IN THE CLOSET UNTIL SHE GOES TO SCHOOL TOMORROW MORNING. SHE'LL HAVE CALMED DOWN BY EVENING.
THEN MAYBE SHE'LL BE SATISFIED WITH JUST A FEW PUNCHES.

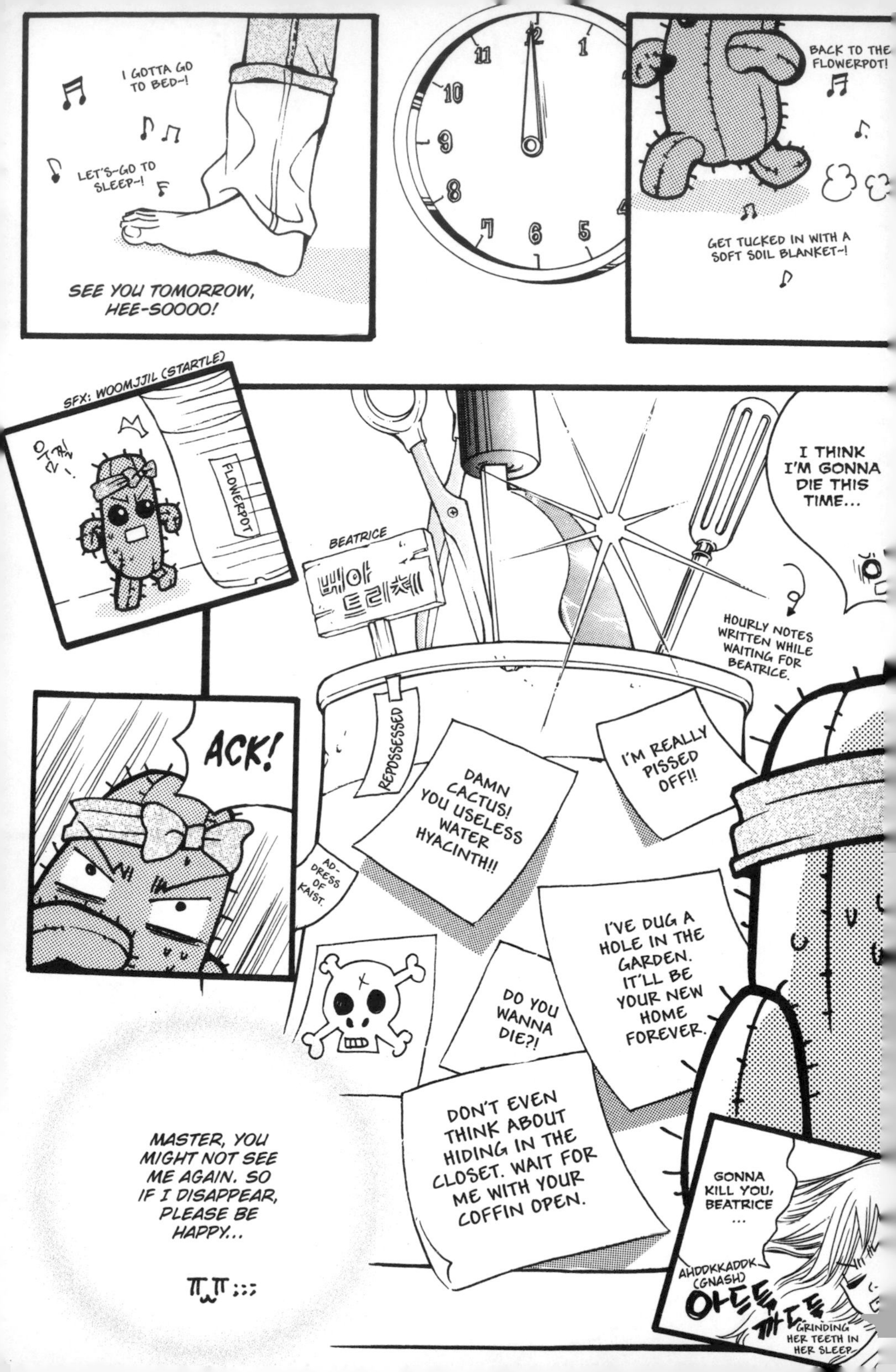

I GOTTA GO TO BED~!
LET'S~GO TO SLEEP~!
SEE YOU TOMORROW, HEE-SOOOO!
BACK TO THE FLOWERPOT!
GET TUCKED IN WITH A SOFT SOIL BLANKET~!
SFX: WOOMJJIL (STARTLE)
FLOWERPOT
ACK!
BEATRICE
빼아
트리체
REPOSSESSED
AD-DRESS OF KAIST.
DAMN CACTUS! YOU USELESS WATER HYACINTH!!
I'M REALLY PISSED OFF!!
I THINK I'M GONNA DIE THIS TIME...
HOURLY NOTES WRITTEN WHILE WAITING FOR BEATRICE.
DO YOU WANNA DIE?!
I'VE DUG A HOLE IN THE GARDEN. IT'LL BE YOUR NEW HOME FOREVER.
DON'T EVEN THINK ABOUT HIDING IN THE CLOSET. WAIT FOR ME WITH YOUR COFFIN OPEN.
MASTER, YOU MIGHT NOT SEE ME AGAIN. SO IF I DISAPPEAR, PLEASE BE HAPPY...
π_π ;;;
GONNA KILL YOU, BEATRICE ...
AHDDKKADDK (GNASH)
GRINDING HER TEETH IN HER SLEEP

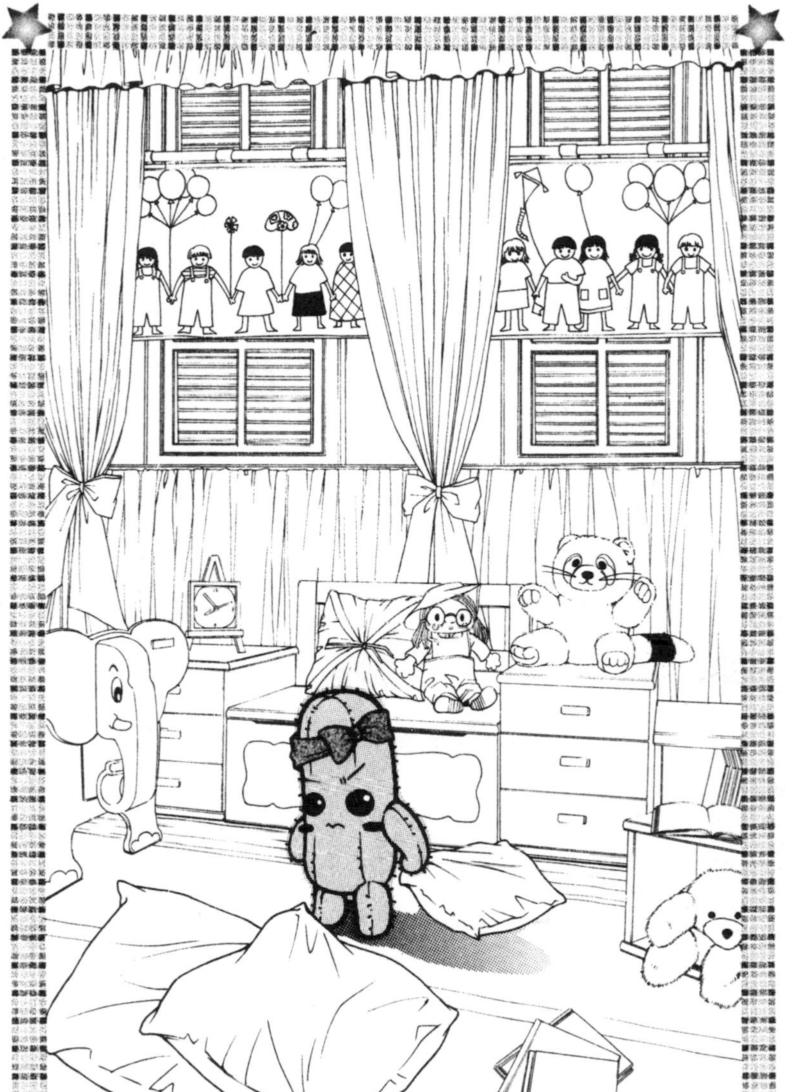

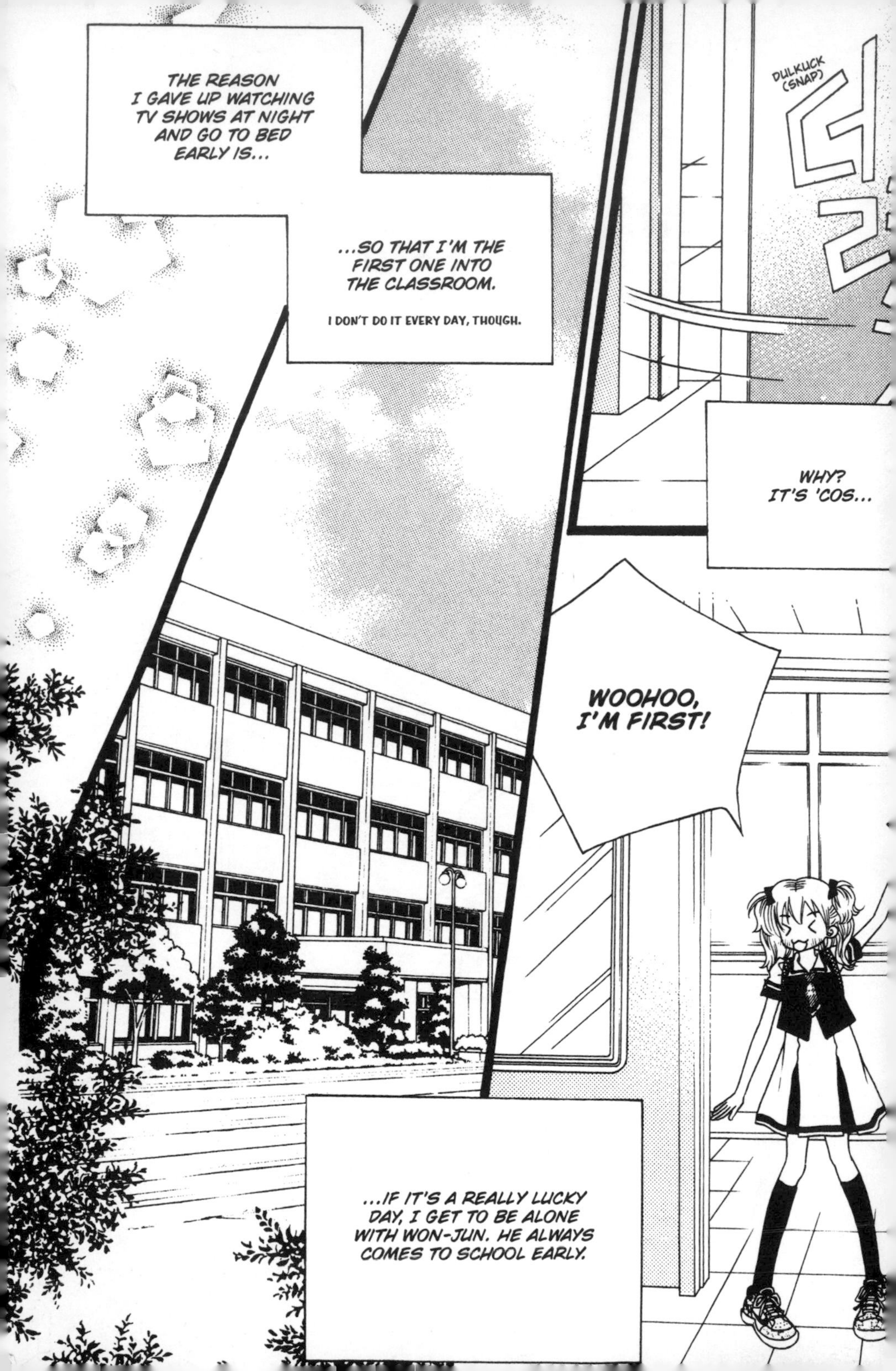
THE REASON I GAVE UP WATCHING TV SHOWS AT NIGHT AND GO TO BED EARLY IS...
...SO THAT I'M THE FIRST ONE INTO THE CLASSROOM.
I DON'T DO IT EVERY DAY, THOUGH.
DULKUCK (SNAP)
WHY? IT'S 'COS...
WOOHOO, I'M FIRST!
...IF IT'S A REALLY LUCKY DAY, I GET TO BE ALONE WITH WON-JUN. HE ALWAYS COMES TO SCHOOL EARLY.

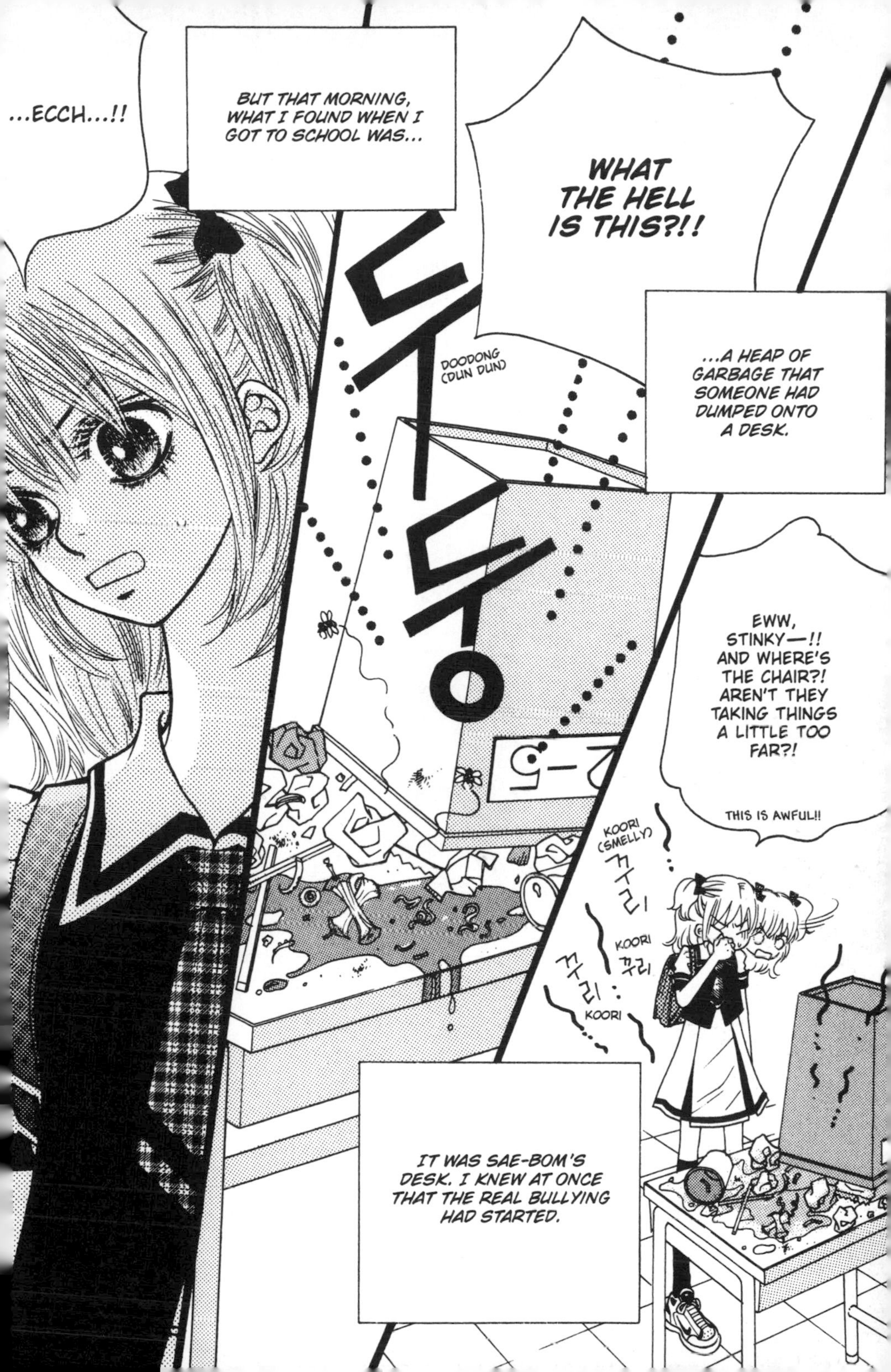

...ECCH...!!
BUT THAT MORNING, WHAT I FOUND WHEN I GOT TO SCHOOL WAS...
WHAT THE HELL IS THIS?!!
DOODONG (DUN DUN)
...A HEAP OF GARBAGE THAT SOMEONE HAD DUMPED ONTO A DESK.
EWW, STINKY—!! AND WHERE'S THE CHAIR?! AREN'T THEY TAKING THINGS A LITTLE TOO FAR?!
THIS IS AWFUL!!
KOORI (SMELLY)
KOORI
KOORI
IT WAS SAE-BOM'S DESK. I KNEW AT ONCE THAT THE REAL BULLYING HAD STARTED.

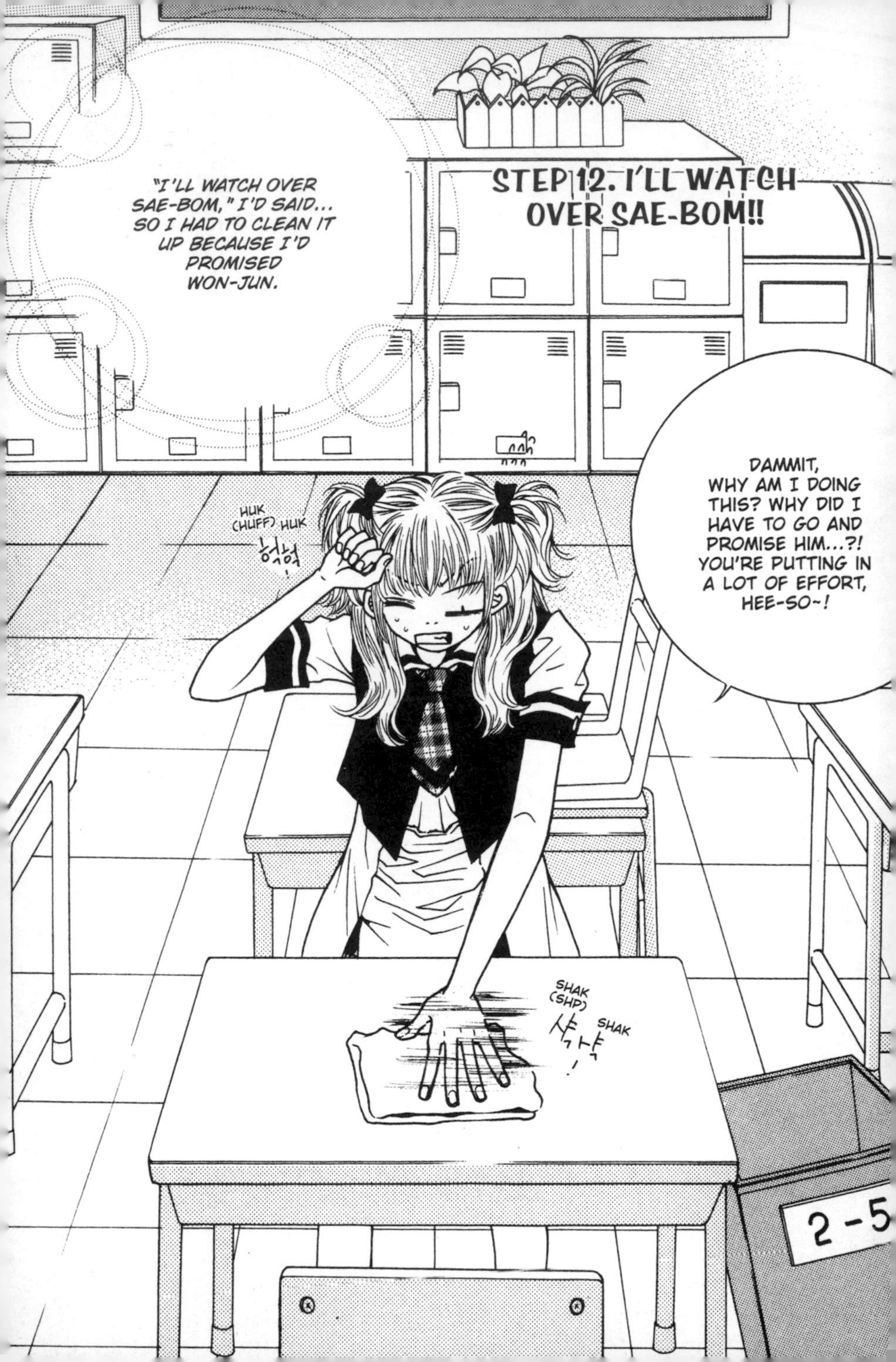
"I'LL WATCH OVER SAE-BOM," I'D SAID... SO I HAD TO CLEAN IT UP BECAUSE I'D PROMISED WON-JUN.
STEP 12. I'LL WATCH OVER SAE-BOM!!
HUK (HUFF) HUK
헉헉!
DAMMIT, WHY AM I DOING THIS? WHY DID I HAVE TO GO AND PROMISE HIM...?! YOU'RE PUTTING IN A LOT OF EFFORT, HEE-SO~!
SHAK (SHP) SHAK
2-5

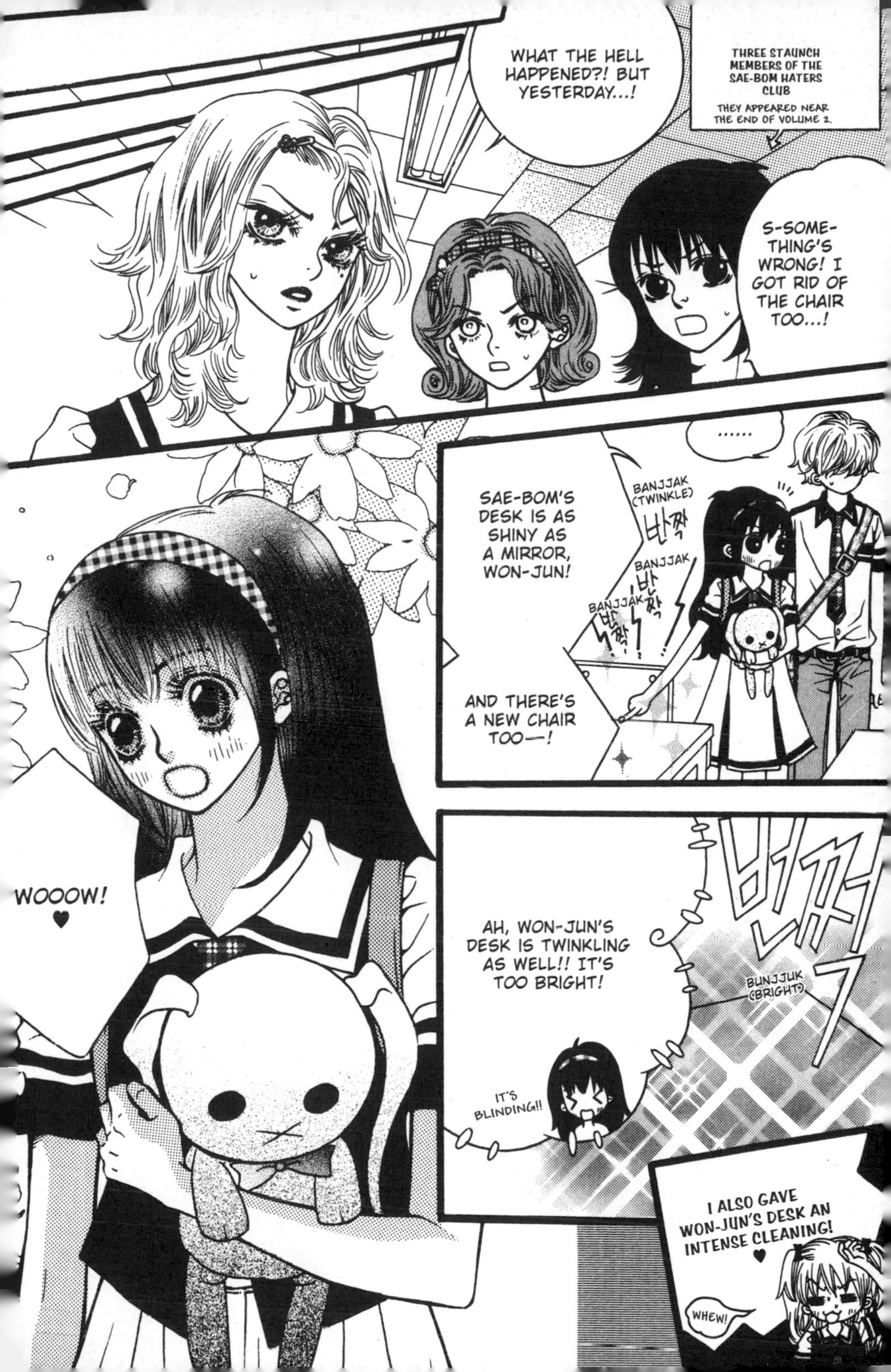
WHAT THE HELL HAPPENED?! BUT YESTERDAY...!
THREE STAUNCH MEMBERS OF THE SAE-BOM HATERS CLUB
THEY APPEARED NEAR THE END OF VOLUME 2.
S-SOMETHING'S WRONG! I GOT RID OF THE CHAIR TOO...!
WOOOW! ♥
......
SAE-BOM'S DESK IS AS SHINY AS A MIRROR, WON-JUN!
BANJJAK (TWINKLE)
반짝
BANJJAK
반짝
BANJJAK
반짝
AND THERE'S A NEW CHAIR TOO—!
AH, WON-JUN'S DESK IS TWINKLING AS WELL!! IT'S TOO BRIGHT!
BUNJJUK (BRIGHT)
IT'S BLINDING!!
I ALSO GAVE WON-JUN'S DESK AN INTENSE CLEANING! ♥
WHEW!

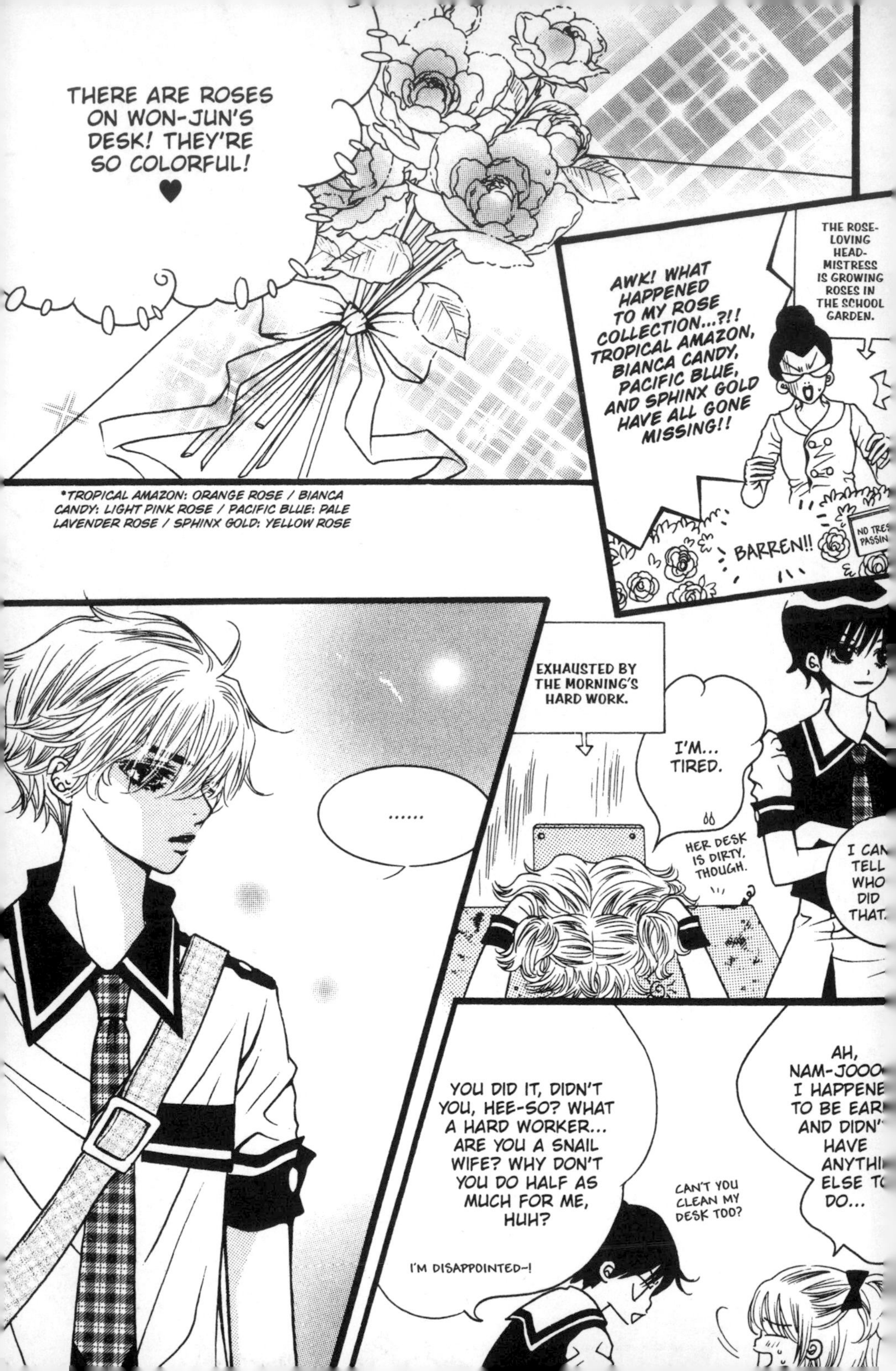

THERE ARE ROSES ON WON-JUN'S DESK! THEY'RE SO COLORFUL! ♥
AWK! WHAT HAPPENED TO MY ROSE COLLECTION...?!! TROPICAL AMAZON, BIANCA CANDY, PACIFIC BLUE, AND SPHINX GOLD HAVE ALL GONE MISSING!!
THE ROSE-LOVING HEAD-MISTRESS IS GROWING ROSES IN THE SCHOOL GARDEN.
BARREN!!
NO TRES PASSIN
*TROPICAL AMAZON: ORANGE ROSE / BIANCA CANDY: LIGHT PINK ROSE / PACIFIC BLUE: PALE LAVENDER ROSE / SPHINX GOLD: YELLOW ROSE
......
EXHAUSTED BY THE MORNING'S HARD WORK.
I'M... TIRED.
HER DESK IS DIRTY, THOUGH.
I CAN TELL WHO DID THAT.
YOU DID IT, DIDN'T YOU, HEE-SO? WHAT A HARD WORKER... ARE YOU A SNAIL WIFE? WHY DON'T YOU DO HALF AS MUCH FOR ME, HUH?
CAN'T YOU CLEAN MY DESK TOO?
I'M DISAPPOINTED~!
AH, NAM-JOOO I HAPPENE TO BE EAR AND DIDN' HAVE ANYTHI ELSE T DO...

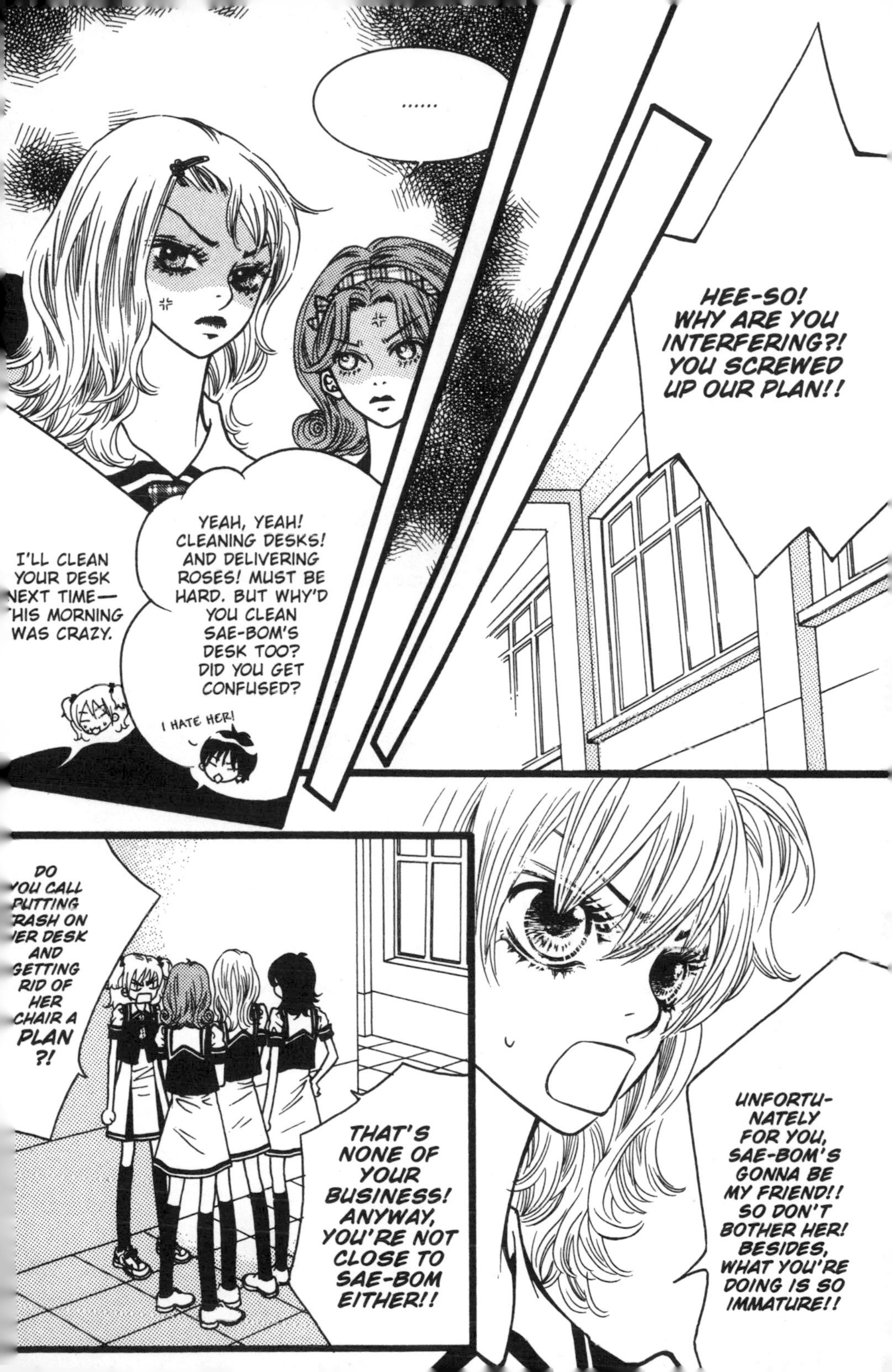
......
I'LL CLEAN YOUR DESK NEXT TIME— THIS MORNING WAS CRAZY.
YEAH, YEAH! CLEANING DESKS! AND DELIVERING ROSES! MUST BE HARD. BUT WHY'D YOU CLEAN SAE-BOM'S DESK TOO? DID YOU GET CONFUSED?
I HATE HER!
HEE-SO! WHY ARE YOU INTERFERING?! YOU SCREWED UP OUR PLAN!!
DO YOU CALL PUTTING TRASH ON HER DESK AND GETTING RID OF HER CHAIR A PLAN ?!
THAT'S NONE OF YOUR BUSINESS! ANYWAY, YOU'RE NOT CLOSE TO SAE-BOM EITHER!!
UNFORTU-NATELY FOR YOU, SAE-BOM'S GONNA BE MY FRIEND!! SO DON'T BOTHER HER! BESIDES, WHAT YOU'RE DOING IS SO IMMATURE!!

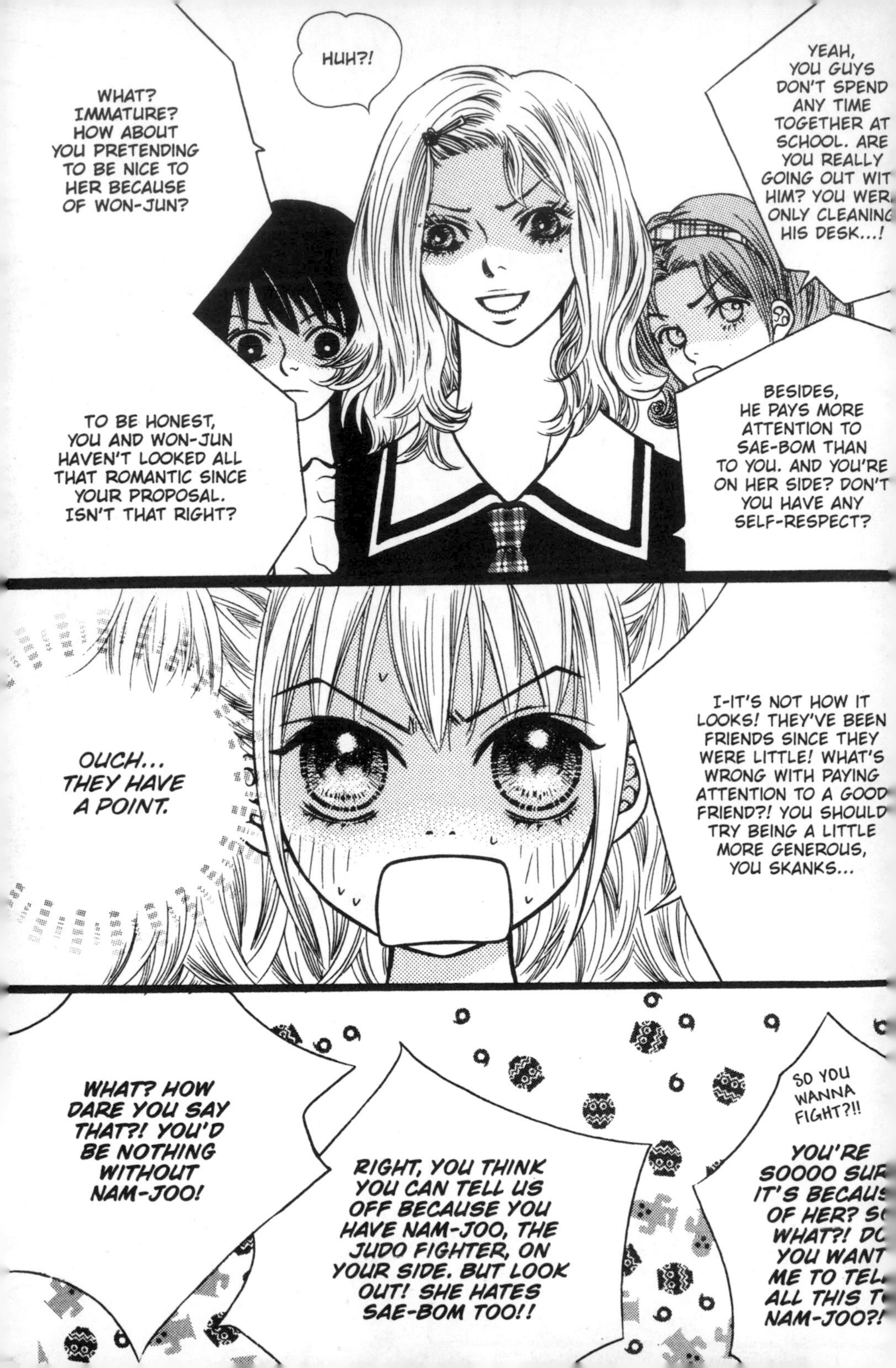

WHAT? IMMATURE? HOW ABOUT YOU PRETENDING TO BE NICE TO HER BECAUSE OF WON-JUN?
HUH?!
YEAH, YOU GUYS DON'T SPEND ANY TIME TOGETHER AT SCHOOL. ARE YOU REALLY GOING OUT WIT HIM? YOU WER ONLY CLEANING HIS DESK...!
TO BE HONEST, YOU AND WON-JUN HAVEN'T LOOKED ALL THAT ROMANTIC SINCE YOUR PROPOSAL. ISN'T THAT RIGHT?
BESIDES, HE PAYS MORE ATTENTION TO SAE-BOM THAN TO YOU. AND YOU'RE ON HER SIDE? DON'T YOU HAVE ANY SELF-RESPECT?
OUCH... THEY HAVE A POINT.
I-IT'S NOT HOW IT LOOKS! THEY'VE BEEN FRIENDS SINCE THEY WERE LITTLE! WHAT'S WRONG WITH PAYING ATTENTION TO A GOOD FRIEND?! YOU SHOULD TRY BEING A LITTLE MORE GENEROUS, YOU SKANKS...
WHAT? HOW DARE YOU SAY THAT?! YOU'D BE NOTHING WITHOUT NAM-JOO!
RIGHT, YOU THINK YOU CAN TELL US OFF BECAUSE YOU HAVE NAM-JOO, THE JUDO FIGHTER, ON YOUR SIDE. BUT LOOK OUT! SHE HATES SAE-BOM TOO!!
SO YOU WANNA FIGHT?!!
YOU'RE SOOOO SUR IT'S BECAUS OF HER? S WHAT?! D YOU WANT ME TO TEL ALL THIS T NAM-JOO?!

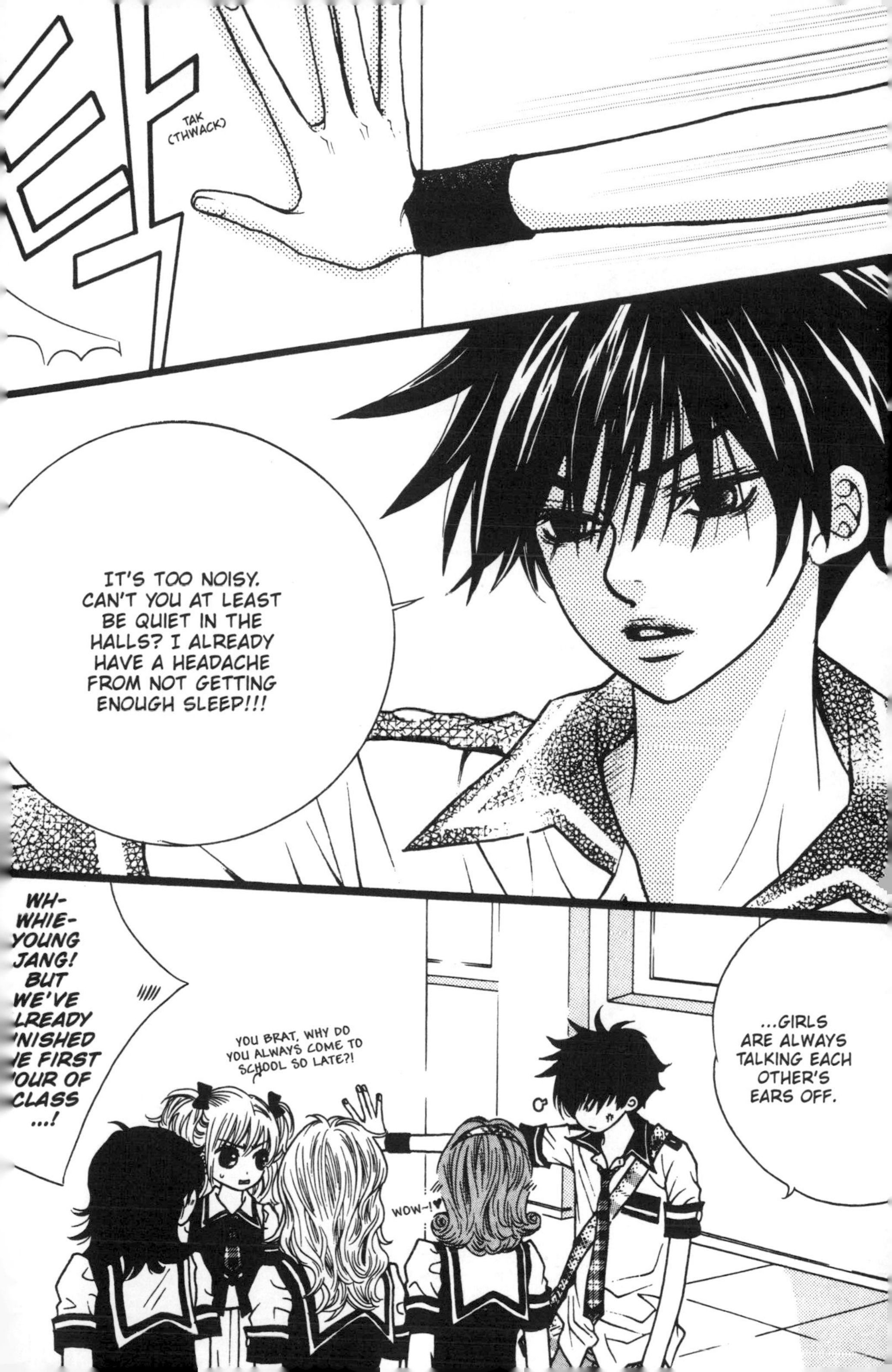

TAK (THWACK)
IT'S TOO NOISY. CAN'T YOU AT LEAST BE QUIET IN THE HALLS? I ALREADY HAVE A HEADACHE FROM NOT GETTING ENOUGH SLEEP!!!
WH- WHIE- YOUNG JANG! BUT WE'VE LREADY NISHED E FIRST OUR OF CLASS ...!
YOU BRAT, WHY DO YOU ALWAYS COME TO SCHOOL SO LATE?!
WOW~!♥
...GIRLS ARE ALWAYS TALKING EACH OTHER'S EARS OFF.

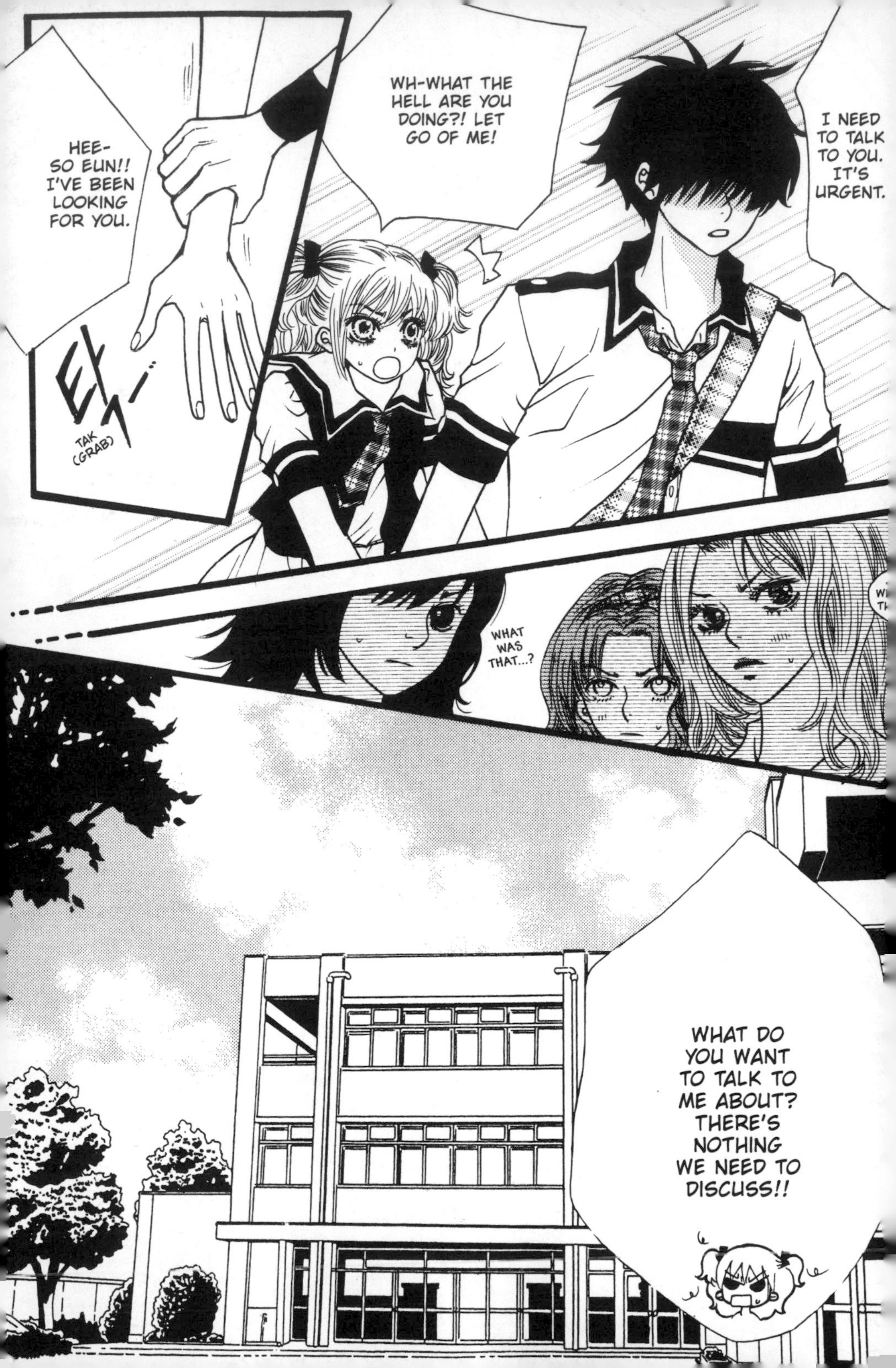
HEE-SO EUN!! I'VE BEEN LOOKING FOR YOU.
TAK (GRAB)
WH-WHAT THE HELL ARE YOU DOING?! LET GO OF ME!
I NEED TO TALK TO YOU. IT'S URGENT.
WHAT WAS THAT...?
WHAT DO YOU WANT TO TALK TO ME ABOUT? THERE'S NOTHING WE NEED TO DISCUSS!!

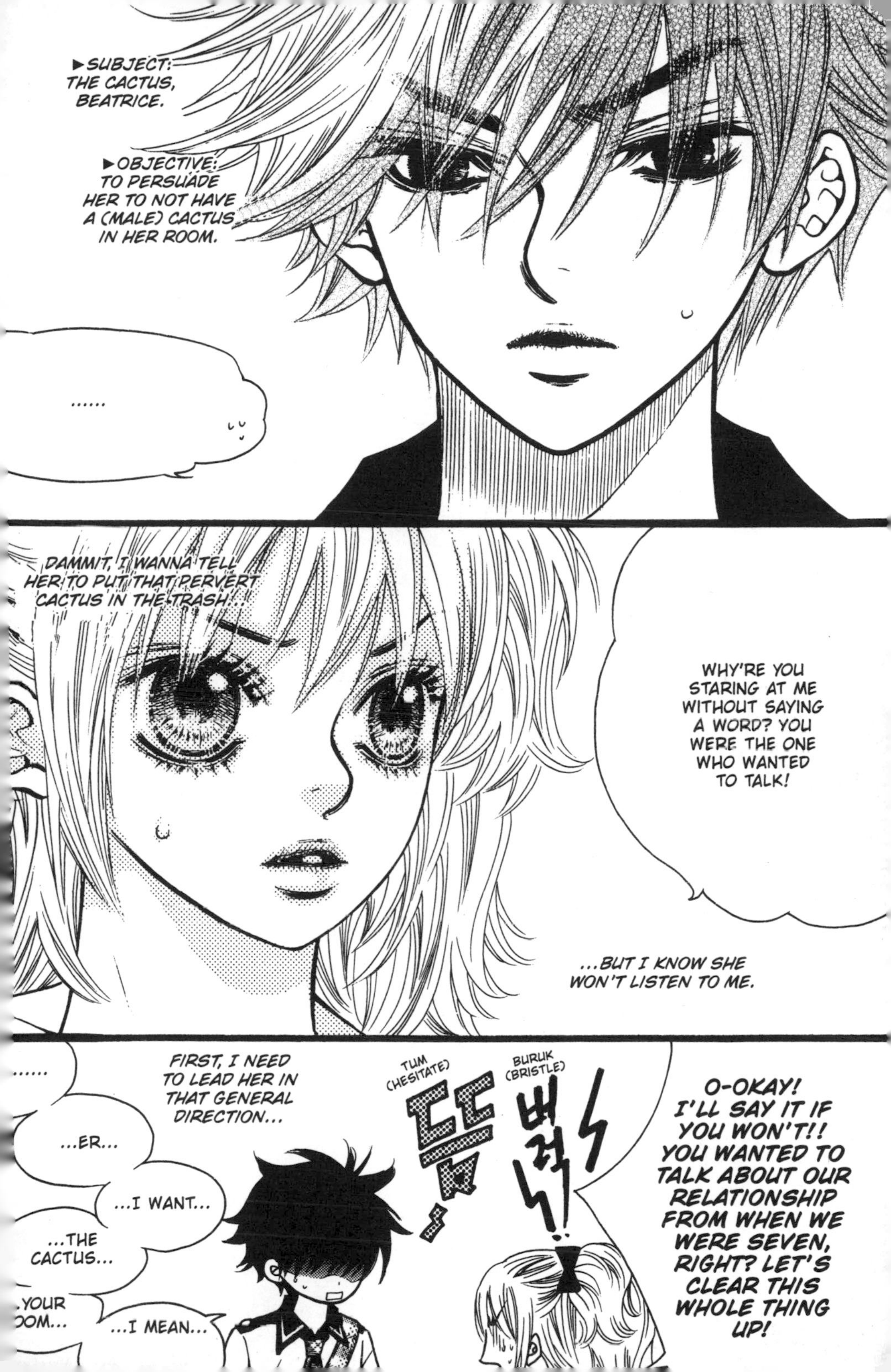
►SUBJECT: THE CACTUS, BEATRICE.
►OBJECTIVE: TO PERSUADE HER TO NOT HAVE A (MALE) CACTUS IN HER ROOM.
......
DAMMIT, I WANNA TELL HER TO PUT THAT PERVERT CACTUS IN THE TRASH...
WHY'RE YOU STARING AT ME WITHOUT SAYING A WORD? YOU WERE THE ONE WHO WANTED TO TALK!
...BUT I KNOW SHE WON'T LISTEN TO ME.
......
...ER...
...I WANT...
...THE CACTUS...
.YOUR OOM...
...I MEAN...
FIRST, I NEED TO LEAD HER IN THAT GENERAL DIRECTION...
TUM (HESITATE)
뚱
BURUK (BRISTLE)
버럭
O-OKAY! I'LL SAY IT IF YOU WON'T!! YOU WANTED TO TALK ABOUT OUR RELATIONSHIP FROM WHEN WE WERE SEVEN, RIGHT? LET'S CLEAR THIS WHOLE THING UP!

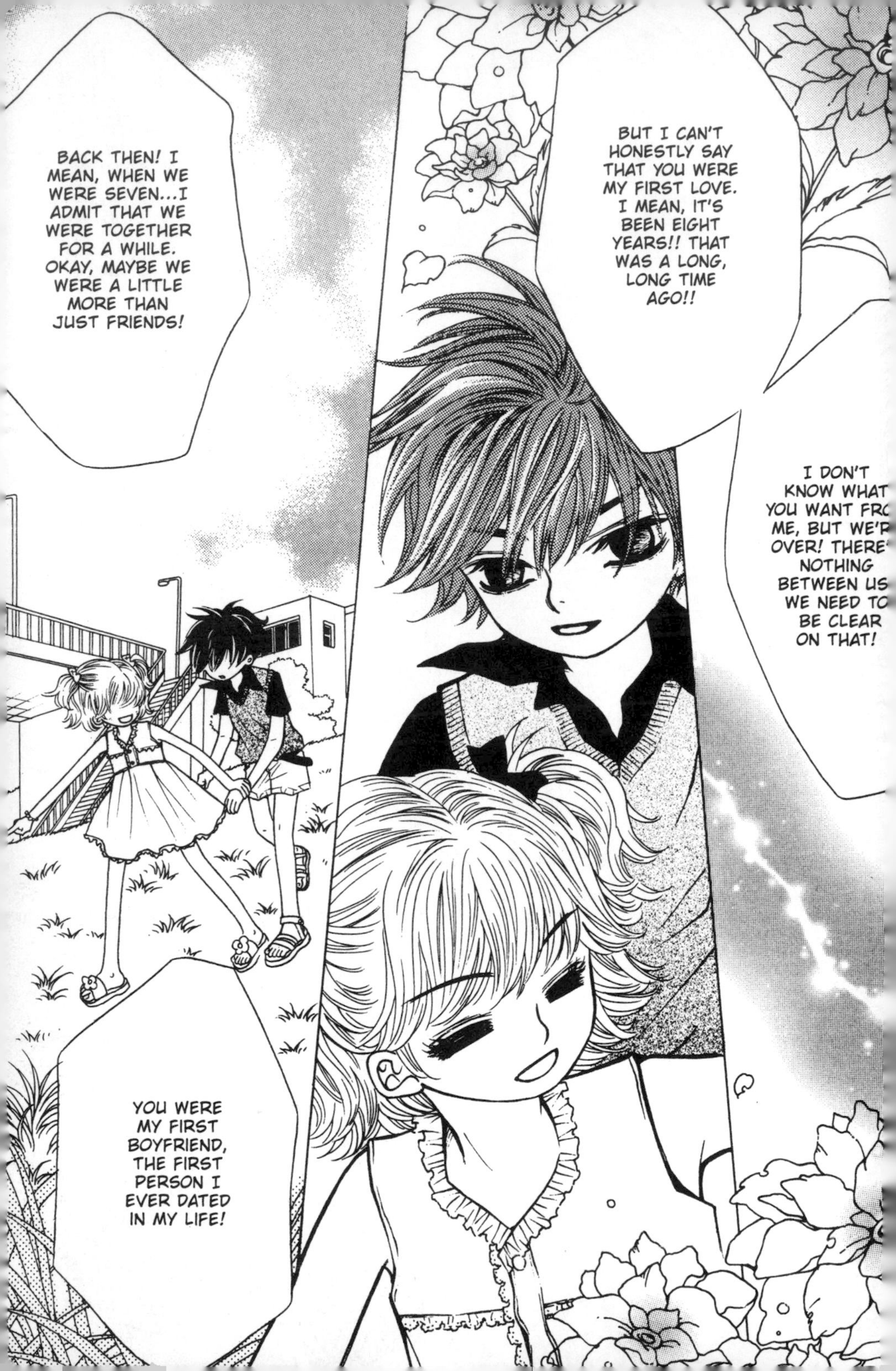
BACK THEN! I MEAN, WHEN WE WERE SEVEN...I ADMIT THAT WE WERE TOGETHER FOR A WHILE. OKAY, MAYBE WE WERE A LITTLE MORE THAN JUST FRIENDS!
YOU WERE MY FIRST BOYFRIEND, THE FIRST PERSON I EVER DATED IN MY LIFE!
BUT I CAN'T HONESTLY SAY THAT YOU WERE MY FIRST LOVE. I MEAN, IT'S BEEN EIGHT YEARS!! THAT WAS A LONG, LONG TIME AGO!!
I DON'T KNOW WHAT YOU WANT FRO ME, BUT WE'R OVER! THERE' NOTHING BETWEEN US WE NEED TO BE CLEAR ON THAT!

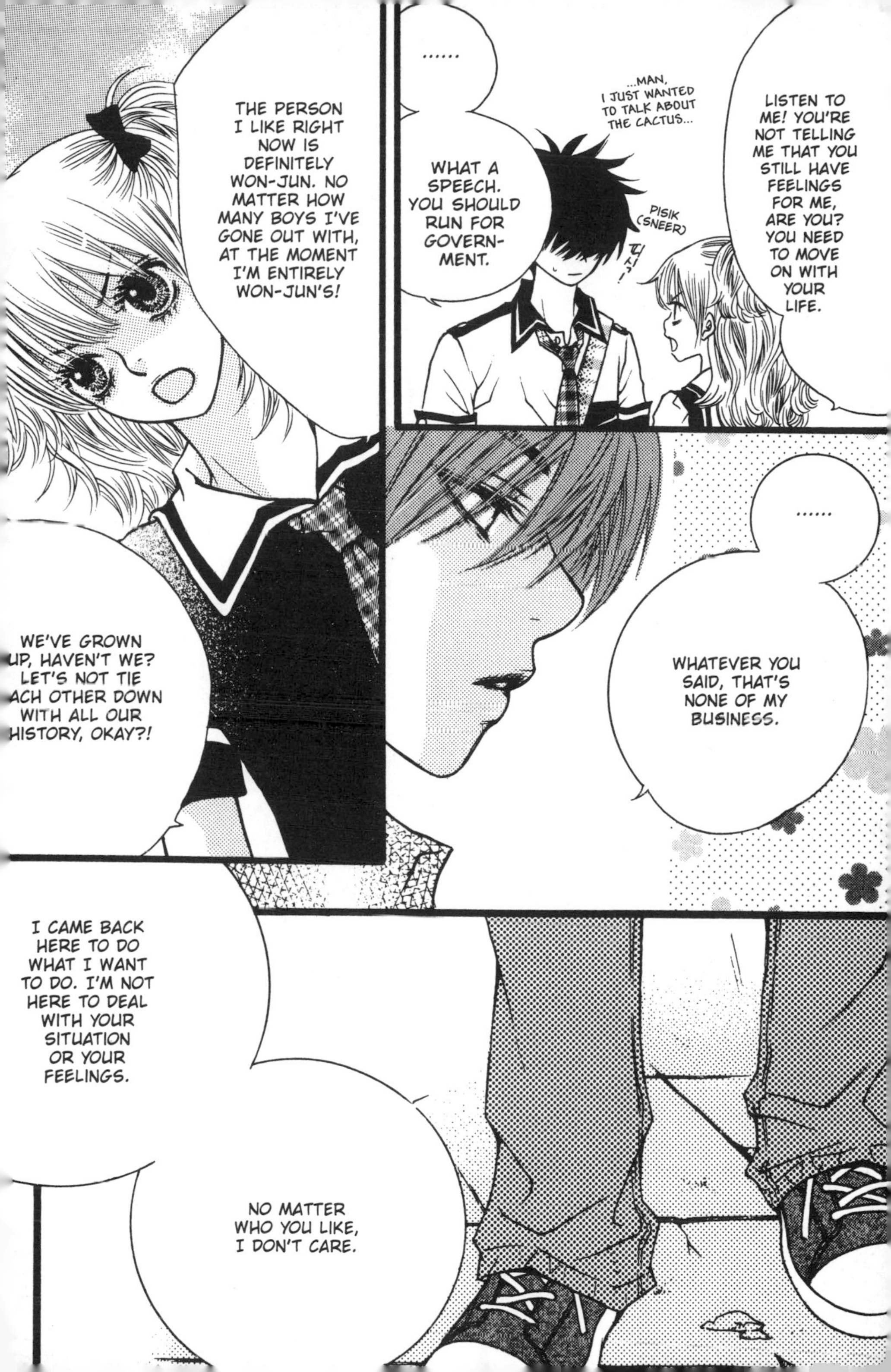
THE PERSON I LIKE RIGHT NOW IS DEFINITELY WON-JUN. NO MATTER HOW MANY BOYS I'VE GONE OUT WITH, AT THE MOMENT I'M ENTIRELY WON-JUN'S!
WE'VE GROWN UP, HAVEN'T WE? LET'S NOT TIE ACH OTHER DOWN WITH ALL OUR HISTORY, OKAY?!
......
WHAT A SPEECH. YOU SHOULD RUN FOR GOVERN-MENT.
...MAN, I JUST WANTED TO TALK ABOUT THE CACTUS...
PISIK (SNEER)
LISTEN TO ME! YOU'RE NOT TELLING ME THAT YOU STILL HAVE FEELINGS FOR ME, ARE YOU? YOU NEED TO MOVE ON WITH YOUR LIFE.
......
WHATEVER YOU SAID, THAT'S NONE OF MY BUSINESS.
I CAME BACK HERE TO DO WHAT I WANT TO DO. I'M NOT HERE TO DEAL WITH YOUR SITUATION OR YOUR FEELINGS.
NO MATTER WHO YOU LIKE, I DON'T CARE.

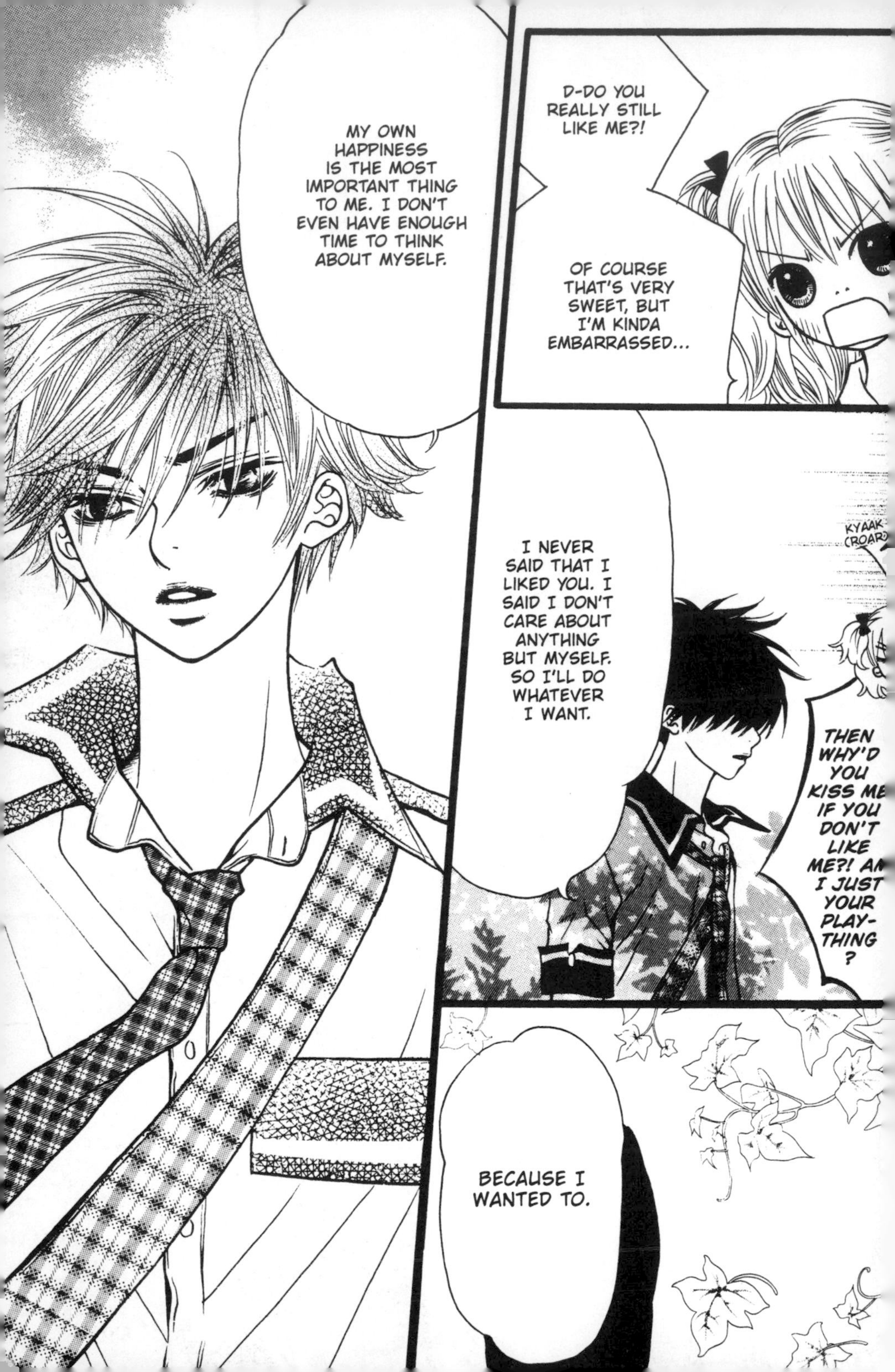

MY OWN HAPPINESS IS THE MOST IMPORTANT THING TO ME. I DON'T EVEN HAVE ENOUGH TIME TO THINK ABOUT MYSELF.
D-DO YOU REALLY STILL LIKE ME?!
OF COURSE THAT'S VERY SWEET, BUT I'M KINDA EMBARRASSED...
I NEVER SAID THAT I LIKED YOU. I SAID I DON'T CARE ABOUT ANYTHING BUT MYSELF. SO I'LL DO WHATEVER I WANT.
KYAAK (ROAR
THEN WHY'D YOU KISS ME IF YOU DON'T LIKE ME?! AM I JUST YOUR PLAYTHING?
BECAUSE I WANTED TO.

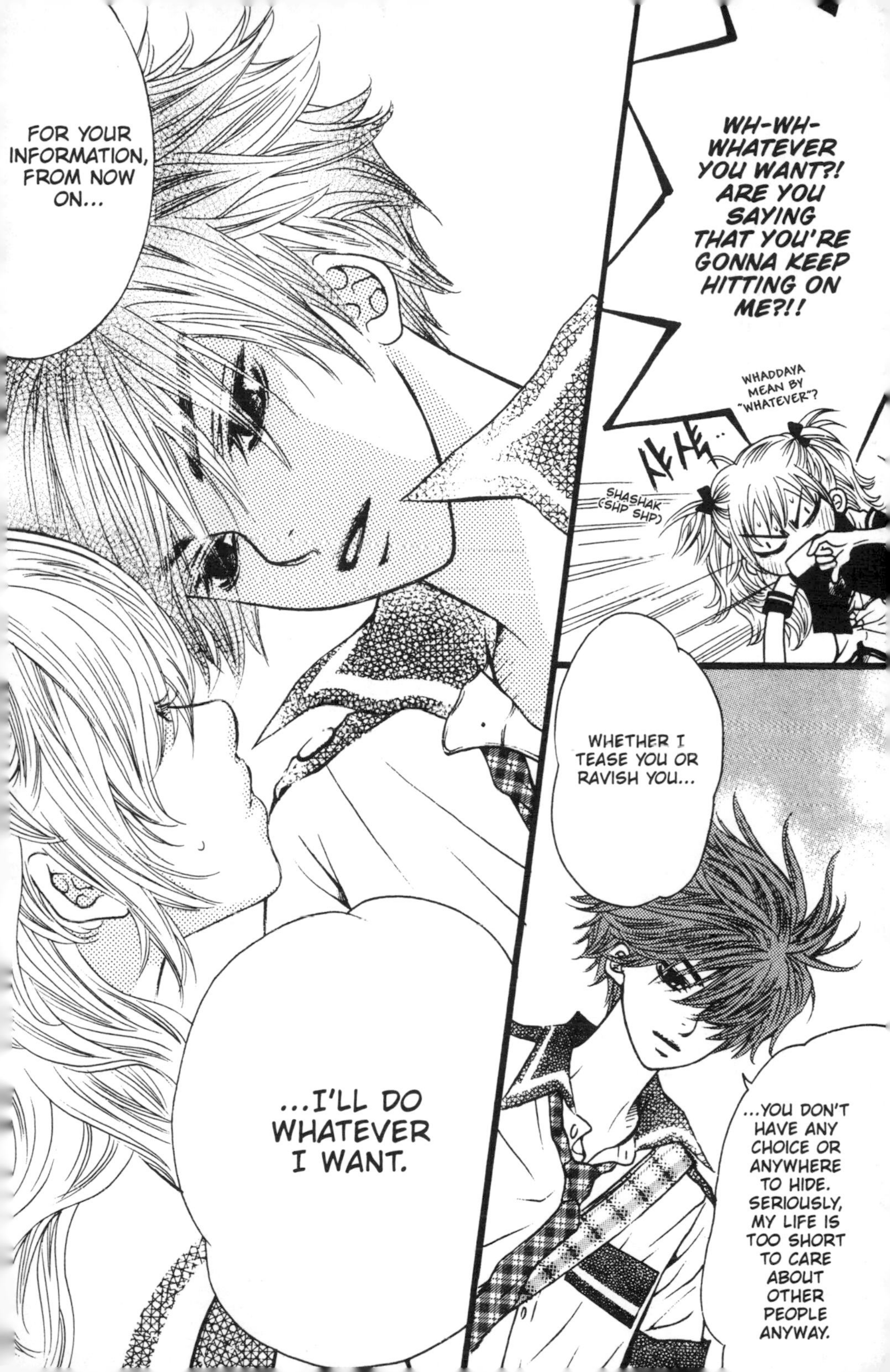
FOR YOUR INFORMATION, FROM NOW ON...
...I'LL DO WHATEVER I WANT.
WH-WH-WHATEVER YOU WANT?! ARE YOU SAYING THAT YOU'RE GONNA KEEP HITTING ON ME?!!
WHADDAYA MEAN BY "WHATEVER"?
SHASHAK (SHP SHP)
WHETHER I TEASE YOU OR RAVISH YOU...
...YOU DON'T HAVE ANY CHOICE OR ANYWHERE TO HIDE. SERIOUSLY, MY LIFE IS TOO SHORT TO CARE ABOUT OTHER PEOPLE ANYWAY.

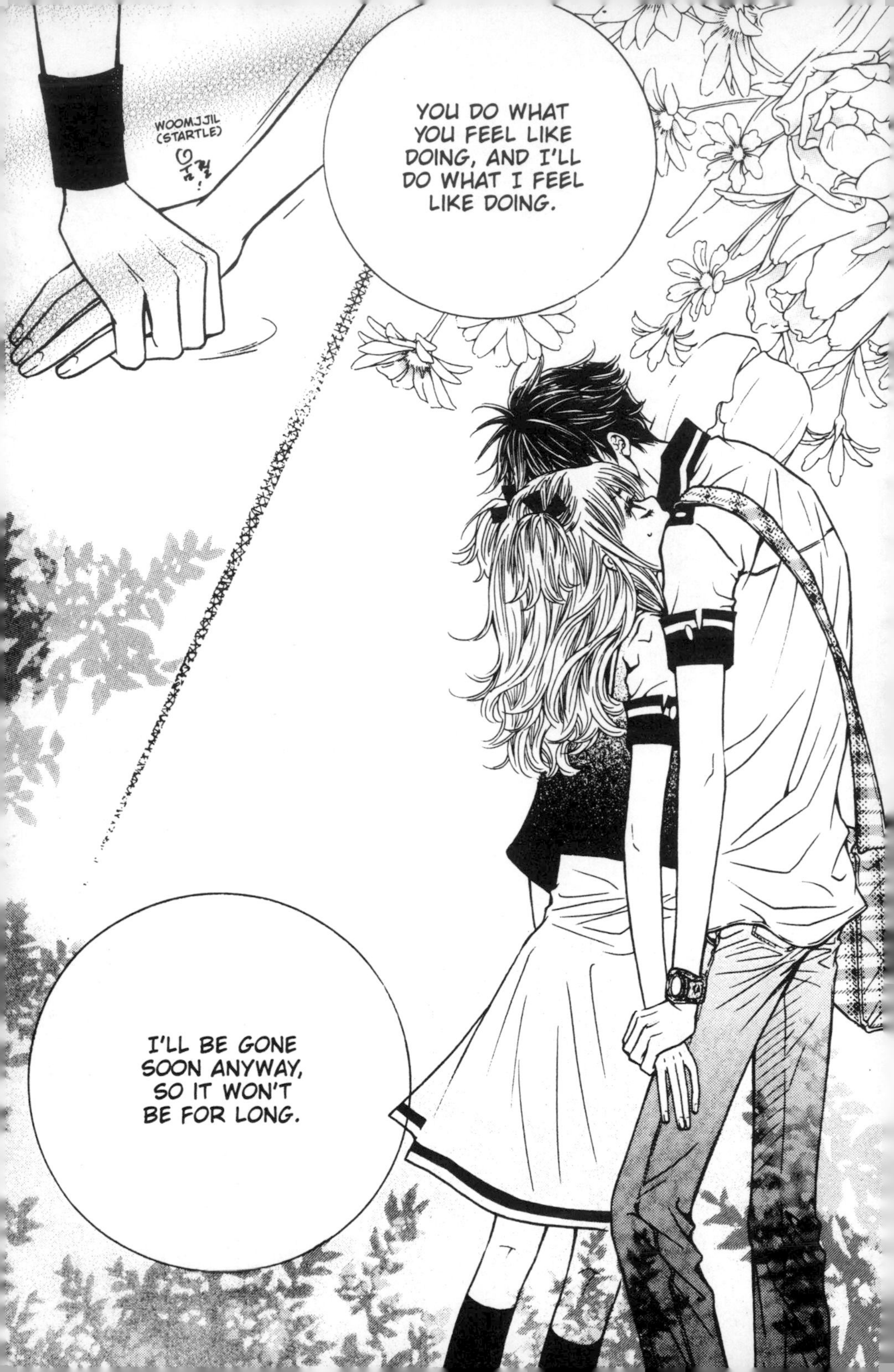
WOOMJJIL (STARTLE)
YOU DO WHAT YOU FEEL LIKE DOING, AND I'LL DO WHAT I FEEL LIKE DOING.
I'LL BE GONE SOON ANYWAY, SO IT WON'T BE FOR LONG.

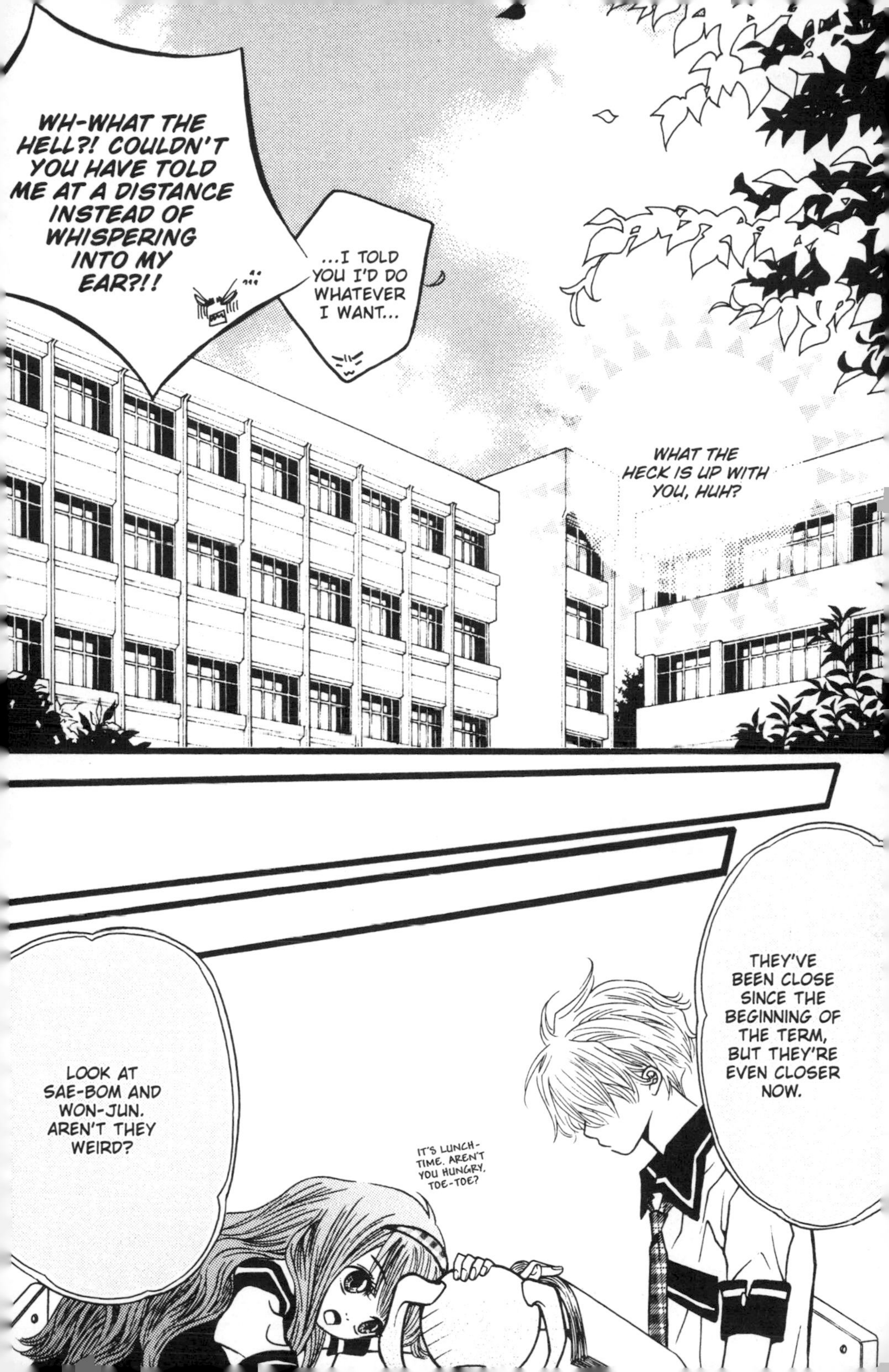
WH-WHAT THE HELL?! COULDN'T YOU HAVE TOLD ME AT A DISTANCE INSTEAD OF WHISPERING INTO MY EAR?!!
...I TOLD YOU I'D DO WHATEVER I WANT...
WHAT THE HECK IS UP WITH YOU, HUH?
LOOK AT SAE-BOM AND WON-JUN. AREN'T THEY WEIRD?
IT'S LUNCH-TIME. AREN'T YOU HUNGRY, TOE-TOE?
THEY'VE BEEN CLOSE SINCE THE BEGINNING OF THE TERM, BUT THEY'RE EVEN CLOSER NOW.

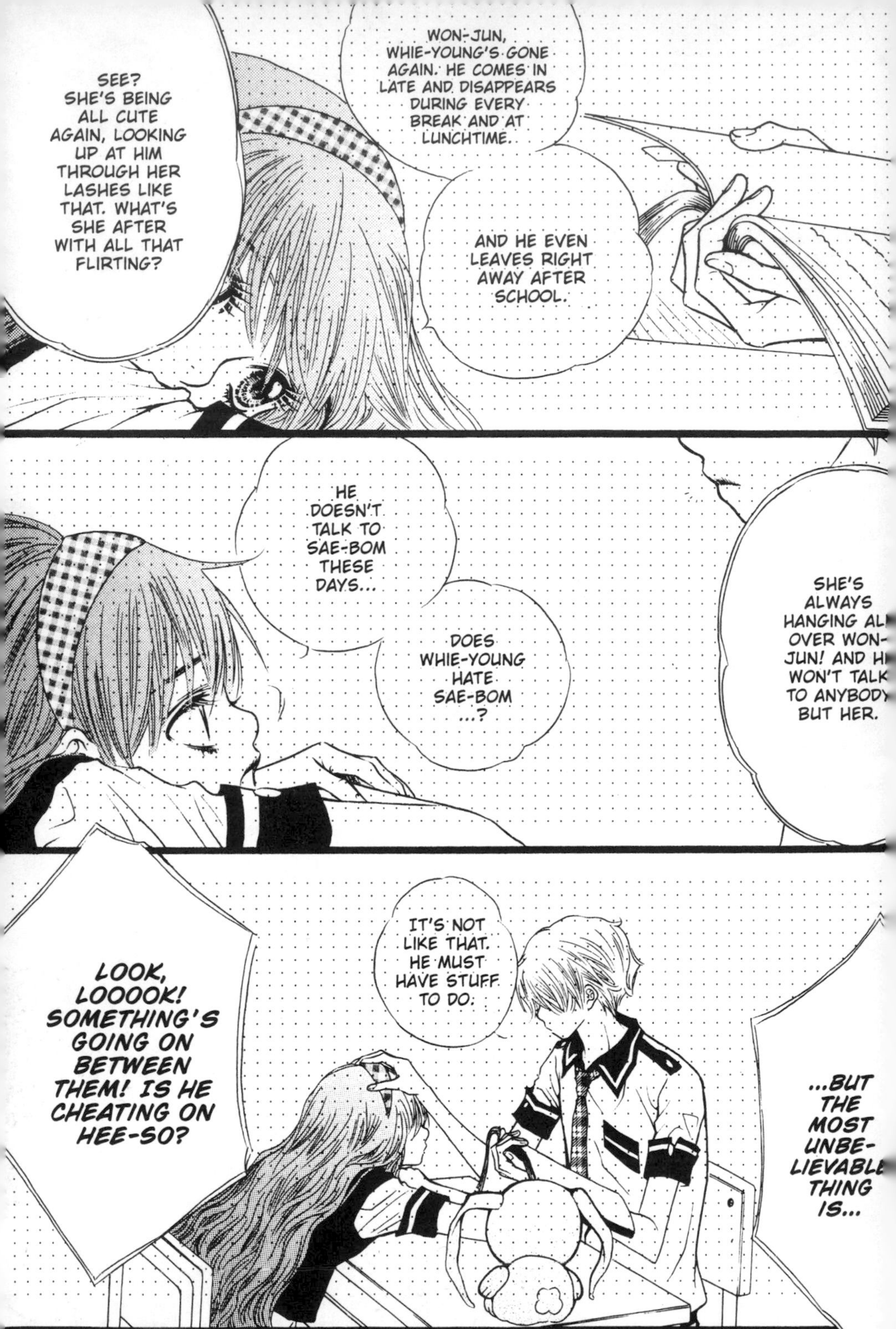
SEE? SHE'S BEING ALL CUTE AGAIN, LOOKING UP AT HIM THROUGH HER LASHES LIKE THAT. WHAT'S SHE AFTER WITH ALL THAT FLIRTING?
WON-JUN, WHIE-YOUNG'S GONE AGAIN. HE COMES IN LATE AND DISAPPEARS DURING EVERY BREAK AND AT LUNCHTIME.
AND HE EVEN LEAVES RIGHT AWAY AFTER SCHOOL.
HE DOESN'T TALK TO SAE-BOM THESE DAYS...
DOES WHIE-YOUNG HATE SAE-BOM ...?
SHE'S ALWAYS HANGING AL OVER WON-JUN! AND H WON'T TALK TO ANYBODY BUT HER.
LOOK, LOOOOK! SOMETHING'S GOING ON BETWEEN THEM! IS HE CHEATING ON HEE-SO?
IT'S NOT LIKE THAT. HE MUST HAVE STUFF TO DO.
...BUT THE MOST UNBE-LIEVABL THING IS...

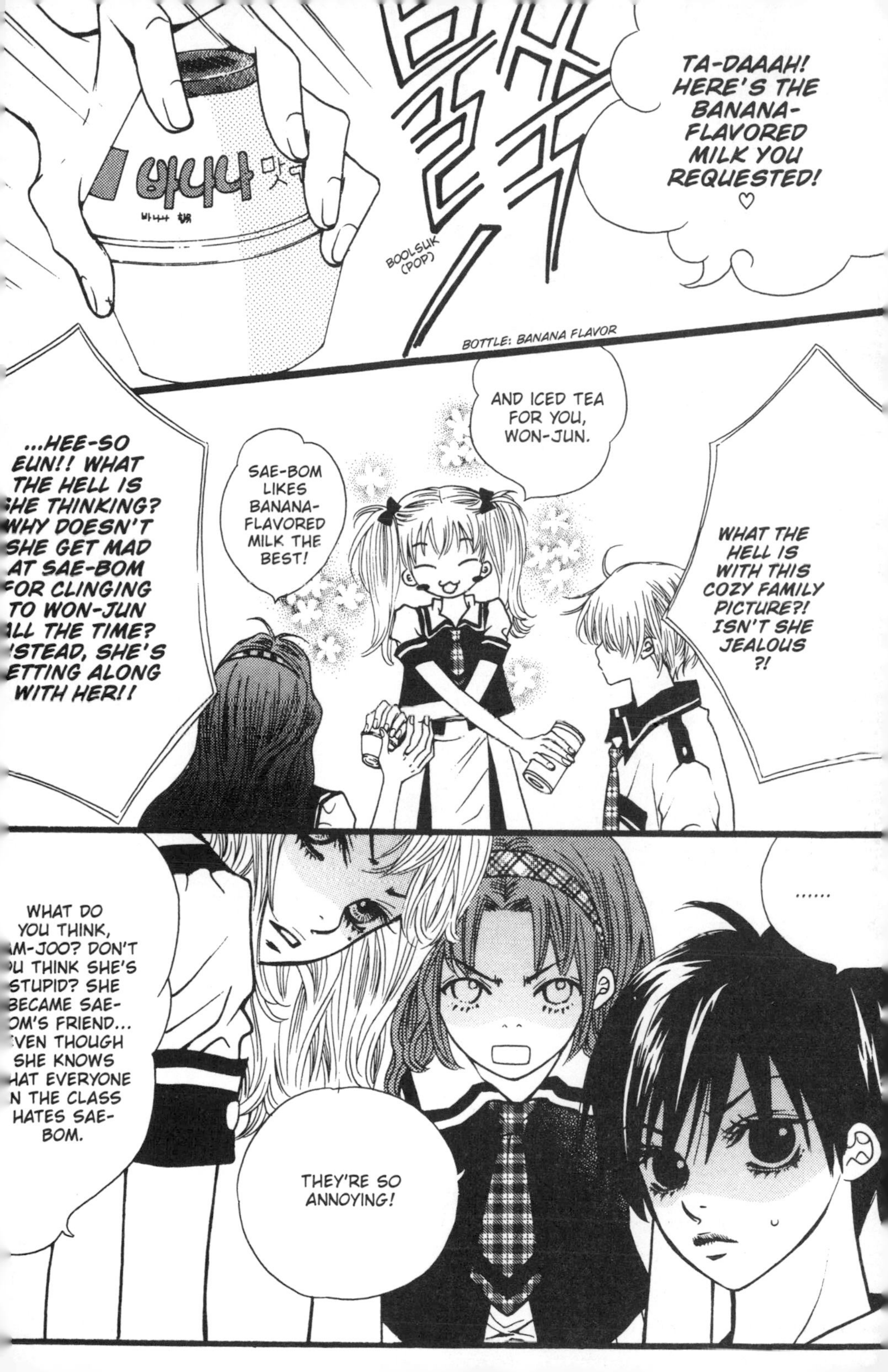
불쑥
BOOLSUK (POP)
TA-DAAAH! HERE'S THE BANANA-FLAVORED MILK YOU REQUESTED! ♡
BOTTLE: BANANA FLAVOR
...HEE-SO EUN!! WHAT THE HELL IS HE THINKING? WHY DOESN'T SHE GET MAD AT SAE-BOM FOR CLINGING TO WON-JUN ALL THE TIME? NSTEAD, SHE'S ETTING ALONG WITH HER!!
SAE-BOM LIKES BANANA-FLAVORED MILK THE BEST!
AND ICED TEA FOR YOU, WON-JUN.
WHAT THE HELL IS WITH THIS COZY FAMILY PICTURE?! ISN'T SHE JEALOUS ?!
WHAT DO YOU THINK, AM-JOO? DON'T OU THINK SHE'S STUPID? SHE BECAME SAE-OM'S FRIEND... EVEN THOUGH SHE KNOWS HAT EVERYONE N THE CLASS HATES SAE-BOM.
THEY'RE SO ANNOYING!
......

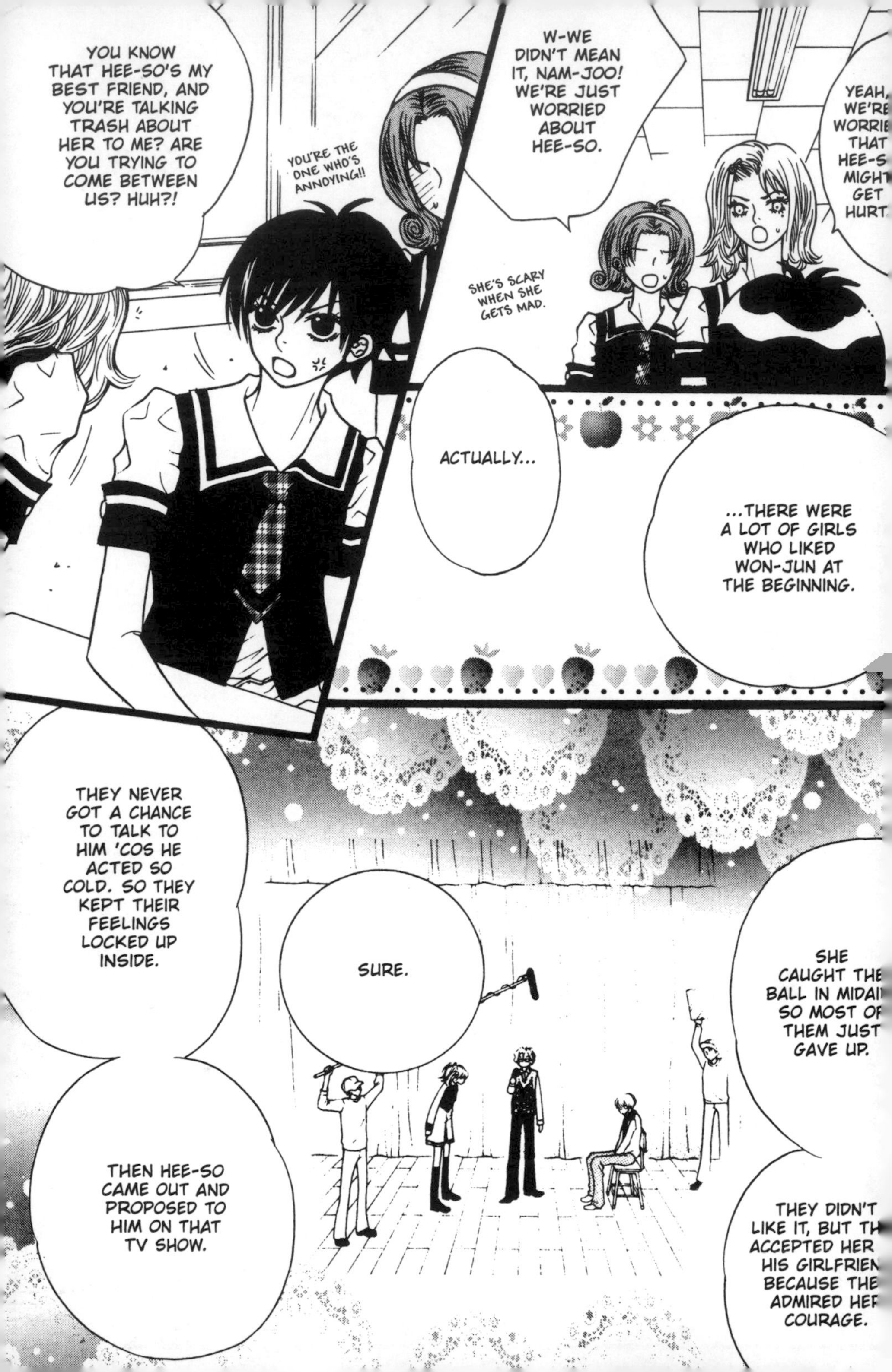
YOU KNOW THAT HEE-SO'S MY BEST FRIEND, AND YOU'RE TALKING TRASH ABOUT HER TO ME? ARE YOU TRYING TO COME BETWEEN US? HUH?!
YOU'RE THE ONE WHO'S ANNOYING!!
W-WE DIDN'T MEAN IT, NAM-JOO! WE'RE JUST WORRIED ABOUT HEE-SO.
YEAH, WE'R WORRIE THAT HEE-S MIGHT GET HURT.
SHE'S SCARY WHEN SHE GETS MAD.
ACTUALLY...
...THERE WERE A LOT OF GIRLS WHO LIKED WON-JUN AT THE BEGINNING.
THEY NEVER GOT A CHANCE TO TALK TO HIM 'COS HE ACTED SO COLD. SO THEY KEPT THEIR FEELINGS LOCKED UP INSIDE.
SURE.
SHE CAUGHT THE BALL IN MIDAI SO MOST OF THEM JUST GAVE UP.
THEN HEE-SO CAME OUT AND PROPOSED TO HIM ON THAT TV SHOW.
THEY DIDN'T LIKE IT, BUT TH ACCEPTED HER HIS GIRLFRIEN BECAUSE THE ADMIRED HER COURAGE.

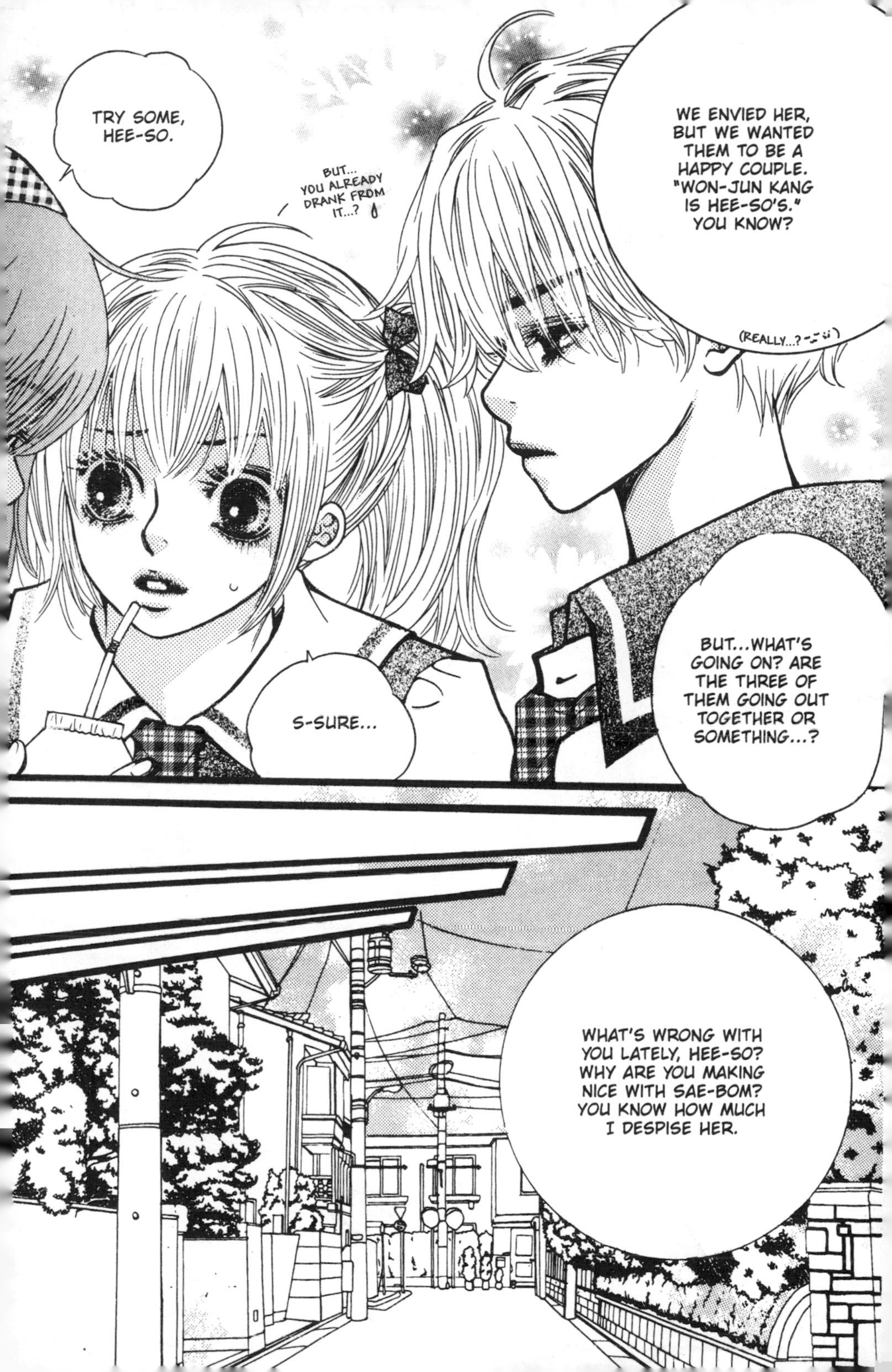
TRY SOME, HEE-SO.
BUT... YOU ALREADY DRANK FROM IT...?
WE ENVIED HER, BUT WE WANTED THEM TO BE A HAPPY COUPLE. "WON-JUN KANG IS HEE-SO'S." YOU KNOW?
(REALLY...?
S-SURE...
BUT...WHAT'S GOING ON? ARE THE THREE OF THEM GOING OUT TOGETHER OR SOMETHING...?
WHAT'S WRONG WITH YOU LATELY, HEE-SO? WHY ARE YOU MAKING NICE WITH SAE-BOM? YOU KNOW HOW MUCH I DESPISE HER.

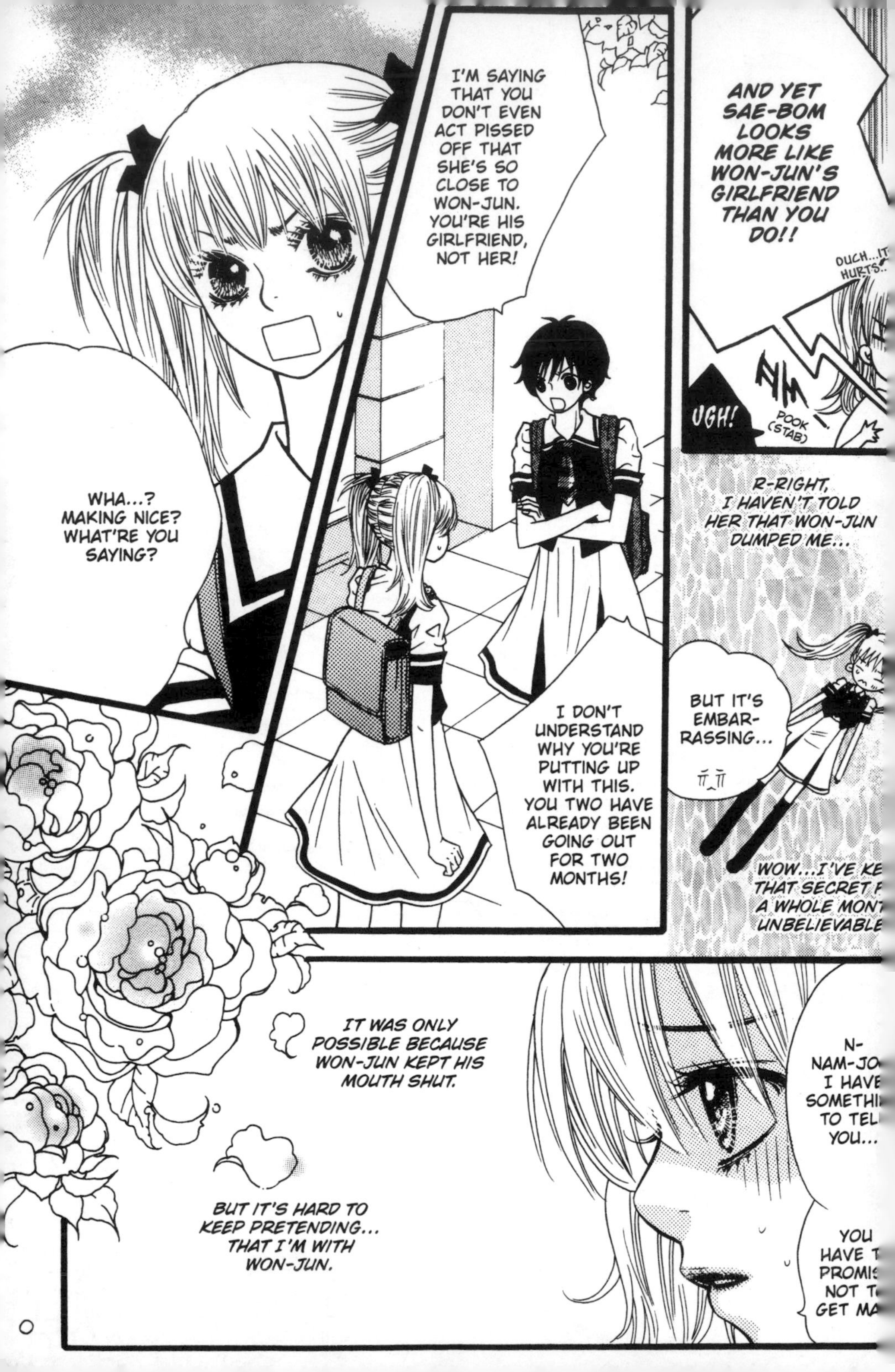
WHA...? MAKING NICE? WHAT'RE YOU SAYING?
I'M SAYING THAT YOU DON'T EVEN ACT PISSED OFF THAT SHE'S SO CLOSE TO WON-JUN. YOU'RE HIS GIRLFRIEND, NOT HER!
I DON'T UNDERSTAND WHY YOU'RE PUTTING UP WITH THIS. YOU TWO HAVE ALREADY BEEN GOING OUT FOR TWO MONTHS!
AND YET SAE-BOM LOOKS MORE LIKE WON-JUN'S GIRLFRIEND THAN YOU DO!!
OUCH...IT HURTS...
UGH!
POOK (STAB)
R-RIGHT, I HAVEN'T TOLD HER THAT WON-JUN DUMPED ME...
BUT IT'S EMBAR-RASSING...
WOW...I'VE KE THAT SECRET F A WHOLE MONT UNBELIEVABLE
IT WAS ONLY POSSIBLE BECAUSE WON-JUN KEPT HIS MOUTH SHUT.
BUT IT'S HARD TO KEEP PRETENDING... THAT I'M WITH WON-JUN.
N- NAM-JO I HAVE SOMETHI TO TEL YOU...
YOU HAVE T PROMIS NOT T GET MA

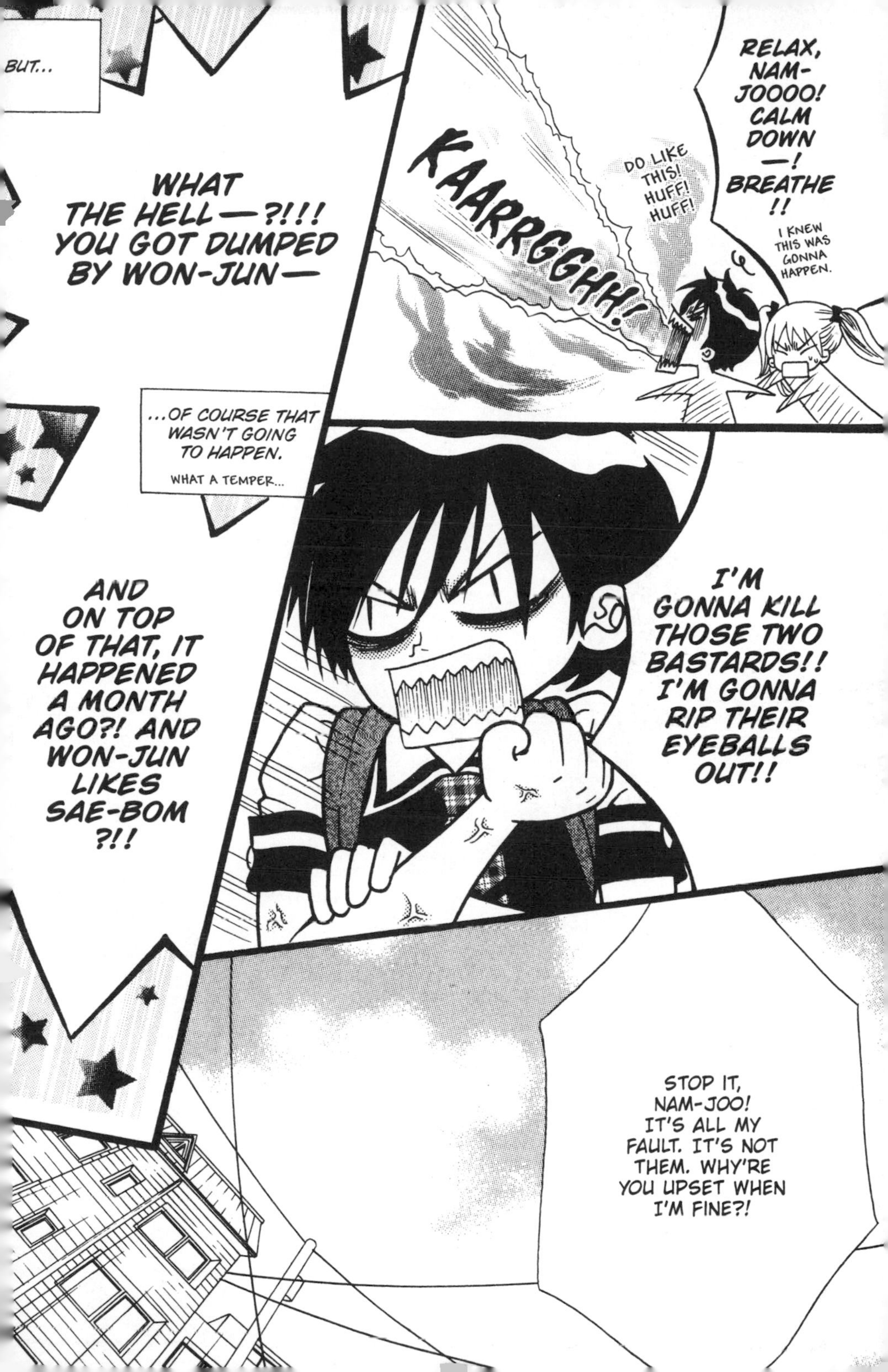
BUT...
WHAT THE HELL—?!!! YOU GOT DUMPED BY WON-JUN—
KAARRGGHH!!
DO LIKE THIS! HUFF! HUFF!
RELAX, NAM-JOOOO! CALM DOWN—! BREATHE!!
I KNEW THIS WAS GONNA HAPPEN.
...OF COURSE THAT WASN'T GOING TO HAPPEN.
WHAT A TEMPER...
AND ON TOP OF THAT, IT HAPPENED A MONTH AGO?! AND WON-JUN LIKES SAE-BOM?!!
I'M GONNA KILL THOSE TWO BASTARDS!! I'M GONNA RIP THEIR EYEBALLS OUT!!
STOP IT, NAM-JOO! IT'S ALL MY FAULT. IT'S NOT THEM. WHY'RE YOU UPSET WHEN I'M FINE?!

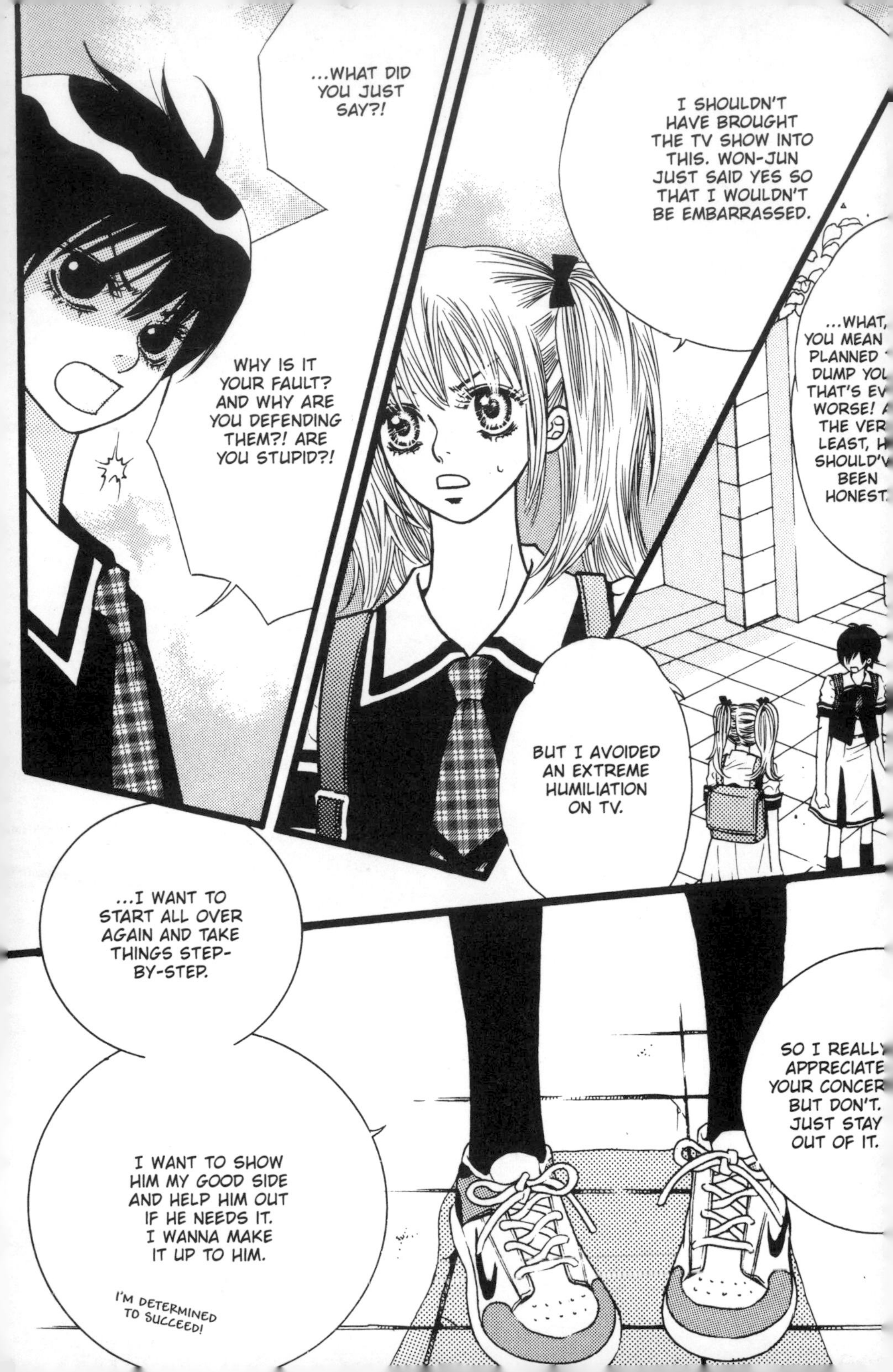
...WHAT DID YOU JUST SAY?!
WHY IS IT YOUR FAULT? AND WHY ARE YOU DEFENDING THEM?! ARE YOU STUPID?!
I SHOULDN'T HAVE BROUGHT THE TV SHOW INTO THIS. WON-JUN JUST SAID YES SO THAT I WOULDN'T BE EMBARRASSED.
...WHAT, YOU MEAN PLANNED DUMP YOU THAT'S EV WORSE! A THE VER LEAST, H SHOULD'V BEEN HONEST.
BUT I AVOIDED AN EXTREME HUMILIATION ON TV.
...I WANT TO START ALL OVER AGAIN AND TAKE THINGS STEP-BY-STEP.
I WANT TO SHOW HIM MY GOOD SIDE AND HELP HIM OUT IF HE NEEDS IT. I WANNA MAKE IT UP TO HIM.
I'M DETERMINED TO SUCCEED!
SO I REALLY APPRECIATE YOUR CONCER BUT DON'T. JUST STAY OUT OF IT.

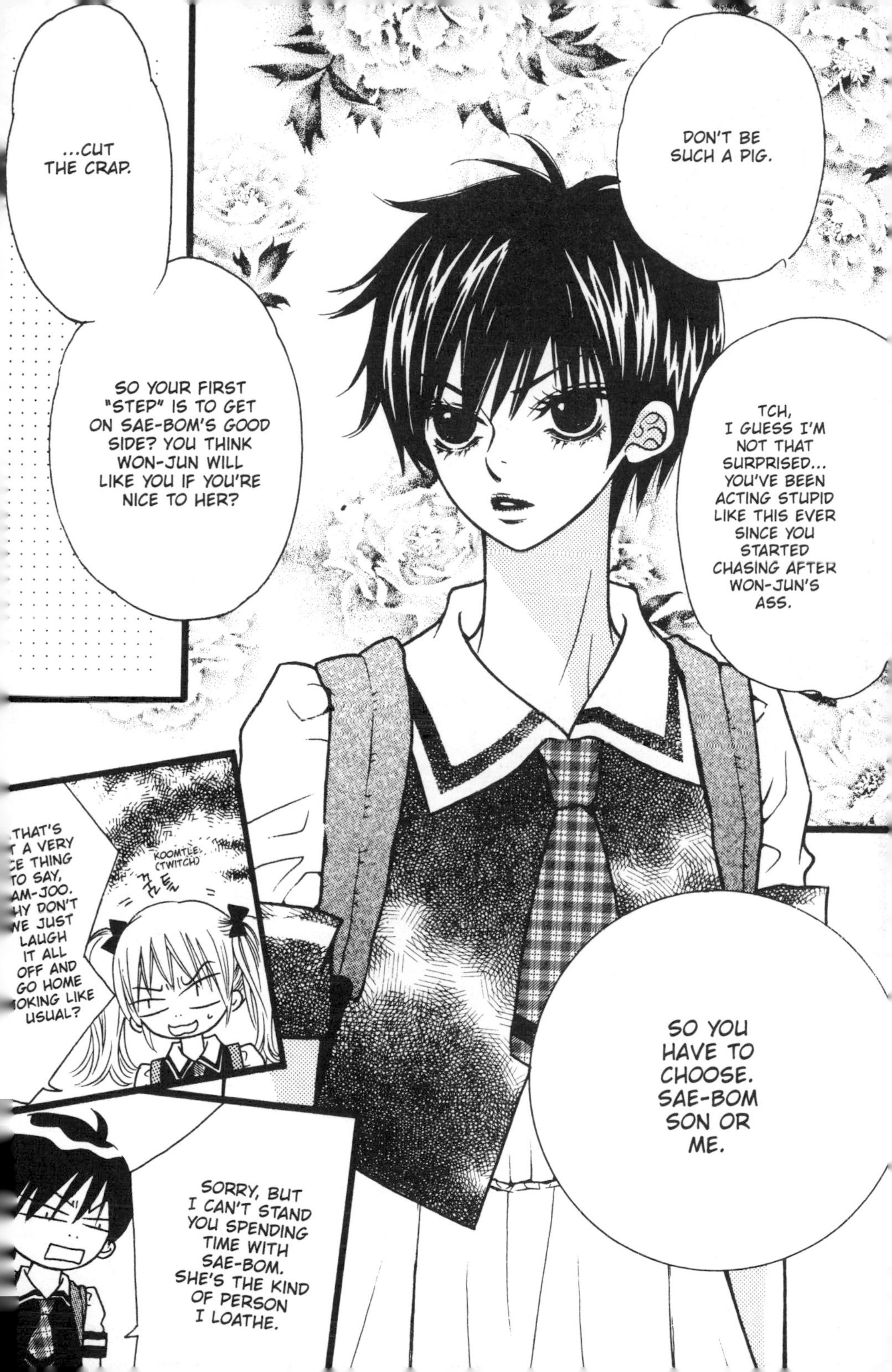
...CUT THE CRAP.
SO YOUR FIRST "STEP" IS TO GET ON SAE-BOM'S GOOD SIDE? YOU THINK WON-JUN WILL LIKE YOU IF YOU'RE NICE TO HER?
DON'T BE SUCH A PIG.
TCH, I GUESS I'M NOT THAT SURPRISED... YOU'VE BEEN ACTING STUPID LIKE THIS EVER SINCE YOU STARTED CHASING AFTER WON-JUN'S ASS.
THAT'S T A VERY CE THING TO SAY, AM-JOO. HY DON'T WE JUST LAUGH IT ALL OFF AND GO HOME OKING LIKE USUAL?
KOOMTLE (TWITCH)
SORRY, BUT I CAN'T STAND YOU SPENDING TIME WITH SAE-BOM. SHE'S THE KIND OF PERSON I LOATHE.
SO YOU HAVE TO CHOOSE. SAE-BOM SON OR ME.

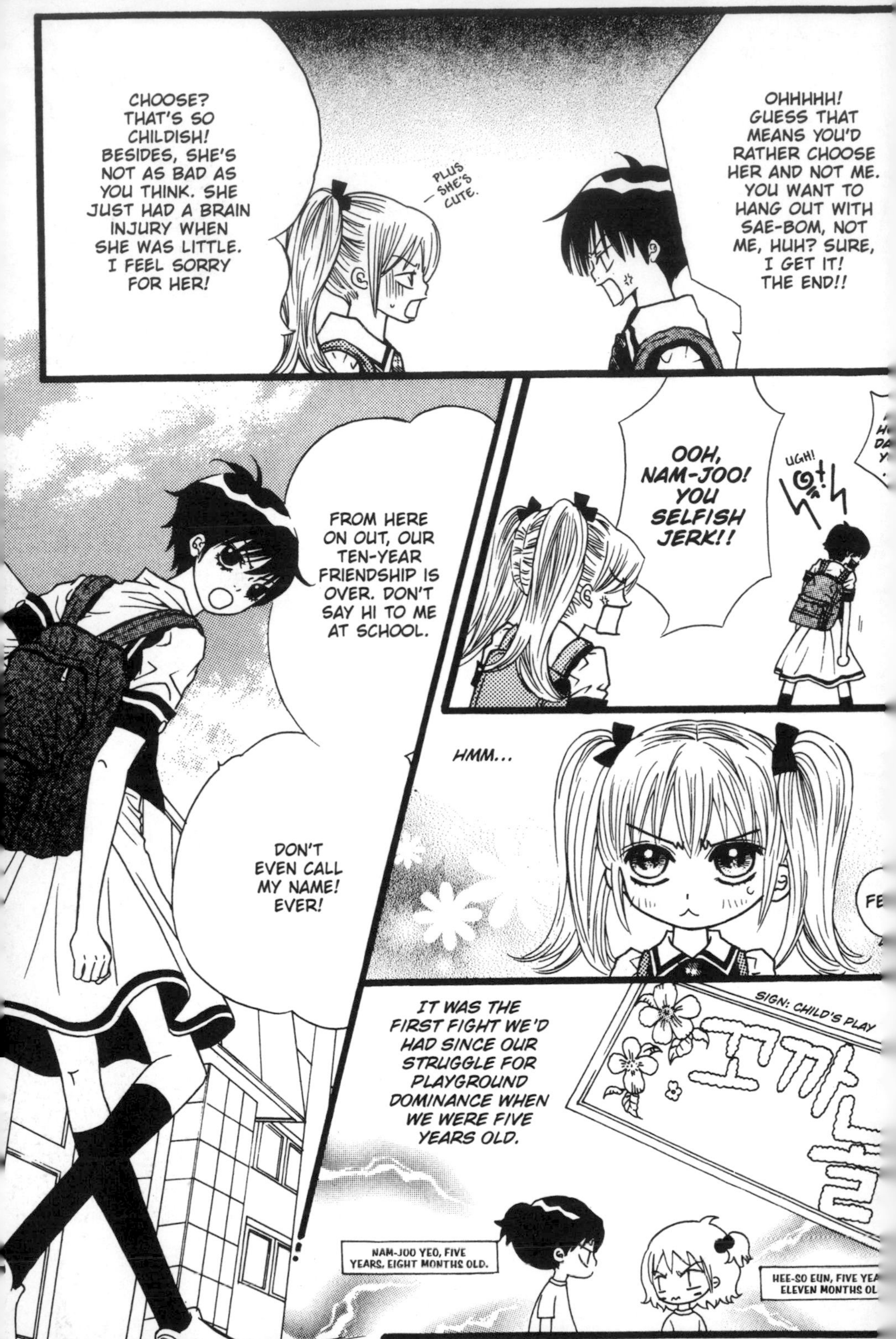
CHOOSE? THAT'S SO CHILDISH! BESIDES, SHE'S NOT AS BAD AS YOU THINK. SHE JUST HAD A BRAIN INJURY WHEN SHE WAS LITTLE. I FEEL SORRY FOR HER!
PLUS SHE'S CUTE.
OHHHHH! GUESS THAT MEANS YOU'D RATHER CHOOSE HER AND NOT ME. YOU WANT TO HANG OUT WITH SAE-BOM, NOT ME, HUH? SURE, I GET IT! THE END!!
FROM HERE ON OUT, OUR TEN-YEAR FRIENDSHIP IS OVER. DON'T SAY HI TO ME AT SCHOOL.
DON'T EVEN CALL MY NAME! EVER!
OOH, NAM-JOO! YOU SELFISH JERK!!
UGH!
HMM...
IT WAS THE FIRST FIGHT WE'D HAD SINCE OUR STRUGGLE FOR PLAYGROUND DOMINANCE WHEN WE WERE FIVE YEARS OLD.
SIGN: CHILD'S PLAY
NAM-JOO YEO, FIVE YEARS, EIGHT MONTHS OLD.
HEE-SO EUN, FIVE YEA ELEVEN MONTHS OL

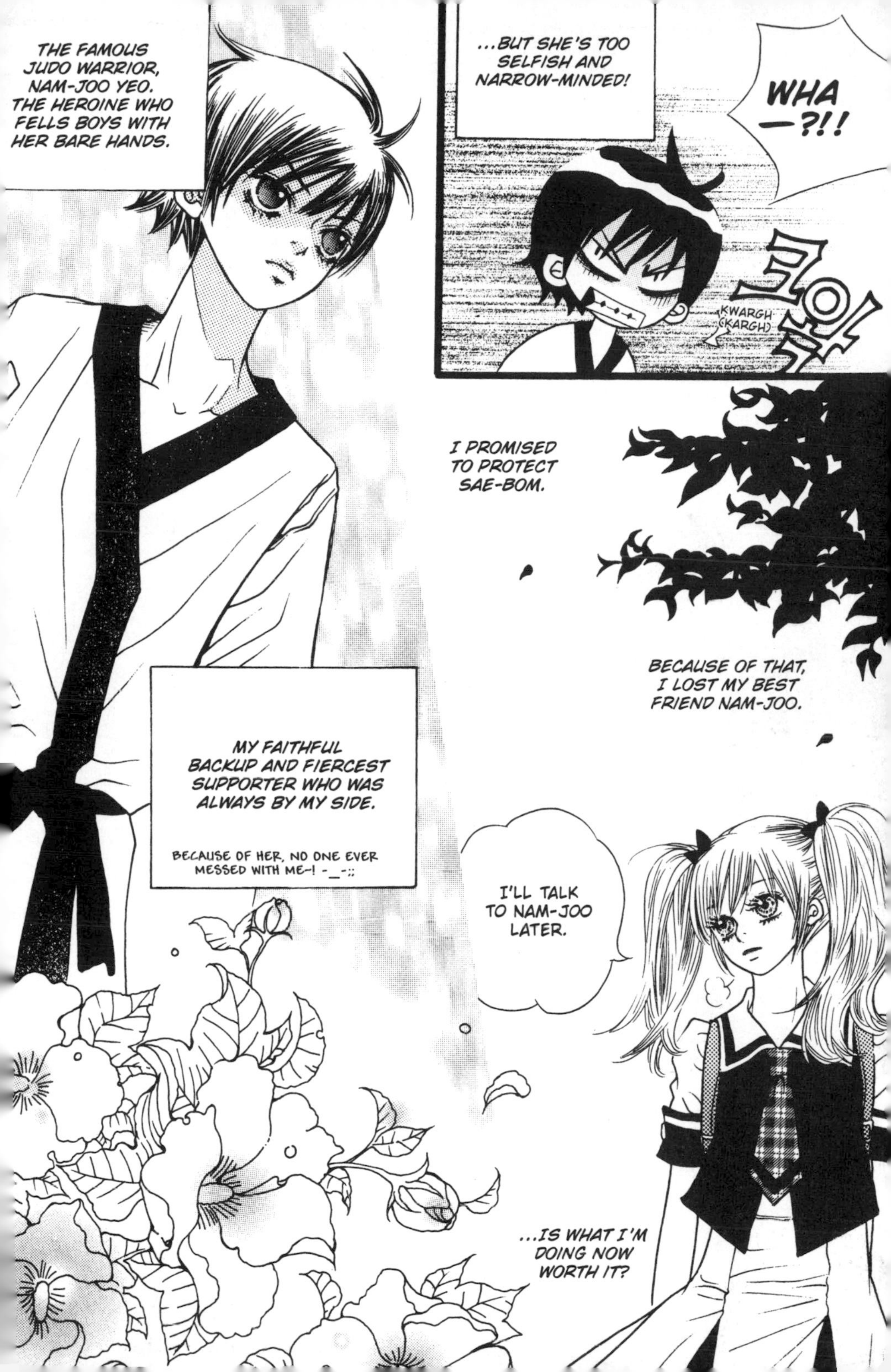
THE FAMOUS JUDO WARRIOR, NAM-JOO YEO. THE HEROINE WHO FELLS BOYS WITH HER BARE HANDS.
MY FAITHFUL BACKUP AND FIERCEST SUPPORTER WHO WAS ALWAYS BY MY SIDE.
BECAUSE OF HER, NO ONE EVER MESSED WITH ME-! -_-;;
...BUT SHE'S TOO SELFISH AND NARROW-MINDED!
WHA—?!!
KWARGH (KARGH)
I PROMISED TO PROTECT SAE-BOM.
BECAUSE OF THAT, I LOST MY BEST FRIEND NAM-JOO.
I'LL TALK TO NAM-JOO LATER.
...IS WHAT I'M DOING NOW WORTH IT?

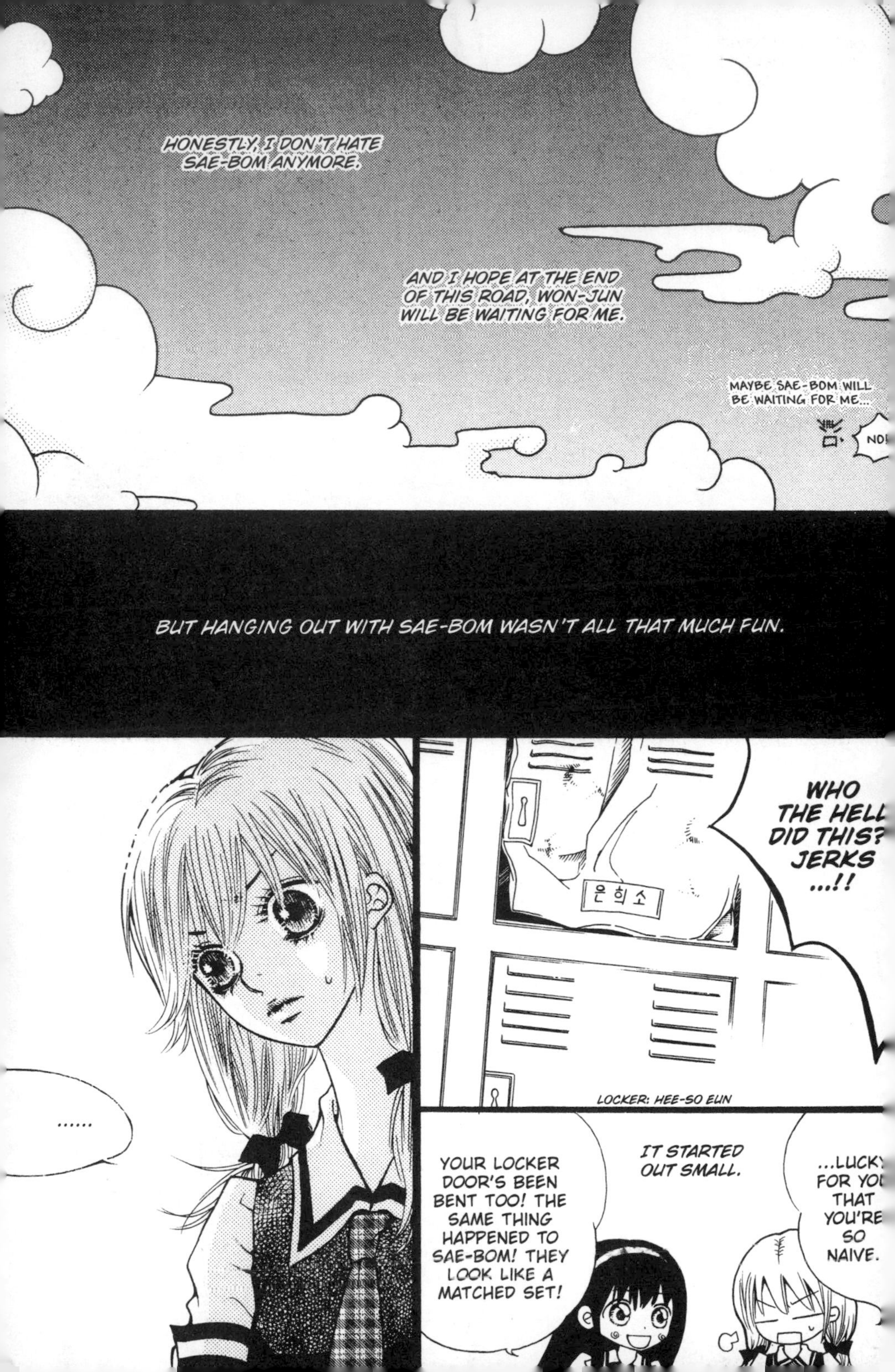
HONESTLY, I DON'T HATE SAE-BOM ANYMORE.
AND I HOPE AT THE END OF THIS ROAD, WON-JUN WILL BE WAITING FOR ME.
MAYBE SAE-BOM WILL BE WAITING FOR ME...
NO!
BUT HANGING OUT WITH SAE-BOM WASN'T ALL THAT MUCH FUN.
......
은희소
WHO THE HELL DID THIS? JERKS ...!!
LOCKER: HEE-SO EUN
YOUR LOCKER DOOR'S BEEN BENT TOO! THE SAME THING HAPPENED TO SAE-BOM! THEY LOOK LIKE A MATCHED SET!
IT STARTED OUT SMALL.
...LUCKY FOR YOU THAT YOU'RE SO NAIVE.

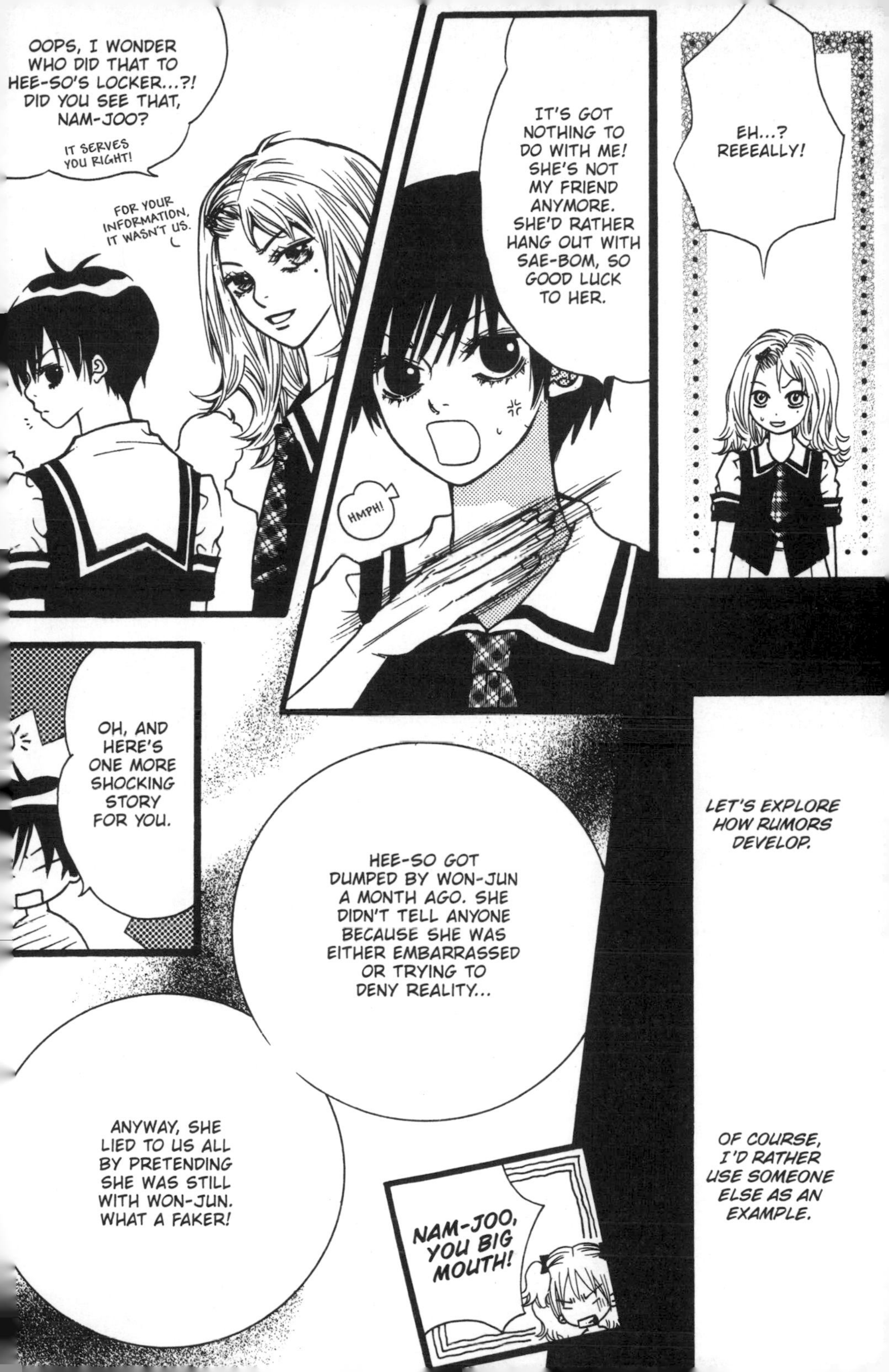
OOPS, I WONDER WHO DID THAT TO HEE-SO'S LOCKER...?! DID YOU SEE THAT, NAM-JOO?
IT SERVES YOU RIGHT!
FOR YOUR INFORMATION, IT WASN'T US.
IT'S GOT NOTHING TO DO WITH ME! SHE'S NOT MY FRIEND ANYMORE. SHE'D RATHER HANG OUT WITH SAE-BOM, SO GOOD LUCK TO HER.
HMPH!
EH...? REEEALLY!
OH, AND HERE'S ONE MORE SHOCKING STORY FOR YOU.
HEE-SO GOT DUMPED BY WON-JUN A MONTH AGO. SHE DIDN'T TELL ANYONE BECAUSE SHE WAS EITHER EMBARRASSED OR TRYING TO DENY REALITY...
ANYWAY, SHE LIED TO US ALL BY PRETENDING SHE WAS STILL WITH WON-JUN. WHAT A FAKER!
NAM-JOO, YOU BIG MOUTH!
LET'S EXPLORE HOW RUMORS DEVELOP.
OF COURSE, I'D RATHER USE SOMEONE ELSE AS AN EXAMPLE.

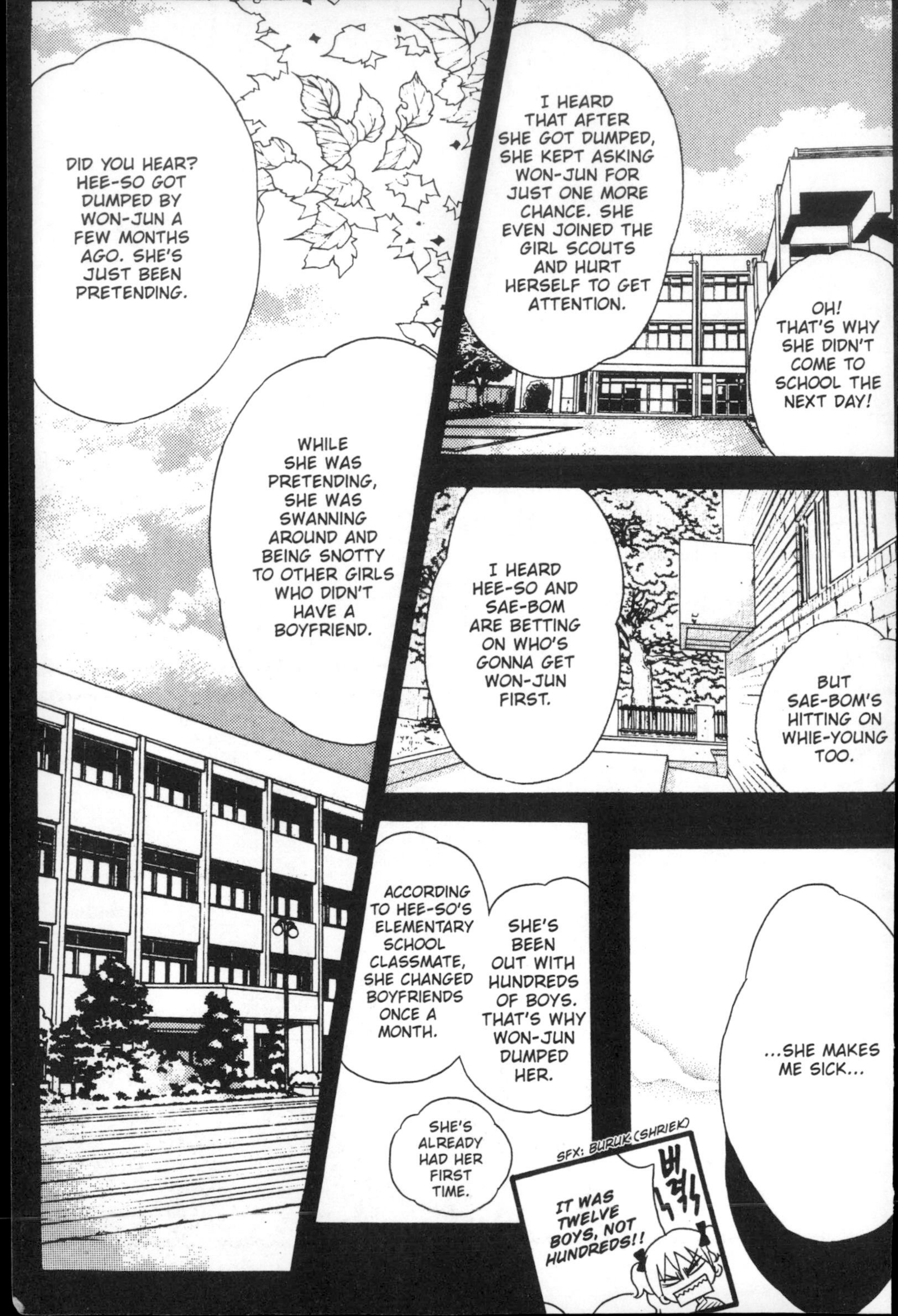
DID YOU HEAR? HEE-SO GOT DUMPED BY WON-JUN A FEW MONTHS AGO. SHE'S JUST BEEN PRETENDING.
WHILE SHE WAS PRETENDING, SHE WAS SWANNING AROUND AND BEING SNOTTY TO OTHER GIRLS WHO DIDN'T HAVE A BOYFRIEND.
I HEARD THAT AFTER SHE GOT DUMPED, SHE KEPT ASKING WON-JUN FOR JUST ONE MORE CHANCE. SHE EVEN JOINED THE GIRL SCOUTS AND HURT HERSELF TO GET ATTENTION.
OH! THAT'S WHY SHE DIDN'T COME TO SCHOOL THE NEXT DAY!
I HEARD HEE-SO AND SAE-BOM ARE BETTING ON WHO'S GONNA GET WON-JUN FIRST.
BUT SAE-BOM'S HITTING ON WHIE-YOUNG TOO.
ACCORDING TO HEE-SO'S ELEMENTARY SCHOOL CLASSMATE, SHE CHANGED BOYFRIENDS ONCE A MONTH.
SHE'S BEEN OUT WITH HUNDREDS OF BOYS. THAT'S WHY WON-JUN DUMPED HER.
SHE'S ALREADY HAD HER FIRST TIME.
...SHE MAKES ME SICK...
SFX: BURUK (SHRIEK)
버럭
IT WAS TWELVE BOYS, NOT HUNDREDS!!

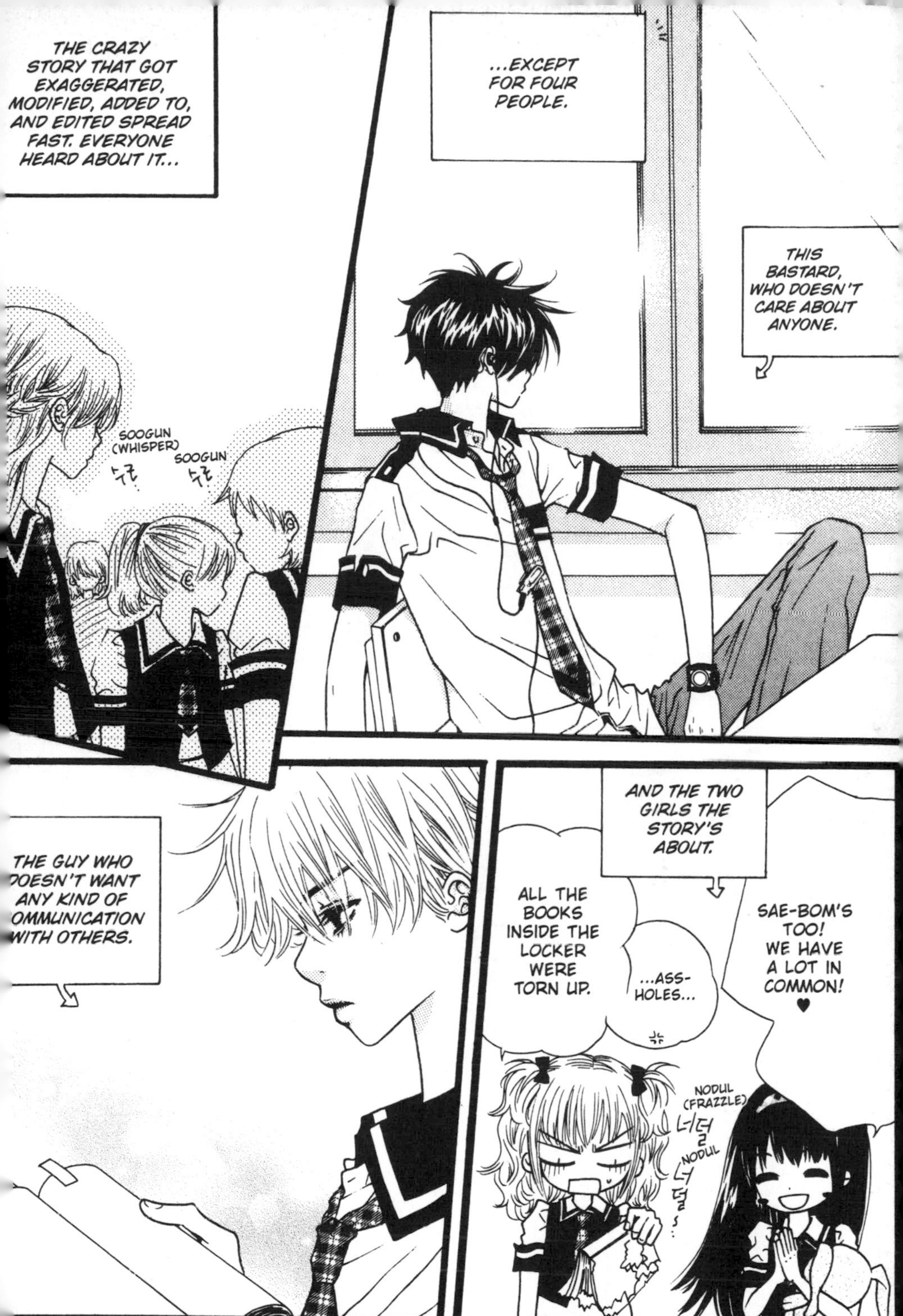
THE CRAZY STORY THAT GOT EXAGGERATED, MODIFIED, ADDED TO, AND EDITED SPREAD FAST. EVERYONE HEARD ABOUT IT...
SOOGUN (WHISPER)
수군
SOOGUN
수군
...EXCEPT FOR FOUR PEOPLE.
THIS BASTARD, WHO DOESN'T CARE ABOUT ANYONE.
THE GUY WHO DOESN'T WANT ANY KIND OF COMMUNICATION WITH OTHERS.
AND THE TWO GIRLS THE STORY'S ABOUT.
ALL THE BOOKS INSIDE THE LOCKER WERE TORN UP.
...ASS-HOLES...
SAE-BOM'S TOO! WE HAVE A LOT IN COMMON! ♥
NODUL (FRAZZLE)
너덜
NODUL
너덜

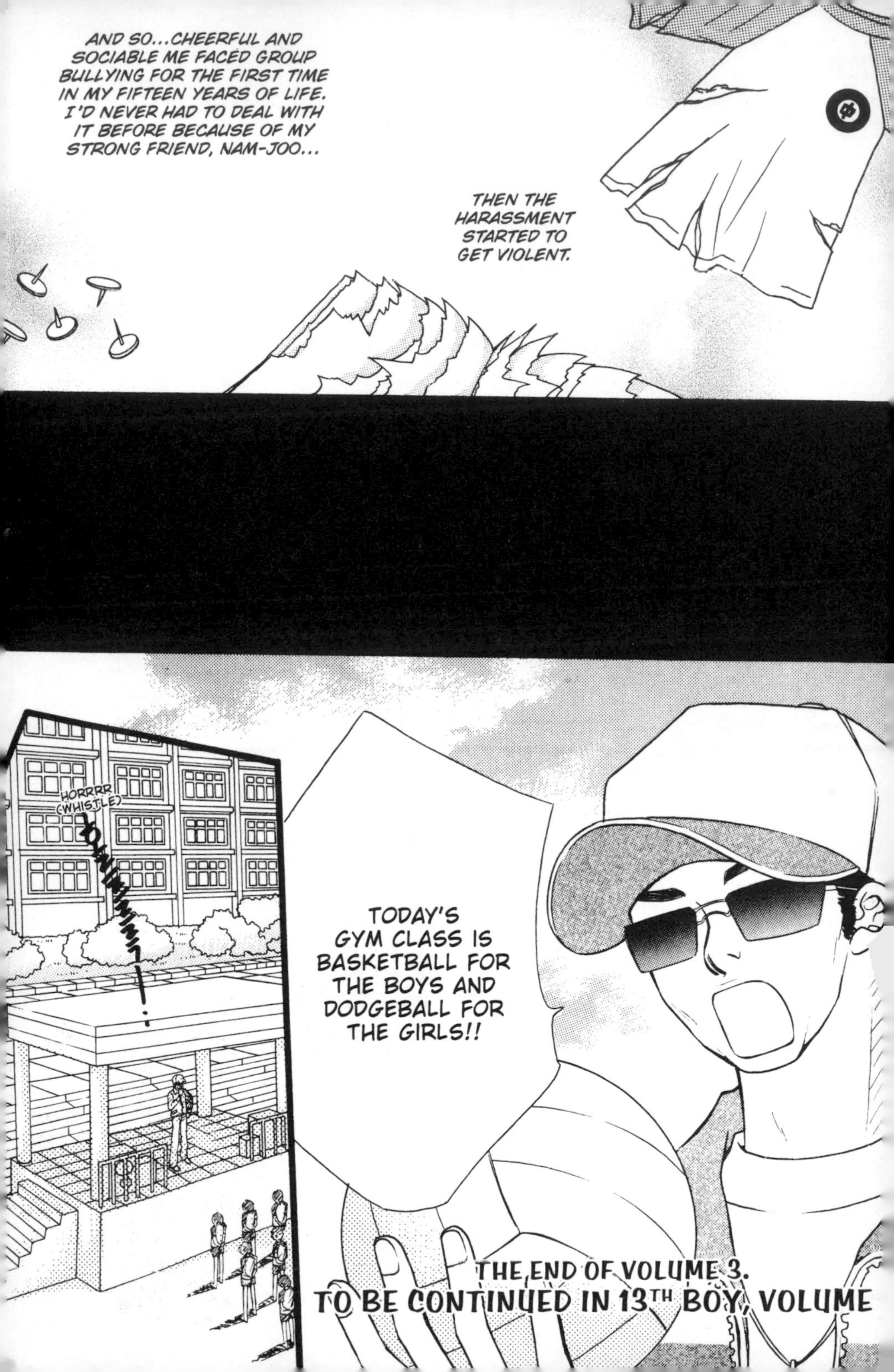
AND SO...CHEERFUL AND SOCIABLE ME FACED GROUP BULLYING FOR THE FIRST TIME IN MY FIFTEEN YEARS OF LIFE. I'D NEVER HAD TO DEAL WITH IT BEFORE BECAUSE OF MY STRONG FRIEND, NAM-JOO...
THEN THE HARASSMENT STARTED TO GET VIOLENT.
HORRRR (WHISTLE)
TODAY'S GYM CLASS IS BASKETBALL FOR THE BOYS AND DODGEBALL FOR THE GIRLS!!
THE END OF VOLUME 3.
TO BE CONTINUED IN 13TH BOY, VOLUME

13th Boy Translation Notes

Page 11
***Kyungki-do*:** One of the largest provinces in South Korea.

Page 24
***Kimchi*:** Famous Korean side dish made of cabbage and chili sauce.

Page 48
Ddong-Min: The boy's name is "Dong-Min," but Hee-So thinks of the first part as spelled "Ddong," which is the Korean word for "shit."

Page 63
***Won*:** Korean monetary unit. A rough conversion rate is 1,000 won to $1 USD. So the fine here is roughly $10,000 US.

Page 68
Seoul: Capital city of South Korea.

Page 142
***Hyungnim*:** Korean title a woman would use to address her husband's older brother's wife.

***Dongseo*:** Korean title a woman would use to address her husband's younger brother's wife.

Page 172
Snail wife: A reference to a Korean folktale about a woman who creeps out of a snail shell every night and secretly cooks and cleans for her love.

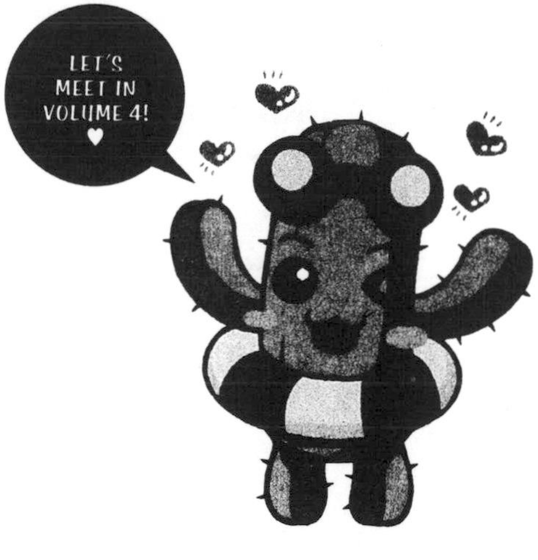
LET'S MEET IN VOLUME 4! ♥

13th BOY③

SangEun Lee

Translation: JiEun Park
English Adaptation: Natalie Baan

Lettering: Terri Delgado

13th Boy, Vol. 3 © 2005 SangEun Lee. All rights reserved. First published in Korea in 2005 by Haksan Publishing Co., Ltd. English translation rights in U.S.A., Canada, UK, and Republic of Ireland arranged with Haksan Publishing Co., Ltd.

English translation © 2010 Hachette Book Group, Inc.

Yen Press
Hachette Book Group
237 Park Avenue, New York, NY 10017

www.HachetteBookGroup.com
www.YenPress.com

Yen Press is an imprint of Hachette Book Group, Inc.
The Yen Press name and logo are trademarks of Hachette Book Group, Inc.

First Yen Press Edition: February 2010

ISBN: 978-0-7595-2996-0

10 9 8 7 6 5 4 3 2 1

BVG

Printed in the United States of America